Wealth and Rebellion

Publication of the American Folklore Society

NEW SERIES
General Editor, Patrick B. Mullen

WEALTH
AND
REBELLION

Elsie Clews Parsons,
Anthropologist and Folklorist

ROSEMARY LÉVY ZUMWALT

Foreword by Roger D. Abrahams

UNIVERSITY OF ILLINOIS PRESS
Urbana and Chicago

Publication of this book was supported in part by a grant
from Davidson College.

This book is printed on acid-free paper.

Library of Congress Cataloging-in-Publication Data

Zumwalt, Rosemary Lévy, 1944-
    Wealth and rebellion : Elsie Clews Parsons, anthropologist and
folklorist / Rosemary Lévy Zumwalt.
        p.   cm. — (Publications of the American Folklore Society. New
series)
    Includes bibliographical references and index.
    ISBN 0-252-01909-1 (alk. paper)
    1. Parsons, Elsie Worthington Clews, 1875-1941.
2. Anthropologists—United States—Biography. 3. Folklorists—
United States—Biography. 4. Indians—Folklore. 5. Indians—
Social life and customs. I. Title. II. Series: Publications of
the American Folklore Society. New series (Unnumbered)
GN21.P37Z86 1992
301'.092—dc20
    [B]   91-36288
                                                              CIP

To my daughter, Heather Allyson Elrick

Contents

Illustrations follow pages 2 and 122.

Foreword

Roger D. Abrahams

This book reclaims Elsie Clews Parsons as an intellectual force in American life in the twentieth century. Drawing on relationships forged in radical feminist and aesthetic circles, Parsons became a major player in the social sciences, especially in the development of modern American anthropology and folklore study. Operating largely outside the academy, she saw her own role as that of encourager through word and deed and financial resource management. While Parsons herself made little claim as an intellectual, her immense energy and dedication to understanding human expressive capabilities placed her again and again at the center of the most important discussions of her times.

Rosemary Lévy Zumwalt's biography of Parsons is more than a "life in the profession." Zumwalt gives us an interesting essay in the sociology of knowledge, revealing how research projects and ideology interact and are propelled by people of strong principle and vision. Here we see the young prodigy, Elsie Clews Parsons, the suffragist and early feminist, writing powerful early books on sociological perspectives drawing on labeling theory. We are led to the formation of that group of thinkers who gave substance to the idea of "the New York intellectual": Clarence Day, Randolph Bourne, Walter Lippmann, Mabel Dodge, and the many others involved in starting the *New Republic* and other radical publications. The Heretic Club, with Bourne, Day, Van Wyck Brooks, and others, provided further opportunities for Parsons to refine her social and cultural ideas. It was in these relationships that she really found her vocation. And then there is the remarkable transformation that occurred in her life when she discovered the friendship and intellectual stimulation of Franz Boas, who was then engaged in developing the field of cultural anthropology.

Margaret Mead has long been known for her ability to sustain her friends as they carried out their fieldwork and then wrote up their discoveries. It is fascinating to see how widely such practices were shared by that generation of anthropologists, especially the students of Franz Boas, including Elsie Clews Parsons. Boas may have set the pattern, but Parsons and the others of this group were just as adept at communicating and encouraging. Some of this comes to light in the works by Mead concerning her friend Ruth Benedict and in Edward Sapir's deep and personal implication in their lives and works. With Parsons's story, our understanding of these times broadens and deepens immeasurably. Moreover, Mead's and Benedict's ability to translate anthropological ideas for a popular audience was preceded by Parsons's books on manners and morals of Americans, such as *The Old-Fashioned Woman* and *Fear and Conventionality*.

For some years there has been a growing feeling that folklore as a discipline has failed to see its relation to the other humane and scientific pursuits that were in formation during this century. With this biography, we begin to see some of the most important features of investigation that are shared by folklore and anthropology, and why this interrelationship should have developed in the ways it did. In league with Boas, her mentor, Parsons attempted to cover systematically the major cultural zones in the American sphere of influence, especially American Indians and Afro-Americans. She was, in fact, the most thoroughgoing comparatist of her generation, in theory and practice. More than any literary folklorist, Parsons saw folklore and culture in terms of dissemination as well as in the unique kinds of cultural configurations that her student and friend Ruth Benedict was to characterize as "patterns of culture."

Parsons took it as her special province to carry out systematic collecting, on her own and with other fieldworkers, throughout Afro-America, starting in Rhode Island and Massachusetts among the Cape Verdeans living there and extending south, to Virginia, North Carolina, and into the sea-lanes of the western Atlantic and eastern Caribbean. One of her last great works was the three-volume collection of West Indian lore, published by the American Folklore Society. More than anyone else, Parsons began the new-world Afro-American fieldwork and generally energized that whole endeavor, sustaining it until a Hurston and a Herskovitz could catch hold.

But Parsons was just as deeply involved as a fieldworker in the American Southwest, joining with the great team of Boas's students and colleagues in collecting in the pueblos throughout that region.

This she followed up with work in cognate communities in Mexico. The results as a collaborative project have never been discussed as such; they need a work as comprehensive as this biography of Parsons. Meanwhile, Rosemary Zumwalt provides us with a glimpse of how Parsons achieved her life-project. Zumwalt demonstrates how the personalities of the fieldworkers affected not only the intensity by which the common endeavor was approached but how the lives of those involved were changed. The three-cornered relationship between Pliny Earle Goddard, Alfred Kroeber, and Parsons is opened up for us through letters and other personal documents in a way that cannot fail to excite anyone interested in the work of this great generation of cultural anthropologists and folklorists.

By taking the Boasian method of working culture by culture, carefully going from community to community, but asking the same questions of each group and using her knowledge of one to elicit in the contiguous groups, Parsons carried out comparative fieldwork that only now is being paralleled, and then only in certain very well collected areas in which a number of fieldworkers have descended, such as Papua New Guinea, Highland Chiapas, and the Amazon.

One of the most significant outcomes of the American Folklore Society's centenary celebration (1988–89) has been the increased interest in its important figures over the last century. This biography, by a distinguished folklore historian, is a direct tangible result. By and large, folklorists had remembered Elsie Clews Parsons as a wealthy "angel," especially during the very hard times of the Depression, when the Society was hinted to be near bankruptcy. She was said to have kept it going during a time when, according to legend, it had been nearly subsumed by the anthropologists. She was also remembered, by anthropologists as well as folklorists, as an indefatigable fieldworker about whom several not entirely complimentary stories circulated in oral tradition. In reality, no one was more central than Parsons to the continuing presence of folklore on the scholarly landscape in the 1920s and 1930s. Most visibly, she served as president of the American Folklore Society in 1919–20.

When Zumwalt began this project, no one suspected how rich the Parsons papers would prove and how central a player Parsons had been in a great many of the most important intellectual discussions of the twentieth century. Parsons's folklore activities turned out to be only a small passage in the very large painting of her life. The life story we have before us is so very much more interesting than anything we might have expected, for Zumwalt has brought forth an abundance of humanizing detail. Amassing and editing a tremendous number of important texts was the least of Parsons's effort. She converted a stubborn temperament into practices of dogged persistence in observing, recording, and understanding human expressive capacities. She developed a model for refining techniques of elicitation and comparative analysis. She had the ability to deal strongly with others at a time when this was far from common with women. With money and ideas and abundant energies she encouraged the work of many others who went into the field. We will never again be able to think of Parsons as simply a wealthy and well-connected person who did folklore collecting as a frenzied avocation from her yacht as she toured the Sea Islands and the West Indies.

Wealth and Rebellion is a book that folklorists, anthropologists, intellectual historians, those concerned with the cultural critique and women's issues, and lovers of strong biographies will read with fascination. However, it is far from the first step taken in resuscitating Parsons's life and career: Zumwalt details in her preface all of the recent work that has been done, and certainly a great deal more will be carried out in the near future, now that Parsons's feminist and regionalist writings are being read and discussed a good deal. But future discussions will have to begin with this biography, for Rosemary Lévy Zumwalt has put the life in good order for us, and she has done so with an infectious spirit that reflects Parsons's own enthusiasm for everything she touched.

Preface

History can never be dead, I am convinced, when it is experienced through the voices of those who lived it. To approach these figures of the past, to put flesh on their bones, to clothe their bodies, to hear the sound of their voices, one must dig through the attics of their memories. One must find the letters creased with age, covered with the dust of time, and unfold them. Surrounded by scraps of paper inked with sweeping script or illegible scrawl, one must immerse self in this other reality, read, and absorb. One must be willing to follow the course of the story, to be pulled along by the then-powerful currents. And one must surface to bring order to these pieces of lives once lived.

Just such a process I went through in making the acquaintance of Elsie Clews Parsons, née Elsie Worthington Clews. With the encouragement of my friend and colleague, Roger Abrahams, who first suggested to me that I write a biography of Elsie Clews Parsons, I turned to the mirrors of our memory. As a folklorist and anthropologist, I looked first at her reflection in these disciplines. Here she was primarily remembered for her generosity—she had, after all, been benefactor to the American Folklore Society, the American Anthropological Association, and the American Ethnological Society. She was also remembered with fondness for her personal eccentricities: she customarily wore beaded Indian moccasins and, once, tennis shoes under her long, formal lace gown. And she smoked incessantly. Also not so fondly, she was remembered for an outburst of temper, for reprimanding the treasurer of the American Folklore Society for not keeping accurate records. These were memories of those who had seen her when they were young graduate students.[1] And then there were those who simply reacted to her, using the present, which is numbed by a certain amnesia about the influential figures of the past, as their gauge. A folklorist, with a patronizing nod, admitted, "Yes, she was very kind to folklore, very generous," but he implied by tone that there was nothing much more to her. I had already begun my research on Parsons, and I knew that she was much more than the sum of her eccentricities, and more than simply a worthy benefactor. So I continued with her letters, papers, and books. And as I became absorbed in the richness of her correspondence, I realized that I could not follow the initial course that I had charted—I could not limit myself to a consideration of Elsie Clews Parsons as a folklorist and anthropologist. The other facets of her life were too strong. They pulled me to them with an irresistible fascination. As I explored more and traced the paths of her letters, I realized that Elsie Clews Parsons was at the nexus of an intellectual community—or rather intellectual communities. She was friend, colleague, confidant of leaders in the arts, literature, politics, and anthropology. Her letters and the letters to her recorded crucial issues and concerns as they were being addressed at the time. I could not excise from her life the two strands of anthropology and folklore, golden as they may be, and follow them. So I decided to take all the vibrant hues of her life and blend them together. This, then, is a portrait of Elsie Clews Parsons, one rooted in the materials of her making—her letters, articles, books, journals. I have sorted through these materials carefully, assessing what must be presented to give an accurate portrayal, what adds color and line and thus brings life. I have snipped out that which, in my judgment, does not add to the image, or is too intensely personal. So I measure and weigh—that which is necessary must be included; that which adds only a quickening of tone is background or is omitted.

A biographer, it seems to me, has a charge, to etch in words a portrait that reveals the strengths and the vulnerabilities of the subject. The wrinkles must be as readily apparent as the beauty mark. There is a slight irony here. In life, Elsie Clews Parsons would have authorized no such portrait. She was a very private person, one who did not seek acclaim. Writer and feminist Signe Toksvig had once suggested compiling a biography of Elsie. The matter was not pursued. And an ambitious artist who offered to paint a portrait of Elsie drew this response from her, "I don't fancy my face, and yet, as it is mine, I can't be wholly indifferent on the subject. So that I have always had a horror of being painted or photographed. The former catastrophe has never occurred and the latter but rarely and under very severe pressure."[2]

The task, then, in a biography is to write a life, that is, to present the events and achievements of a lifetime, to give the spirit and the personality of the individual, and to provide a certain thematic ordering to this complex whole. During the course of this writing, Elsie presented me with many challenges, but none was quite so difficult as the puzzle of how to provide order for the richness of her life. How might I, for example, tell of her life with her husband, Herbert Parsons, while discussing her scholarly work written during her years of marriage? Were the two to be intertwined, or, more realistically, as they were in Parsons's life, were they to be separated? I chose the latter, to disengage the personal from the scholarly, and further to disengage the conceptual and theoretical from the descriptive. Thus Parsons's intellectual approach to issues of individual freedom—the content of her writings on feminism and the constraint of the individual—are separated from her feminist and pacifist political activities. Her fieldwork in folklore is presented in a chapter apart from her theoretical approach to folklore; the same is done for her ethnographic fieldwork and her theoretical approach to ethnography. Still, I have attempted to combine a chronological ordering with a thematic treatment. There are times, however, when the reader will encounter a "flash forward," a topic or individual will be introduced in an early chapter according to chronological ordering, to be discussed in more detail in a later chapter according to thematic treatment.[3]

This book begins with "A Portrait in Words," Chapter 1, which introduces Elsie, gives an overview of her life, a sense of her concerns in life, and of her personality. Chapter 2, "The Clews Family," traces Elsie's relationship with her father and her mother from birth to her teenage years and situates her in her social milieu. Chapter 3, "College Years," focuses on Elsie's undergraduate work at Barnard, and her graduate study at Columbia, as well as her years teaching sociology at Barnard. Chapter 4, "Elsie and Herbert," tells of her marriage to Herbert Parsons. The focus here is on the personal—the intense attachment of the two, their young love, marriage, the birth of their children, and their later disappointments. Chapter 5, "The Closed Circle," examines Parsons's works on social psychology, her analysis of classification as a means of social control, her critique of contemporary society, and her call for sexual equality. Chapter 6, "The Heretics," explores Parsons's work for social change, specifically in the pacifist resistance to World War I. Here she is linked to her liberal and radical friends, to Ralph Lippmann, Randolph Bourne, Frances Hackett, Signe Toksvig, and Clarence Day. Chapter 7, "Observations of Other Worlds," shifts, as Parsons did, from contemporary American problems to her newfound field, anthropology. Chapter 8, "The Scientists," introduces her anthropologist friends, Franz Boas, Alfred Louis Kroeber, Robert Lowie, and Pliny Earle Goddard. Chapter 9, "Of Tales, Riddles, and Proverbs," examines Parsons's work in folklore. Chapter 10, "The Filigree of Cultures," traces the concepts and theories that guided her work in anthropology. Chapter 11, "In the

Southwest," takes its title from an unpublished manuscript of Parsons's that described in such living detail her work in this area that so enchanted her. Tied together in this chapter is a complex web of her creation, her fieldwork experiences, her publications, and her support of others, as well as her involvement in the opposition to the Bursum bill, a blatant attempt to divest the Pueblo Indians of their lands. Chapter 12, "Mayo-Yaqui, Cora, Huichol, and Mitleño," moves on to Elsie's work in Mexico, part of it conducted in collaboration with Ralph Beals. Chapter 13, "Peguche," describes Elsie's last place of fieldwork in Ecuador. Chapter 14, "A Position of Power," examines Parsons's contributions to the American Folklore Society and the American Anthropological Association. Chapter 15, "A Legacy to Folklore and Anthropology," tells of Elsie at the apogee of her career in 1941, as the first woman president of the American Anthropological Association, and of her sudden and tragic death.

There has been a surge of interest in Elsie Clews Parsons within the past few years. This can be traced to several factors. Peter Hare, as grandnephew of Parsons, had had access to letters and manuscripts that had been stored in the attic of the family home in Rye, New York. In 1985 he published his work, *A Woman's Quest for Science: Portrait of Anthropologist Elsie Clews Parsons*. Hare's intent was to present Elsie as an individual, and not to provide a detailed examination of her as an anthropologist. With his provocative book, he engendered a further interest in Parsons's scientific contributions. At the same time that Hare's book was being published, plans were underway for the celebration of the 1988 Centennial of the American Folklore Society. As a crucial figure in the society, Parsons was a natural focus for research. There has been a desire on the part of feminist anthropologists and folklorists to rediscover the women whose contributions to the disciplines have been so completely forgotten. In "Taking Liberties, Writing from the Margins, and Doing It with a Difference," a paper presented as part of the feminist panels for the 1986 American Folklore Society Meeting, Barbara Babcock stated this clearly: "The history of folklore studies is the history of the male line. How can we, in Virginia Woolf's words, think back through our mothers if we don't know who they are? When even the mother of us all, who literally kept both the society and the journal alive, is absent from official texts and histories, we will have to read our history 'into the scene of its own exclusion. It has . . . to be invented—both discovered and made up.'"

For folklorists, "the mother of us all," was, as Babcock said, "the indomitable and 'indefatigable' Elsie Clews Parsons." In *Pueblo Moth-*

ers and Children: Essays by Elsie Clews Parsons, 1915–1924, Babcock has assembled a selection of Parsons's writings concerned "with the cultural construction of gender, sexuality, and reproduction—with motherhood as experience, as discourse and as institution." In *Daughters of the Desert: Women Anthropologists and the Native American Southwest, 1880–1980,* Barbara Babcock and Nancy Parezo joined together in compiling a museum exhibit, a videotape, and a catalogue that documented the contributions of women anthropologists, among them, Elsie Clews Parsons, to southwestern research. Judith Friedlander contributed an entry on Parsons to *Women Anthropologists: Selected Biographies,* a reference work intended precisely for a feminist reclamation of the past. For the 1988 American Anthropological Association Meeting, Beverly Chiñas organized a panel on Feminist Perspective on Elsie Clews Parsons and Her Works. And, finally, for the 1989 distinguished lecture, delivered to the American Ethnological Society, Louise Lamphere discussed "Feminist Anthropology: The Legacy of Elsie Clews Parsons."[4]

I have been blessed in this research on Elsie Clews Parsons with a wealth of material. The Elsie Clews Parsons Papers, housed at the American Philosophical Society, in Philadelphia, Pennsylvania, are the richest collection of personal and professional papers that I have ever had the opportunity to consult. In my time there in the summers of 1985 and 1986 and the summer and fall of 1987, I made my acquaintance through Parsons's letters with the Parsons family and with Elsie's friends and colleagues. I pursued Herbert Parsons further in his papers, which are housed at the Columbia University Rare Book and Manuscript Library, and I read through the interview with Elsie's daughter, Lissa Parsons Kennedy. I followed the path of the letters to the National Anthropological Archives at the Smithsonian Institution in Washington, D.C., to the University of Pennsylvania Folklore and Folklife Archives, and the Bancroft Library at the University of California, Berkeley. At the Bancroft Library, I would find, like pieces to a puzzle, answers to letters that I had read on the opposite side of the continent. In the vividness of the correspondence, these figures of the past—Elsie Clews Parsons, Herbert Parsons, Franz Boas, Gladys Reichard, and Robert Lowie—stepped off the pages of their letters and came to life. I felt for a time immersed in their concerns, their hopes, disappointments, and victories. While in my rational mind, I knew that these people had been dead for years, in my emotional present, they were alive. As I read through their letters, I felt that I had lived through their lives; and when I came to the death notices, I felt the loss of close and dear friends.

In the course of this work, I have built up a debt of gratitude to many friends and colleagues. I am grateful to Florence Baer, who generously shared biographical research that she had conducted on Elsie Clews Parsons. Sally Peterson opened her home to me while I was doing archival work in Philadelphia. Patricia Mason and Don Rosick kindly took time on their trip to Mitla to visit and photograph La Sorpresa for me. Lucinda Manning, Barnard College Archivist, located information for me on courses taught by Elsie Clews Parsons at Barnard. Margaret Rose, College Archivist at the New School for Social Research, informed me about the course taught by Parsons in 1919. The manuscripts archivists at the Bancroft Library, the Columbia Rare Book and Manuscript Library, the National Anthropological Archives, and the University of Pennsylvania Folklore and Folklife Archives were generous with their assistance. At Davidson College, Mary Beaty, Assistant Director of the Library, and Edward Proctor, Automation Project Librarian, were more than willing to assist me with my research questions and with my search for books through interlibrary loan. I am grateful to Patricia Richart, head of Faculty Secretarial Services at Davidson College, for her help at all stages of manuscript preparation. My stepdaughter, Catherine Lévy Gottlieb, has always been efficient in obtaining books for me through the interlibrary loan. I am grateful also to the reference librarians at the Thomas Cooper Library, University of South Carolina, for assisting me so frequently. Stacy Rooker, work-study student for the Department of Anthropology and Sociology at Davidson College, has with great competence searched through microfilms of the *New York Times* and traced obscure references for me. I am grateful to Robert C. Williams, Vice-President for Academic Affairs and Dean of the Faculty at Davidson College, for his support and encouragement of my research. Grant D. Jones, as head of the Department of Anthropology and Sociology at Davidson College, has been consistently helpful and supportive of my research.

I am especially indebted to Roger Abrahams for suggesting to me in his comfortable, casual way—which always belies deep seriousness—that I write a biography of Elsie Clews Parsons. Not only did he plant the seed of the idea, but also he and his wife, Janet Anderson, provided me with a place to stay in Philadelphia for the summer—their own home. Roger has been a constant source of encouragement throughout the research and the writing of this book. For this, I am deeply grateful. Dan Ben-Amos and Alan Dundes have also been a source of support and encouragement in my work. Judith McCulloh, of the University of Illinois Press, has been patient with me, and always encouraging about the progress of my work. I am indebted to her for her kindness, and I am ever respectful of her professionalism. I am grateful for the suggestion of the readers of my manuscript, to Roger Abrahams, Nancy Oestrich Lurie, and Patrick B. Mullen, and for the careful editing of Susan L. Patterson.

For so many weeks, over the period of so many summers, I have made my home at the American Philosophical Society Library. There I was greeted by the quiet efficiency of Beth Carroll-Horrocks, Manuscripts Librarian. I admire her professionalism and am very grateful for her continuing interest in my research. Martin L. Levitt, Assistant Manuscripts Librarian, has always been willing to answer my questions and to search for yet another letter in the collection. Frank Margeson, Photographer, has reproduced many of the pictures that appear in this book. Often, the prints he has had to work with have been old, grainy, and fuzzy. With skill, he makes the past come into focus.

I want to thank especially Susan Morison, Director of the Rye Historical Society, for allowing me to visit the Lounsberry House before it was officially open as a facility of the society. The excitement of that afternoon stays with me. Susan Morison, Isaac Jack Lévy, and I walked through the wide expanse of the attic, viewed the engraved plates of Parsons's books, and saw the stacks of membership cards for the Barnard College Settlement organization, which Elsie had helped to establish. And, then, in one small room off to the side of the attic, we found a large box of letters, many still in their original envelopes, covered with a fine layer of dust. And underneath this box was another, which contained Elsie Clews's graduation gown and her riding habit, complete with her hat and leather boots, which she wore on her fieldtrips in the Southwest. Indulgent of my scarcely contained excitement, Susan Morison allowed Isaac Jack Lévy and me to settle down in Elsie Clews Parsons's former bedroom, which had been converted into a temporary office for the cataloguing of the Parsons Papers. There we were able to spend the afternoon hours reading through some of the letters that we had uncovered.

I am grateful to the following institutions for granting me permission to quote from items in their collections: the American Museum of Natural History; the American Philosophical Society Library; the Bancroft Library and the University Archives, University of California, Berkeley; the Beinecke Rare Book and Manuscript Library, Yale University; the Bentley Historical Library, University of Michigan; the Rare Book and Manuscript Library, Columbia University; the Joseph Regenstein Library, University of Chicago; the National

Anthropological Archives; the Rye Historical Society; and the University of Pennsylvania Folklore and Folklife Archives. I am grateful to the American Philosophical Society, the Bancroft Library, the Rye Historical Society, and to Fanny Parsons Culleton for allowing me to reproduce the photographs in this book. Professor Karl Kroeber has kindly given me permission to quote from the letters of his father, Alfred Louis Kroeber. Fanny Wickes Parsons graciously granted me permission to quote from the material in the Elsie Clews Parsons Papers. And Fanny Parsons Culleton kindly granted me an interview in July 1988, which made her grandmother live for me.

My research has been supported by assistance from Davidson College Faculty Research Grant, the National Endowment for the Humanities Travel Grant, and the Southern Education Research Board. The L. J. Skaggs and Mary C. Skaggs Foundation provided funds that allowed me to take a leave of absence from Davidson College in the fall term of 1986. From the Skaggs Foundation, I want to thank especially Jillian Sandrock, who was so enthusiastic about this biography. For all this support, I am truly grateful. My husband, Professor Isaac Jack Lévy, has in this project, as in all my work, been a companion and a colleague. He has traveled with me from archives to archives, has listened to me "talk Parsons" for these past years, and has read and commented on the manuscript. I am grateful for his lively support and constant encouragement. My daughter, Heather Allyson Elrick, has the spirit and enthusiasm that, to me, make her a model of the new woman of whom Elsie Clews Parsons wrote. It is to Heather that I dedicate this work.

NOTES

1. For an account of "derogatory anecdotes" about Parsons, see Barbara A. Babcock's provocative, "Taking Liberties, Writing from the Margins, and Doing It with a Difference," *JAF* 100 (1987): 395–96. See also Richard Dorson, "Elsie Clews Parsons: Feminist and Folklorist," *AFFWord* 1–3 (1971): 4, for a listing of her eccentricities.

2. ECP, EC to Davis, 25 July 1899. Throughout this work, all quotations from Parsons are rendered exactly as written, including spelling and punctuation. This will at times result in apparent inconsistencies. For instance, Parsons included an accent for "Zuñi," while other writers did not.

3. Nancy Lurie in her reading of my manuscript referred to this organizational format as "flash forward."

4. Peter Hare, *A Woman's Quest for Science* (Buffalo, N.Y.: Prometheus Books, 1985). Babcock, "Taking Liberties," p. 395; Babcock included a quote from Peggy Kamuf, "Penelope at Work: Interruptions in *A Room of One's*

Own," Novel 16 (1982): 9. Babcock, *Pueblo Mothers and Children* (Santa Fe, New Mexico: Ancient City Press, 1991), p. 1. Babcock and Nancy Parezo, *Daughters of the Desert* (Albuquerque: University of New Mexico Press, 1988). Judith Friedlander, "Elsie Clews Parsons (1874–1941)," in *Women Anthropologists*, Ute Gacs et al., eds. (Urbana: University of Illinois Press, 1989), pp. 282–90. Beverly Chiñas, panel on Feminist Perspective on Elsie Clews Parsons and Her Works, American Anthropological Association, Phoenix, Arizona, 1988. For this panel, I discussed "Elsie Clews Parsons as Folklorist," a paper I also presented to the American Philosophical Society's reception for the American Folklore Society in October, 1989. In addition, I have delivered the following papers on aspects of Parsons's work: "Elsie Clews Parsons's Feminist Work" (invited lecture, Women's History Month, University of South Carolina, March, 1989); "A Friendship of Substance: Franz Boas and Elsie Clews Parsons" (American Folklore Society, October, 1988, Cambridge, Massachusetts); and "Commissioner Burke's and Senator Bursum's Threat to Pueblo Life: The Opposition Responds" (American Folklore Society, October, 1989, Philadelphia, Pennsylvania). Louise Lamphere, "Feminist Anthropology: The Legacy of Elsie Clews Parsons," *American Ethnologist* 16 (1989): 518–33.

Abbreviations

AMNH	American Museum of Natural History
AA	*American Anthropologist*
ECP	Elsie Clews Parsons Papers
JAF	*Journal of American Folklore*
NAA	National Anthropological Archives
UCA	University of California, Berkeley, Archives. Department of Anthropology
UM	University of Michigan, Michigan Historical Collection, Bentley Library
UPFFA	University of Pennsylvania Folklore and Folklife Archives

1

A Portrait in Words

> Her society had encroached on her; she studied the science
> of society the better to fight back against society. It had
> shown her little quarter, and she became not only a persis-
> tent but an attacking foe, whose self-respect earned re-
> spect. Endowed by environment with a degree of status and
> affluence, as well as by nature with intelligence and cour-
> age, she never scrupled to use the former against its origin.
> —Alfred Louis Kroeber[1]

Elsie Clews Parsons was a rebel against her social class. Child of the
wealthy Henry Clews and the socially prominent Lucy Worthington
Clews, she was marked from birth as privileged. But she was not to be
one who would placidly go through the paces of upper-class society
life, changing gait and trappings for her proper age set. For as well as
privileged, she was marked from birth as different. And this difference of mind, of view, of opinion, she nurtured. Elsie grew up in the
family's fashionable home in New York City and their castlelike resort
in Newport, Rhode Island. As a young girl, she went to the right
schools, was connected with the right people. She made her debut at
age sixteen. But with all the marks of her social pedigree, the careful
breeding and grooming, Elsie would yield to no master. She struck
her own gait. And she did this with head held high, in pride, sometimes in disdain, sometimes in defiance. Elsie's nature was not, however, that of the free, unfettered spirit. She charted her own course
most definitely, but this was done with the firm anchor of reason. One
who enjoyed pleasure, not one for unnecessary self-denial, still Elsie
was disciplined. Her inner dynamic was ever, by fierce choice, rebellion against conformity.

Against her parents' wishes, Elsie Clews entered the newly founded
Barnard College in 1892 and graduated Phi Beta Kappa in 1896. Still
fighting her family's expectations, she continued her study of sociology at Columbia University, where she worked with Nicholas Murray
Butler for her master's degree, and with Franklin Henry Giddings for

her Ph.D., granted in 1899. Awarded a Hartley House Fellowship in 1899—just one year prior to her marriage to the progressive Republican politician, Herbert Parsons—Elsie directed the fieldwork section in sociology for Giddings. In 1903, as a Hartley House Lecturer, she taught her own course on family organization. Elsie gave up her position at Barnard in 1905 and devoted herself to her own scholarly work and to her young family. Much of Elsie's energy during the first years of her marriage was spent raising four children. Still, while occupied with the demands of family life and of her husband's political career, Elsie continued with her work in sociology. In 1903, her translation of Gabriel Tarde's *Laws of Imitation* was published, and in 1906, her textbook, *The Family*, appeared.

By 1912, Parsons's interest had begun to shift from sociology to anthropology. Influenced by a trip that she had made with Herbert in 1910 to the Southwest, Elsie felt she had found what she had been searching for—a place where she could work that was totally apart from the world of New York society and Washington politics, and from the demands of children and husband. Parsons began making periodic fieldtrips to the Southwest and initiated her studies of that which she rejected in her own society—rituals, customs, and ceremonies. Her work in the Southwest was carried out during the same period that she was conducting research in black folklore in the Caribbean, Nova Scotia, and the eastern and southern United States. Parsons switched with ease from research in folklore to work in anthropology. She worked simultaneously in both fields, drawing on field research that she had conducted in different geographical areas.

Parsons never allowed herself to be solely identified with one geographical area. Just at the point when the anthropological world had come to regard her as a preeminent specialist in Pueblo Indian studies, Elsie moved south to Mexico. In 1930 she began research of village complexes that resulted in her well-known *Mitla, Town of the Souls* (1936); and in 1932 Elsie undertook joint fieldwork with Ralph Beals among the Mayo-Yaqui, Cora, and Huichol. In 1940 she moved still farther south to Ecuador, where she began a study of acculturation that resulted in the posthumous publication of *Peguche* (1945). In her folklore research, she was also on the move. Attempting to trace the path of black folktales, Elsie had journeyed to Spain (1923), from whence she was convinced the merchantmen of the Iberian Peninsula had sailed forth to Africa and the New World to wreck havoc and spread folktales. She followed the path farther to Egypt and Sudan (1926), where her spirit quickened to hear some of the same tales that she had collected from the blacks of the Caribbean.

Elsie as a young girl, circa 1886 (courtesy of the American Philosophical Society).

Barnard College Class of 1896. Elsie is in the top row, far left (courtesy of the American Philosophical Society).

The Rocks (courtesy of the American Philosophical Society).

Elsie and Lissa, 1902 (courtesy of Fanny Parsons Culleton).

Not only was Parsons an energetic and ceaseless fieldworker, but she was also a prolific writer. She wrote twenty-eight books, edited four books, translated two, and wrote well over two hundred articles. She is best known for *Pueblo Indian Religion* (1939), *Mitla, Town of the Souls* (1936), and her publications on the southwestern pueblos, including among others *Taos Pueblo* (1936), *Isleta Paintings* (published posthumously in 1962), *Hopi and Zuñi Ceremonialism* (1933), and *Notes on Zuñi* (1917), as well as for her monographs in folklore, such as *Folk-Lore of the Sea Islands, South Carolina* (1923), and *Folk-Lore of the Antilles, French and English* (1933). Some treasures now largely forgotten that deserve more recognition grew out of her work in social psychology. *Social Freedom* (1915) and *Social Rule* (1916) are provocative examinations of the molding of the individual to conform to social custom. *The Old-Fashioned Woman* (1913) and *Religious Chastity* (1913), both of a more dated approach than the former two works mentioned, still merit attention for the comparative and historical approach to gender study.

Elsie Clews Parsons had moved with brilliance and ease from sociology, to work in feminism and pacifism, to anthropology and folklore. Ultimately, however, it was to anthropology and folklore that Parsons dedicated herself with singleness of purpose, self-discipline, and enormous energy. In her southwestern work, she moved gradually from one pueblo to the next, using a systematic approach to each, and building up a base of information that fleshed out in complex detail the similarities and differences of southwestern Indian cultures. Hers was an approach grounded in the Boasian tradition, which required careful study based on thorough research of contiguous cultures. In this way, over the years of work in the Southwest, Parsons effected comparative fieldwork studies that have only been duplicated by elaborate group endeavors, such as the Jesup North Pacific Expedition of 1897, and the more recently organized efforts in Papua New Guinea, Highland Chiapas, the Amazon, the trans-Himalayan area, and certain regions in West and East Africa.[2] Parsons's achievements in anthropology and folklore were recognized by professional societies. In 1919 she served as president of the American Folklore Society; from 1923 to 1925, as the president of the American Ethnological Society; and in 1941, she became the first woman president of the American Anthropological Association.

The discipline and singleness of purpose requisite for such mighty achievements were frequently remarked upon by family, friends, and colleagues. Elsie had what sociologist Franklin H. Giddings referred to as an "unconquerable energy . . . equal to almost anything." Others remarked on this, too. The anthropologist, Frank Waters, wrote her, "I can't tell you how good it is to meet vitality. You have it." The feminist and author, Signe Toksvig, queried, "From what well, I wonder, do you draw energy." And others referred to her indefatigable nature.[3]

Elsie carefully channeled her energy, giving structure to her time. She had scheduled hours for study—as a college student, hours spent in the library, or, during summer vacation, mornings spent pursuing her own scholarly interests; as a mature scholar, in daily blocks of time set aside for writing. Both Elsie's granddaughter and her daughter spontaneously described her work habits. Her granddaughter, Fanny Parsons Culleton, remarked: "What I remember is Elsie sitting in her living room . . . in Lounsberry, and working. She sat in a Morris chair . . . by the fireplace, writing and smoking. . . . Elsie had a secretary who lived with us called Ann Nagle. . . . And I remember her scurrying back and forth from the library which was down some steps from Elsie's room with manuscripts." Elsie's daughter, Lissa, recalled: "She loved, she had a passion for working." Lissa remembered her mother's cabin as a solitary place of refuge. Elsie's good friend, the artist Grant La Farge, had designed the cabin that was built up in the woods behind the Stonover Farm at Lenox. "And she'd go up there. She had no electric light up there, and no telephone, and she could get away and be quiet up there and get away from us children. None of us enjoyed climbing the hill, for one thing. And when lunch was ready we'd take out the big dinner bell and ring it, and she'd come down the hill for lunch with us."[4]

A central element of Elsie's personality was her generosity. That she gave from an inner feeling of concern for others and for their work, not just because she was wealthy, is crucial for understanding this aspect of her being. In truth, the total dollar amount of her philanthropic contributions was so large that it might well overshadow the real source, her caring nature. Elsie was approached for financial assistance by diverse people. It is their words that most clearly reveal her reputation for giving. One man who had lost his job wrote asking for letters of reference, or any help she might give: "Two years ago when I was doorman at 320 E. 72 St. you were kind enough to give me tickets . . . to the Opera. You were very kind to me then and now I'm in serious trouble and I hope you might be able to help me." A woman, who said she had nowhere else to turn, wrote Elsie about the failure of the family business. She asked for help in establishing a boardinghouse on the beach, "I would beg of you to help us out with a little money so we could make an honest living. We are desperate."

A college classmate wrote, "This letter will take you back to the days when I knew you as Miss Clews in my French classes at Barnard. I have your address from Miss Mabel Parsons who is aware that things have not gone well with me in recent years." She asked if "on the off-chance . . . someone in the circle of your family or friends might need a French tutor." A man wrote to her from Leavenworth, Kansas, where he was in prison, asking for fifteen dollars for the day of his release, for, as he said, "As there is no one els [*sic*] in the out side world seems to care to cheerish [*sic*] me while I am here but you and I feel sincere that what soever [*sic*] I ask of you why you will grant me." Elsie continued to correspond with him while he served out the rest of his term, attempted to intercede for his early parole, and encouraged him to write to her for assistance. In January, 1940, a medical doctor in New York acknowledged the receipt of her check for $750, which enabled a Jewish scientist from Poland, resettled in the United States, to send for his wife and children. The doctor added, "Elemina, our Dutch West Indian cook, when I told her the story of your generosity, crossed herself and said, 'Moi! Moi! Moi!' "[5]

Elsie's giving was quiet. She was not one to seek acclaim for what she did. This was true also of her contributions to professional societies and for scholarly work, both of which were in the hundreds of thousands of dollars. Much of this was done anonymously, channeled through other individuals or foundations to disguise the source. Of course, there was good sense in this as well as modesty. With a reputation for being wealthy and generous, Elsie Clews Parsons was inundated with requests. Indeed, in reading her correspondence—with letter after letter of requests for financial assistance—one reaches the conclusion that she was regarded as either a lending institution or a scholarly funding agency. She seemed eminently patient with these requests.

It was not only money that Elsie gave. She gave of her time and her energy. She helped young anthropologists plan their fieldwork and then read through drafts of their manuscripts, marking them with her precise script. Her correspondence with them was voluminous. They came to depend on her for suggestions and advice, as well as for financial support. So extensive was this network that to trace it brings one to the leading American anthropologists of her time. It is not an exaggeration to say that one cannot understand the development of American anthropology between the years of 1916 to 1941 without taking into account the influence of Elsie Clews Parsons. Again, this is not to be measured in dollars alone. Hers was a mental power as well. Morris Opler, who benefited from Parsons's assistance, wrote of her,

"She was always willing to go over my material critically and to put her impressive comparative knowledge at my service. And she sponsored field work and publication for me at a difficult time. I had an ambitious plan of remaining in the field for a number of years, going from one Apache tribe to another. . . . I started out on the venture during the depression years, when support and encouragement for this sort of thing were not very plentiful, and Dr. Parsons' role often made the crucial difference."[6]

This did not go unmarked by others as well. Her dear friend and colleague, the anthropologist Alfred Louis Kroeber, commented, "Toward the young and the dependent she was uniformly helpful. . . . The extent of her benefactions, including the most precious of all possessions, her time, will probably never be fully known."[7] And the anthropologist of whom she was perhaps most fond, Franz Boas, eulogized her: "In her researches she welcomed the help that other competent observers were able to give, and much of the research work that has been done during the last few decades is due to her stimulation of young scientists, to whose attention she called problems and whom she enabled to carry through field work that otherwise would have remained undone. It was her good fortune that she was able to render such material assistance. It was her merit that her devotion to science prompted her to use her position unselfishly for the promotion of scientific work that she considered important."[8]

Elsie's interest in observing and analyzing social behavior was apparent even as a young girl. At sixteen, she visited Washington, D.C., and wrote to a friend commenting on the contrast with the style of life in New York: "The whole city seems to pass such an easy going life. No bustle, no business. In the streets, I miss more than anything else that quick rush of life, so bewildering to those who do not share it and so invigorating to the initiated. People saunter along in the streets in a very American manner. It seems to me that the passing faces are more restful than in New York, but perhaps it is because I myself feel carefree, and in crowds people seem to wear our own expression, glad when we are joyful, tired when we are depressed."[9] She included comments on the family life of her hosts, and, in so doing, showed a perceptive reading of emotions that she would later use in the analysis of her own society: "Alice is an only child, the hope of her parents. Her mother is a practical, worldly woman, encrusted with life's daily dust. She only shows what she once may have been in her love and tenderness to her daughter. The father has a larger nature and sometimes, I fancy, misses sympathy in his wife."[10]

Elsie showed a healthy skepticism for the easy answer to social problems held forth by those who framed utopias. In a letter written to her friend, Alice, she reflected on the meaning of Edward Bellamy's *Looking Backwards*. She had found it "very interesting although like all books of that character entirely impractical." She continued, "Our human nature, as it now exists and as it will exist so far as I can see, would have to be materially changed to render Bellamy's scheme possible."[11] She showed her pragmatism in the study of politics that she had undertaken "in a most diligent manner." She had observed "the different types of politicians," and included among these was "the blustering, handshaking westerner," who made his breezy way through Washington.[12]

As a child, Elsie was precocious, with a keen, inquisitive mind that took her from art, music, and literature to politics and observations of human nature. As an adult, her mind ranged as widely, and her intellect was honed to a fine edge that cut through sham and artifice, through the accepted and the conventional. Never was her sharpness blunted with the years, or her rebellious nature tamed. Always she resented the expected, the socially correct way of behaving, of thinking, of living. As Elsie expressed it, she disliked "appropriate sentiments." These included shaking hands, giving "institutional" kisses, saying good-bye, wishing people a Merry Christmas, and writing "bread and butter" notes of thanks. Elsie's disdain for these customs was a fascination to her friends, and they delighted in violating her wishes. One wrote, "You told me once that you disliked appropriate sentiments so I suppose that it is not permissible to wish you the traditional Merry Christmas." Another remarked, "You are uncommon tolerant . . . Mrs. Parsons—with no apologies of course as I know how you disapprove of them." Still another referred to her "good-bye theory." He wrote, "My glimpse of you at New Haven was delightful. . . . I said 'good bye' purely by reflex—and I won't do it again." Familiar with her many dislikes, he said in another letter, "In spite of your objection to the direct personal, I'd like to see you again." As years passed, Elsie apparently modified her adamant rejection of all expected conventions, for, in 1924, a friend remarked, "It was very pleasant to see you, even though you are willing now to shake hands." To her husband, Herbert, she also avowed her dislike of the expected, while assuring him of the spontaneity of his words: "I don't like institutional letters any more than I do institutional kisses. But your letters have never seemed institutional."[13]

Elsie's disdain of the perfunctory was the basis of an essay for the radical magazine, *The Masses*. Contrasted with ever-renewing spontaneity was what she portrayed as the stranglehold of custom that drained the life between two people. The scene was set with a young woman and an older woman before "the fire of a winter night" in a

New England farmhouse, contemplating the style of "Meetings." The younger woman recounted:

"Years ago I would go to meet George, anticipating the delight of it. You've seen George kiss me in a railway station or when he comes home to tea. He's always done it. Just what that kind of a kiss means to George I don't know, but I find it depressing. It was particularly trying at first, when I cared so much. It was depressing, but I'd get over it quickly and begin to express my joy in our meeting. It generally took the form of eagerness to tell him about whatever interesting or amusing things had been happening in his absence, or perhaps the book I'd just read or the story I'd heard or some new idea exciting me."

The man's calculated reception of her spontaneity eventually cooled her ardor.

"George would listen in a taciturn sort of way, sometimes almost as if he were irritated. Sometimes he'd shut me up with a sarcasm, sometimes and still more effectually with a joke about my hat or the coat he didn't like. That sort of thing went on for years. The same anticipation on my part, the same disappointment. I was a hopeful young fool."

The young woman broke the pattern by "being irregular" about meeting George at the station. This upset him: " 'He was used to my meeting him. So I became regular again; but now I am taciturn too and full of the same kind of inhibitions George feels. We open the conversation with inquiries—weather, children, health, you know the sort of impersonal thing.' " The older woman affirmed, " 'Yes, I know . . . It takes the heart out of you, I know that too.' "[14]

In this fictionalized account, there is much of Elsie's spirit and soul. After years of being ready to battle the expected and the conventional, she was a bit worn down. She acquiesced on occasion, as the young woman did here when she met the train and spoke of the mundane. This did not mean that her spirit was submerged; it meant that it was expressed elsewhere. Still this to her was a disappointment, because she wanted to be true to her beliefs and not to give in to the deadening effects of custom.

Elsie was drawn to adventure. She felt most alive when on a quest, mind and body fully engaged. For Elsie, the sea quickened her spirit. Its mist and movement, its salty essence, called forth the strength of her spirit. Just such a challenge she met in the waters of the Mediterranean. Along with Alexander Sedgewick, of the *New York Times*, and his wife, Elsie sailed among the Greek Isles. Sedgewick told of an occasion when the captain of the yacht was struck with fear at the danger of sailing through one particular spot. As Lissa Parsons recalled his account, "There was nothing timid about mother on the water. She was a great sailor and a passionate sailor. When he wouldn't go . . . out of harbor when she wanted him to, she'd take the boat out. She had great courage." Lissa added, "I think my mother had a great deal of moral courage as well as physical courage."[15]

A close friend and colleague, anthropologist Gladys Reichard, said of Elsie, "If one trait of her sturdy character were to be stressed more than another it must be her absolute regard for truth." Another friend referred to this trait as her "thesis concerning the importance of intellectual honesty." Anthropologist Ruth Bunzel valued this in Elsie. After a difficult episode in Bunzel's Guatemalan fieldwork, she wrote Parsons, "I do want to say that when you wrote me last summer that I could count on you, I knew that that was absolutely true; I knew that you were a truly loyal and generous person, and that knowledge stirred me deeply. I know how rare such persons are."[16] This regard for truth translated into a directness of behavior. Elsie was straightforward. As Reichard said to her, "You are the only person who is definite, & how we do need definiteness." And La Farge remarked, "You have quite a wonderful place in you that is compounded of directness . . . and a very generous sweetness."[17] In her work, this was expressed in her regard for, above all, the facts. She abhorred the sentimental and the emotional; she was a rationalist to the core. For her, truth was the unadulterated rendering of the empirical. Analysis most certainly had its place, but this, too, must be rooted in the rational.

Her reaction to those who effused emotion was harsh. Of George Sand and the romantic movement, Elsie wrote, "What a vulgar sentimentalist she was. She changed her lovers like her gloves and always calling God in to witness her sincerity. The Romanticist movement of the early 19th century never made any appeal to me at any rate." Weighing her judgment, she added, "I wonder how much we owe to it. Perhaps in part the idea of women 'leading their own lives' even if at that time the idea was expressed in freedom for a sentimental promiscuity."[18] She was impatient also with those who rationalized aspects of culture by appealing to an outside, mystical force, be it God or deified evolutionary principles. She railed against what she saw as "that very common error of describing the savage as an erratic, wayward, improvident creature, and civilization as a progress from savagery, thanks to its exceeding ability in taking thought for the morrow."[19] In a review of *The Primitive Family as an Educational Agency,* Elsie sympathized with the author's goal, "the cornering of the sentimentalist."[20] She would gladly join him, though for her it would more likely be an attack on the sentimentalist. She had chosen her weapons, those "put into our hands by the study of comparative culture."[21] Armed with these, she turned against "the established morality" of the elders and against the lazy acceptance of the norm. However, in order to be successful in this marshaling of facts, Elsie insisted on "the scrupulous raking through of ethnographic data." No haphazard listing of ethnographic examples or data assembled in misleading ways to support one's point would be acceptable.[22] The facts presented without emotionalism would speak in reasoned and truthful tones.

Elsie was remarkable not only for her generous spirit, the scope of her interests, and the incisiveness of her intellect, but also for her physical appearance. Tall and slender, but in every line a woman, Elsie cast a spell on those around her. She moved with a rhythm and grace undoubtedly molded by years of outdoor life. Hers was a healthy beauty. As Clarence Day commented, "You looked like a beautiful gypsy at that dinner among a lot of pale soft-living indoor-people. What is Spring doing to you?" In a similar vein, La Farge referred to her as his "Gypsy Queen" in a poem he had written for her, entitled "Elsie, Time and the Map." Kroeber spoke of "her erect carriage, chiseled features, level look, and slow direct smile." He recalled memories of her at Columbia: "Her statuesque figure floated through the seminar alcoves of the Low Library on Morningside Heights as a memorably astonishing sight."[23] Even her voice drew attention, for she spoke in low tones with carefully chosen words, never in the heat of emotion, always with reason. Of her, an admirer wrote: "You are a different order, like a well moulded marble figure that would come up fresh and new out of even the deepest buried city of splendor."[24] This image of classic beauty appeared to another admirer: "I never quite made up my mind as to what you were most: American or 'old worldly.' I finally compromised with the problem and it used to be one of my pet fancies to picture you in some Roman atrium with the light falling from above on young roses and old armour. When you forbade me calling you 'Lady' I wondered a long time whether you would allow 'Domina.' . . . That is . . . what I shall call you—simply— 'Domina.' " It was her perceptive spirit that impressed him: "From the first . . . I consciously classified you. I remember first you were, 'She who would see things' (i.e., as they are), then you were 'She who does see things.' Then gradually as I grew to know you a little better you were 'She sees and "savvys" ' (understands), then again she who laughs and she who loves and laughs at things."[25]

One comment on Elsie's beauty came in the form of an apology from Alyse Gregory, a leader in the American suffrage movement. She wrote Elsie in October, 1939, from Switzerland. Years earlier she had been working with Gilbert Cannan to raise funds for D. H. Lawrence's journey to the United States, and she had approached Elsie for a contribution. The memory of this remained with Gregory as an unpardonable breach of manners. With the world embroiled in war, her apology was mingled with a sense of doom: "Gilbert Cannan is in an insane asylum, Lawrence, who is as over rated as he used to be under rated, is in his grave, Randolph [Bourne] is in his grave. Europe is once more turning out machines more and more expert, to kill more and more quickly, more and more young men, and yet these human incidents survive." With all the death and destruction of a way of life, Gregory still carried with her the image of Elsie two decades earlier. She recalled: "On the few occasions that I saw you, you seemed, with your unusual personal charm, your beauty, the firmness and reserve of your mind, its daring and its pride, the sense of distinction that surrounded all that you said and did, someone whom I longed to know but felt too shy and uncertain to approach. Your friendship for Randolph Bourne, who was perhaps my greatest friend at that time, made me feel that we must both have appreciated in him the same qualities and what he told me of you had always for me so much charm and interest."[26]

Her uniqueness was noted by many. In response to an article that she had written for a journal, the sociologist Albion Small said, "We cogitated for a long time on the problem—will not Mrs. Parsons' brilliancy in the company of our dry as dust style of material look like a diamond on a gentleman in overalls? We have taken the chance, however, and hope the contrast will not be too conspicuous." A U. S. circuit court judge conveyed her appeal: "Elsie Clews Parsons gave a most brilliant paper in a symposium on ideals before the City Club. Hers was the ideal 'Society.' Graceful, witty, sarcastic, brilliant in every way." Her husband, Herbert Parsons, perhaps offered the best encapsulation, "Elsie is not as other women are and everyone who knows her so realizes."[27]

The most poignant memories of Elsie come from her granddaughter, Fanny Parsons Culleton, who remembered her time with her in the Lounsberry house, in Rye, New York, where, Fanny lived with her father, John Parsons, her mother, Fanny Wickes Parsons, her two younger brothers, and her grandmother, whom she called simply

Elsie: "Lounsberry had at that time about forty acres of land, with a walk down to the . . . inlet. And one of the things I was proud of was that Elsie was able to find four-leaf clovers, and sometimes five and six. And I inherited that and my father did too. So we would all go out and carry home our little bunches of four-leaf clovers! And I think it is that particular way of being able to look for the odd . . . pattern in the normal that . . . Elsie . . . had."

Fanny recalled hearing stories about the Stonover Farm, in Lenox, Massachusetts, another of the Parsons's homes. "Like all her houses," Fanny said, "it was very uncomfortable, because Elsie didn't do any housekeeping, didn't look after anything in particular." The farmer and his family lived in the kitchen wing, and all of the Parsons children, as Fanny said, "hung out doing farm things all the time." She remembered the house in Vinal Haven, Maine, where Fanny as a young child would spend her summers with her grandmother. "You can go there by train which is what I did as a child. You get off in Rockland and you get on the ferry, and the ferry goes to North Haven where Elsie's launch would meet you and take you to the island of Vinal Haven. . . . Now Elsie lived kind of in the bay, in her bay." Fanny would arrive by boat, walk up the long gangplank, and across the boardwalk to "a little trail through piney woods, spruces and there were clamshells on the path so if it was nighttime you could see the path. . . . And you'd come to the house." There, up behind her house in a cabin, Elsie would work all day. Fanny and Elsie would have lunch together, and then later in the afternoon, they might go for a sail in one of the dinghies. Elsie taught Fanny to row when she was nine years old. Of this, she recollected, "I would put on my life jacket in the morning and I was given a rowboat of my own and I rowed [across the bay] everyday." There she had found Ernest Holt, the pediatrician, and his family of adopted children. At the Holts, Fanny learned a game that she brought back across the bay and taught Elsie:

> I do have one wonderful memory and I just love it. It must have been maybe when I was ten or eleven. I was over at the Holts, I learned a game. And the game was called the Parson's Hat. And I brought it home and Elsie nearly freaked she liked it so much. . . . When [Elsie's son], Herbert and [his wife], Margot, and my mother and father came to visit she made everybody play the Parson's Hat every evening. And they thought it was terribly boring. And it was just like her. . . . What happens is that you have one person who's the parson, and you have everybody else sit . . . in a complete circle around them and each chair . . .

has a color attached to it in the order of the rainbow. . . . And there's a ritual, you see this is a ritual. . . . It went like this. Somebody starts and they say, "The Parson's lost his hat. Some say this and some say that. But I say" and then you say "red" and red has to be right on and you say, "I sir," "Yes, you sir," "Not I sir," "Then who sir?" "Green!" And the object of the game is to unseat the Parson, so once in a while you say, "The Parson." And the Parson has to be right on. You have to answer [immediately]. Then he has to say, "Not I sir." "Then who, sir?" And this goes on very fast. . . . If you don't answer right, then you go to the end of the rainbow. . . . Everybody moved up to a different chair . . . and got to be a different color and you were supposed to remember what the color was, or you'd have to ask your neighbor quickly.

Fanny concluded, "Well, it was just too close to her work, the things that she'd known. I can still remember her glee. . . . I still remember her playing it. Of course, she loved to be the Parson. Her one idea was to sit in that chair!"[28]

Reichard remarked that Parsons was among the women "whose very casualness" in their endeavors "was in large part a result of her own efforts." From the work of Parsons and others for women's equality, Reichard said, "Many conventions had broken down so that a woman need not fight to be allowed to think; women in anthropology at least did not even question their willingness to do fieldwork or to express their conclusions about it."[29] Nonetheless, women's equality in the anthropological endeavor had not always been accepted. In 1927 the Santa Fe Laboratory in Anthropology began sponsoring summer research groups in ethnology and archeology. Alfred Kidder had arranged for the organizational meeting to be held at the Yale Club, which excluded women. As Kidder wrote Boas, " 'I am afraid that I cannot manage to include Mrs. Parsons.' " He asked Boas to attempt to explain the situation to Elsie, and said that he had been " 'incredibly stupid' " in making the arrangements. This initial "oversight" in the exclusion of women carried through to the summer research groups as well. Parsons criticized Kidder for this, and he responded, "I think you are a bit rough on me in the matter of women's participation in the field training courses." He referred to "this business of women in anthropology" as "perplexing." First, Kidder asserted, it was difficult to accommodate women in the field. Second, the professional opportunities for women did not match those for men, so why train women who could then not be employed? And finally, Kidder admitted, "Another handicap, and a very real one . . . is that a young woman, because of the liklihood [*sic*] of her marriage, is an unreliable element to build into the foundation of a staff structure."[30] Reichard provided an inside view of this conflict in the 1929 season of the Santa Fe Laboratory in Anthropology. Kidder, Edward Sapir, and Kroeber were the group leaders, and women had been excluded from the archeological group. Reichard wrote: "Kroeber's answer to your message, 'Tell Elsie I never was a feminist, & I'm not an anti-feminist now, appearances to the contrary notwithstanding.' The main contention of them all is that girls are all right, entertaining, etc., but no good in science because you can't do anything with them. Kroeber ends all remarks with 'Boas will place her.' It never seems to occur to any of them that if he can others might be able to were they sufficiently interested."[31]

Elsie Clews Parsons was a woman who made things happen, for herself, for others, for anthropology, and for folklore. She was directed, she was determined, and she had an inner strength that came from harnessing a stubborn temperament toward positive ends. Once a willful child, Elsie became a disciplined woman, who, as Kroeber said, "valued control preeminently: first in herself, next in others."[32] Her ability, her energy, and her wealth placed Elsie in a position to influence and to guide the work of others. At a time when women did not ordinarily wield much power, Elsie Clews Parsons became a force in anthropology and folklore.

NOTES

1. Alfred Louis Kroeber, "Elsie Clews Parsons," *AA* 45 (1943): 252.

2. I am grateful to Roger Abrahams for suggesting the parallel between Parsons's systematic fieldwork in the Southwest and other, more elaborate group efforts.

3. ECP, Giddings to ECP, 13 Oct. 1906; Waters to ECP, 1 Mar. 1940; Toksvig to ECP, 12 Jan. 1940; Gladys E. Reichard, "Elsie Clews Parsons," *JAF* 56 (1943): 45; Keith S. Chambers, "The Indefatigable Elsie Clews Parsons— Folklorist," *Western Folklore* 32 (1973): 197.

4. Fanny Parsons Culleton, interview by Rosemary Lévy Zumwalt, 6 July 1988; Elsie (Lissa) Parsons Kennedy, "The Reminiscences of Mr. and Mrs. John D. Kennedy" (New York: Oral History Research Office, Columbia, 1966), pp. 19, 24.

5. ECP, anonymous correspondence.

6. ECP, Morris Opler to Peter Hare, 26 Oct. 1970.

7. Kroeber, "Elsie Clews Parsons," p. 255.

8. Franz Boas, "Elsie Clews Parsons, Late President of the American Anthropological Association," *Scientific Monthly* 54 (May 1942): 480.

9. ECP, a rough draft of a letter to an unnamed friend. Though giving no date, in these letters written during her trip to Washington and on her return to New York, Elsie referred to "the lost one," and to having "a great sorrow in the heart." With this internal evidence, I suggest the date as circa 1890, sometime after the death of her brother, Robert.

10. ECP, EC to anonymous, [c. 1890].

11. ECP, EC to Alice, [c. 1891].

12. ECP, EC to anonymous, [c. 1890].

13. ECP, anonymous to ECP, [1908?], [1913?]; ECP to HP, 27 Oct. 1910.

14. Elsie Clews Parsons, "Meetings," *The Masses* 6, no. 7 (Apr. 1915): 11.

15. Kennedy, "Reminiscences," p. 21.

16. ECP, Bunzel to ECP, n.d. For the difficulties in Bunzel's fieldwork situation, see ECP, Bunzel to ECP, 16 July 1934.

17. Reichard, "Elsie Clews Parsons," p. 48; ECP, anonymous correspondent, 1935; Reichard to ECP, 13 Sept. 1940; La Farge to ECP, 29 July [1913?].

18. ECP, ECP to HP, 18 June 1909.

19. Elsie Clews Parsons, "A Communication in Regard to the 'Discovery of Time,' " *The Journal of Philosophy, Psychology and Scientific Methods* 12 (1915): 713–14.

20. Elsie Clews Parsons, review of *The Primitive Family as an Educational Agency*, by James Arthur Todd, *Science* 39 (May 1914): 654.

21. Elsie Clews Parsons, "The Sin of Being Found Out," *New Review* 3 (15 Dec. 1915): 361.

22. Parsons, review of *The Primitive Family*, p. 655.

23. ECP, Day to ECP, Friday [1918?]; La Farge, 24 July 1918; Kroeber, "Elsie Clews Parsons," pp. 252, 255.

24. ECP, anonymous to ECP, 13 Oct. 1923.

25. ECP, anonymous to ECP, 19 Jan. [1915?]; 15 Dec. 1914.

26. ECP, Alyse Gregory to ECP, 15 Oct. 1939.

27. ECP, Small to ECP, 3 Dec. 1913; anonymous, 28 Apr. 1916; HP to Hamilton Angus, 22 May 1913.

28. Culleton, interview, 6 July 1988. While "Lounsberry" is actually in Rye, the location referred to in all of Parsons's correspondence was Harrison, New York.

29. Reichard, "Elsie Clews Parsons," p. 46.

30. Margaret M. Caffrey, *Ruth Benedict* (Austin: University of Texas Press, 1989), p. 261, quoting Franz Boas Papers, Kidder to Boas, 13 Feb. 1931; ECP, Alfred Kidder to ECP, 30 Mar. 1929; 8 Apr. 1929.

31. ECP, Reichard to ECP, 25 Aug. 1929.

32. Kroeber, "Elsie Clews Parsons," p. 255.

2

The Clews Family

You were born on Friday, November 27, 1874 at 7:30 p.m.
in the Grosvenor House, 5th Ave. and 10th St. This morning I spent at your mother's getting figures for her personal
tax assessment and while there she got out her keys and her
tin box and her Bible and gave me the above extract.
—Herbert Parsons[1]

Elsie Worthington Clews was the firstborn child of Henry Clews and
Lucy Madison Worthington Clews. She was healthy and full of life
and would be both a pleasure and a problem for her parents. As she
grew older, she was to challenge all of the conventions of social etiquette, until finally, one day, she would incorporate in her writings
the conflicts she had had in the society of her youth. Perhaps her father, buoyant as was his nature, missed that which marked his baby
girl as different. Her mother did not. Elsie was a puzzle to her from
birth. As Elsie's daughter, Lissa, remarked, "My grandmother told me
that she never could understand Mother from the time she was a
little girl." This was reflected in the remark that Lucy Clews made
to Elsie on the birth of Lissa, her first grandchild, "I can only hope
the little girl is as attractive and as interesting as her mother was
at the same early age. As you have often been told, you were an unusual baby!"[2] Part of the enigma derived from Elsie's total disinterest
in all things that her mother valued. The conflict started early and
lasted long.

Her parents' world was one of wealth and social standing. Their
marriage had been a merger of sorts to assure them a place in society.
Henry Clews was a self-made millionaire, and Lucy Madison Worthington came from a family whose good name survived the financial
devastation of the Civil War. Though raised in Iowa from the age of
five until her marriage, Lucy Madison Worthington was fiercely attached to her southern roots. She was born in Lexington, Kentucky,
in 1852. Her father was General William Hoard Worthington, and
her mother was Anna Eliza Tomlinson, of Harrodsburg, Kentucky.

Lucy's middle name of Madison marked her relationship with President James Madison whom she thought was her great-uncle, though later genealogical research conducted by her grandson showed him to be a second cousin. She was also related to Andrew Lewis, who had been next in command to General George Washington during the Revolutionary War. Lucy never accepted her father's northern sympathies. He had freed his slaves before the Civil War, organized the Fifth Iowa volunteers, and served as the colonel in this Union regiment.[3]

Her marriage to Henry Clews, in 1874, brought her uncomfortably close to the despised Yankee past. A man eighteen years her senior, Henry Clews had been acquainted with President Abraham Lincoln and had worked with President Ulysses S. Grant. Indeed, Henry and Lucy had met at a White House ball given by Grant. These days in Washington became a taboo subject in the family because, as Lissa Parsons Kennedy later explained, "Grandmother was Southern and she was ashamed of all this." She was especially ashamed of Henry Clews's friendship with Lincoln. Lissa recalled one story that escaped the careful censorship of Lucy Worthington Clews: "I always understood that when Lincoln lay in state . . . [Grandfather] was one of the men that stood guard. . . . But that was before he was married to my grandmother." After her husband's death, Lucy Worthington Clews destroyed all evidence of Henry Clews's friendship with Lincoln. Lissa remembered returning to the New York house with her uncle, Henry Clews, Jr. There were fire engines in front of the house, smoke was bellowing from the chimneys, and her grandmother was sitting calmly in the upstairs sitting room, dropping letters in the fire.[4]

Born on August 14, 1834, Henry Clews was the son of Bessie Kenrick and James Clews, the master potter of Cobridge, England. As the youngest of four boys, Henry was to have entered the ministry and to have acted as curate for his cousin, the vicar of Wolstanton. At the age of fourteen, his training for the Anglican Church was interrupted by a trip to New York City. As he recalled years later, "I came to this country from England . . . expecting to stay for merely a short visit. I had barely learned the localities of the public buildings and the principal streets, when I began to perceive the possibilities that presented themselves to a young man. . . . I liked the hustle and the bustle that contrasted so vividly with the slow and easy style which prevailed in my native country. I could not escape being drawn into the spirit which surrounded me, and I made up my mind that I would make my stand in life in New York."[5] He worked as a clerk in the dry goods importing house of Wilson G. Hunt and Company. Through good business sense, Henry Clews was able to move from the importing house to Wall Street. He described the way in which he gained admittance to the New York Stock Exchange: "I . . . inserted an advertisement in the newspapers, and proposed to buy and sell stocks at a sixteenth of one per cent" when the going rate was an eighth of one percent. The "old fogies," as Clews said, were stunned by this move: "What rendered it more distasteful to them still was the fact that, while they lost customers, I steadily gained them. The result was that they felt compelled to admit me to their ranks."[6]

Clews organized the firm of Stout, Clews & Mason, which was later changed to Livermore, Clews & Company, and finally to Henry Clews & Company. He brought his brother, James Clews, over from England to manage the Broadway and Broome Street branch of the brokerage.[7] The success of Henry Clews has not gone unnoticed by financial historians. As Robert Sobel remarks in *Panic on Wall Street: A History of America's Financial Disasters*, "Men like Henry Clews, a pillar of his church, a person of eminent respectability, a chatty social climber, and a shrewd analyst, made up the large majority of those who worked in the financial district. An upright Victorian, Clews was considered a broker of honor and integrity, which meant that he would participate in raids, pools, and corners but did not associate with known criminals."[8]

In an assessment of his work, Clews would recall from the vantage of retirement, "Above everything else in my business life, I regard with most satisfaction the work I did in marketing the Civil War loans of the Government of this great and glorious country of ours." This financial work for the benefit of the Union was undertaken not with patriotic fervor, but with wise business sense. By the end of the Civil War, Clews's firm was second largest seller of U.S. war bonds.[9]

Henry Clews's life followed the course for the successful man, which had been suggested in mock earnestness by Charles Dudley Warner as he toured American resorts in 1886. In order to transpose oneself from a businessman to the " 'full-blown existence of a man of fashion,' " Warner prescribed the following: " 'The process is perfectly charted. Success in business, membership in a good club, tandem in the Park, introduction to a good house, marriage to a pretty girl of family and not much money, a yacht, a four-in-hand, a Newport villa.' "[10]

In matters of fashion, Clews was meticulous. He was "very careful about his clothes . . . very *soigné* . . . always immaculately dressed."[11] As he grew older, he playfully attempted to conceal his age. At his eighty-second birthday party in 1916, "he would permit no more than forty-four candles on the cake, and for long in answer to questions as to his age he gave the smiling answer: 'Upward of 46.' " Three years later, at his eighty-fifth birthday party, "he felt compelled to make a slight concession to the date, for he then replied: 'I guess that after today I'll have to tell my friends I am upward of 47.' "[12]

Clews prided himself on retaining his youthful appearance, and jokingly linked this to his premature baldness. He recalled that he posed as a youth in his adult years, being aided by having "no hair on top of my head, in the place where other people's hair usually grows." Thus, he presented the same appearance as he had the day he was born. His "perpetual bloom of youth" was tarnished by the financier, William R. Travers. An issue of Frank Leslie's *Illustrated Weekly* had included a photograph of Henry Clews among several of New York businessmen who were designated as self-made men. In the main hall of the Union Club, Travers seized the moment. To the bankers and brokers present, Travers, who was known for his wit and his stutter, said, " 'Hallo, boys! Here comes Clews, the self-made man. . . . I s-s-say, Cl-Cl-Clews, as you are a s-s-self-made man, wh-why-why the d-d-devil didn't you p-put more h-h-hair on the top of your head?' "[13] On another occasion, Clews was musing about what he should wear to a fancy dress ball, when Travers suggested a costume that would highlight his baldness, " 'Why d-don't you g-g-gild your h-head and g-go as a p-pill?' "[14]

In an interview with the *New York Times* on "The Pet Economies of Well Known Millionaires," Henry Clews denied undue concern about frugality. " 'There's no little thing that I cut down on financially, . . . absolutely none.' " On his chief concern, he elaborated: " 'But the secret of my success is my energy, my enthusiasm. I push matters. I'm always going ahead, doing things other people don't think to do. Well, that vigor absolutely depends on my health. My health is my lucky star. If it should go down I believe my business would too. My favorite economy is husbanding my health. I'm as careful of myself as an opera singer is. I never drink, I never smoke, I take a moderate amount of exercise every day, and I go to bed early.' "[15]

Though Henry Clews regarded himself as a patriotic supporter of the Union, apparently his wife thought he passed as a foreigner. Lissa Parsons Kennedy coolly commented about her grandmother's choice of mate, "If she had to marry money, I suppose the fact that he was an Englishman—so that you couldn't consider him a Northerner . . . she didn't feel she was betraying the South as much." Henry Clews treated his wife with "great kindness and solicitude." Still, as Lissa characterized the marriage, it was "a business proposition." This was especially so for her grandmother, who, as was the custom of the time, always addressed her husband by his surname, "Mr. Clews," and never used any form of endearment or showed any signs of affection.[16]

In her recollections of her grandfather's personality, Lissa Parsons recalled, he was formal, and not spontaneous. But in the right setting, Henry Clews could be less restrained: "He let go more when Grandma wasn't there. She used to fix him with a look . . . and he'd go back to eating his meal." Of his disposition, she remarked: "He was always very cheerful. At the table, if one of the family got into a discussion and it seemed to be getting at all acrimonious, or one of the children got a little noisy, he'd always quiet us and say, 'Now, we'll all relax. We mustn't have serious conversation while we're eating because it's bad for the digestion. We will all relax and we will sing a song.' And he'd begin it. The song that he always sang was, 'I Dreamt I Dwelt in Marble Halls.' " Lissa said this worked for everyone, except her grandmother, who regarded it as improper to sing at the table and "would get a little tense over this."[17]

Lucy and Henry Clews had three children, two boys and one girl. Their younger son, Robert Bower, died in 1890, at the age of thirteen from a cerebral hemorrhage. "Little Robert Clews's Sudden Death" was reported in the *New York Times:* "The lad was a pupil at the Cushing Academy, Dobbs Ferry, and came to this city on Saturday evening, to spend Sunday at home. For some years he had been subject to fainting fits of an epileptic nature. On Sunday evening, about 7 o'clock, while playing with the other children in the house the lad was suddenly stricken down, and became unconscious. . . . The family physician was summoned but when he reached the house, the boy was dead."[18]

Their surviving son, Henry Clews, Jr., was an artistic child who pursued his interest in photography and turned his hobby to profit at school as a young child by selling pictures to his friends. Elsie proved to have a more discriminating eye for photography than did his clients. After sending her a packet of pictures and receiving her response, he wrote, "I am sorry that you don't like those Photos. I think that you are very hard to please." Scholarship was not his forte, a theme he conveyed to his sister in two separate letters: "I have not got very much to tell you, but that I have been very bad this week, and that I have gotten terrible lot of black marks;" and later, "I have tried to study hard but I don't think it is any use, I never *shall* become a *scholar*, I am too fond of play, and out door exercise."[19]

In the years when their children were young, Henry and Lucy Clews were frequently separated from them by business and pleasure trips. Both wrote long letters filled with love, concern, and instructions. On July 12, 1888, Elsie's father wrote,

My Dear Elsie:
  I suppose you and the boys have been very lonely since your Mamma and myself left you at the dock and your loneliness doubtless has caused you to think of us both very often since our departure. Your Mamma was a good deal worried fearing that you might not get home safely, but not getting a telegram from you the next morning she construed it into an evidence that you had reached home safely.

Henry Clews expected Elsie, as the eldest child, to watch over her younger brothers and to tend to the dogs:

I hope you will not fail to exercise your influence in keeping Henry and Robby in good order while your Mamma is away. Make them keep their feet off the furniture, from sliding on the floors and from taking the dogs into the house, and also keep an eye upon Topsy. Don't fail to whip her whenever she is naughty as it is only in that way you can get her into good training.[20]

Twelve days later, angered at the lack of correspondence from the children, Henry Clews wrote Elsie a stern letter:

The fact that neither you nor the boys have written to your Mother during the past week that she has been absent excepting one epistle from you in the Dutch language which she couldn't read a word of any more than if it had been written in hieroglyphics and which you must have known at the time, and about one line from Bob, is not performing the part of loving children to your parent. It was the duty of one of you to have written every day, as you certainly must have known how anxious your Mother was to hear from you. On receipt of this do not therefore fail to write to her and make the boys do the same, and one of you write a letter every day thereafter until she returns.[21]

In a postscript, he reminded Elsie, "I hope you have kept the boys and their little boy friends from injuring the floors and the furniture of the house. Look sharply after them while your Mother is away." Elsie, Henry, and Robert responded to their father's command; each wrote a letter to their mother. Their father acknowledged receipt:

My Dear Chicks,

   I was glad to hear through Bobby's letter that the house re-
mains in the same place, as I was quite of the opinion that you
three children with the aid of a few others called in from outside
had put your shoulders under the foundation and carted it into
the valley below and then claimed on my discovery of its re-
moval, that it had been a land slide.

His sternness had passed, and his affectionate tone returned:

You don't know how much I missed my usual trip last week to
Newport and also the one this week, mainly because it deprives
me of seeing and being with you all. I sometimes wonder
whether you miss me half as much as I do you. Sometimes I
think that you all have so much fun from the time you get up
until you go to bed (you only go there because you are tired, the
result of excessive exuberance of spirits) that your poor Mother
and myself are forgotten through it all. Isn't that so now? Give
me your honest opinion when you write, and give me credit for
guessing right once in my life at least.[22]

Henry Clews was proud of Elsie, whom he addressed in one letter
as "My Dear *Tall* Daughter."[23] He encouraged her to work hard, to be
industrious, and to invest her earnings. In 1888 he commissioned her
as his "agent" to sell copies of his book, *Twenty-Eight Years in Wall
Street,* to the residents of Newport. He suggested that she might offer
"a small commission for services rendered" to her brothers who could
act as her subagents. He continued: "Just make the bargain to start
with, 'no work, no pay.' Henry can cover one section of the city and
Bob can take another section. In that case the whole of Newport can
be covered in three directions. You take the North, Henry the South
and Bob from east to west. In that way by starting out together, one
of you I am sure will have the wind in your favor, which will give you
an additional impetus to speed. . . . There's money in it and don't let
the grass grow under your feet. The only way to do in business is to
make it grow under the feet of your competitors."[24] The profits, he
playfully suggested, could be invested in his firm.
   This same jovial and hearty rapport was not present in Elsie's relationship with her mother. Certainly there was love between the two,
but not necessarily understanding. Neither mother nor daughter
could fathom the other's approach to life. Values, concerns, goals—
these were at opposite poles for them both. Lucy Worthington Clews
was acquisitive, concerned with clothes and fashion, bent on having a

good time and enjoying life as it came. Elsie, with no fascination in the world of fashion, developed an interest at a young age in the social problems of poverty, hunger, and disease. And as a young adult, she began working toward applying her knowledge in a way that might help change society. Part of their divergent approach to life was apparent in a letter that Elsie's mother wrote to her in 1906: "You see I view it like this. *This* life is the only one we are to live, and we must make what we can from it, not always fighting conditions, as you and Henry are so inclined to do. . . . As for me, life is our existence *only*. I think it must be so always, where there is *one vital* personal interest. However I make the most of all that offers, not expecting the impossible. And trying to do all I can for the happiness of those I am fond of. Love and service are the finest things in life, even if they don't bring *control*."[25]

In Lucy Clews's letters to her young daughter, one can still hear a tone of exasperation as well as of affection. For several years, the challenge was to mold Elsie into a young lady with proper manners, decorum in behavior, and a modulated voice. During the summer of 1888, Elsie was staying for several weeks with friends. Her mother wrote fondly, "We all miss you very much, and the boys have several times exclaimed how very strange it seems without sister! and Papa who is home is disappointed in not seeing you." She continued with an entreaty for Elsie to mind her manners, "I hope you will enjoy yourself and *adapt* yourself to Mrs. Adams wishes, and do not try to force any of your own ideas no matter how convinced you are of being right; the Adams girls always *gave up* most pleasantly when they were with us." The next week, Elsie's mother again wrote encouraging proper behavior, "I am glad to hear you are having a pleasant time, and are enjoying yourself. You are making a longer visit than intended. But I do not object to it, as long as you are a good girl, and give no trouble. Continue to be careful of your manners, and *your voice*." Lucy Clews was still cautioning Elsie concerning voice modulation and manners the following summer, "Remember not to insist and control the *voice* and pray be careful with your toilette—you know how to be agreeable and can make yourself most charming in a home circle."[26]

Elsie, in addition to holding strongly to her own opinions, and stating them emphatically—or to quote her number one New Year's resolution, "I promise to mean what I say and say what I mean"—was full of energy, and not always full of caution. Her mother, who preferred to indulge her children rather than punish them, was forced to be firm with her: "I have decided to deprive you of riding for a time, as you must admit my dear daughter, you deserve some deprivation for your *wild ride* . . . Friday. Don't you think so? Your poor horse is in a most shocking condition. . . . I am made nervous now when I think of the risk you took with *your life*. You know I am not severe, and always try to make you happy. Try and realize this if you are disappointed about riding."[27]

The greatest difference between Elsie and her mother was the amount of importance placed on material items, especially on clothes. For Elsie, these held little value; for her mother, they were, as Elsie herself said, her chief interest in life. Lucy Clews was finally able to bestow gifts on a grateful child when her granddaughter, Lissa, was born. Concerning one such present, she wrote to Elsie, "I am so glad the ring gave her pleasure. You can't tell how much she wanted it. But *I* know. When you were a small child, you had no special longing for material things. *I* had, and I was not gratified. So I know."[28]

Lucy Clews's interest in clothes was not a mere fancy; it was her passion in life. Cleveland Amory, an historian of high society, noted that Lucy Clews was "reputed to be Newport's best-dressed lady of her era, [and] declared that each summer she set aside $10,000 for 'mistakes in her clothes.' "[29] In tenacious style, she took hold of Elsie's wardrobe and tried to make it respectable. On one of her yearly shopping trips to Paris, she wrote, "Upon my return I will have some things I am sure you are much in need of. I have taken much trouble in my selections. I would write you in detail but think it is as well you should tell *what* you need first."[30] Her mother tried to entice her to Paris, "How I wish you could be here for two weeks. *Not* for *clothes* but to see Paris in November and enjoy yourself." And again, two years later, she wrote: "I do wish you would come over here for a few days and attend to your wardrobe. You might sleep on the roof!! Seriously I do wish you would come. I have things I can have arranged for you but you should have a look over them and a fitting. I will do the *pisé* [foundation]. You can take in the Opera and have some friends to dinner. Can't you come?"[31]

Lucy Clews was not just concerned that Elsie would not be dressed à la mode, but she was also convinced that her daughter's health problems were connected with her careless attitude about clothes: "I am afraid you may look shabby and feel *cold* until I get home. You know those severe colds are all from want of proper clothes!" She was alarmed about Elsie's care of her figure after the birth of her first two children: "I am not surprised you go *curlless*, but that will do no harm. I am afraid you also go *corsetless*, and that is harmful. Before you have an expense, you must learn to hold up and get back some *lines*." Knowing that Elsie relaxed at the Rocks, her mother added, "I am hoping you will soon go to Newport. It would be good for all of you. And you know '*The Yellow Rock*,' and perfect climate, etc., sea and sky!" This continued to be her wish for Elsie, "I hope this will find you in comfort at Newport. Do pay attention to your costumes. And *hats*. Buy anything you require to be *dressy* and charge to me. Do amuse yourself."[32]

Following the birth of Elsie's fourth baby, her mother quickly sent her something to wear: "I'm sure you would find the tea gown a *necessity*. Does it close? If not, I have another one I can lend you." And in the next letter written from Paris on black-bordered mourning stationery, which marked the death of Elsie's infant, her mother took up the subject of proper clothes for mourning: "I am afraid you have not made adequate provisions for clothes under the circumstances. A black net gown and long woolened net coat would see you to October in a *seemly* comfortable manner. *Crane* could make it for you. [It] should be *simple*, no belt, like a *shirt*, and the coat *no* sleeves. Like the . . . lace one I gave you, only *long*. I will *give* it to you if you will write and order it. But do so at once as Crane leaves *very soon*."[33] Elsie's mother added in a postscript, "N.B. I have written to Crane myself!!"

The Clews family spent their summers in Newport, Rhode Island, the most prestigious resort community in the country. For Henry Clews, Newport provided a blending of the social and business worlds. Participation in this society was crucial, for as social historian Cleveland Amory remarked, "The Big Businessman who did not attend at least one resort in season was socially suspect."[34] Lucy Clews was in her element: the focus of life was on fashion, elaborate dinners, and ornate parties. For Elsie, the attraction had nothing to do with finance or fashion, but rather with the freedom she felt. She thrived on the combination of the sea and the open land.

As with other elite vacation spots, the residents referred to themselves as "the cottagers," or "the cottage colony." Amory remarked, "To the historian of the future, looking back on the great American resort extravaganza, it is quite possible that its most outstanding single feature may be the use of the simple word 'cottage.' Through the years this word has been used, with remarkable aplomb, to denote the million-dollar mansions, marble palaces and chateau castles."[35] The Clews' cottage was called the Rocks. An elegant and enormous structure of rough-hewn limestone, perched on the edge of the sea, it was described as rising "from the rocks as if it were a part of them."[36] From her memories as a young child amidst the grandeur, Lissa recalled: "As you walked into 'the Rocks' . . . you came into a hall. It was an enormous hall, like a very big, big drawing room. The stairs going up divided. Then there was a little platform, and this divided again. This hall was two stories high, and at one end of it was a balustrade." It was so dark there and the balustrade was so high that "we children could crawl along on our tummies and look through and see them coming in after they had taken off their coats."[37]

A veranda extended around the front and the side of the house and overlooked an expanse of green lawn that spread to the edge of the sea wall. Cliff Walk, a four-mile long footpath, wound along the edge of this sea wall. As one resident of Newport described it: "The best time to take the Cliff Walk is in the late afternoon, when surf breaks like pearl against the yellow sands, the rocks are glamorous with brown and rose seaweed, and the air pungent with scent of flowers and tang of sea. When one tires of the glorious view of beach and cliff and the ocean that stretches unbroken to the shores of Spain, he can turn landward to another feast of beauty. No velvet is smoother than the lawns of emerald green dotted with twisted pines, and with shrubbery cunningly planted to shield the dwellings that lie along the Cliff Walk." In spring, the land was carpeted with daffodils and crocuses. This soon was followed by bowers of rhododendrons, and then a profusion of roses, growing wild in the hedgerows, as well as restrained in the gardens. In summer, heavy blooms of hydrangeas splashed the landscape with lavender and blue.[38]

Newport became known as the summer resort where wealth was put on display. The tone had been set by August Belmont, Sr., and his wife: they held elaborate ten-course dinners, with gold and silver service in abundance and each guest attended by a liveried footman. Such affairs were ornate, though, as described by the Honorable Herbert Pell, not necessarily scintillating. He had begun attending formal dinners at Newport in 1899, at the young age of fifteen. There was, he candidly admitted, a shortage of men. As he described it, " 'The richest man present always sat at the hostess's right, and the next richest at her left, and so on right down the table. After dinner, when the men were separated, we sat around and listened to the richest man tell us how to make money.' "[39]

By the end of the nineteenth century, flamboyant excess was de rigueur. The opportunity for such a tapestry of delight drew new and very rich blood to the seashore. This fresh wave of summer residents did not establish their beachhead without a nod of permission from the entrenched elite. Samuel Ward McAllister, whose social pedigree could not be questioned, named the Four Hundred, a number that fluctuated according to his whim, but always included "the elect of the social world in the metropolis. . . . McAllister made a career out of social arbitration, of acting as adviser to the dowager queens, of serving as grand vizier over their courts and cotillions. Indubitably he was a throwback to older courts on another continent, courts equally obsessed with relieving the boredom of having too much of everything."[40]

The boredom of privilege was punctuated with fetes of such an elaborate nature as to occupy the hostess in planning, arranging, and decorating, all on a grandiose scale. The night of a full moon was the most desired time, and invitations were sent out at least a month in advance in order to lay claim to the evening blessed with the fullest lunar glow.[41] One such festivity was given by Mr. and Mrs. Pembroke Jones who converted their estate into a sylvan fantasy: "The supper tent was decorated to represent a woodland scene, the sides entirely enclosed and the ceiling hung thickly with the beautiful southern bamboo vine, brought especially from the South for the occasion. The temporary ballroom and theater combined was eighty-five feet long and forty wide; it was made of substantial material and entirely enclosed so as to be serviceable in any kind of weather. The decorative scheme was white and pale green in tone, lavishly emphasized by the use of 10,000 water lilies arranged in streamers on the ceiling and walls where they showed to the best advantage near the score of large plate-glass mirrors that lined the walls from floor to ceiling."[42]

The decorative theme of one dinner centered on the stream that flowed down the middle of the table wherein "vivid fish swam pleasantly." At another, the pièce de la résistance was a cage filled with parrots of varying hues. "At still another the center of the table was covered with sand; at each place was a small sterling silver pail and a matching shovel. At a given signal, half a hundred guests dug frantically into the sand in front of them for their favors—thousands of dollars worth of rubies, sapphires, emeralds and diamonds." The sparkle, dazzle, and display of wealth struck the Grand Duke Boris, brother-in-law of Czar Nicholas II, who "compared preincome tax Newport and pre-revolution Russia. 'I have never dreamed of such luxury as I have seen at Newport. . . . We have nothing to equal it in Russia.' "[43]

Whether it was the result of the imagination played to the limit, or the urge to parody, some of the Newport hosts and hostesses held parties that mocked the idiosyncracies of their social mates. One such was the Dogs' Dinner, the brainchild of Harry Lehr, given by Mrs. Stuyvesant Fish and Mrs. Elizabeth Drexel Lehr at the latter's estate of Arleigh. Invitations were sent to one hundred dogs and to their owners. Received on the veranda, the pets, many in fancy dress, were seated around the leaves of dinner tables that had been placed together and were supported on a foot-high trestle. Waited on by Mrs. Lehr's servants, the dogs enjoyed a three-course meal of stewed liver and rice, fricassee of bones, and crumbled dog biscuits. " 'It must have been appreciated,' Mrs. Lehr remembered, 'because Elisha Dyer's dachshund so overtaxed its capacities that it fell unconscious by its plate and had to be carried home.' "[44]

Henry Clews, Jr., exploited his talent for the theater when he staged the Servants' Ball. The invited guests dressed in costume as their favorite servant. Shy of carrying the jest too far and exposing themselves to the critical eye of their servants, the elite of Newport gave the night off to all in their employ. As one participant recalled, Freedbody Park, located in the center of Newport and frequented by domestics, was filled to capacity at the hour when the guests departed for the ball. They were greeted at the front door of the Rocks by "young Clews, holding a duster in one hand and a pail in the other . . . disguised as his own valet. Behind him in the entry hall Tessie Oelrichs was mopping the floor and O. H. P. Belmont was presiding as cloakroom attendant. Harry Lehr was impersonating the butler. Later the guests adjourned to the kitchen and prepared a curious menu of scrambled eggs, lobster Americaine, and spaghetti, which served as dinner. It was agreed that the spectacle of representatives of the greatest fortunes in America actually doing housework, taking off their own coats and hats and cooking their own food was excruciatingly funny."[45]

In addition to the diversion of the parties, a major activity for the elite of Newport was bathing at Bailey's Beach. Here the exclusivity was established by admittance and not decor. Simple wooden cubicles served as changing houses. A pail of cold salt water was provided for rinsing off the sand. As one member of the club recalled: "Only the elite could bathe at Bailey's Beach. It was Newport's most exclusive club. The watchman in his gold-laced uniform protected its sanctity from all interlopers. He knew every carriage on sight, fixed newcomers with an eagle eye, swooped down upon them and demanded their names. Unless they were accompanied by one of the members, or bore an introduction from an unimpeachable hostess, no power on earth could gain them admission. If they wanted to bathe, they could only go to Easton's Beach—'The Common Beach' as the habitués were wont to call it. There they would have the indignity of sharing the sea with the Newport townspeople, referred to by Harry Lehr, who was fond of quoting the sayings of Louis XIV, as 'Our Footstools.' "[46]

At Bailey's Beach, the giants of Wall Street and the lights of society could don their bathing costumes and frolic in the surf without fear of journalistic exposure. (It was not until 1947 that a photographer was permitted on the premises, and then one from the *National Geographic*.) Thus, in the selective company of their peers, the rich indulged in their seaside eccentricities. James Val Alen bathed "in the full glory of a monocle and white straw hat," puffing all the while on his Havana cigar. Mrs. O. H. P. Belmont never parted with her green parasol, even while bathing. And Herman Oelrichs, "a short fat man with the contours of a walrus," floated out from Bailey's Beach on his raft, supplied with a lunch pail, a flask of whiskey, and a waterproof cigar case: "He would drift for hours offshore, a bulbous shape on the horizon, eating, quaffing, smoking and reading undisturbed by other swimmers. Sometimes he would drift a mile out from shore and be swept back to the beach by an incoming tide; frequently he had to be rescued by the Coast Guard before he could drift halfway to Nova Scotia on the Gulf Stream." Mrs. James Kernochan definitely could not float in her bathing costume. In an effort to protect her porcelain complexion, she garbed herself in a black bathing costume consisting of shoes, blouse, pantaloons and thick stockings, a full skirt and jacket with billowing sleeves tied at the wrists.[47]

While for a lady, an excess of body covering was viewed only as a precautionary cosmetic measure, an absence of a part of the costume was scandalous. And it was Elsie Clews Parsons who, just prior to World War I, set the precedent by appearing on Bailey's Beach without her heavy stockings. Bare-legged, she waded into the surf. Newport did not recover for years. Mrs. August Belmont, Jr., recalled that when she first came to the Belmont summer home, By-the-Sea, Newport was still trembling from the shock of Elsie's misconduct: "That first year—unfamiliar with the ancient or modern feuds of Newport—my mistakes were many and varied. One couple, who hadn't been invited to By-the-Sea for years by the Senior Mrs. Belmont, accepted my invitation with alacrity. I placed the lovely, modern-minded Elsie Clews next to the formal, old-school chairman of Bailey's Beach, not knowing that he had refused to speak to her after she went in bathing there without stockings, in spite of the committee ruling in the summer of 1910 that long stockings were required articles for ladies at the beach. . . . After that dinner Newport buzzed with gossip for days."[48]

The events at New York society resorts, no matter how mundane or frivolous, were regarded as important news. Lucy Clews's swim at Bailey's Beach made the front page. The title in bold capitals read, "Mrs. Henry Clews in Danger, Banker's Wife in Trouble while Bathing and Mrs. C. W. Dolan Saves Her." The story began: "Mrs. Clarence W. Dolan of Philadelphia received many congratulations at the Casino today for having helped Mrs. Henry Clews, who was yesterday in trouble in the surf at Bailey's Beach. The sea was quite rough, and Mrs. Clews, who had ventured out too far, called for help. Mrs. Dolan, who is one of the strongest swimmers among the women here, by good fortune chanced to be near Mrs. Clews. She swam quickly to her side and brought her to shore before the life guards could reach her."[49]

Newport continued to be a lodestone for Elsie, even when as a young woman she so emphatically rejected the trappings of society. In a letter to Herbert, she wrote, "I . . . went out to the moon, the honeysuckle and the water. Tonight I shall sleep out. I have just had breakfast out here on the porch and am rejoicing over the whole day in just about this same blue and breezy spot."[50] However, in spite of Elsie's enthusiasm, Newport would remain for Herbert a place of ostentatious display. It offended him deeply. This disagreement over the essential character of Newport ran like a thread through their correspondence. Comparing his assessment with her own, Elsie wrote, "I think your view of Newport is fair. It is a place of 'wealth, waste, and vanity,' but that aspect I am able to ignore in very large measure for a variety of reasons. Some of which you may surmise and some of which you can not. Strange as it may seem to you, one of Newport's chief charms to me is its possibility for privacy. . . . I am never any where so much alone as here. I spend many solitary hours every week on a little beach out of view and call of humans. On your next visit I promise to give you a new impression of it all and make you understand the hold it has on my affections."[51] Though Elsie understood Herbert's objections, she still maintained a hope that he, like her, could find pleasure there. Nine years after her marriage to him, she wrote: "I hope you will enjoy Newport. With tennis and swimming and pleasant company and no servants standing about, you ought to. It is always a regret to me that you don't get my degree of satisfaction out of the ocean. It is part of my sub consciousness which I can always bring up over the threshold of consciousness."[52]

Elsie resigned herself to Herbert's aversion. As she wrote, "Newport disagrees with your body and so hampers your spirits." She saw "something of that" in their son, John, "whereas Lissa soars."[53] The pleasure for Elsie remained in spite of this continual disagreement with Herbert: "Almost all the way here I kept asking myself your question, why? But as soon as I got out on the roof among the stars and in the sea breezes I stopped asking. Nor have I asked once on this blue day. I came for pleasure and I am getting it."[54]

The Rocks received the Clews family for the years the young family was growing. It housed the Parsons family, even though Herbert found the stone facade chilling. It remained for Lucy Clews as her fashionable summer home after she was widowed. But it could not withstand the force of a storm from the sea. In 1938 the Rocks was destroyed by a hurricane.

NOTES

1. ECP, HP to ECP, 28 Nov. 1924. There had been confusion about Elsie's date of birth, which had been recorded as 1875 in biographical entries about her. See Peter Hare, *A Woman's Quest for Science* (Buffalo, N.Y.: Prometheus Books, 1985), p. 27.

2. Elsie (Lissa) Parsons Kennedy, "The Reminiscences of Mr. and Mrs. John D. Kennedy" (New York: Oral History Research Office, Columbia, 1966), p. 33.; ECP, LC to ECP, 19 Aug. [1901].

3. A biographical sketch of Lucy Madison Worthington Clews is given in Hare, *A Woman's Quest for Science*, p. 27. He interviewed John E. Parsons, grandson of Lucy Clews, for much of this information. See also "Mrs. Henry Clews is Dead Here at 93," *New York Times*, 20 May 1945, sec. 1, p. 31, col. 1; "Henry Clews Dies in His 89th Year," *New York Times*, 1 Feb. 1923, sec. 1, p. 4, col. 4–5; and Kennedy, "Reminiscences," p. 9.

4. Kennedy, "Reminiscences," p. 4.

5. Henry Clews, *Fifty Years in Wall Street* (1908; rpt. New York: Arno Press, 1973), p. 1061.

6. Henry Clews, *Twenty-Eight Years in Wall Street* (New York: Irving Publishing Co., 1887), p. 8.

7. "James Clews," *New York Times*, 9 June 1903, sec. 1, p. 9, col. 6.

8. Robert Sobel, *Panic on Wall Street* (New York: MacMillan Co., 1968), p. 116.

9. Clarence L. Barnhart, ed., *New Century Cyclopedia of Names* (New York: Appleton-Century-Crofts, 1954), Vol. 1, p. 999.

10. Cleveland Amory quoting Charles Dudley Warner, *The Last Resorts* (New York: Harper and Brothers, 1952), p. 43.

11. Kennedy, "Reminiscences," p. 1.

12. "Henry Clews Dies," p. 1, col. 2; p. 4, col. 4–5.

13. Clews, *Twenty-Eight Years*, pp. 414–15.

14. Maud Howe Elliott, *This Was My Newport* (Cambridge, Mass.: The Mythology Company, 1944), p. 159.

15. "The Pet Economies of Well Known Millionaires," *New York Times*, 5 June 1910, pt. 5, p. 11, col. 6–7.

16. Kennedy, "Reminiscences," pp. 11, 8.

17. Ibid., pp. 1–3.

18. "Little Robert Clews's Sudden Death," *New York Times*, 25 Feb. 1890, sec. 1, p. 8, col. 2.

19. ECP, Henry Clews, Jr., to EC, [1890?]; ECP, Henry Clews, Jr., to EC, [n.d.]; 21 Apr. 1890. Never attracted to the financial world of his father, Henry continued with his interests in literature, the theater, and art. After his graduation from Amherst in 1898, he went to France where he studied sculpture under Rodin. His art was well received both in France and the United States. Two exhibitions of his sculpture were mounted in New York City, one in 1914, and one, posthumously, at the Metropolitan Museum of Art in 1939.

20. ECP, HC to EC, 12 July 1888.

21. ECP, HC to EC, 24 July 1888.

22. ECP, HC to EC, 27 July 1888.

23. ECP, HC to EC, 15 June 1888.

24. ECP, HC to EC, 9 Oct. 1888.

25. ECP, LC to ECP [1906?].

26. ECP, LC to EC, 20 Aug. 1888; 28 Aug. 1888; 24 Sept. 1889.

27. ECP, LC to EC, 20 Aug. 1888.

28. ECP, LC to ECP, Sunday [1906?]. In this, as well as in all subsequent quotations from Lucy Clews, the emphasis is hers.

29. Amory, *Last Resorts*, p. 175.

30. ECP, LC to ECP, 4 Nov. [1908?].

31. ECP, LC to ECP, Friday, [1910?].

32. ECP, LC to ECP, 4 Nov. [1908?]; [1906?]; 25 July [1914?].

33. ECP, LC to ECP, [1907?]; [1907?].

34. Amory, *Last Resorts*, p. 8.

35. Ibid., pp. 3, 11.

36. Elliott, *My Newport*, p. 132.

37. Kennedy, "Reminiscences," p. 7.

38. Elliott, *My Newport*, pp. 161, 132.

39. Amory, *Last Resorts*, pp. 8, 36, 47.

40. Richard O'Connor, *The Golden Summers, An Antic History of Newport* (New York: Putnam, 1974), p. 37.

41. Elliott, *My Newport*, p. 165.

42. O'Connor, *Golden Summers*, p. 250.

43. Amory, *Last Resorts*, pp. 175, 176.

44. O'Connor, *Golden Summers*, p. 251.

45. Ibid., p. 252.

46. Ibid., pp. 262–63.

47. Ibid., pp. 264–65.

48. Ibid., pp. 263–64.

49. "Mrs. Henry Clews in Danger," *New York Times*, 14 July 1910, sec. 1, p. 1, col. 6.

50. ECP, ECP to HP, 11 July 1911.

51. ECP, EC to HP, 19 June 1898.

52. ECP, ECP to HP, 4 Aug. 1909.

53. ECP, ECP to HP, 15 July 1913.

54. ECP, ECP to HP, 9 Sept. 1913.

3

College Years

As a young adult, Elsie Clews charted her own course. With singleness of purpose, she choose to go to college; and with determination
she met the opposition head-on, for this was not the approved aspiration of young girls from her social class. She choose to attend Barnard College, which, newly founded and located "in a brownstone
residence on Madison Avenue in the Forties,"[1] did not even offer the
secure status of established colleges for women.

Elsie's personality and style as a young adult carried through patterns that had been etched in childhood. She surrounded herself with
interesting friends, plunged into work and pleasure with equal intensity, burst the bonds of social decorum, and faced the world as her
own person. Elsie was conscious of the questioning and criticism that
she directed toward the accepted. She was also aware of the difficulties posed by this process. As she wrote a friend, "I sometimes almost
envy these pure minded, simple natures who only see one road before
them and one means of traveling on it. Their heart and head are
never at variance." On a scrap of paper, she penciled, "It is easy to
shut one's eyes to discrepancies in logic and action. . . . It is hard to
acknowledge that deep rooted beliefs have lost their significance or
have been supplanted by others."[2]

While challenging accepted beliefs and practices, Elsie was not rejecting ideals. In notes that must have been intended for a school essay, she wrote, "To loyally cherish high ideals is ennobling." Ideals
lifted "us above ourselves" and allowed us "to know our fullest powers." Without them, "ambition is evil, love and friendship nil." She
contrasted the ideal, which gave "strength [and] determination," to
the real, which was the "purely practical."[3] Commitment to ideals was
the heartbeat of Elsie's life. She placed this above all else, even above
family and friends. An understanding of this provides a key to her inner strength and utter tenacity.

In a draft of another essay, whose title was to be either "Moods" or
"Experiences" (though apparently the latter was favored since it was
heavily underlined), Elsie focused on the stages of life, from the mysteries of infancy to the exuberance of childhood, the cynicism of

youth, and the maturity of adulthood: "The course of life we project for ourselves is determined by our own views of life. As they change, our plans change. In early childhood the mystery of life seems to be most inexplicable. The strangeness of existing impresses us with a curious intentness which is dulled in after life. We do not think that we will ever live to take a place in the great world. We see no future." In the next step, the early questioning passes away, and the surge of greatness is upon us: "We are absorbed in ourselves. We anticipate a glorious future. We will be great, we will accomplish something." But the reality of the adult world impinges, and the questions arises, "Why do the men and women about us lead such humdrum lives? Soon we faintly realize the obstacles in the path and understand that average souls are not strong enough to overcome these obstacles. One must possess a certain unknown something to rise above the crowd. But there is still belief in our own power. What! must I pass into oblivion like the millions of human beings who have been born, have lived, have died. The word fame is dear to us." To attain fame, "to live in the memory of after generations," one must possess genius. And the gradual realization of this cools exuberance and leads to a rejection of boundless hope: "Experience is waking us from our dreams. Ah! but we can not give up our ideal, so we go on hoping and trusting to the future. A sharp awakening to find the ideal of childhood swept away by a fuller realization of life. Fame is worthless. All effort is futile. We become cynical. All bearings are lost. Life turns its worst side to us. . . . It is a bitter struggle, this outward loyalty for objects growing valueless." The final change in this progression is one of growth "in true knowledge of life," and with this "superciliousness, cynicism, and misanthropy drop away from us as an out-grown garment."[4] While "Moods—Experiences" has nowhere in the text an indication of date, the essay was clearly the work of one who had lived through the exuberance of childhood and the cynicism of coming-of-age. The last lines, which were struck out in dark ink, suggest this: "Then . . . the shadows fade away and leave a true appreciation of the duties and aims of life." Elsie was facing adulthood.

And she was facing a struggle with her parents. Lucy and Henry Clews anticipated that their daughter would attend Miss Ruehl's school in New York City. Here she would be instructed in subjects necessary for a lady's refinement, and care would be taken not to overtax the mind. Elsie insisted on attending Barnard College, which, having been founded in 1889, had not yet produced its first graduates. Mr. and Mrs. Clews were not pleased with their daughter's choice. As Lissa phrased it, "I think she had quite a ruckus to get to Barnard." Elsie's mother had a twofold concern: first, about Elsie's lack of attention to social grace and decorum, and second, about her overly studious nature. Attendance at Barnard would remedy neither. As Lissa explained, "My grandmother deplored . . . her lack of interest in clothes, and in dress, and in décor, and in housekeeping . . . and her lack of interest in social life, the kind of social life you think of as starting with a capital 'S.' "[5] Elsie herself wrote about this conflict, "When I wanted to go to college, I was called selfish. I should stay home, I was told, and be companionable to my mother. I had never noticed that my mother found me companionable. In those years we were not at all congenial."[6]

Elsie's father was convinced that women were not mentally suited for competitive endeavors. So fervent was he that he delivered several lectures on the subject that were later published in a collection of his speeches. In one such talk, "Shall the Suffrage Be Given to Women?," delivered to the National League for the Civic Education of Women in November, 1909, Clews made recourse to "natural law [and] natural instinct." Women needed the protection of men, and this was best attained through marriage and homelife. Henry Clews emphasized that this was the proper order for life. It was the plan of creation as stated in the Bible, which he referred to as woman's Magna Carta; and it was the civil charter, as stipulated in the Constitution of the United States, a document that, he pointed out, did not mention women, but only spoke of men.[7] In another talk, "Woman in Politics, Nature, History, Business and the Home," delivered to the National Society of New England Women in February, 1910, Clews stressed that woman "is endowed and equipped by nature for a higher and more important sphere of action, and her activities should centre in her home life." With this proper and natural focus, woman could find her "crowning glory in home-making and her domestic life."[8] Women who insisted on rejecting their proper role in life, and entering the man's domain of business, politics, and education, posed a serious threat. This was especially apparent in colleges and universities: "Women in politics, as in business, would also, in time threaten to crowd out the men, just as the university girls are already threatening to crowd out the university men in this country." Henry Clews traced the history of this problem in his address on suffrage:

The first woman admitted to a college here made her entry at Oberlin in 1833. She made the world wonder. But now sixty per cent. of the students in all our colleges open to them are women. In seven of the thirteen Western universities the women outnumber the men this year, while Nebraska, Minnesota, and California have nearly twice as many women as men students; and Stanford University, to protect the men from exclusion, has just decided to limit to five hundred the number of women that may be admitted in each year.

Tufts College, too, has had such an overwhelming rush of women students that, to prevent its becoming a woman's college exclusively, it has asked for a special fund of $250,000 so that it may segregate the women from the men.

Henry Clews had a solution for the problem posed by those women who strained at the traditional bonds: "Let woman stick to her natural sphere; let her rejoice in the fact that she is a woman; let her worship womanly standards; let her throne remain firmly established in the home protected by the man of her choice and let her stop aiming to be manly."[9]

It was not, of course, just Elsie's parents who objected to her attending college. Elsie often encountered this attitude, though frequently it was veiled as praise of her achievements. Years later, after she had finished her undergraduate and graduate work, she wrote to Herbert, "The ladies afterwards sat around and extolled me for going to college, for 'doing so much,' etc. until I made shift to turn the conversation. Not one of them would dream of sending their daughters to college. I find that sort of talk, and I have had endless doses of it, very tiresome. It is so unreal."[10] In her book, *The Old-Fashioned Woman,* Elsie recalled these encounters, "Brought up in a circle of society opposed to college-going for girls, the rather curious formula most commonly used to put me in my place during my college years was 'I hear you are so *literary,* Miss Clews.' "[11]

Elsie was not one to follow her father's advice or to succumb to the pressures of her social circle. Indeed, she attempted to hurdle every barrier placed in her path, whether it be one of social convention or gender expectation. She brought to the Clews's home the very conflicts that Henry Clews spoke about from the podium. Still, as Lissa recalled, "Grandfather was very proud of her intellectual capacity." And, most certainly, Elsie did insist! She took her entrance examinations in the spring of 1892, and an official from the college informed her father that "Miss Clews passed . . . in Latin, Ancient History and Geography, and Greek." The letter continued: "About the results in the first two subjects I believe she had no fear, but neither she nor I felt sure of the outcome in Greek. In fact, she went away with the impression that . . . Greek prose was in store for her. I write this therefore that . . . [you] may set her mind at rest on that score."[12]

Elsie enrolled in Barnard College in the fall of 1892. At the end of the first year, Miss Ellen Meed wrote her that she had "passed a very excellent examination" and that she had "only one condition,—Arithmetic." Miss Meed concluded, "I congratulate you very cordially, especially on your work in Greek, which I consider surprisingly good."[13]

Elsie was serious about her classes and pursued reading and research avidly. In a letter written during her sophomore year, she thanked her friend, Sam Dexter, for the etiquette book that he had playfully sent her, and then spoke of her work: "Many thanks for Dear Lady Disdain. She arrived yesterday, but I have been too busy with Euripides, Tacitus and such like worthies to have paid my respects to her as yet. Those worthies take all my time; I don't have even a flying dive and swim. I live at the Redwood Library. . . . I love to read in the atmosphere of a library, it makes me feel learned."[14] Then she returned to her teasing tone, questioning, "Do you think I am growing pedantic?" The Redwood Library of Newport held an enduring attraction. Years later she wrote to Herbert, "I have been reading Darwin's autobiography in the Life and Letters this evening. I found it extremely interesting as Prof. Osborne had promised me. I have spent most of the day in the Redwood Library. . . . So far my hours in the library have been spent in browsing, a most enjoyable pastime to me, for I am at heart a great book lover."[15]

Among the mementos from Barnard that Elsie had pasted in her scrapbook was a schedule of classes from her junior year: "Mon. 9:30-11:30—zoology, philosophy, economics, sociology, Greek, and American history."[16] Her study of Greek carried over to Proedros, the Greek Club. Elsie, as president, wrote the description of it in the *Barnard Annual* as "a weekly meeting for the discussion of an assigned passage in the Greek with the reading of a paper by one of the members concerning some subject suggested by the text."[17] Active in extracurricular activities, Elsie was a member of the Hap-Hazard Club, a Greek letter society. During her senior year, she was elected chair of the Executive Committee of the Undergraduate Association of Barnard. She was one of the founders of the Barnard Chapter of the College Settlement Association. A handwritten note pasted in her scrapbook recorded the first meeting of this organization:

There will be a meeting of all the students of Barnard College on Thursday, Feb. 21st, at 3:30 o'clock, to consider the representation of Barnard College in the College Settlement organization.

E. W. Clews

After the chapter was formed, she served as the student elector and presided over all the meetings. Later, Elsie extended her organizational work for the College Settlement Association to other college campuses.[18]

In 1896, among a class of twenty-three women, Elsie graduated Phi Beta Kappa from Barnard College. She continued the next year at Columbia University, where much of her study was done in the history of education and government with Nicholas Murray Butler. Her master's thesis in sociology, "On Certain Phases of Poor-Relief in the City of New York," was conducted with the sociologist, Franklin Henry Giddings. For her Ph.D. oral examinations, which she took in 1899, Elsie's major subject was listed as education, with minor subjects in philosophy, sociology, and statistics.[19]

Under Butler's direction, Elsie began work on her doctoral dissertation. In a letter to Herbert, she touched on her research and asked him to make arrangements for her to use the library of the New York Bar Association: "My subject is a dissertation concerning the relation of our colonial governments to education to be presented in partial fulfillment of the requirements for the degree of Doctor of Philosophy in Columbia University and I expect to find in the library of the Bar Asso. certain colonial laws on the subject, those notably of North Carolina which I am unable to find in the Columbia library." She thought that "three mornings would suffice" for the research. In a postscript to a subsequent letter, she wrote "Woolsey's International Law has proved just what I want."[20]

Apparently Elsie was under pressure from her family to finish her graduate work. She wrote Herbert about an offer of a fellowship: "I have a piece of news. I have been offered and accepted the Hartley House fellowship for next year." And then she added, "In view of the one year compromise which I had about decided to make with the family, the prospect is very timely."[21] That same year of 1899, Elsie completed the dissertation, *The Educational Legislation and Administration of the Colonies,* which was published as part of Columbia University Contributions to Philosophy, Psychology and Education.

Giddings had selected Elsie Clews as the recipient of the Hartley House Fellowship, an award established to provide "training in accurate habits of social observation for the technical study of advanced problems in sociology or for the active work in philanthropy and social reform."[22] Elsie explained to Herbert: "The fellowship does not seem to be much associated with Hartley House; it is virtually a teaching fellowship in sociology in Columbia. Professor Giddings made me the proposition. I am to take in charge all the laboratory work of his

Barnard undergraduate students and this part of the work is to be made required in the course. I am also to develop it along my own lines more or less. I think it will be pretty good fun and very useful work too."[23]

Herbert must have felt that he had been excluded from Elsie's plans for such a fellowship. She wrote in response to his objections, "I could have said nothing to you before about the sociology fellowship, for I didn't know anything about it until last Thursday morning." Then she explained, "Once last year when I was telling Prof. Giddings about my public school plan, he said something rather vaguely about wishing me instead to develope the sociological work. I remember telling you of that too."[24]

Even before her appointment to the Hartley House Fellowship, Elsie had taught Barnard students. In 1898 she had conducted classes for the members of the College Settlement Chapter at her alma mater. The purpose was to provide instruction on methods of conducting social work among indigent families. Indeed, Elsie had drawn on her experience as a volunteer for the Penny Provident Fund, which was a system of banking developed by the Committee on Provident Habits of the Charity Organization Society for low income people, specifically as a means of encouraging frugal habits among children.[25] The community work provided the basis for the laboratory section of Giddings's course, for, as she said, "I started in on a career of penny provident collecting for the local charity organization society yesterday afternoon to get my hand in for the benefit of my sociological students next winter." She told Herbert of the enthusiastic response of one particular student, "I am enclosing a letter from one of my settlement girls which I had in mind to show you before, but forgot. Of course it is school girl gush, but it touched and pleased me nevertheless; for the writer is a very simple genuine little girl. No don't laugh at her or at me." She continued with thoughts on her philosophy of teaching, and allusions to Herbert's critical view: "My relations to my classes have always been singularly undemonstrative and I have sometimes wondered if the obvious advantages of that policy were not outweighed by the results of the more personal methods of other teachers. Do you remember what I told you once about my refusal ever to tack my own personality on. . . . You disagreed and said that I thereby lost influence. And so it pleases me in view of my own doubts and your criticism, to see that in this instance, at least, my method has been successful in the way that I wished it to be—the girl does think for herself. This I know from other sources than her letter—and yet I seem to have a strong hold over her too."[26] Years later, in 1939, a former student recalled her impression of Parsons in the classroom: "Writing to you . . . takes me way back to 1900 when I used to report to you as Penny Provident Collector. You used to petrify me as having intellectually achieved far beyond the aspiring pupil in Socialigy [*sic*]."[27]

Elsie taught sociology at Barnard as a Hartley House Fellow from 1899 to 1902, when her title changed to Hartley House Lecturer, a position that she held from 1903 to 1905.[28] The direction of her work was described in the Barnard College catalogue as follows:

> Mrs. Herbert Parsons, Ph.D., . . . will give personal direction to students wishing to undertake observational work, and the entire instruction will be under the general charge of the Professor of Sociology. The advantages offered will include opportunities to become familiar with the work of the more important private institutions for social betterment in New York City, such as the State Charities Aid Association, the Charity Organization Society, the New York Association for Improving the Condition of the Poor, and the various social settlements, as well as to study the organization and working of various public agencies charged with the welfare of the community.[29]

In her classroom instruction, Parsons combined her graduate fields of specialization. From her master's work, she continued her focus on poor relief in New York City; and from her Ph.D. research, she pursued her interest in pedagogy. Both areas were within the scope of sociology, which at the end of the nineteenth century and the beginning of the twentieth, was closely linked to directed social change. The course that she offered as a lecturer was listed in the Barnard College catalogue as:

> 16—Family Organization. Field work in the study of family groups. Study of the sacred law codes. Consultations. Dr. Elsie Clews Parsons. One point.
> Tu. at 3.30 bi-weekly.
> Open to Seniors.[30]

Recognizing the need for a general introductory text in sociology, Elsie wrote to Livingston Farrand of the Department of Anthropology at Columbia University, to inquire if there was such a book in anthropology. Farrand responded, "All of us threaten from time to time to write some general book but it would have to be rewritten about as soon as it were out and the game seems hardly worth the candle."[31] Elsie decided to compile a text by drawing on her teaching and her fieldwork experience. The result was *The Family,* which was published in 1906.[32] In the preface and the introduction, she gave a clear and comprehensive statement of her opinions on education. Concerned about the development of effective methods of instruction, she discussed the need to improve teaching at the college level. Colleges, she suggested, like poor stepchildren, suffered from attention given to the elementary schools and the universities and professional schools. At the elementary level, there had been changes in curriculum and in teaching methods. The universities and the professional schools, remaining aloof from progressive "pedagogic method," had retained the lecture as the primary means of instruction. Improvement in college instruction—the broadened curriculum and the addition of laboratories—had been made "as a reflex from elementary school-teaching." Part of the difficulty in effecting change at the college level had to do with the work load of the professors. As she explained it, the "borrowed university scientist" was overtaxed and simply transferred the lectures and seminars from the university to the college, without any attempt at adaptation for a different teaching environment.[33]

There was a crucial need for planned and directed change in college education, according to Parsons. The subjects of study and the methods of instruction needed to be clearly differentiated from those of the lower grades and those of the professional schools and universities. Reliance on assigned readings and lectures should be abandoned in college. As she emphasized: "It is the universal experience of college instructors that text-book or lecture-imparted information is rarely assimilated by their students. How seldom does one see any effort to apply the facts or methods learned in one course to another course, or to personal experiences outside of college walls. The college note-book is a kind of intellectual graveyard." College instruction, Parsons stressed, must actively engage the students. To accomplish this, each student should have a special area of study that would result in a particular area of expertise. The professor would draw on this knowledge in the class setting, thus challenging the individual student and stimulating the interest of all. New subject matter could be introduced through "anticipatory questions," which, in turn, might relate to the student's special areas of study.[34]

The discipline of sociology, Parsons maintained, was a particularly suitable subject for college instruction. Students would need to classify "social facts from written records and personal observations," and they would then analyze the material. While appropriate for colleges, sociology, according to Parsons, did not lend itself to high school instruction. Unless very exceptional, students of that age were not ready for such a study. Parsons also questioned the usefulness of sociology for the university curriculum. As she expressed it, "Such a discipline is . . . essentially preliminary to university work." She was not of the opinion that sociology was less sophisticated or more elementary than other university disciplines. Rather, she maintained, the university student had not received the proper training to approach the subject in a useful manner. As she said, "Much of the effort of university students in sociology, not to speak of other subjects, is futile because of their lack of training in scientific method."[35]

The study of the family would offer a strong addition to the college curriculum. Tied as it was to broader sociological concerns, it introduced the student to other issues. As she said, "The family's function and structure are so closely connected with the social organisation in general that in their study an outlook is opened upon other social groups and upon the working of far-reaching social laws." For this purpose, that a course be taught at the college level, Parsons organized *The Family* as a text, with the lecture material given in the chapters and marginal notes providing topics for discussion. As she said, "The lecture outlines are reduced to the presentation of a few important and well-established deductions and to schemes of classification"; the theories were relegated to notes. Four sections following each chapter had been compiled for a specific purpose. Notes "A" gave references and fuller discussions of topics. Notes "B" contained brief summaries of theory relating to topics of the lectures, and Notes "C" gave suggestions for original research. Notes "D," which Parsons called "time economies," provided bibliographic summaries of the suggested readings to "enable the instructor to keep a close watch without expenditure of time upon the special work of each student."[36]

Parsons suggested the manner in which the textbook might best be used. At the first meeting, the student would choose from the groups listed in the introduction, which included the Veddahs, Yaghan, natives of Australia, Eskimo, Wyandots, Thompson River Indians, Melanesians, Slave and Gold Coast Africans, Kabyles, ancient Arabs, ancient Hebrews, ancient Babylonians, ancient and modern Chinese, ancient Hindus, ancient Greeks, ancient Romans, ancient Welch, ancient Irish, Anglo-Saxons, modern French, and the people of the United States. Throughout the course, the student would research the selected group and follow the plan for organizing the information. In this way, each class member would be involved directly in contributing specialized knowledge to the discussion. As Parsons explained: "The student will be expected to bring with him to class that part of his classification which concerns the topics to be immediately discussed. In developing the topics, the instructor will then be able to call upon the class for illustrative facts."[37]

In addition to bibliographic research, the students were expected to pay weekly visits to two or more families. Ideally, these families would be located in the same neighborhood, thus saving time for the student and providing "the student opportunities to learn of the relations of neighbours to neighbours." The visits could be arranged, Parsons suggested, through "the local Charity Organisation Society, or through any relief society that makes use of the volunteer 'friendly visitor' in its work."[38] Parsons stipulated that contacts with the families must be systematic and that "there must be some reason other than that of getting information." This could most readily be established through the guise of a business relationship rather than charitable work, through, for example, penny provident collecting, or insurance or rent collecting. In her article, "Field Work in Teaching Sociology at Barnard College, Columbia University," which was based on the laboratory portion of the course she taught under Giddings in 1899–1900, Parsons detailed the way in which the students would establish contact and collect information from families. She selected families who had been participating in the Hartley House penny provident bank: "It was a simple matter to suggest sending a collector to them instead of continuing to receive their deposits at the Hartley House station." The circle of families broadened, Parsons said, because the student collectors were referred by the families to friends and relatives, but all under the guise of charitable banking.[39]

In Parsons's discussion of establishing contacts with families, there was no intimation that the subjects should be informed of the study, or told of the true identity of the student collectors. Parsons defended the approach in both "Field Work in Teaching Sociology at Barnard College, Columbia, University," and *The Family*. Clearly, there had been objections, some of which apparently came from students. In *The Family*, Parsons noted that a sensitive student might be troubled by the fieldwork because "she feels constrained by the idea that she is an unwarrantable and deceptive intruder upon family privacy. She feels hypocritical in asking questions or in directing conversations." For these remarks on the need for sensitivity in fieldwork, Parsons switched explicitly to the feminine gender, since as she said, "This particular style of visiting has been followed only by women students." Parsons suggested that the instructor could indicate to the student the ways in which she might prove helpful to the families—by encouraging the children to attend school regularly, finding a kindergarten for a young child, encouraging a family member to join a church or settlement club, helping to locate medical assistance, or assisting them in joining a circulating library.[40] The benefits gained by the families through contact with the students included help with employment, education, and job-training. As she stressed, "I have been glad to emphasize the practical good accomplished by the student investigators because of the objection that has once or twice been urged against the so-called unwarrantable intrusion into private life entailed by this method of social observation." For Parsons, the chief justification of this approach to fieldwork was the learning process. The students became "more intelligent and therefore more useful members of society."[41]

Each student would keep a notebook for the family in which the observations were recorded following every visit. The student was "to record whatever she considers a social fact or a fact which bears in some way or other upon the social life of the family."[42] The instructor would present the students with a series of schedules to provide structure and organization for the complexity of material gathered. The format of the schedules would be coordinated with the material presented in lecture. For example, observations would be recorded on "Utilization (Economy)," which included information on "Term of residence, residence, position of house," and "Sources of authority," at the same time that these items were being discussed in lecture. For each schedule, there was a section for "Interesting facts still unclassified," which allowed for inclusion of information that might not have otherwise been recorded. This, Parsons hoped, might encourage diversity in observation and flexibility in fieldwork.[43] Included also was a section to note lacunae in the record and the reasons for the lack of information. This, Parsons thought, would foster thoroughness in research and might allay frustration by allowing the student to explain the reasons for the lack of information. In the course of study, the student would develop social tact and sympathy, both of which were necessary for successful fieldwork. If the student did not naturally possess such qualities, then it was incumbent on the instructor to foster these by "leading the student to note the resemblances as well as the differences between herself and those visited, and in suggesting subjects for friendly conversation."[44]

Parsons referred to the course on the family as "education in practical philanthropy."[45] She visualized the fieldwork as training for social service, which was to be the ultimate goal for the student. In Parsons's work, both as a teacher and as a community activist, there was a definite applied focus. One learned with the intent of doing, and this action was to be socially useful.

In the last chapter of *The Family,* Parsons released what was to be a bombshell. She put forth her suggestion for trial marriage. In the reception of the book, this fifteen-page discussion of "Ethical Considerations" totally eclipsed the preceding 339 pages of text. Of these fifteen pages, it was really only seven that were seized by ministers, journalists, and public speakers for their attack on what they regarded as a threat to the moral fiber of the nation. Parsons's argument was predicated on the assumption that monogamy offered distinct advantages for women and was the highest form of marriage. In contrast, "polygyny, including concubinage [and] prostitution," channeled specific functions to different women: "the concubine, prostitute, or mistress serve for sexual sympathy and gratification, the chief or legal wife for reproduction"; economic activities were also distributed unequally. As a result, women developed only certain aspects of their personality and were subsequently handicapped in the full education of their children. Under monogamy, the various "womanly functions" were fulfilled by one woman. "The resulting type of woman is a better educator and her children fall heir to a richer inheritance of personality than is the case where women are differentiated into child-bearing and non-child-bearing or productive and non-productive classes."[46]

Monogamy necessitated mature judgment. Young people were neither educated for nor predisposed to such careful selection of a life-long mate. Parsons opined: "An abiding argument against early marriage lies . . . in the differences of sexual choice at different ages. When sexual choice resulting in sexual intercourse and child-bearing occurs after maturity, mental and moral are more apt than merely physical traits to influence the choice and therefore, according to the law of sexual selection to be propagated in the offspring."[47]

Thus, the success of the monogamous family depended upon postponement of marriage. This, however, was coupled with another problem: the expectation of female chastity and the permissive nod toward the release of male desire. The pressure of this combination yielded prostitution, an institution about which Parsons was not sanguine. As she viewed it, democracy and freedom were incompatible with prostitution. The choice was quite simple: "If we desire monogamy we must condemn prostitution, but we must necessarily condemn male as well as female prostitutes." If promiscuity is regarded as acceptable for men, then, Parsons argues, "it must be . . . that their nature is radically unadapted to monogamy and that monogamy is undesirable." Given this situation, there should not then be discrimination against the female prostitute. Parsons continued, "If the social stigma were taken off the prostitute, if she were no longer a segregated person, prostitution might become, in the sense of a division of labour, more consistent with a democratic point of view." Still, this acceptance of prostitution would also be an acceptance of specialization of woman's functions, which would "be untrue to democracy in its large meaning, *i. e.*, equal opportunities for total development of man or woman."[48]

Following her argument, if marriage was to be postponed for the benefit of mature judgment, and prostitution was to be abandoned as a violation of democratic principles, Parsons concluded that there were two alternatives: "the requiring of absolute chastity of both sexes until marriage or the toleration of freedom of sexual intercourse on the part of the unmarried of both sexes before marriage, *i. e.*, before the birth of offspring." This, she coolly reasoned, would require a change of attitude: "Sexual intercourse would not be of itself disparaged or condemned, it would be disapproved of only if indulged in at the expense of health or emotional or intellectual activities in oneself or in others." She continued: "It would, therefore, seem well from this point of view, to encourage early *trial* marriage, the relation to be entered into with a view to permanency, but with the privilege of breaking it if proved unsuccessful and in the *absence of offspring* without suffering any great degree of public condemnation."[49]

The trial marriage proposal, Parsons stressed, could not be easily engaged until certain social issues were clarified and specific technologies developed. She referred to "the present experiments in economic independence for women" and to "the discovery of certain and innocuous methods of preventing conception." Economic independence of women and the development of methods to control birth would drastically alter the patterns of marriage. Parsons anticipated that if these factors were conjoined with an increased knowledge concerning the importance of biological, psychological, and social factors, that parenthood would be "a more enlightened and purposive function than is even dreamed of at present." For Parsons, marriage began in earnest when there were children. At that point, the union between husband and wife was no longer one of choice, but of obligation. With children, the maintenance of the marriage ties was of the most serious concern. As she said, "From our standpoint . . . the effect of divorce upon the children of the separating parents is the foremost consideration." She suggested that there might be a differential treatment of divorce cases, in which childless couples could more easily obtain a divorce than could couples with children.

Whatever the circumstances of the divorce, Parsons did propose the abolition of legal separation and divorce laws that prohibited remarriage of the defendant.[50]

Parsons's main concern was for the equal treatment of partners in marriage—as she phrased it, the application of democratic ideals to marriage—and for the responsible and enlightened treatment of the children. She did not view the regulation of sex, apart from these two considerations, as necessarily a component of marriage. She cautiously extended the argument from trial marriage to the possibility of sexual freedom in marriage: "If . . . with this increase of knowledge a higher standard of parental duty and a greater capacity for parental devotion develop, then the need of sexual restraint as we understand it *may* disappear and different relations between the sexes before marriage and to a certain extent within marriage may be expected."[51]

Parsons's suggestions were put forth in a dispassionate tone; the responses were not. An article in the *New York Times* appearing on Sunday, November 18, 1906, was captioned, "DR. DIX ON TRIAL MARRIAGES. Rector of Trinity Says Mrs. Parsons's Views are Barbarous." Dr. Morgan Dix was to preach a sermon at Trinity Church addressing "doctrines advocated in Mrs. Parsons's book, 'The Family.' " He wanted one point clearly understood, "he had not read the book," though he had read excerpts of the book in the newspapers. He expostulated,

> "The idea of men and women living like animals, separating at will, and contracting new alliances, leaving the children to be nobody's children, and to be cared for by the State, is barbarous.
>
> The proposal to abolish the clause in the divorce law prohibiting the remarriage of divorced couples is almost as reprehensible. No divorced person can be remarried in any of the nine churches in my parish, no matter for what cause the divorce may have been granted.
>
> The proposal to reduce the number of children in a family and keep down the progeny of married couples is also most offensive, and is a menace to morality and the stability of society. I consider Mrs. Parsons's theories outrageous, and deny them with all the force there is in me."[52]

Dr. Dix preached his sermon on "Childhood and the Home from the Christian Point of View" to "a congregation composed largely of women." He inveighed against "the radicals of the day [who] are pushing their schemes of social revolution." The most dangerous notion afoot, Dr. Dix said, was "the plan to abolish marriage and break up the home." These ideas were put forth "in books in wide circulation," the goal being "to make converts in places frequented by the seditious communists and the murderous Anarchist."[53]

Dr. Dix's condemnation was followed less than two weeks later by others. "TRIAL MARRIAGE IDEA DENOUNCED IN CHURCHES," the *New York Times* caption read: "People of all creeds thronged the churches of New York City yesterday morning for the Thanksgiving services. . . . Two clergymen, the Rev. D. Parkhurst at the Madison Square Presbyterian Church and the Rev. David G. Wylie at the Scotch Presbyterian Church, condemned Mrs. Herbert Parsons's book in which 'trial marriages' are suggested." The Reverend Parkhurst commented, " 'The last blow upon the sanctity of marriage comes from a source from which we would not have anticipated a stroke of such kind. . . . It has come in the shape of a book entitled *The Family.*' " The Reverend Parkhurst acknowledged that there was worth in the book, that, indeed, it was "replete with evidence of research."

> "The book is rigidly scientific—cold, hard, and bloodless, but I shall content myself with commenting upon what I do not hesitate to stigmatize as the abominable suggestion advanced in the fifteenth chapter, the matter of what the writer calls 'trial marriages'—that is to say, probationary marriages, marriage for experimental purposes, matrimonial contracts that two human animals, one of each sex, enter into for the purpose of seeing how they like it, and then if, after a time, if they decide that they do not like it, breaking away from each other and starting in, in the same experimental way, somewhere else."

While not attaching any semblance of moral disrepute to Mrs. Parsons, the Reverend Parkhurst charged that this book would ultimately contribute to "matrimonial looseness," by imputing a certain respectability to it. He continued:

> "Let us distinctly understand that half a dozen experimental wives, espoused one after the other, is not a whit less than the same number of contemporaneous ones; that from a moral point of view a consecutive harem is no improvement on a simultaneous one, and that what our author designates as 'trial marriage' is simply a form of polygamy graduated to the tastes of people who are not quite so abandoned as to assent to polygamy of the Brigham Young type."[54]

The Reverend Dr. Wylie was more succinct and more damning in his criticism.

> "While we are celebrating this day we ought to consider the dangers that beset this Nation. There is the danger to the family life in the theories now being promulgated. There has been advocated the idea of trial marriages. It is a disgusting theory. I wonder if the author of it would advocate trial marriages to a daughter?"

He alerted his congregation: the author of the book proposed that her book be used as a textbook in the nation's schools. He called for a unified response from people across the land that would make "the users of such books ashamed of themselves."[55]

The *New York Times* editorial dispensed with the book as "a success of scandal," which had been unanticipated by "the authoress."[56] Indeed, such recognition was unanticipated and unwelcome. Elsie wrote Herbert on June 18, 1907, "I . . . am visited by World impertinence as the enclosed slip shows. Fortunately the reporter was decenter than his directive, & took my sad smile & usual answer quite like a gentleman." The reporter had been instructed as follows: "See Mrs. Herbert Parsons at Lenox and ask her if she can trace any analogy between her trial marriage plan and the plan of Judge McPherson of Iowa who orders that the railroads give the 2 percent rate a 3 months' trial." Herbert himself had met the representatives of the press in front of his apartment in Washington and answered their repeated questions with a cryptic statement, " 'Mrs. Parsons has nothing to say, and will have nothing to say. Neither has Mr. Parsons.' "[57]

There was embarrassment for Elsie in all this. She was one who cherished her privacy and who did not seek public acclaim. She was also the wife of a politician who could ill afford such publicity. In an effort to head the critics off at the pass, as it were, she had sent President Theodore Roosevelt a copy of *The Family*. She wrote:

> Dear Mr. President,
>   I am sending you a copy of my unhappily notorious book. The outcry against it has been so grotesquely clamorous that I want you to know what the book really is. If you can spare ten minutes . . . I suggest that you glance over the preface and Lecture 15. The rest is purely descriptive for teaching purposes & of course dry reading.

Elsie assured Roosevelt that she had learned from "the public reaction . . . that a writing wife is a distinct handicap to a politican and so henceforward in our family authorship is going to yield to states-manship after as well as before elections." He responded, "I thought your note very amusing, and I am really glad to have the chance of reading the famous book. Very soon I shall get you and Herbert to come round to lunch, and then we will talk it over."[58]

Elsie did not give up her research on controversial topics. She simply avoided unsought attention by keeping her work out of the public eye. Of her attendance at the 1908 American Sociological Association Meeting, she wrote Herbert: "My Atlantic City trip was a success . . . for I enjoyed meeting with my kind, my little paper took well and didn't get into the papers. I think I have found a way to outwit the reporter."[59] For a wider audience, she used a pseudonym when expedient, as she did for *Religious Chastity: An Ethnological Study,* published under the name of John Main in 1913. She discarded this subterfuge when her husband was out of national politics, and she would write bluntly again on the subject of sexuality and marriage. She returned to the subject of trial marriage when in her 1924 article, "Changes in Sex Relations," she would write, "Advocates of the monogamous family would do well to consider how essential to an enduring union . . . experience in love may be, together with restraint from child-bearing before experience is achieved."[60]

Elsie received praise as well, though more subdued and select than the criticism. In 1916, an eighty-one-year-old man wrote, "You were not to be criticized or condemned but merited the thanks of all thinking people."[61] And Hamilton Holt, president of Rollins College, wrote her in 1938: "I wonder if you have forgotten me. It seems an age since the old days when your husband ran the Republican Party and you started the Trial Marriage Argument. . . . You always impressed me as being a woman of real intellectual curiosity and one who liked to contemplate new ideas."[62]

Elsie's years as a college student had merged with her years as a Hartley House Fellow. She hoped that her work with the college settlement organization would, as she wrote, "bring opportunities for culture and social development into a neighborhood more or less destitute of these opportunities."[63] And she saw sociology as a way of inculcating such concerns in students. Elsie had charted a course for herself as an intellectual with a social agenda.

NOTES

1. Alfred Louis Kroeber, "Elsie Clews Parsons," *AA* 45 (1943): 252.
2. ECP, EC to unnamed friend, n.d.; penciled notes of EC.

3. ECP, Elsie Clews's notes on ideals.

4. ECP, EC, "Moods—Experiences," unpublished essay. An estimated date of 1885 was penciled on this document by one who was attempting to establish a chronological sequence for Parsons's undated manuscripts and letters, though, as stated, I am certain that this was written at a later date. The essay was not the work of an eleven-year-old child, even one as precocious as Elsie Clews.

5. Elsie (Lissa) Parsons Kennedy, "The Reminiscences of Mr. and Mrs. John D. Kennedy" (New York: Oral History Research Office, Columbia, 1966), p. 16.

6. ECP, EC, "Selfishness," undated essay.

7. Henry Clews, "Shall the Suffrage Be Given to Women?," in Henry Clews, *Financial, Economic, and Miscellaneous Speeches and Essays* (New York: Irving Publishing Company, 1910), p. 258.

8. Henry Clews, "Woman in Politics, Nature, History, Business and the Home," in *Financial, Economic, and Miscellaneous Speeches*, pp. 317, 320. See also Henry Clews, *Twenty-Eight Years in Wall Street* (New York: Irving Publishing Company, 1887), p. 437, with the chapter heading, "Wall Street No Place for Women. They Lack the Mental Equipment."

9. Henry Clews, "Shall the Suffrage Be Given to Women," pp. 268–69.

10. ECP, EC to HP, 14 Aug. 1900.

11. Elsie Clews Parsons, *The Old-Fashioned Woman* (New York: G. P. Putnam's Sons, 1913), p. 285.

12. Rye Historical Society, G. M. Nelson to Henry Clews, 13 May 1892.

13. Rye Historical Society, Ellen Meed to EC, 16 June 1892.

14. ECP, EC to Sam Dexter, 17 Oct. 1893.

15. ECP, EC to HP, 27 July 1899.

16. ECP, penciled notes in scrapbook. Though not dated, this had been a semester from her junior year, since three of the courses—philosophy, history, and political economy—were required of third-year students, and since sociology courses taught at Columbia were not open to Barnard students until 1894–95. The earliest college catalogue on file at the Barnard College Archives is for the year of 1895–96. I am assuming that the requirements for the junior year in 1894–95 were essentially the same as those listed in the following source: *Courses in the School of Arts, Leading to the Degree of Bachelor of Arts in Columbia College, 1895–1896* (New York: Columbia College), p. 21. While Franklin Henry Giddings was listed in the *Barnard College Announcement, 1899–1900*, as professor of sociology and as offering Sociology 15, Principles of Sociology (pp. 2, 21), according to R. Gordon Hoxie, it was not until 1894 that Dean John Burgess would permit women students from Barnard to attend classes in his department of political science. Rosalind Rosenberg, *Beyond Separate Spheres* (New Haven: Yale University Press, 1982), p. 149, quoting Hoxie, *A History of the Faculty of Political Science, Columbia University* (New York: Columbia University Press, 1955), pp. 64–67, 176–77, 286–89. This change was finally reflected in official form in the catalogue issued by Barnard College for the academic year of 1896–97: *Barnard College, Courses in the*

School of Political Science in History, Economics, and Sociology, under the Charge of the Faculty of Political Science of Columbia University, 1896–1897.

17. Peter H. Hare, *A Woman's Quest for Science* (Buffalo, N.Y.: Prometheus Books, 1985), p. 36.

18. ECP, handwritten note in scrapbook; Hare, *A Woman's Quest for Science,* p. 36.

19. Hare, *A Woman's Quest for Science,* p. 38. For an assessment of Giddings's work, see Clarence H. Northcott, "The Sociological Theories of Franklin Henry Giddings: Consciousness of Kind, Pluralistic Behavior, and Statistical Method," in Harry Elmer Barnes, ed., *An Introduction to the History of Sociology* (Chicago: University of Chicago Press, 1948), pp. 744–65. For an appraisal of Giddings's influence on Parsons, see Rosenberg, *Beyond Separate Spheres,* pp. 147–77.

20. ECP, EC to HP, n.d.

21. ECP, EC to HP, 20 Apr. 1899.

22. Barnard College catalogue, 1902, p. 48.

23. ECP, EC to HP, 20 Apr. 1899.

24. ECP, EC to HP, Apr. 1899.

25. Elsie Clews Parsons, "Field Work in Teaching Sociology," *Educational Review* 20 (1900): 160, n. 3.

26. ECP, EC to HP, 7 Aug. 1898.

27. ECP, anonymous correspondent to ECP, 3 Nov. 1939.

28. Personal communication from Virginia Shaw, Registrar, Barnard College, 26 Oct. 1987. Parsons was on leave from Barnard College in 1905–6 and did not subsequently return to teaching.

29. Barnard College catalogue, 1902, pp. 49–50.

30. Ibid., p. 51.

31. Rye Historical Society, Farrand to ECP, 1 June 1905.

32. Elsie Clews Parsons, *The Family* (New York: G. P. Putnam's Sons, 1906), p. 10.

33. Ibid., pp. v–vii.

34. Ibid., pp. ix, 8–9.

35. Ibid., p. vi. She cited Sebald Rudolf Steinmetz, *Classification des types sociaux et catalogue des peuples* in *L'Année sociologique,* 1898–99, pp. 43–147, for failure of method on part of sociologists.

36. *The Family,* pp. vi, viii, 7.

37. Ibid., pp. 1–4.

38. Ibid., pp. 11, 10.

39. Parsons, "Field Work," p. 162.

40. *The Family,* pp. 14; 10, n. 1; 14–15.

41. Parsons, "Field Work," pp. 163–64, n. 7.

42. *The Family,* p. 11.

43. Parsons, "Field Work," p. 164, and *The Family,* p. 12.

44. *The Family,* pp. 12, 14. On page 13, Parsons included actual notes from a student's schedule, along with the instructor's corrections, and on pages 16–19, she included sample schedules.

45. Ibid., p. 15.

46. Ibid., p. 345.

47. Ibid., p. 347.

48. Ibid., pp. 347, 348.

49. Ibid., pp. 348, 349.

50. Ibid., pp. 351, 350.

51. Ibid., pp. 350–51.

52. "Dr. Dix on Trial Marriages," *New York Times,* 18 Nov. 1906, p. 12, col. 3. For reactions to *The Family,* see also Hare, *A Woman's Quest for Science,* pp. 11–14.

53. "Dr. Dix Speaks out to Save the Home," *New York Times,* 19 Nov. 1906, p. 5, col. 2–3.

54. "Trial Marriage Idea Denounced in Churches," *New York Times,* 30 Nov. 1906, p. 6, col. 1–2.

55. Ibid., p. 6, col. 2.

56. "Trial Marriages," editorial, *New York Times,* 2 Dec. 1906, p. 6, col. 3–4.

57. ECP, ECP to HP, 18 June 1907; Hare, *A Woman's Quest for Science,* p. 13, quoting an article in the *New York Herald,* 18 Nov. 1906.

58. Manuscript Division, Library of Congress, ECP to Theodore Roosevelt, 22 Dec. 1906; ECP, Theodore Roosevelt to ECP, 22 Dec. 1906.

59. ECP, ECP to HP, 1 Jan. 1908. The paper to which she referred was entitled "Higher Education of Women and the Family," and appeared in the 1909 *American Journal of Sociology* 14:758–63.

60. Parsons, "Changes in Sex Relations," *The Nation,* 14 May 1924, p. 552.

61. ECP, anonymous correspondent to ECP, 7 Aug. 1916.

62. ECP, Hamilton Holt to ECP, 8 Sept. 1938.

63. ECP, ECP to Editor of *Charities,* n.d.

4

Elsie and Herbert

Stationed in France during World War I, Herbert Parsons wrote a letter to his children:

> My dear Children,
>   This is mother's day and General Pershing has asked us all to write a letter. As I have no mother living in this world to write to I naturally think of writing to your mother and so this letter is addressed to her. But knowing her dislike of ceremonials in practice—a dislike only equalled by her avidity for them in research—I have decided to spare her by writing to you about her.

He continued, recalling the time he and their mother had met:

> It was 23 years ago in December that I first met mother. It was on the way to Lenox in a private car in a party that the Stohese were giving over New Year's in the present Carnegie house. Mother was then regarded as a wonderful person because she was in college and enjoyed herself also. Some game was played in the train which called for intelligence. How she did at it I don't recall but it was assumed that she was superior at it. I first got to know her the next day. There was a lot of snow and all Stohese's Bowl was frozen over. I in skates pulled her on a sled to the outlet and back and walking up we talked and we were late for lunch and that was the beginning of it all. She had many admirers. One was coming up a few days later bringing some boots for her—she was accustomed to make practical use of her admirers—and I remember that Mr. Gerard, our recent ambassador to Berlin, and I teased her much about him. I once wrote a poem about him—he was a friend of mine—that I thought was witty and she disliked. Mother was a good sort on a house party and did everything.
>   A few weeks later I walked around New York so much in the cold and wet without overcoat or overshoes that I came down with pneumonia and as I convalesced I spent a great deal of time

thinking about mother. She did not know it. I was anxious to see her and I thought I might run into her if I walked in 5th Ave. My first day out I took too long a walk there, fainted when I got home and had something of a relapse. Though I missed her there I commenced to see a great deal of her after I had convalesced. And we did . . . things together. And will you believe it—when the Spanish war came in 1898 and I was trying to go to it I found that she was fond of me. How long I would have had to wait to find it out if it had not been for the war I don't know. And I doubt if she would have been fond of me if I had not wanted to go to the war! At least she discarded one admirer for lack of physical courage.

Her views may have changed. They have in many things. It is a sign of her perpetual youth.[1]

Conveyed in this letter was the charm, the fascination, the challenge, and the admiration that were woven into the fabric of Herbert's love for Elsie. High-spirited at parties, surrounded by admirers, she had them do her bidding; serious of thought, possessed of opinions, she let them be known. Here also was irony. For Herbert's willingness to serve in the Spanish War of 1898 forced Elsie to acknowledge her love for him, while his insistence on enlisting in the army in 1916 evoked her persistent disapproval. And here was power, Elsie's power of mind and spirit. She was possessed of a presence that profoundly affected those around her.

From this December day in 1895, Herbert continued in his attentions to Elsie. She responded in playfulness and teasing. A year later, after receiving pictures and poems from Herbert, she wrote to him: "I think the pictures are very good and the 'inscription' very cheeky. I got even with you though by reading it aloud to the family. I warn you that Mama took the last verse most solemnly to the extent even of delegating Papa to interview Mr. Parsons Senior concerning his son's intentions and prospects. You had better be on your guard. I don't think a breach of promise suit would be a pleasant experience. What evidence I have already in my hands—poetry and 'a buggy ridin'.' "[2]

Flirtatious and slightly outrageous, Elsie hatched a plan to go to the Klondike: "How soon can you be ready to start with me for Alaska? The Klondikes are exerting an over-powering attraction upon me and I am eager to go at all sacrifices."[3] She teasingly played one admirer off against Herbert, inviting both of them to accompany her.

Both the Clews and the Parsons apparently felt the need to rein in the budding romance between Elsie and Herbert. First, Herbert's parents squelched plans for Elsie's visit to their Lenox home in August of 1897. She wrote him, "I confess that I too am disappointed about Lenox. I have been thinking of some long rides over the hills with you, getting home very late for dinner; but I thought all along that it would be natural of your family not to want visitors, and I believe 'it is not personal.' " Herbert then suggested a trip to the Adirondacks for the following month with his sister Eunice and Dr. Walton. Elsie was enthusiastic about the plans. She wrote Herbert that she liked his sister and wanted to get to know her better. As she said, "I have never been in our mountains and the camping out plan appeals to me greatly." Elsie plotted the strategy to gain her parents' approval: "I have just written a most diplomatic letter to my father about the plan. Unless he takes to it at once it might not be amiss for you to pay him a visit and present details with your accustomed skill. The more I think of the details the more keen I become. You know I am only too easy in matters of expedition."[4] Elsie's parents, however, did not approve the plans. They forbade her to go on the Adirondacks trip. Elsie wrote in explanation that they did not like group expeditions. She added, "There is nothing 'personal' to use your expression."[5] The letter, written not in her usual meticulous hand, but in a scribble, reflected her mood of depression. She was upset about not getting her way with her parents—or more specifically, with her mother, since her father had said it was her mother's decision.

Elsie closed the letter with a tender note that would sound again, "One thing I shall remember, however. The proof that you have given that even if you can not say about my company what I say about yours, at any rate, you like it in a certain measure." Subsequently she would remark on Herbert's reluctance to show his feelings, to make himself accessible. And when he did, she responded with pleasure, "Your last letter made me so happy. Neither you nor I are naturally so-called expressive people and so I judge in your case as in my own that a thing said or done means a great deal."[6]

Pleased with the closeness and the newfound expressiveness, she wrote, "I am glad that I have made you happy. I am very happy, too, to have those painful barriers down."[7] In this came a revelation about herself: "I told you much more about myself than I have ever been able to before. Do you know I never realized as of late what a clam I really am. So many of my thoughts and feelings I have always kept so utterly to myself that I find it difficult to put them into words and still more difficult to speak out the words—even to you."[8]

The early letters were full of Elsie's fresh new love. As she wrote Herbert, "I may have charmed before—to use one of your expressions—but no one ever loved me the way I think you do, and it seems a wonderful thing."[9] She wrote of her day spent with him in her imag-ination: "You may be surprised to learn that you have been with me almost all day. . . . This afternoon I read to you the Portuguese son-nets from beginning to end and then we drove out to see the sunset at Coddington's Point—just you and I and the nameless mare—and home again over the hills of the Peninsula *in time for dinner.* Tonight we sat on the rustic bench and looked at the moon's wake."[10]

Elsie and Herbert shared an intense appreciation for the outdoors. They were drawn to the hills for hiking, riding, and camping. Elsie wrote frequently to Herbert of her swimming, biking, ice skating, fishing, tennis, golf, sailing, and, on occasion, hunting. As she said of one July day in 1898: "You would have to admit that I had assumed my old true form could you have seen me Friday playing golf in the morning and swimming and running with Miss Alice Dexter and then shooting, bicycling and crabbing in the afternoon." Of her hunting, she reported, "I killed two birds today to my own great astonishment. I do not seem to be as successful with a shot gun as with a rifle." One letter Elsie wrote on a perfect piece of birch bark from their va-cation resort at Roberval Lac, St. Juan, Canada: "This is a most child-ish pastime my dear Herbert, but I got the birch bark yesterday when I was wishing for your presence at the foot of the finest falls I have ever seen."[11]

While totally caught up in her love for Herbert, Elsie kept clearly in mind her opposition to marriage. She related a dinner-table con-versation on the subject of matrimony: "We had a lively matrimonial discussion this evening in which the family and guests stood divided and the one month bride and groom were most entertaining. . . . They have no imagination and no humor. He has already begun to tell her that she *cant* do things and she asks him about his mail." If she ever were to advocate matrimony, Elsie said, "It would be on very dif-ferent lines from what I see these people are taking." She added, "I think that I would like to be married for a while just to show people how."[12] Indeed, as their relationship grew more serious, she became more adamant: "I have not changed in my aversion to matrimony; in-deed it is stronger than ever, or rather I am more convinced than ever that I shall never marry. For, although I love you better than I love or can conceive of loving anybody else,—moreover if I had to choose be-tween you on one side and all my family and friends on the other I would choose you,—yet I should let you get entirely out of my life rather than marry you. There can be no stronger test than this. I say all this unnecessarily you may think, to show you how extremely un-likely it is for me to change even if the time came when you really wanted to marry me. And to show you, too, how free and justified you would be to break off our relations whenever you saw fit."[13]

Jestingly, Elsie "had made matrimony a forbidden topic." When she spoke of it, she made reference to offending Herbert with her "peculiar views." Then suddenly, the jests were spent. The taboo was serious; marriage was not to be mentioned. The intensity that she had poured into expressing her love was now directed toward maintaining silence on this issue: "Sweetheart, after much thought and trial I find that when I am not with you the thought that we are not 'keeping the rule' disturbs me greatly. Please be good and humor this whim. Part of it is not to talk about the subject anymore." And yet she scolded him when he wrote of their separate lives: "Don't ever again say that 'our paths in life lie wide apart.' It is not true. I can't help your thinking it; but it annoys me greatly for you to say it and so I know that you won't say it again."[14]

A pattern was beginning to emerge in their relationship, which would continue through the years. Elsie set the tone concerning emotional and intellectual issues, and Herbert endeavored to please her, never to annoy her. In this particular exchange, she even told him that he must not look at her "with that wish in your eyes" because, as she said, "I am sufficiently remorseful and discouraged as it is."[15] Of course, Elsie attempted to please Herbert as well, and, on occasion, Herbert gave vent to his displeasure through sarcasm. But the undercurrent was one of Elsie leading strongly, and Herbert attempting to smooth out the surface tension.

To maintain her position, Elsie called on her store of self-discipline. She limited Herbert's visits: "No you must not come tomorrow night. I have manufactured a new set of strict rules—a very selfish set of rules you will think." And she dramatized the degree of separation: "To me it seems like goodbye for ever. Please send me no flowers. I must adopt my own rigorous measures, chief of which is silence."[16]

Elsie was ardently committed to personal freedom. At this time, she was carrying out the battle on the academic front, where against the objections of her family and the expectations of her social class, she was completing her graduate work. She brought the struggle to her relationship with Herbert by taking a strong stand for freedom from marriage. For her this was linked to abhorrence of convention and wariness of the ever-threatening grip of social custom. She established this forcefully in her letters. And yet, with her rejection of matrimony, she did not reject her love for Herbert. She was caught between the cool rationality of her ideal and the fervent surge of her emotion. Thus, in the same beat, she pushed Herbert away and pulled him to her. Convinced of the finality of Elsie's position, and undoubtedly in an effort to maintain his sanity, Herbert took "the first step" in making a separation between them. Elsie was torn. In an effort to be true to her ideal, she discussed the necessity of the break, which should not be gradual, but sudden. "I was never patient of long continued adjustments and I probably shall be spared more by a 'once for all' than by any gradual process." Then she referred to Herbert's initiative and how he could continue easily in this direction. If he were to visit during the week, they would not "refer again to the situation." Elsie had reached her "own settlement" and the talks caused her more pain than she was willing to admit either to Herbert or to herself. Then in the postscript, she gave vent to her pain: "I have been trying to get used to your first step all day. I can't. And so good-bye. Perhaps next winter, if you still want to see me then, I shall have myself well enough in hand to be a reasonable and agreeable companion."[17]

In a return to her ardor and passion, she sent a telegram to Herbert, "Come tonight at eight."[18] And exactly one month later, she restated her place in Herbert's life: "Sweetheart, many of the happiest days of your life you are to spend without my presence. I wish it so. It would grieve me very much otherwise. Some other time we must discuss this matter. I wish to make your life so much fuller by being in it. I could not bear to shut you off from anything."[19]

Elsie resolved, in spite of Herbert's overtures of love—the bouquets, the letters, the embraces—to be "very hard and set." While this was her position, she said, "I can't appear like that when you hold me in your arms. For I am not like that then; nor am I like that in the usual currents of my thought of you when we are separated."[20] For both of them, Elsie said, their idea of love and marriage was tied to their ideals in life: "You and I are both people of very firm ideals. I can not marry you for it would be giving up my ideals . . . ; you must not go on loving me as you have done for it would be giving up your ideals. . . . I want to see you married in accordance with your own ideals. And so, dear, whatever does come in the future to really 'make our paths lie far apart,' I will not take it amiss. I shall rejoice in any proof that after all our relation did not stand in the way of your ideals."[21]

Elsie was to accept the bouquets of flowers once again from Herbert. She wrote him that she "wore the lilies to college today" and, in her happiness, gave a few to the man at the library check-out desk. She recounted her mother's remark, "Mama told me with earnest emphasis that the best thing that could happen to me was 'to fall desperately in love.' . . . I don't think I can be desperately in love. What do you think about it?"[22] But she was intensely in love. She gave herself over to Herbert, to engagement, and to marriage. In her euphoria, Elsie fell so thoroughly into his arms and so enthusiastically into the role of fiancée and new bride that she could not fathom her previous objections to marriage. Not one cautiously or partially to commit herself, Elsie had a gift for total immersion. She was energy, intellect, and body in motion. Without doubt she was stunning in her publicly admitted love of Herbert. For his part, he had weathered the storm and endured the year and a half of her rejection of marriage.

Elsie was now absorbed in planning the honeymoon, keeping a record of the wedding gifts, and decorating their new home. Excited about the prospect of a honeymoon to the Southwest, she sent Herbert the letter which her friend, Howard Cushing, had written her about a possible itinerary: "*Very* beautiful landscape—Indians, pink cliffs, snow mountains probably in September, religious dances, etc. From Flagstaff to Canyon Diablo where J. Volz an Indian trader provides horses and equipment etc. for the Pueblo Indian trip. Two days ride across the desert to Oraibi (Moqui Indian Village). Probably dances in September—and very strange." Elsie added, "That in comparison with a driving trip in New England [Howard] advises us by all means to go West."[23] But behind all her enthusiasm and her plans for the honeymoon, she insisted: "Sweetheart when I speak of Mexico or Colorado or Costa Rica or any other old place I don't want you to think (as I fear you may have) that I want anything in this world during September but your happy company. It merely amuses me to be fertile in suggestions, just as it would amuse a child to say that sometime it was going to the moon. I have a very strong feeling that time should be peculiarly yours to spend as *you* most like."[24]

Elsie kept Herbert informed in detail about the wedding gifts. She enclosed a complete list of the people who had given gifts, along with a note of the item, and her assessment of it. A tea service from Mr. and Mrs. Jesup she liked, even though, as she noted, it was Queen Anne; a pair of bookends she found "very pretty and nice for our library table"; a Sevres china vase she found ugly, as she did a glass and silver inkstand; and a silver dish marked with initials she found showy. She wrote, "Presents are flooding in as you predicted—too numerous to describe. . . . A tea table from Mr. Thoms. Barnes I must mention however. This beautiful and one of the most satisfactory things we have received."[25]

They were caught up in a whirl of domestic decisions. Concerning wallpaper, Elsie wrote, "I would prefer plain green canvas for the dining room, but I don't feel very strongly about it and so if you like the gold and green, please decide upon it." For dishes, she decided, "I think we want both the glass salad bowl and the water pitcher. . . . If they can't get the 4 or 5 inch size vegetable dishes, let us have 2 of the 7 inch. If you want the green and gold entree plates . . . , I have not the slightest objection." She was learning the domestic skills necessary to care for all their new acquisitions. She told Herbert of "taking a lesson in cleaning silver from Ashton. It really amuses me very much to learn how such things are done."[26]

The two were married on September 1, 1900, in what was described as a simple ceremony at home. It was reported in a special to the *New York Times* from Newport:

Miss Elsie Worthington Clews, only daughter of Mr. and Mrs. Henry Clews, was united in marriage to Herbert Parsons of New York, at 12:30 to-day. The ceremony was performed in the Clews Summer home, The Rocks. The lawn was tastefully ornamented with tents and other decorations so familiar to the cottage life of the place. . . . The broad lawns were dotted here and there with large clumps of hydrangeas, and the main piazza entrance was lined with choice palms. Inside The Rocks, the decorations were chiefly American Beauty roses in tall vases. Mr. Parsons and Miss Clews were married in the oval shaped music room under a canopy of flowers in the form of garlands and a large wreath of white roses and lilies of the valley, tied with broad white ribbons caught up among the palms which formed a background for the wedding party.

Elsie's gown was "of liberty satin trimmed with chiffon and lace, with a high neck and long sleeves of Duchess lace." Her bouquet was of white orchids, and her veil of tulle was accented by orange blossoms, as was the chiffon trim of the skirt. After the ceremony, the guests arrived for the wedding breakfast, which was held in the main hall. The table for Elsie and Herbert was profusely decorated with bride roses and jasmine. In the afternoon, "Mr. and Mrs. Parsons left on their wedding trip, and as they departed there was a shower of rice and slippers, and another send-off at the Wickford boat landing."[27]

Instead of the honeymoon to the Southwest aboard the Santa Fe Railroad, Herbert and Elsie went on a quiet driving trip through New England. At the same time, in New York City, the Republicans gathered to nominate candidates for Congress. Charles A. Hess, one of the party leaders, rose and addressed the convention: " 'Mr. Chairman and Gentlemen: In behalf of the Republicans of the Twenty-fifth Assembly District and its Republican majority of 2,500, and in the interest of peace, harmony, and good will, I take pleasure in presenting the name of the Hon. Herbert Parsons as the candidate of the Republicans of the Twelfth District.' [Great cheering.]"[28] Parsons was lauded as a man of integrity, ability, knowledge, and charity. Mr. Hess continued, " 'I have only this to add, that if you accept him as your candidate I pledge him unreservedly the enthusiastically loyal support of all my friends. Men of the Twentieth, does that go?' [Cheers.]" Mr. Parsons was declared the unanimous nominee.

News had been carried to Herbert and Elsie on their honeymoon of the intention to nominate him for Congress. As their daughter, Lissa, related, "It was up in the back country of Massachusetts or Vermont where they located [my father] to tell him he would have to run for Congress."[29] Herbert Parsons was clearly ready for the plunge. He immediately sent a wire to General Greene, who was then able to announce to the Republican Convention, "A telegram had been received from Mr. Parsons, who is on his wedding tour, accepting the nomination if tendered him, and promising to return to New York forthwith to begin an energetic campaign."[30] Thus ended what was to have been a tranquil honeymoon. As Peter Hare recounts, "He and Elsie immediately took a train to New York City where he waged a strenuous but unsuccessful campaign. Exhausted and discouraged by the election returns, he lay down on the sofa for an hour, the only time in his entire life Elsie ever saw him sleep during the day."[31]

Herbert Parsons had a strong educational background and impeccable social standing. As the *New York Times* typified his origins, "he sprang from a 'silk-stocking' district, having lived from the time he was born until toward the end of his political career in the Twenty-fifth Assembly District."[32] In a biographical sketch of Parsons, on the occasion of his election to the presidency of the Republican County Committee in New York, he was characterized as "far removed from the ordinary type of district leader. He is of aristocratic lineage, highly educated, the possessor of wealth, and with the best of opportunities for social distinction. His inclination has been for politics rather than society . . . , and while other young men of his set have been devoting their leisure time to social functions, Mr. Parsons has used all the time he could spare from the practice of the law to making a political career for himself."[33]

Herbert Parsons was born in New York City on October 28, 1869. His mother was Mary Dumesnil McIlvaine, and his father, John Edward Parsons, was a wealthy New York lawyer and a well-known independent Democrat. As a young boy, Herbert attended Everson School in New York City, spent one year in Paris at age ten, and then enrolled in St. Paul's College in Concord, New Hampshire. He graduated from Yale University in 1890 and studied economics and history for one year at the University of Berlin. In 1893, he completed Harvard Law School, and in 1895 joined the firm of Parsons, Shepard and Ogden. In 1902, the name of the firm was changed to Parsons, Clossen and McIlvaine. Herbert served in the National Guard as a private and then as a corporal in the Seventh Regiment, and as judge advocate of the First Brigade. He was a staff officer in organizational work for the Spanish-American War. When the United States entered World War I, Parsons, then forty-eight years old, immediately volunteered for service as a combatant. He was in the aviation branch of the army and rose to the rank of lieutenant colonel.

Active in the Presbyterian Church, Herbert took his religion seriously and worked with dedication toward charitable causes. He served for many years as board member of the Greenwich Settlement House and was also a board member of the New York Association for Improving the Condition of the Poor, the House of Refuge on Randall's Island, the Manhattan Eye and Ear Hospital, and the Anti-Poverty Society. He was president of the Fresh Air Fund, the Memorial Hospital for the Treatment of Cancer and Allied Diseases, the board of trustees for the Canton Christian College, and the Friends of Russian Freedom. The latter organization assisted Russian intellectual and political exiles who had been impoverished by the revolution. As a lawyer, Parsons defended Russian revolutionaries from extradition. Along with his daughter, he attended rallies in support of the struggle for liberation being fought in Russia. Lissa said that whenever the Russian national anthem was played, he stood in respect and insisted that his daughter stand by his side.[34] When the Russian ambassador, Boris A. Bakhmeteff, visited the Henry Street Settlement House, a shelter for revolutionists, Parsons, along with hundreds of others, was there to greet him. Addressing the ambassador and the crowd, Parsons said, " 'I know of nothing which has appealed to American idealists as much as has the Russian revolution.' "[35]

At Yale University, Herbert Parsons registered as a Republican. He made this conscious break from his father's political affiliation in the Democratic party with the intent of fighting the graft and corruption of Democratic politics in New York. This very theme was highlighted in a political advertisement that began, "Mr. Parsons is a young man who abandoned the political party of his ancestors to become a Republican. . . . This epitome of his political career tells what all young

men should do. . . . Every young man should think for himself. No
political tradition, no family tendencies, should sway him from exer-
cising his suffrage as his highest sense of civic duty impels."[36] The editor of the *New York Herald Tribune* wrote of his political career,
"Herbert Parsons will be remembered in this city chiefly for what he
did to lift the level of leadership in local politics." Ever opposed to
Tammany Hall and to their methods, Parsons was "deeply in earnest
and could be as ruthless and exacting in the causes of cleaner politics
as Tammany's most noted chieftains have been in the cause of politics
for the pocket only." With equal vigor, Parsons waged battle against
the Republican party bosses, such as Thomas C. Platt, who had controlled the organization of the Republican party in New York state
from the 1880s until the turn of the century, and Benjamin B. Odell,
Jr., who was governor of New York. Not alone in his struggle, Parsons
had the ample support of President Theodore Roosevelt, who was determined to reform and reorganize the Republican party in his home
state of New York.[37]

Parsons's political career began in 1899, when he was elected to the
New York City Board of Aldermen, a position to which he was reelected in 1901. In 1904 he waged a successful campaign as representative to the U.S. Congress, and he served three terms, from 1905 to
1911. In 1905 Parsons was elected chairman of the Republican
County Committee, a position he held until 1910. His nomination for
this position came after a battle of wills with and a final blessing from
Theodore Roosevelt. The *New York Times* reported these events in an
article entitled, "ROOSEVELT TO PARSONS: SAY YOU HAVE NO
BOSS, But Candidate for County Leadership Isn't Inclined to Do It.
He's Independent, Anyway; Has Said So Twice, and Doesn't Want it
to Appear That He's Dominated from Washington;" and the next
day, a follow-up article, "NO MACHINE, NO BOSS FOR ME, SAYS
PARSONS, If Any Man Supports Me to Get Favors, He needn't. BIT-
TER FIGHT PREDICTED; Congressman's Statement Taken as Evidence of President Roosevelt's Determination to Oust Odell." In
twenty-four hours, enough pressure had been exerted to elicit a statement from Parsons that he was not beholden to any political boss in
New York State. Roosevelt was assuaged. On December 22, 1905, his
victory was announced, "PARSONS THE WINNER IN ALL-NIGHT
STRUGGLE, Stormy Meeting of Republican County Committee."[38]

Once Parsons had gained the support of Roosevelt, he retained it.
With grand flourish, Roosevelt hosted Parsons at the White House
and made sure that there was appropriate news coverage. As the
New York Herald reported, "PRESIDENT STRIKES BLOW AT

'MACHINE' [by entertaining] at a luncheon . . . Mr. Herbert Parsons, Representative from New York and Chairman of the New York County Republican Committee, whom the Odell-Platt combination is trying to defeat." The president's secretary issued a statement, "The President's cordial sympathy with the purposes and methods for which Mr. Parsons stands in public life and which the President believes must obtain in the Republican party if the party is to fulfill its full measure of usefulness to the nation. . . . The President thinks it is not his business to interfere in state or local contests, but he has not made any secret of his sympathy with such men as Mr. Parsons, who enter politics with the intention of rendering service to the public."[39]

This image of closeness between President Roosevelt and Representative Parsons was carefully fostered by well-placed press releases. In a November 15, 1907, special to the *New York Times*, it was reported that "PARSONS VISITS ROOSEVELT. Entertains President with a Recital of His Explorations of Salt Creek." Parsons, the article reported, had visited the president two times during the day. When he first stopped by the White House, "he was able to see the President without delay." The president invited Parsons to lunch with him, "whereupon Mr. Parsons hustled home, arrayed himself in fine linen and a pot hat and was back at the White House on the dot."[40]

The following year, Parsons met with Roosevelt at the president's home in Sagamore Hill. Though tight-lipped about the substance of their discussion, Parsons told reporters, " 'I came down here at the President's request to discuss the political situation in the State.' " After a long and private conference with the president, Parsons returned to New York in what was described as "a record-breaking trip." He left "Sagamore Hill in the Government automobile to catch the 2:40 P. M. train for New York. As it was, the train was held up for several minutes when a cloud of dust in the distance betokened the coming of the County President. As Mr. Parsons made a flying leap for the train he called in reply to the correspondents' questions: 'Oh, we talked Taft, the campaign, Hughes, pretty nearly everything. Sorry I haven't time to tell you what it was all about.' "[41]

Herbert Parsons was to play a crucial role in local politics. He directed his efforts toward eliminating fraud in county elections. For his brand of politics, Parsons wanted an honest registration list of enrolled voters rather than a fabricated list of nonexistent voters, so he and his co-workers began organizing election districts by going door to door to enroll voters.[42] He countered the fraudulent tactics of his opponents through sponsoring a voter identification law. In his own words, he recalled: "I became county chairman, and I appointed a committee to investigate the report that 40,000 fraudulent votes were cast in this city. . . . Tammany men in the legislature admitted privately that they cast 30,000 fraudulent votes. . . . Then the national campaign came on, and every one was surprised when under the signature law of 1907, the registration seemed to be 30,000 to 40,000 votes short. At the election my views were sustained. . . . You may remember that Roosevelt lost the city by 20,000—but Taft only lost it by 5,000. A sufficient proof of what had been happening in other years."[43]

Elsie was supportive of Herbert's political career. When there was word of the possible nomination for the 25th Assembly District in 1900, she wrote her encouragement, "I am much excited about the possibility of an assembly nomination. Unselfishly I would like it greatly for you."[44] She did, however, have certain reservations. First, if the chances were slight that he would receive the nomination, then it would possibly be a mistake to consider the proposition, "for it would make many of the people in the district misunderstand your really disinterested political stand. And it might weaken you in your anti-Hess fight. But if there is a good chance, I agree with your father. Of course you would find a congressional experience interesting and I suppose it would be valuable too." Elsie voiced agreement with Herbert's position that there was a "greater need of people like you in New York than in Washington" and that this recognition made "it difficult to be enthusiastic about your immersion in national politics." Still, Elsie added, "you might be all the more valuable locally after a larger experience."[45] Further, she pointed out, the national political arena might offer him more opportunities to work for the good than the city or state level.

Herbert had tackled the bosses in New York, and the battle had not been easy. In October, 1905, he wrote Elsie, "The campaign continues to be an awful mix-up. I wish it was over. . . . One thing is certain—Tammany is white under the gills with fear."[46] On the eve of the 1906 election, he wrote Elsie: "The outlook is excellent. We are cheerful and the others are glum. The fight, however, will be hot and hard. We are up against the Sullivan influence used illegitimately south of 14th Street. I shall go around in an automobile with a bodyguard of 2 detectives who will probably be sworn in as deputy sheriffs. . . . There may be a good deal of trouble down there during the day."[47] The next day, he wrote of the defeat of the party bosses: "Quigg is beaten in his own district. Odell is therefore down and out. . . . I will be renominated for Congress. The disorder and fraud beat anything I have ever seen. It was barefaced. Henry O'Brien was nearly stabbed. Other men in the 25th were knocked around. . . . I am very tired but so relieved."[48]

Elsie was both proud and protective of Herbert. She wrote him, "I wish I could hear some of your speeches—even if you don't." In response to a critical statement made by Judge Parker that implied that Herbert had compromised his principles, Elsie seethed, "How can he or anyone else think that you who have had such high standards from their own point of view have suddenly dropped these standards? The intolerant egotism of the reformer beats all. I realize now that I once had it myself and that only because of association with you have I dropped at least part of it."[49]

Herbert sought Elsie's opinions about his legislation. She encouraged him to continue in his progressive leadership, specifically with his plan to sponsor an item of social reform each year having to do with health care and children's welfare. As she wrote, "It seems to me that Congress is so conservative that it can never be expected to initiate new legislation. But if it has the progressive legislation of our states and of foreign countries continually thrust upon it, in course of time it will follow."[50]

As a congressman, Herbert had been invited to join in the "Philippine Junket," or the "Taft Tour." Under the auspices of Secretary of War William Howard Taft, a party composed of congressmen, their wives, journalists, and other unofficial representatives of the United States sailed to the Philippines for a tour of the islands, specifically to make a case for the free admittance of tobacco, cigars, and sugar to the U.S. market. Of this group, Taft was later to write, " 'I doubt if so formidable a Congressional representation ever went so far.' " After two months at sea, he was able to boast, " 'We took eighty people with us and came back so harmonious that everyone was able to speak to everyone else.' "[51]

Elsie compiled her recollections of this in "Memoirs of Washington & Outlying Provinces: 1905, by a Political Wife." She wrote: "In April 1905 we went to Washington, house hunting for our Congressional term. . . . I had had a lively desire to meet Secretary Taft, & so one morning put on a smart hat and dress and met H[erbert] at the War Department. The interview was charming. Taft had already urged H[erbert] to go on the trip and now he included me."[52]

Elsie began to prepare almost at once for the trip. She wrote Herbert, "Bring up some of the Philippine books as I wish to start in."[53] Impromptu instruction was conducted on board ship by Colonel Clarence R. Edwards, Bureau Chief of Insular Affairs. He would gather the group around his maps that he had unfolded on the deck and, with pointer in hand, discuss the public works projects. Formal lectures were also given by Colonel Edwards and by James Leroy, whom Elsie described as "a scholarly young man who . . . knew more about the Islands than anyone on board."[54]

The group congregated in San Francisco for the departure on July 8, 1905, aboard the Pacific mail steamship, *S. S. Manchuria*. Elsie recalled the scene at the dock: "Our bustling and mishapless departure . . . was very gay. Perhaps I enjoyed most as an anticipation of the East the sight of our Chinese sailors and of the little group of Chinese women who waved goodbyes from the dock to their steerage friends. As we moved away a shower of little colored papers thrown aloft by the orientals to bring good luck filled the air."[55] Herbert and Elsie were assigned to Secretary Taft's table. The seating order, explicitly detailed, reflected care toward rank as well as etiquette. Secretary Taft sat at the head of the table, and Colonel Edwards sat opposite him. Miss Alice Roosevelt sat to his left. She was named "the princess" of the party by the young men on board and was received quite literally as such by the Japanese and the Filipinos.[56] The others at the table included Senator Francis G. Newlands of Nevada, and his wife, Edith McAllister Newlands, Representative Frederick H. Gillett of Massachusetts, Representative Nicholas Longworth of Ohio, Captain James K. Thompson, aide-de-camp to Secretary Taft, Miss Mabel T. Boardman of the American National Red Cross, and Miss Amy McMillan of Washington, D.C. Elsie described Taft's custom of sitting at table after meals: "Those of us who liked to hear him talk—I for one did above everything else—moved down to his end. The Colonel and his girls (as we called Misses Boardman and McMillan), Alice Roosevelt and 'Nick' always left early. The Secretary, H[erbert] and I were very apt to outstay even the others." The table talk, Elsie said, "was not always of a serious character, altho' Taft used to dub Senator Newlands and me 'the heavy middle layer.' "[57]

Taft clearly took an interest in Herbert and Elsie, for he wrote his wife, "Mr. and Mrs. Herbert Parsons are people whom I am anxious to have you know." He continued, "He is the son of John E. Parsons and she is the daughter of a beautiful New York belle who married Clews, a New York banker. They were our particular party on the Manchuria and added much to our pleasure." Taft described Elsie as "a bright woman who attends in some way as an instructress at Columbia. She was brought up in fashion, but seems to break away from it some. They are well to do and will take a house in Washington."[58]

The Taft party stopped off in Japan on their way to the Philippines. Not simply an amusing diversion, this visit was a carefully arranged act of diplomacy that was tied to the policy in the Pacific. Through all the fanfare, receptions, and celebrations, Secretary Taft was shrewdly attempting to ascertain the Japanese position on the Philippines. Stretched taut beneath this all was the tightrope of neutrality on which the United States was poised in the dispute between Japan and Russia.

The *S. S. Manchuria* steamed into Yokohama on July 25, 1905. Elsie recalled waking up that morning and peering through the port-hole at "a tug filled with little frockcoated, silk-hatted Japanese, waving American and Japanese flags and sending off fantastic paper balloons." From the ship, the party was escorted on to rikshas, of which Elsie remarked, "I shall never forget the entrancing ten-minute riksha ride to the imperial waiting room. . . . Our route was filled with a banzaiing crowd and bands of school children waved American flags at us."[59]

Miss Alice Roosevelt had been invited to be the guest of the emperor, but her father, cognizant of Japanese-Russian neutrality, had quickly cabled a refusal. She stayed at the American legation. Secretary Taft and his military staff of four were received at one of the imperial palaces. The rest of the party went to the homes of American, German, and Japanese officials. Elsie and Herbert were guests of Sho-saku Matsukata, a secretary in the Foreign Office.[60] Elsie recalled, "Our considerate host met us at the station at Tokyo and after passing thro' the cheering and flag-waving crowd around the station . . . took us to his home." Actually, the Matsukatas had two homes, side by side, one of European style, and the other Japanese. To Elsie's dismay, they were never taken into the Japanese home, but instead were received in the European home. She described it as being "not bad looking on the outside," with an inside that showed "the pitiable things that Europe and America were doing to Japanese taste." All sense of the balance and line of Japanese aesthetic was abandoned. In its place was a profusion of things European, "furniture, wall papers, knick knacks, everything, was of garish pattern and color, and all very expensive. Even the flowers on the elaborately served dining room table were bunched together regardless of form or color. The well-trained butler and footman were in European liveries."[61]

The official party was invited to lunch with the emperor at his palace. In a letter to his father, Herbert wrote of their reception, "Wednesday at 11:30 we each made 3 bows & shook the Mikado's hand, & in another room similarly greeted the princess, the empress not being there because of an illness." In his diary, Herbert expanded on the formal reception by the Mikado, "Most of us wore white gloves. McKinley of Illinois loaned his left to Otjen [of Wisconsin] and wore his right. As our turns came in close file we bowed at the sill of the room, advanced 3 or 4 steps and bowed again & then advanced, shook hands with his majesty and bowed, Griscom standing on the son of Heaven's left & announcing our names. Driscoll's shoes squeaked horribly." The delegation was served lunch in the imperial dining room. Herbert wrote that "Elsie looked very well in afternoon costume, but I was in evening clothes & a Japanese silk hat, having failed to bring my own."[62]

The Japanese, from the emperor down, had been relaxing their usual set form of etiquette to accommodate the Americans. The emperor "gave the cue by going around informally and shaking hands with the members of the official party, over fifty in number, whom he invited to lunch with him after the formal audience was over."[63] He then invited them all to see his private garden, never before shown to foreigners. Lloyd C. Griscom, U.S. minister to Japan, rather breathlessly recalled the event: "We climbed into imperial barouches and drove through a narrow gate in a high green fence surrounding a beautiful park. In front of us was a lake, covered with pink flowering lotus. We walked across an old mossy stone bridge, sharply curved in the middle, and reached a forested island, crisscrossed by little trails. The nightingales were singing, the first time most of the party had every heard them."[64]

The warmth of feeling carried through to the departure. The Taft party was ushered out with masses of people lining the streets, "shouting '*Banzai!*' and waving red and white lanterns, and throwing bouquets at the daughter of the Peacemaker."[65] As the *S. S. Manchuria* steamed through the Inland Sea, people crowded the banks to shout their farewell: "While in the strait between Moji and Shimonoseki there was a salute from a Japanese gunboat, and tugs with Japanese officials and army and navy officers steamed alongside the ship for several miles, shouting 'Banzai!' setting off the always unique Japanese fireworks and having bands play American patriotic airs."[66]

The main purpose for the trip still lay ahead, in the Philippines. The party arrived there on the fifth of August. While ostensibly the delegation was to become acquainted with governmental and economic aspects of the Philippines, and was to assess the future of the U.S. involvement, Secretary Taft had a more direct goal in mind. He aimed to convert the opposition. Those hostile to the further development of U.S. and Philippine relations had been specially targeted for the trip. As Colonel Edwards would say, " 'We have all our enemies with us.' "[67] The real work was to win them over, and this was done with parties, dinners, and lavish accommodations. A tour of the islands was included, and the members of the party were greeted by the colorful and the exotic: "At Jamboanga . . . the party [was] received at the pier by 2,300 Moros, representing ten different tribes. A parade, fencing bouts and a baseball game between a Filipino and Moro team occupied the afternoon, and in the evening there was a boat parade and a sham battle with canoes. At Cebu they were met by a procession of 2,000 school children. . . . The Sultan received the party in the open fields outside the walls of Jolo, where 8,000 Moros mounted on decorated ponies were assembled. The entertainment consisted of native sports, including a spear dance and a bull fight."[68]

The members of the party were protected from the real problems of the people. As one critic remarked, the size of the party, the shortness of time, and the number of festive occasions, all meant that crucial things were overlooked. It was the life in the countryside that required study: "The *tao*, or 'the man with the hoe,' is by long odds the most important person in the Philippines, but he does not appear to best advantage or in truest character on a gala day in a provincial capital. Our visitors, it may be said, never really saw him or heard his voice."[69]

Just as the party was protected from the Filipino of the countryside, so also were they kept apart from the Filipino of the city. After her return from the trip, Elsie wrote of "American Snobbishness in the Philippines": "The entertainment of the Taft party furnished many illustrations of this neglect of native society. It was stated to me, and as far as I could I verified the statement, that not a single Filipino lady was invited to meet Miss Roosevelt or the ladies of the party at any of the dinners given in their honor."[70] This was so even though at the grand ball held in the marble hall of the government house, Miss Alice Roosevelt, the guest of honor, wore a costume that Filipino women had spent three months making.[71]

The Americans living in the Philippines openly disparaged the ability of the Filipinos to entertain properly members of the Taft party. Elsie recalled, "One Filipino lady who has always kept an excellent table was told that if she wished to entertain two members of the unofficial party she must engage a Chinese cook." Elsie remarked on statements that appeared in American newspapers published in the Philippines, "that it was hoped that Miss Roosevelt would not be seen dancing with any 'gugu'—the American term of contempt for the Filipino."[72]

The social division was nurtured and maintained by the Americans, and specifically, Parsons said, by American women: "Excepting three or four school teachers and the wife of one American official who was interested in introducing housekeeping classes into the school system, I met during the week in Manila not a single American woman who expressed an interest of any kind in the welfare or progress of the Filipinos."[73] The underlying problem, Parsons said, was the "unintelligent and selfish race prejudice." The irony was that this should feature so prominently in the reception of the Taft party, since, as Parsons stressed, it contrasted so with "the tone set by Governor and Mrs. Taft." As governor of the Philippines, Taft had been expansive and open. Parties at the governor's palace were an equal balance of American and Filipino guests. Furthermore he journeyed throughout the islands, attending banquets, fiestas, and balls.

The Taft party left the Philippines for Hong Kong, arriving there on September 2. Two days later, they traveled to Canton for a reception at the American Consulate. This was an important symbolic visit, for Taft wanted to stress the goodwill of the United States toward China and to bring about an end to the boycott of American goods.[74] Here the party separated, with some going to Korea, and others going to Peking. Elsie and Herbert joined the latter group, and thus were included in the audience with the empress. The women of the party were without the requisite black hats that had to be worn in the presence of the empress, and as Elsie's daughter recounted, "And mother, who was the least dressy of all of them and cared the least about clothes, made blacks hats for all of them, which they wore." Lissa added, "So you can imagine what the old Empress thought of the chic of the American women."[75]

Departing Peking, Herbert wrote to Taft of their "delightful and interesting trip." He ended his letter, "But not in a generation has a nobler mission been offered or accepted than yours. So much in public life is sordid & self-centered that it is uplifting to come across such work as yours." Elsie's acquaintances were not, however, interested in the lofty goals of the two-month diplomatic tour. On her return home, she recalled, "The only question that was asked me of experiences and impressions was 'How did you like Alice?' 'How did Alice behave?' "[76]

Herbert's success in politics continued. In 1907 he vanquished the powerful Republican, Benjamin B. Odell. The *New York Times* reported, "PARSONS MAKES HIMSELF MASTER. . . . Congressman Herbert Parsons bids fair to be the absolute boss of the Republican Party in New York County, holding a position more secure than that held by any other man in the party for the last fifteen years."[77] Griscom, who had first met Herbert in Japan, recalled the nomination procedure at the New York County Republican committee: "Just before we were called to order, the district leaders came bustling in, and the whisper circulated, 'Parsons says Otto Bannard for Mayor.' I heard some murmurs of disapproval. . . . However, Parsons' choice was the convention's choice, and Bannard was quickly nominated."[78] With less success, Parsons struggled to deliver the New York State delegation to the presidential candidacy of William Howard Taft at the 1908 national convention. In an astute political move, Taft declared himself opposed to splitting the state delegation over support for him or for New York Governor Charles Evans Hughes. It was reported, "TAFT CALLS OFF FOES OF HUGHES, Tells Parsons to Let the Governor Have the New York Delegation."[79]

With all this, Herbert tired of the pressures of the political world, and by 1908, he was thinking of leaving Congress. He wrote Elsie, "Would you object very much if I declined a renomination for Congress? I am so sick of politics . . . that I feel like getting out bag and baggage and working for myself for pay. Soon I will be so unpopular that I will be kicked out. . . . So why not retire now voluntarily?" Elsie counseled that for Herbert it would be a mistake to leave Congress, though she thought that he had done more than could be expected for the Republican County Committee. She added, "As for me, there would be both advantages and disadvantages in your withdrawing from politics. Our social life would be so much duller that I should want to get some amusement out of writing and I should be free to do so."[80]

Certainly word of Representative Parsons's possible withdrawal from politics alarmed his supporters. Perhaps for this reason, there was a timely exchange of letters between President Roosevelt and William S. Bennet of the New York Committee on Immigration and Naturalization. On September 30, 1908, Bennet wrote Elsie, "I think that the enclosed may interest you. I feel quite certain that Herbert would never send it to you." He attached a copy of a letter to him from the president, dated September 27, 1908: "I have your letter of the 26th & agree with every word you say about the County organization & the credit due to Parsons. It is simply fine & I have taken the liberty of sending some of it to Parsons because he is such a good fellow & deserves all encouragement."[81] Elsie had received praise of Herbert's political efforts from others as well. Franklin Giddings wrote, "Mr. Parsons' sturdy fighting against the Quigg gang is one of the two or three political developments that I have attempted to follow! All success to him!"[82]

Herbert Parsons stayed on for another term in Congress, and he won the support of yet another president. William Howard Taft wrote Elsie in 1910, "I have your note of March 25th. I know just how you feel, and if what I said about Herbert gave you any pleasure I am doubly repaid for saying what I was anxious to say—the truth."[83]

In the first years of their marriage, there was joy. Elsie was totally devoted to Herbert. She wrote him, "I miss you *awfully*, Herbert. You have become a part of every bit of me." On December 4, 1900, Elsie wrote Herbert of her pregnancy, "That is very satisfactory, isn't it? I want so much to help in bringing *everything* to you that you want, that I can't help being pleased." When Lissa was born, Elsie's letters were full of her, "Lissa receives universal admiration—naturally. She wore her new sunbonnet today and *couldn't* have looked sweeter." With fondness, Elsie remarked on an aspect of Lissa's personality that would later nettle her, "Lissa's delight in playfulness is intense. What a social creature she is going to be."[84]

Elsie observed her children carefully, noting the development of their personalities. Of their three-year-old son, Elsie wrote Herbert, "John's masculine sense is already too developed for my liking. He often says boys do this, girls that, etc." She likened John to Herbert, for as she said, "John's lunch party was, I think, a success. Altho' I haven't heard much about it yet. John, like you, chooses his own time for his story." Of a party for Lissa, she wrote: "The fancy dress party was a great success—except that the prize was awarded to the one child here that Lissa dislikes. . . . She was a newspaper, and probably had done more of her costume herself than the others. . . . Lissa was really charming. The crook [was] very pretty and she carried a woolly lamb. . . . I gave John my pistol on condition that he wouldn't flourish it, and he didn't, but one request he had to take it out and explain it to the children, said Lissa—'and there were some very big boys there.' So he must have had a good time too."[85]

Elsie was convinced that children should be taught at a young age about sex. Lissa was eight when her mother, in response to a question from Lissa, explained "something of one of the mysteries of creation." As Elsie wrote Herbert, "She was pleased to hear. 'Now I know how people get babies,' she commented with satisfaction. She herself then changed the subject and was not unduly impressed." Elsie was also of the opinion that a relaxed attitude toward nudity was healthy for the children. With this, Herbert disagreed. Elsie resigned herself: "I will do as you wish about John. (I suppose you don't mind underclothes *yet*.) As I am uncertain about the working of my theory—on him at least. It is rather hard for me to get at your point of view at first hand. Altho' I haven't had the advantage of being the daughter of a painter, nudeness *per se* has never stimulated any sex feelings in me. But a sunset, waves, singing, a fanciful turn of speech, a jest, do. It is strange that you don't know that about me."[86]

Herbert was emphatic in his view, and thoroughly impatient with his wife's liberal attitude toward nudity. He wrote her, "Why do you think that John, a boy, should be like you and unlike other boys! More than surmise seems to me necessary to set at naught the views and experience of those who have had most to do with boys." He continued, in exasperation, taking issue with Elsie's formulation of opinion: "I am frequently astonished at your novel propositions entirely self-made, not based on the views of those most experienced and almost universal reason and belief, but in direct opposition to them without reason. [Your brother] Henry was more correct than I when he denominated naiveté what I am wont to call your lack of knowledge of human nature. I want what is best for the children, new or old, but I trust the old until real reasons are given for the new."[87]

Elsie's liberal views clearly impressed her children as well. John had absorbed in his own speech Elsie's disdain of materialism. She wrote Herbert, "I was jumped 50 years or more ahead in the morning, hearing John add to his terms of insult to passersby 'oh you private property.' " Lissa was searching for a topic for "her experience story;" her mother suggested that she might write about her father. Elsie recorded the dialogue for Herbert, " 'I don't know anything about Father,' was her objection, 'except that he is a Congressman and we like him.' 'Well, try me.' 'The only things I could say about you are that you are rather tall, that you like to write books and go without clothes.' "[88]

During these early years of her marriage, Elsie rarely wrote to Herbert of her work. Clearly, she was actively engaged in research and writing. In September 1900, her article on "Field Work in Teaching Sociology" appeared in the *Educational Review*. In 1903, her translation of Gabriel Tarde's *Laws of Imitation* was published; and in 1905, three articles, as well as a preface for E. G. Herzfeld's *Family Monographs*, were completed. Additionally, she was teaching sociology at Barnard College during the first five years of marriage. However, from her letters to her husband, it would seem that her concerns were all babies, teas, and visits. In this vein, she wrote, "I had quite a social day. Lunched with Miss Cram. . . . Afterwards I drove to Mrs. George Tumures. . . . Then to Mrs. Jessup's. . . . When I dress my hair elaborately I must make an occasion of it." If Elsie did mention her work, it appeared as a parenthetical comment or an apologetic demurrer. Appended to her declaration of devotion to Herbert, she added, "(Perhaps I ought to expect a still lingering fondness for studying the development of the family . . .)." She clearly felt guilty about expenses incurred through her work, unless she was able to defray them through her stipend as Hartley House Fellow at Barnard College. She wrote Herbert: "I enclose a letter from Professor Osgood because of its reference to the printing of the minutes of the Common Council. I did not show you the elaborate document of thanks from the Columbia Trustees as it came when I was ashamed of my extravagance and when I thought that my next years *salary* was not to be earned." From time to time, there was a brief mention of her work, a reference to "a quiet day—devoted to the textbook." On occasion, she included Herbert by giving him copies of her writings, as she did in October, 1905, "I am sending you a reprint of my second *Charities* article."[89]

During these years, when Herbert and Elsie maintained an apartment in the Capital, she might have had more professional contact had she sought out the Washington anthropologists. She made it a point to remain abreast of their publications, and on one occasion, she attended a lecture. As she wrote to Herbert on April 16, 1907, "I went to the meeting of the Anthropological Society this evening, but Miss Fletcher wasn't there and so I made no acquaintances. . . . A woman talked about the Navajo Indians. You would have been interested. I was somewhat." What seems to have been a singular lack of contact between Elsie and the Washington anthropologists was the result of several factors. First, Elsie was absorbed with her young family, her teaching at Barnard, and her research. More importantly, Elsie did not really reside in Washington. By choice, she lived with the children either at Lenox or at the Rocks. When she did spend time with her husband in their Washington apartment, this was arranged around Herbert's demanding schedule. In what was a representative expression of the conflict he felt, Herbert wrote her on October 23, 1907, "I both do and don't want you to come down. I love to have you and then on the other hand the rush and stress of things are such that I am easily fretted, can see little of you and generally feel like a mink when I do see you."[90] Finally, the Washington years did not really coincide with the time when Elsie was intensely focused on anthropology. That was to come later, after much change in her personal and intellectual life.

A period of sadness and tribulation began for Elsie in 1906. Her third child died two days after birth. Deeply did she feel the loss, though outwardly she attempted to mask her sorrow. Herbert praised her for bravery, and she responded, "I think I have never in my life been brave except about the baby's death, and I may overestimate myself there because I am so conscious of the effort I have made, for there never has been a time since he died that I couldn't have easily sat down and let myself go to pieces." Elsie focused intensely on her desire for a baby. She wrote Herbert: "It is ridiculous how much I long for a baby, much more than before Lissa or John were born. Besides the unformulated, sort of physiological desire, it seems to me that I shall never quite regain my old *joie de vivre* until I have, *we* have, a baby. Florence asked me the other day, 'Did you mind the baby's dying?' " Her wish was fulfilled, but tragedy followed, for this baby died within an hour of birth on February 11, 1907. Elsie was inconsolable. Yet with characteristic self-discipline, she tried to take herself in hand. She wrote Herbert, "I found William James article last night on human energy quite stimulating, and I began to put my own old system—not a yoga one—into operation today."[91]

By April, 1907, Elsie was pregnant again, and filled with foreboding. She suggested a vacation to Puerto Rico or Cuba: "A trip now would help me out quite a little as I shall have to get in a stock of cheerfulness and serenity for what is ahead again. With you at hand that is comparatively easy. My chief foe under these circumstances is the middle age state of mind." Happily, this time, she gave birth to a healthy, robust boy, Herbert, Junior. Still, her depression continued. Herbert counseled, "Swift told me to-day that Tahawas was the best place for you to go and *that you ought to give up your work* for awhile." Occupied in Washington, Herbert was unable to accompany her to the mountain resort. He wrote, "Yet I am glad you have gone for I realize your real purpose and all the future happiness that it involves. . . . I even asked Swift if you had better go abroad but he said no. . . . Have a glorious time. Don't work much. Do open air pleasures both morning and evening."[92]

Elsie had set in motion her plan for rejuvenation. With determination, she countered the extreme depression she felt from the loss of the two babies, and she fought what she called her chief foe, the middle age state of mind. She flung herself into a gay social life and quite consciously undertook a series of flirtations, all of which she reported in detail to Herbert. From the Tahawas Club, Elsie wrote: "You will be pleased to know that I have not been working at all—thanks mostly to the pleasant companionship of Fitz. He is a very good sort of a boy and man." A week later, Elsie told of her sadness concerning the departure of Reginald Fitz, for, as she said, "He has added very much to my pleasure, making me feel like doing all sorts of young things." The following day, she wrote: "It was over 80 here today, and

I ought to have gone swimming all day; but I didn't as that would have made me miss R. Fitz even more than I did. It was surprising how much I enjoyed his companionship, considering his age and Bostonese ideas. He had a very charming personality. And then he liked me so frankly that I could not help being flattered." Herbert, she said, sounded overworked, and though she wished for a more equitable division of labor, she was certain that he would be pleased, for, as she said, "My experiment up here is doing all for me that I had expected. I don't work and I don't even want to." Herbert reacted in an understandable way; he was jealous of Reginald Fitz. Elsie responded, "Yes, you can be jealous, a little, of Fitz, as far as one can be jealous of a symbol. I could be. My recipe for rejuvenation will always be to have a boy like you."[93]

With her letters replete in detail, Elsie even described the rift in her relationship over the course of the year: "Reginald Fitz I have given up as anything more than a pleasant incident where it comes quite without my initiative. If I were conceited I would say that he acts as if he were awfully afraid of falling in love with me. He thinks that falling in love for years to come is quite incompatible with his profession. But I am not conceited, in that way at least, and so I conclude that to his evasive nature my sincerity is just irksome, altho' it is plain enough that he takes pleasure in my company *when* he is with me."[94]

While Fitz was out, there were still other flirtations. With a candor that must have stung Herbert, Elsie wrote to him from the Rocks: "I . . . telephoned to young Pearson to go out in the evening. We started at 9 and got back at 12, going to Bateman's Beach. We had an overcast moon. I loved it. He paddles well and doesn't talk much. In the two minutes he talked to Mama, while I was dressing, she said she had found out all about him. . . . They pinned him down on our return to supper in the hall. Henry asked how old he was, which question for a youth who is wearing a mustache at 24 is invariably painful. He doesn't compare with Reginald Fitz, but I think we will nevertheless canoe around to the other beaches this afternoon."[95]

Elsie continued in her resolve to fight off age. At times, she felt "not only young, but juvenile." From the constant reiteration of her intent, she must have at least convinced Herbert of her success. She wrote, "I have been gay enough even for you, and I have talked so much about practicing the art of youth that Katherine asked me last night if I meant the art of youth or of youths." Even the German maid noticed her high spirits: " 'Mrs. Parsons. . . . has been getting very gay herself lately.' 'Of course, I'm keeping young,' I said, and was much amused." Elsie included Herbert in her quest for youth. With determination, she said, "You and I are not going to age. All suggestions of it are taboo."[96]

Herbert himself adopted Elsie's plan for rejuvenation, though, it would seem, less out of devotion to the cause than out of insecurity about his relationship with his wife. He cultivated a friendship with Lucy Wilson, who resided in Washington with her husband, the diplomat Huntington Wilson. While Elsie's flirtations involved dates, excursions, even camping trips, Herbert simply visited Lucy and her husband, met them for tea, dined with them, joined them at the opera, and went "motoring" and for walks with them. His adventures were pallid in comparison with Elsie's. There being no balance in affairs of the heart, Elsie descended into a pit of despair. She was alternately tormented by fits of jealousy and besieged with self-revulsion at her emotional outbursts. Instead of reassessing this perilous path of youthful gaiety, Elsie and Herbert maintained their course.

Elsie was especially nettled when she thought her feelings had been divulged to others. She wrote Herbert on July 28, 1909, "I have a letter from Peters in which he writes, 'You will be relieved to know Mrs. Wilson is in Washington and as Herbert drives with me [to Charlottesville] I think need cause you little anxiety.' " While the jealousy raged within, Elsie feigned a calm exterior. To this mildly impertinent comment of her friend, she responded, "Of course I know the Wilsons are in Washington. Thanks to them or rather to her Herbert has had a more agreable time than he would otherwise have had." But of Herbert, she demanded, "Now what did he mean by that? Did you give me away to him?" She was emphatic: no one should take her seriously on the subject of jealousy, not even Herbert. As she said, "The moments when I take myself seriously are quite enough."[97]

Always conscious of proper etiquette, Herbert suggested that Elsie invite Lucy and her husband for dinner as a repayment for the hospitality they had extended to him in Washington. She responded: "I cant ask the Wilsons to come here. It seems and it is ungenerous to you—not to them, as I cant see that you are at all in their debt, the company of an agreable man always pays a woman in itself. Another time I would make myself ask them but just now I cant take the physiological risk. It is evident that you cant understand my state of mind—an occasional and pathological one perhaps. I hope to get over it in course of time. But until I do, I shall never see L. W. for my own pleasure. Suppose we drop the subject until it becomes historical."[98]

Elsie became fixated on the subject of Lucy Wilson. She wrote to Herbert, "You are a poor psychologist: You cant joke *obsessions* away."

She asked Herbert not to discuss "the subject." In a letter dated February, 1910, written in a scrawled hand, with lined-out words and blotches of ink, Elsie warned, "Such reference will only add to the train of unpleasant associations & it involves me in a fresh waste of time and energy. I made a pretty good start this morning and now your two references have put me back into the wretched state I was in yesterday and I shall have to start over again putting the matter out of my mind. You can help me only by absolutely avoiding the subject between us from the time you get this note. Remember I have no sense of humor about myself."[99]

In the midst of her fury over Lucy Wilson, Elsie still buoyed her spirits with male companions, and she did not follow the rule of "shutting down" on the subject, as Herbert had willingly done. She wrote him about her trip with George Young and said that it proved his "impertinent maxim 'Give a calf a long rope.' " George she found to be "a charming companion in many ways, but exacting." Then she added, "You are too, but then I love you and that changes things." One year later, she took a canoe trip with him. She wrote Herbert, "George Young and I went to Great Falls yesterday afternoon, canoed across the river, walked down & looked at the gorge. . . . He was cranky & would neither stay out there to supper nor come home with me. He makes me curious as no one ever did before." Elsie reported to Herbert about having tea with George's wife, Helen Young, who leveled an eye at Elsie, and asked, " 'Do you think anybody is loyal in Washington?' " Elsie added, "If I could only tell her how flimsily George thinks about me and how much more in love with you I am. . . . As a matter of fact I have never been in the least in love with him—altho he charms me in some ways more than anyone I have ever met."[100]

In her more tormented moments, Elsie was convinced that Herbert thought of nothing but Lucy Wilson. Detailed accounts of his social engagements were taken as indications of his guilt feelings. When Elsie imposed silence on the topic, she could still feel the presence of Lucy in Herbert's letters. As she wrote him, "You haven't the art to keep her out of your letters even when you dont mention her."[101] In truth, the style of Herbert's writing did change during this period. Instead of the rather perfunctory remarks about his political work, he became more chatty and included details on his social life. Elsie found Herbert comparing her to Lucy, and took offense. On one occasion, he remarked on how quickly Lucy Wilson had dressed for dinner, "12 minutes by my watch," and then added a postscript, "Don't take this letter as a criticism on your slow dressing. I prefer that you should be late your way, *very much!*"[102] In exasperation, Elsie accused Herbert of not knowing the difference between Lucy and herself: "Since we can not depend on your perceptions & you will go on mixing up L. W. & E. C. P. together, I suggest that you make a rule, i. e. institutionalize the situation. Whenever L. W. is in evidence (i. e. when E. C. P. can not get out of the way in time) and for one week afterwards do not make love at all to E. C. P."[103]

Elsie puzzled over the question as to whether Herbert would have been happier and better off married to a woman like Lucy Wilson. With this thought in mind, she fell asleep on her bedroom porch at the Rocks: "I woke up from a dream of myself in a flaming scarlet dress in a picture gallery and Merry sitting upright in a bed declaring that he was in love with me. Of course, married to one of them you wouldn't be so likely to fall in love with them whereas you might fall in love with one of my type and find yourself in a distressing situation."[104]

Herbert tried repeatedly to convince Elsie that she was the only woman he loved, or ever wanted to love. On July 27, 1909, he wrote to his distraught wife, "Don't you observe how more & more convinced I become that there is only one girl in the world for me." After a fight, he expressed himself, "I left you without any sign of the love I so much felt. Darling you are so splendid & good that I hate myself when at such moments I behave like a cad." In a mood swing, Elsie was able to bring herself to speak obliquely of Lucy Wilson in a light-hearted way. She joked with Herbert that while she had adjusted to the thought of polygyny, she could not yet accept a harem. And then she suggested, "I think if you would enlarge your real harem it would be a help to me. Cultivate a N. Y. girl at once." Herbert responded not in jest, but quite seriously: "What is the distinction between polygyny & harem? I don't catch the point. I don't want to cultivate any one here or any one elsewhere, but if it does not annoy you, I want to like a person when I do like the person. You exaggerate the matter & fail to realize the reservations I always make & the elements of dislike that mingle with those of like; also the comparing with you that I make which is always fatal to them."[105]

Herbert had been forewarned. In the initial stages of their relationship, Elsie had playfully chastised him concerning "a midnight call" on her friend, Alice Duer. She reminded him that it was "in very bad taste" to call on people of the opposite sex at late hours. Then she added, "Would it surprise you very much to learn that I have a jealous disposition? I am beginning to surprise myself with that piece of information. It threatens to be a very great bore to myself." The last sentence was starred, and in the margin she added, "Don't take this too seriously. I think jealousy is a most ignoble thing and I hope it will never touch me." Years later, when she was at the mercy of this ignoble emotion, Elsie wrote Herbert, "How modern we are. . . . I asking for discipline and you declining to give it. You never heard or read of a jealous wife treated that way. We out Galsworthy Galsworthy."[106]

Elsie fixed her mental energy on jealousy, hoping to be able to understand it rationally and thus to master it. She and her friend, Alice Duer Miller, the same Alice of the late-night visit so many years ago, discussed the topic. Elsie wrote Herbert: "Alice and I had a most illuminating talk last night in the moonlight over jealousy and remorse, my specialty and yours. We agreed that in spite of the possibility of thin ice, interest in the other sex . . . shakes you up out of any settled sodden conjugality and was therefore desireable. A much weightier conclusion for me than for her, for like you, as a superior type, she doesn't really know what jealousy is like and can only see with her reason the advantages to the woman of a man's interest in other women. I see them just as clearly as she does—with my reason. The capacity for remorse she analyses as lack of foresight."[107]

Present also in the early letters was evidence of the jarring juxtaposition between Elsie's possessiveness of Herbert, and the freeness with herself. Here, too, was candor. She wrote of a young Lawrence Butler who came to say farewell, "He is such a simple hearted boy, that his liking for me gives me great pleasure." In September, 1898, four days after having written to Herbert about the intensity of her love and her dependence on him, Elsie told of a plan to go to Egypt with Mr. Abbott. Then, with revealing honesty, she confessed to her ambivalence, "I want you to miss me and yet I don't want you to miss me. It is a very confused emotional state."[108]

The confused emotional state had become the tormented. In August, 1909, Elsie determined the cause of her depression: "The trouble with me is the lack of a time-compelling job. I always knew that my character couldn't stand against idleness. Lately I have taken to copying ms. in which there is no mental effort, but which keeps me occupied, and I am much better off." However, the intense emotional swings and severe depression continued. She attempted to mask this in the letters and revealed only a portion to Herbert when she could no longer remain silent. Woven in with the spurts of introspection and accusation was her method at work for the retention of youth. During the late summer and fall of 1910, Elsie stopped her forced gaiety. She was pregnant with her fourth child. In a concerted attempt to break away from her obsessions about Lucy Wilson, Elsie took a trip to Española, New Mexico, in August.[109]

Her daily letters to Herbert reflected her attempt to channel her energies in directions other than jealousy. She began to write of her new undertakings. When Lissa started cooking and sewing lessons at the age of nine, Elsie wrote, "I too am learning a lot about cooking. Have mastered scrambled eggs and omelette, several vegetables, sour milk things and today make butter." She listed her activities for the day, "I cooked, studied Spanish, went over ms., lived awhile in the Southwest, watched H. P. Jr., arranged flowers, waited on table, taught reading, writing, spelling, drawing, nature, poetry. Drove Mlle to and from the French lesson, brushed Lissa's teeth, did exercises with her and alone, read a story aloud, etc.. etc.." Of her time with the children, Elsie wrote, "I am with them regularly 5 or 6 hours a day, with many extra hours. It is the hardest sort of work . . . for me given my disposition."[110]

Elsie became involved again in her work. She continued studying Spanish and began work on what she referred to as "an Ethnological study." While en route from Concord to Boston, she wrote of "a good time at the library." And the next month she mentioned bicycling to the National Museum, where she "spent an hour . . . with the Indians (shockingly bad collections on view)."[111]

Though she did not mention it to Herbert, Elsie had begun a fictionalized account, "The Imaginary Mistress." Clearly the work of her obsession about Herbert and Lucy Wilson, Elsie had incorporated passages of her own letters and of Herbert's. Lois Fair, the female protagonist, suspected her husband, Anson Barnes—a thinly veiled Herbert Parsons—of having an affair with Alice Smith, the wife of an archeologist. Threaded through the pages of this manuscript were slices of Elsie's own agony. Reflecting on her husband's newfound attachment, Lois Fair spoke with the same words that Elsie had written to Herbert, "I knew in fact a long time before he did. It was his very self-deception which in the beginning aggravated me almost beyond endurance." Lois's emotional dilemma was based on Elsie's reality: "He had many chances to be considerate of me that winter, for I was to have a child in May and for a while I was physically miserable. I was miserable too in spirit. Instead of being a delight to me, as it was before Bobbie was born, Anson's gentleness was hard to bear. It easily made me hysterical, particularly when I could not escape quickly enough to my room. Alone there I had long fits of weeping. Indeed whenever I was alone, my eyes had a senseless way of filling with tears.

Why had it all happened? Why couldn't it be as before between us? What I had most cared for I had lost."[112] The ending was a flight of fancy. Lois separated from her husband and moved to the Yucatan where her home became an intellectual center.

Herbert and Elsie were pulled apart in their interests. For Elsie, this was part of her plan to reclaim the inner strength that she had lost during the siege of jealousy over Lucy Wilson. Herbert tried hard to resist it; he yearned for time spent together: "Friday, Saturday and Sunday afternoons I wanted to be with you, hupping for lack of any other method of chumming together. Friday you went, Saturday you went only for a little because as I supposed you felt ill and Sunday you went not at all. The happiest times I used to have in Lenox were our afternoon drives together. . . . And while I may never have been devoted in manner in getting you to go I took them as an institution which I knew contributed pleasure to me. . . . But when you don't go I feel lost and when you do go I feel pleasantly. It seems to me that your objections to institutionalism goes to the extent of blinding you to the very satisfactory opportunity that institutions are for regular recurrent companionship."

Herbert admitted confusion about Elsie's intentional change: "I confess I don't understand you in some of your new ways. Apparently travel, things new and unconventional are necessary to your enjoyment." He encouraged her to pursue that which made her happy, even though he might feel lonely because of it. Still, he felt displeasure at her behavior during the past year when, as he said, "You went off for Saturdays and Sundays, my freest time, even if you returned for Sunday dinner (generally tired out and fit only to go to bed). . . . My selfish pleasure is in feeling you nearby and my preference would be that your trips and sailings take place at times when I am away or at work."[113] He understood, he said, why she felt compelled to escape: "The imprisonment of child-bearing and maternity makes a person of spirit wish to be free." But he requested that she not leave him on the mistaken notion that he liked to be left alone.

Elsie reacted with an expression of feelings that had been suppressed for years. She spoke of their "different theory of companionship," of which she had always been aware, but had only become apparent to Herbert in recent years. For her, she said, it was her "new experiences . . . new ideas and feelings . . . fresh impressions of persons and places" that she so longed to share with him. And always she felt intense disappointment at Herbert's cool remove from that which concerned her: "From the very beginning of life together it was a great distress to find you indifferent to so much that most mattered to me. It hurt awfully when you didn't want me to hear you make a speech or when you wouldn't read a paper that I had written. Do you realize that apart from the family and the routine of life all my energy and a very large part of my interest have gone into writing which you have never shown the slightest interest in?" Her first book on *The Family*, Elsie said, Herbert had not read. The second, *Religious Chastity*, she continued, was "published anonymously (you being still in public office when it went to print), you didn't even know about." And the one she was writing at the time, *The Old-Fashioned Woman*, she had spoken about with everyone but him, for, as she explained, "it is popular [and] I get help on all sides." This book, she said, he also ignored: "Your indifference or even antagonism once certainly hurt my vanity, but now I have no vanity about writing. . . . To have you absolutely out of so large a part of my life is cutting. It isn't that I want your agreement. Any kind of criticism or ridicule of the ideas themselves would be welcome."

Even on topics of conversation, Elsie felt the need to restrain herself, for there was so much upon which they disagreed: "Religious and many philosophic ideas we can never touch upon." She found that their interests also diverged: "Companionship in new places . . . you don't seem to care for at all with me."[114] In spite of all this, she had been very happy with Herbert until three years ago, and she had, as she said,

> made the most of your theory of companionship—a kind of emotional easy chair. Then Lucy Wilson stepped in, and I saw you acting and reacting with her as *from the time we were married* I had wanted you to do with me. It was awful for me and I *had* to do something about it. Trips with others was one of my most successful devices. But always I had rather have gone with you. The only alternative was staying home with you depressed and so repressed that I knew that at any moment I might be very disagreable in all sorts of unreasonable ways.
>
> Not that I haven't been happy during this time in our *institutional* companionship. I like easy chairs very often myself. Moreover our relation is still the chief thing in the world to me and it seems grotesque to even have to tell you so.

She added, "My trips and occasional flirtations (unfortunately the latter are rare, as so few men are able to work up an interest in me or I in them) keep me from making uninstitutional demands on you which you won't or can't meet."[115] Their current rift was due, she said, to her inability to escape in time, due to the birth of their fourth

child, McIlvaine. "Hence the break in your serenity, and my upset digestion (headaches, obsessions etc.) I am sorry. On the other hand
perhaps the resultant frankness will keep us happier in the future."

Following a strained weekend together, Elsie wrote Herbert, "My
theory is of course that you have been in love with Lucy Wilson these
three years—on and off. Just how much you have yourself realized it,
I don't know, but about the fact itself I have never been uncertain."
She said that she knew that it had not affected Herbert's love for her.
"In fact, as you once told me, that you enjoy my company even more
after having been with her. As far as I can see . . . she does you good."
So in her "better moments," Elsie said, she wanted him to see as much
of Lucy Wilson as possible: "But try as I will, and during the last three
years I have resorted to many devices, I still have despicable moments, moments which I don't understand in the least. Now the only
possible way for you to help me thro' them is not to pay any attention
to them. It is much better for me to be unsocial for an hour or two as
I was this afternoon than to pretend for an hour or two like yesterday
afternoon and the day before and then become hysterical. But I don't
want you to be hurt by my unsociability as you seemed to be tonight."[116] Herbert wrote in response to her theory about Lucy Wilson
that it was all "bosh." Elsie, in turn, responded in anger and disappointment, "Well, I am not sorry I made the try; and now I will be as
conventional and institutional with you as you like, since you do not
want my best."[117]

Herbert defended himself against Elsie's accusations by saying that
he thought he had read all of her articles. He added, "At least all that
I have known about." He admitted that he had read only portions of
The Family: "I suppose cowardice is my reason. I feared that there
would be so many points on which we would not agree that life would
run more smoothly if I did not cross them. . . . I should have read the
book and now will." Herbert claimed ignorance of the second book
having been published: "I supposed that that event was still to happen and that the manuscripts you mysteriously gave me to take to Alice were [parts] of it." He methodically undertook a study of her
works: "Last evening I started reading The Family by E. C. Parsons."
The next day he wrote in a postscript, "Another lecture of The Family was read last night. More would have been read except for sleep-
iness *from other causes.*"[118]

Herbert countered Elsie's assertion that she would have been glad
for any reaction from him, even if it had been critical, for he was sure,
as he said, that Elsie "would find it hard to take criticism or ridicule of
the ideas themselves from *me.*" He was of the opinion that Elsie

learned "only from experience, or from suggestion of those not very close to you." He continued, saying that trips had little appeal to him because he traveled every week for six months of the year. He needed time for his law practice to which he was just returning, and he did not want to be apart from the children who, as he said, in a few years might well be away from home most of the time. In addition, he said, he had been afraid to go on a trip with her after their experience in Yosemite, when the last two days were so unpleasant: "I was probably very disagreeable and my fear is that I would be again, as your unconventional and to my mind insufficiently cautious proceedings prey on my mind in a way that I cannot disguise. Under the circumstances I have felt that there was more happiness for both of us in not attempting it; yet that is an absurd position, the future considered."[119]

Elsie and Herbert both longed for their closeness of years past, when their love was so fresh and so intense. Elsie wrote, "I have been wishing too we could get back our old simple loving relation. Don't you think we can? It has been for the most part a year of misery for me. A little of it you knew about, most of it you didn't. I have been crying almost all day, but perhaps tomorrow I can take a brace and get to work." Elsie was appreciative of Herbert's understanding, and, playfully, promised a change in herself. She wrote him, "I am awfully grateful to you about all of this affair." The last word she had scratched out and had substituted, "situation." She continued, "It has made me more loving—if not more conservative. And that seems to me the only thing that matters. . . . I realize that in many little ways— or big if you like—it is absurd of me to jar you as I do. I will wear a hat in town. I won't talk 'theories'—what else?"[120]

Elsie continued with her travel. She went to the Southwest for three weeks in September, 1912. There she rode horseback through the desert with Clara True to "the great Apache dance." She wrote Herbert, "At times I have missed you awfully, but sometimes on the ride when I lagged behind I was glad you were not there to feel responsible and become annoyed. If only you could get over *feeling* responsible for me, I could make you happier, and we would not have to forego 'trips' together." Her friend had suggested a solution for Elsie's problem: "Merry has just been remarking that if I just hung around, you would go off somewhere with me; but that knowing I have an alternative, you just won't go. I wonder!" She sent a telegram on September 19, "Back from Apaches Great Ride." The next day she wrote of her research, of collecting from the Indians who lived on the ranch, and of exploring the top of the Black Mesa, which, as she explained, was "the height where the Rio Grande Indians made their last stand against the Spaniards." She continued, "I picked up arrowheads and potsherds, and had glorious views, enjoyed ford-ing the river and did not enjoy nearly stepping on a great yellow and red snake."[121]

Elsie intended that her trips would provide a release for the strains in their marriage. On her return from Merida in February, 1913, she wrote: "It is too bad you had such a messy situation. . . . All the good *you* might have got out of my trip you lost. You do mismanage appall-ingly, and you seem incapable of learning. Unless I got relief by going away, we might quite soon begin to dislike each other and so of course part for good."[122]

In 1915, Elsie and Herbert were still trying hard to get along. She wrote him, "I'm more than sorry that I've been hurting you. I'll try to be more considerate, and yet I can't help thinking that freedom rather than consideration is the basis of any real relation between two persons."[123] She continued, "As for the immediate point at issue, the disposal of my time after 7:30 p.m., I can't concede that you have any *a priori* claim on it, for if I did, no matter how much I liked being with you, every evening spent with you would be an abhorrence, in fact the more I liked you, the greater the abhorrence." Their work and their interests still pulled them apart. Elsie did not like New York, save for the evening life, and she much preferred the country, where she felt the tranquility necessary for her writing. However, from the time Herbert had returned to his law practice, they had maintained a res-idence in the city. Elsie felt the need for an honest recognition of their differing desires:

If I'm to get any satisfaction out of living there (and remember I do live there solely on your account and the children's) we had much better face the fact that many of our evening tastes are dis-similar, and not to be satisfied together. It wouldn't give me any particular pleasure, for example, to hear Chvati reminisce or you to hear Francis Hackett tell me I don't know how to write journalism. Why pretend about it, or why pretend that when one of us is tired and liking the end of a sofa and a book, the other is tired too and also preferring the end of a sofa to any-thing else more stimulating?

As for some of my acquaintances, they're not in your line, as some of yours are not in mine, and why pretend about that?

In other words why do we have to pretend to like the same people in the same amusements; what good does either get from that or what sense of friendship?[124]

Their lives became separate spheres, Herbert with his legal, political, and charitable activities, and Elsie with her blossoming interest in anthropology and her radical political interests. Her world, in large measure, became the Southwest. When she was not there, she was writing about it or having guests at Lenox who shared an interest in it. The enthusiasm for the Southwest was hard to share with those at home. As she wrote Herbert, "The stay-at-home rationalizers would not credit what Harry [Miller] had to say when he was prodded by Betty for news, and Harry showed he felt pretty much as I do when I come home from the Southwest—'What's the use talking about it, they like their own preconceptions.' "[125]

Herbert and Elsie were divided over another issue as well, the involvement of the United States in the war that raged in Europe. Elsie was vocal in her opposition, while Herbert saw the fight as "the most sacred cause of history."[126] At forty-eight years of age, Herbert Parsons volunteered his services as a combatant. Elsie was outraged and viewed his enlistment not only as abhorrently militaristic but also as irresponsible to his children. They clashed in heated debate over this issue. In November, 1917, Herbert wrote Elsie:

> It seems to me you are more a victim of militarism than anyone I know, you attribute so much to the war. . . . The men whom I know who are in this war realize that many of them will never come back. They know the facts. They know more than theorists, or people who only know through other's suffering. And they also know that the more talk there is of peace by negotiation, the more likely it is that they will not come back.
>
> With love from
> One of Them

One year later, he wrote from the headquarters of the Fifth Division in France, "I occasionally read a few pages of the New Republic or the Nation and fume at the glib way in which problems are solved which have cost lives." It was Elsie and her radical friends, of course, who had been writing these articles, a point to which Herbert did not allude. "William James," he opined, "was wrong when he thought there were moral substitutes for war. . . . There is nothing else that will bring so many millions of men to the test of courage, bravery & endurance." He told of their "labor through fields heavy with mud. . . . [and their] sleep in holes waterfilled which they must dig." He continued, "They may be killed for they know that many are. Or they may be wounded & lie in a thicket unfound & pneumonia victims in addition from wet & cold. Some do things that mean certain death.

And they are all young with life apparently before them. To me it is wonderful."[127]

When the war was over, Herbert wrote, "My one thought now is of home." Elsie, in turn, wrote of the anticipation of his return, "You should have heard the planning of Lissa and me last night [for] your return. My circle of scientists etc. is not fully satisfying to her and no wonder, and so she counts on you, and so do I, to widen the circle." She requested of him, "Do come home not later than early April. May 20 I have a date with Professor Boas to go to the Southwest for a month to study the Keresan language. I put him off this January because of the children and somewhat because of the vague prospect of your return; but I can't put him off in May."[128]

Herbert returned to his family, though Elsie and he continued in their separate lives. The Southwest had absorbed her intellectually and emotionally. In the fall of 1923, at San Gabriel Ranch in Alcalde, New Mexico, she met the novelist Robert Herrick. Their relationship would last for five years, during which time he would store up "snapshots," as Elsie later said, of her and the Parsons family to use in his novel, *The End of Desire* (1932).[129]

From their intense young love, Elsie and Herbert had passed through to the trials of jealousy. Their years together had been full and challenging, never empty and placid. Throughout it all, even during the most stressful time of their marriage, there had been a basic respect, one for the other. Elsie had, in her reading, found a quote that she thought apt for Herbert and her: "I found rather a good classification for our relationship in 'that rarest and sweetest of all relationships where a strong personal passion is perpetuated and reinforced by a joint participation in the chances . . . of life and the care of children.' "[130]

On September 16, 1925, Herbert Parsons died. Five days earlier, he had been out in the driveway at the Lenox home with his children, showing his son, McIlvaine, how to ride a motorized bicycle that he had bought for him. The bike slipped in the gravel, he fell, and was struck in the kidney by one of the handlebars. An article in the *New York Times* described the accident: "He seemed stunned for a minute after he had been thrown but arose and walked to a stone wall beside the road, where he soon fainted. McIlvaine . . . called to his mother . . . and she brought him some water, which revived him so that with her help he was able to walk to the house. He grew worse rapidly and was taken to the hospital Saturday afternoon."[131] Herbert had been conscious when taken to the hospital, and he told the doctors that he did not know what happened after he had straddled the bike and started the motor. He retained consciousness just up to the point of his death.

There were two services for Herbert Parsons, one at the Trinity Episcopal Church in Lenox, and the other at the Brick Presbyterian Church in New York City. During the hours of the funeral, the stores in Lenox were closed in his honor, and the bells in the church steeple were rung fifty-five times, once for each year of his life.[132] Herbert's body was cremated and buried beside that of his father in the Lenox Cemetery.

Elsie was shattered by Herbert's death. Her son, Herbert, recalled her returning from the hospital with tears streaming down her face, saying, "Your father is dead."[133] She did not, however, attend Herbert's funeral, for to her "death has always meant the end," and she wished to flee from it. When she received an invitation from her friend, Mabel Dodge Luhan, to spend time at her place in Taos, Elsie wrote, "Just right, and the very day of Herbert's death I would have left for the Southwest but for duties to the boys not yet off to school and college." Years later, only a few days before her own death, she told her son McIlvaine of the loneliness she felt without Herbert, " 'There are times . . . when I miss Father awfully. This is one.' "[134]

NOTES

1. ECP, HP to children, 12 May 1918.
2. ECP, EC to HP, n.d. [1896?].
3. ECP, EC to HP, 20 July 1897.
4. ECP, EC to HP, 5 Aug. 1897.
5. ECP, EC to HP, 7 Sept. 1897.
6. ECP, EC to HP, 7 Sept. 1897; 19 June 1898.
7. ECP, EC to HP, 5 May 1898.
8. ECP, EC to HP, 28 June 1898.
9. ECP, EC to HP, 19 June 1898.
10. ECP, EC to HP, 28 June 1898.
11. ECP, EC to HP, 10 July 1898; 21 May 1898; 29 May 1897.
12. ECP, EC to HP, 15 Aug. 1898.
13. ECP, EC to HP, 29 Apr. 1899.
14. ECP, EC to HP, 15 Aug. 1898; n.d.; Apr. 1899.
15. ECP, EC to HP, Nov. 1899.
16. ECP, EC to HP, 12 Apr. 1899; 22 May 1899.
17. ECP, EC to HP, May 1899.
18. ECP, EC to HP, 19 June 1899.
19. ECP, EC to HP, 19 July 1899.

20. ECP, EC to HP, Thursday 11:50 P.M. [1899?].

21. ECP, EC to HP, [1899?].

22. ECP, EC to HP, 7 Apr. 1899.

23. ECP, EC to HP, 14 Aug. 1900.

24. ECP, EC to HP, 22 June 1900.

25. ECP, EC to HP, 28 Aug. 1900.

26. ECP, EC to HP, 27 Aug. 1900; 23 Aug. 1900; 29 June 1900.

27. "Miss Clews Is Married, Wedded to Herbert Parsons in Her Newport Home," *New York Times*, 1 Sept. 1900, sec. 1, p. 5, col. 3.

28. "Republicans Name Congress Candidates," *New York Times*, 12 Sept. 1900, sec. 1, p. 5, col. 1.

29. Elsie (Lissa) Parsons Kennedy, "The Reminiscences of Mr. and Mrs. John D. Kennedy" (New York: Oral History Research Office, Columbia, 1966), p. 17.

30. "Republicans Name Congress Candidates," p. 5, col. 1–2.

31. Peter Hare, *A Woman's Quest for Science* (Buffalo, N.Y.: Prometheus Books, 1985), p. 39. Herbert Parsons lost to George B. McClellan by more than 4,000 votes. See Memorandum for Monte Cutler, Herbert Parsons Papers, Rare Book and Manuscript Library, Columbia University.

32. "Herbert Parsons Dies of Injuries," *New York Times*, 17 Sept. 1925, sec. 1, p. 23, col. 3.

33. "Characteristics of the New President of the Republican County Committee," *New York Times*, 24 Dec. 1905, part 3, p. 2, col. 1.

34. For biographical information on Herbert Parsons, see Hare, *A Woman's Quest for Science*, pp. 39–40, 66; see the *New York Times*: "Characteristics of the New President of the Republican County Committee"; "Who the Candidates Are," 12 Sept. 1900, sec. 1, p. 5, col. 2; "Herbert Parsons Dies of Injuries"; "Services for Parsons Here and in Lenox," 19 Sept. 1925, sec. 1, p. 15, col. 4; and Henry L. Stimson, "The Late Herbert Parsons," 25 Sept. 1925, sec. 1, p. 20, col. 7–8. See the *New York Herald Tribune*: "Herbert Parsons Dies at Hospital in Berkshires," 17 Sept. 1925, Late City Edition, sec. 1, p. 17, col. 4–6; "Herbert Parsons" (editorial), 20 Sept. 1925, sec. 2, p. 6, col. 3. For his work in the Greenwich House and the Fresh Air Fund, see ECP, Mary Simkhovitch to ECP, 18 June 1929; John E. Parsons to Herbert Parsons, Jr., 6 Jan. 1941. For his daughter's recollection, see Kennedy, "Reminiscences," pp. 38–39. For biographical information compiled as a political profile, see Rare Book and Manuscript Library, Columbia University: Bronson Winthrop to the Voters of the Thirteenth Congressional District, 19 Oct. 1904; Memorandum for Monte Cutler; Herbert Parsons to the Voters of the 13th Congressional District, 4 Nov. 1904 in the Herbert Parsons Papers. For information on Parsons work with the Society of Friends of Russian Freedom, see "Fund for Russian Exiles," *New York Times*, 23 Apr. 1917, p. 9, col. 3.

35. "Russian Envoy Thrills East Side," *New York Times*, 10 July 1917, sec. 1, p. 3, col. 1–2.

36. "For Their Pockets' Sakes," *The Evening World*, 3 Sept. 1906.

37. "Herbert Parsons" (editorial), *New York Herald Tribune*. See Robert F. Wesser, "Theodore Roosevelt: Reform and Reorganization of the Republican Party in New York, 1901–1906," *New York History* 46 (1965): 230–52.

38. "Roosevelt to Parsons: Say You Have No Boss," *New York Times*, 29 Nov. 1905, sec. 1, p. 2, col. 3; "No Machine, No Boss for Me, Says Parsons," *New York Times*, 30 Nov. 1905, sec. 1, p. 1, col. 5; "Parsons the Winner in All-Night Struggle," *New York Times*, 22 Dec. 1905, sec. 1, p. 1, col. 5. For Theodore Roosevelt's tactics in the election of the New York County Republican Committee chairman and his reasons for forcing Parsons to declare himself independent of Republican bosses, see Wesser, "Theodore Roosevelt," pp. 230–52.

39. "President Strikes Blow at 'Machine,' " *New York Herald*, 10 Sept. 1906.

40. "Parsons Visits Roosevelt," *New York Times*, 15 Nov. 1907, sec. 1, p. 8, col. 7.

41. "Parsons, All Smiles, at Sagamore Hill," *New York Times*, 11 Sept. 1908, sec. 1, p. 3, col. 4.

42. William Parsons, Jr., "The Progressive Politics of Herbert Parsons," Master's Thesis, Department of American Studies, Yale University, 1965, p. 24.

43. "Parsons, a Politician with Ideals," *Globe and Commercial Advertiser*, 27 Oct. 1910, sec. 1, p. 1, col. 3. For information on Parsons and the identification law, see the following articles in the *New York Times:* "Parsons Scents Tammany Floaters," 4 Oct. 1908, sec. 1, p. 5, col. 1; "Parsons Throws out March Inspectors," 5 Oct. 1908, sec. 1, p. 4, col. 2; and "The Ballot and the Repeater" (editorial), 5 Oct. 1908, p. 6, col. 2.

44. ECP, EC to HP, 7 Aug. 1899.

45. ECP, EC to HP, 29 Aug. 1900.

46. Rye Historical Society, HP to ECP, 30 Oct. 1905.

47. ECP, HP to ECP, 17 Sept. 1906.

48. ECP, HP to ECP, 18 Sept. 1906.

49. ECP, ECP to HP, 25 Oct. 1906.

50. ECP, ECP to HP, 8 July 1910.

51. Henry F. Pringle, *The Life and Times of William Howard Taft* (New York: Farrar and Rinehart, 1939), p. 293.

52. Parsons, "Congressional Junket in Japan, the Taft Party of 1905 Meets the Mikado," *New York Historical Society Quarterly* 41 (1957): 385–406. This is a fragmentary account found among the papers of Elsie Clews Parsons. It was written in the fall of 1906 as the opening chapter of "Memoirs of Washington & Outlying Provinces: 1905, by a Political Wife," p. 385, n. 1; pp. 385–86.

53. ECP, ECP to HP, 3 June 1905.

54. Parsons, "Congressional Junket," p. 394. Parsons referred to Colonel Clarence R. Edwards, U.S.A. (1859–1931) as the "Cook of this Cook's Tour" (p. 386). James A. Leroy was former secretary to Philippine Commissioner Dean C. Worcester and author of *The Americans in the Philippines* (Boston: Houghton Mifflin, 1914).

55. Parsons, "Congressional Junket," p. 389.

56. James A. Leroy, "With Taft in Japan," *The Independent* 59 (14 Sept. 1905): 628.

57. Parsons, "Congressional Junket," pp. 389, 392.

58. *William Howard Taft Papers* (Washington: Library of Congress, 1972), Taft to Helen Taft, 24 Sept. 1905, p. 30.

59. Parsons, "Congressional Junket," p. 399.

60. Ibid., p. 400. Shosaku Matsukata was the son of Count Masayoshi Matsukata (1835–1924), former premier and member of the Privy Council. As finance minister, he put Japan on the gold standard. The wife of Shosaku Matsukata was the niece of Yataro Iwasaki, the founder of the Mitsubishi Company.

61. Parsons, "Congressional Junket," pp. 400–401.

62. Ibid., pp. 403, n. 37; 405. The article ends with a letter from Herbert Parsons to his father, dated 31 July 1905.

63. Leroy, "With Taft in Japan," p. 629.

64. Lloyd C. Griscom, *Diplomatically Speaking* (New York: The Literary Guild of America, 1940), pp. 258–59.

65. Ibid., p. 260.

66. Leroy, "With Taft in Japan," p. 629.

67. Parsons, "Congressional Junket," p. 387.

68. "The Taft Tour," *The Independent* 59 (31 Aug. 1905): 475.

69. Charles H. Brent, "The Visit to the Philippines of Secretary Taft and His Party," *The Outlook* 81 (14 Oct. 1905): 370.

70. Parsons, "American Snobbishness in the Philippines," *The Independent* 61 (8 Feb. 1906): 333.

71. "Secretary Taft's Party in the Philippines," *The Independent* 59 (17 Aug. 1905): 354.

72. Parsons, "American Snobbishness," p. 333.

73. Ibid., p. 332.

74. For information on the visit to Hong Kong and Canton, see William Howard Taft to Helen Taft, 24 Sept. 1905, in *Taft Papers,* and the following *New York Times* articles: "Taft Party at Hongkong," 3 Sept. 1905, sec. 1, p. 1, col. 6; "Canton Cordial to Taft," 5 Sept. 1905, sec. 1, p. 6, col. 6; "Taft Sees Novel Sport," 6 Sept. 1905, sec. 1, p. 1, col. 6. For information on the Chinese boycott of American goods, in response to the harsh treatment of the Chinese in the western United States, see Ralph Eldin Minger, *William Howard Taft and United States Foreign Policy* (Urbana: University of Illinois Press, 1975), p. 166.

75. Kennedy, "Reminiscences," p. 48. For an account of the audience with the empress, see Henry C. Corbin to William Howard Taft, 19 Sept. 1905, in *Taft Papers.*

76. HP to Taft, 23 Aug. 1905 in *Taft Papers;* Parsons, "Congressional Junket," p. 388.

77. "Parsons Makes Himself Master," *New York Times,* 22 Feb. 1907, sec. 1, p. 6, col. 1.

78. Griscom, *Diplomatically Speaking,* p. 326.

79. "Taft Calls off Foes of Hughes," *New York Times,* 24 Jan. 1908, sec. 1, p. 1, col. 7. For further information on Herbert Parsons's role in this political

struggle, see the following articles in the *New York Times:* "No Taft Delegation without a Fight," 18 Aug. 1907, sec. 1, p. 1, col. 3; "Parsons Back; Finds Hughes Men Busy," 8 Sept. 1907, sec. 1, p. 5, col. 3–4; "Trying to Stem Hughes Tide Here," 14 Dec. 1907, sec. 1, p. 2, col. 3; "White House Talk on Hughes's Letter," 23 Jan. 1908, sec. 1, p. 1, col. 7; "Parsons Orders Endorse Hughes," 25 Jan. 1908, sec. 1, p. 1, col. 7; "Mr. Taft and Mr. Hughes" (editorial), 25 Jan. 1908, sec. 1, p. 8, col. 1.

80. ECP, HP to ECP, 5 Aug. 1908; ECP to HP, 10 Aug. 1908.

81. ECP, Bennet to ECP, 30 Sept. 1908; Roosevelt to Bennet, 27 Sept. 1908.

82. ECP, Giddings to ECP, 16 Sept. 1906.

83. ECP, Taft to ECP, 26 Mar. 1910.

84. ECP, ECP to HP, 6 June 1902; 4 Dec. 1900; 9 May 1903; 1 Nov. 1905.

85. ECP, ECP to HP, 16 Oct. 1906; 29 Nov. 1910; 18 Sept. 1911.

86. ECP, ECP to HP, 1 July 1909; 26 July 1910.

87. ECP, HP to ECP, 27 July 1910.

88. ECP, ECP to HP, 9 Apr. 1911; 20 Sept. 1910.

89. ECP, ECP to HP, 7 June 1905; 6 June 1902; 15 June 1902; 13 June 1904; 26 Oct. 1905. The article would have been "The School Child, the School Nurse and the Local School Board," *Charities,* 28 Sept. 1905, pp. 1–8.

90. ECP, ECP to HP, 26 Feb. 1907; 16 Apr. 1907; HP to ECP, 23 Oct. 1907.

91. ECP, ECP to HP, 29 Oct. 1906; 20 Aug. 1906; 19 Mar. 1907.

92. ECP, ECP to HP, 25 Apr. 1907; HP to ECP, 29 July 1908; 26 Aug. 1908. Elsie attributed the death of the first infant to "a long and trying journey" that she had taken just prior to the birth, and the death of the second infant to conceiving too soon after the birth of the former. See ECP, "Remarks at Sanger Dinner," Jan. 1916.

93. ECP, ECP to HP, 18 Sept. 1908; 24 Sept. 1908; 25 Sept. 1908; 2 Oct. 1908.

94. ECP, ECP to HP, 23 June 1909.

95. ECP, ECP to HP, 19 July 1910.

96. ECP, ECP to HP, 23 June 1909; 17 June 1909; 22 Sept. 1909; 4 Oct. 1911.

97. ECP, ECP to HP, 28 July 1909. See HP to ECP, 29 July 1909 for Herbert's response.

98. ECP, ECP to HP, 23 Aug. 1909. For Herbert's letter requesting that Elsie invite the Wilsons, see HP to ECP, 18 Aug. 1909.

99. ECP, ECP to HP, Feb. 1910.

100. ECP, ECP to HP, 3 May 1910; 18 Apr. 1911; 10 Mar. 1911.

101. ECP, ECP to HP, Saturday A. M.

102. ECP, HP to ECP, 28 July 1909.

103. ECP, ECP to HP, Saturday A. M.

104. ECP, ECP to HP, 12 July 1911.

105. ECP, HP to ECP, 27 July 1909; 9 Aug. 1909; ECP to HP, 7 Mar. 1911; HP to ECP, 8 Mar. 1911. For Elsie's response, see ECP to HP, 9 Mar. 1911.

106. ECP, EC to HP, 30 June 1898; ECP to HP, 18 June 1909.

107. ECP, ECP to HP, 27 July 1909.

108. ECP, EC to HP, 14 July 1898; 30 Sept. 1898.

109. ECP, ECP to HP, 4 Aug. 1909; telegram from Española, 5 Aug. 1910.

110. ECP, ECP to HP, 12 Sept. 1910; 13 Sept. 1910; 27 June 1910.

111. ECP, ECP to HP, 31 Oct. 1910; 15 Oct. 1910; 23 Nov. 1910.

112. ECP, unpublished ms., "The Imaginary Mistress," chapter 4, p. 10. See Hare, *A Woman's Quest for Science*, pp. 67–72, for excerpts from this manuscript.

113. ECP, HP to ECP, 4 Aug. 1912.

114. ECP, ECP to HP, 6 Aug. 1912.

115. ECP, ECP to HP, 6 Aug. 1912.

116. ECP, ECP to HP, 4 Aug. 1912.

117. ECP, HP to ECP, 6 Aug. 1912; ECP to HP, 7 Aug. 1912.

118. ECP, HP to ECP, 7 Aug. 1912; 8 Aug. 1912; 9 Aug. 1912.

119. ECP, HP to ECP, 7 Aug. 1912.

120. ECP, ECP to HP, 16 June 1913; 23 June 1913.

121. ECP, ECP to HP, 18 Sept. 1912; 28 Aug. 1912; 20 Sept. 1912.

122. ECP, ECP to HP, 14 Feb. 1913.

123. ECP, ECP to HP, 15 Apr. 1915.

124. ECP, ECP to HP, 5 Apr. 1915.

125. ECP, ECP to HP, 5 Apr. 1918.

126. Stimson, "The Late Herbert Parsons," p. 20.

127. ECP, LC to ECP, [1917?]; HP to ECP, 4 Nov. 1917; 28 Oct. 1918; 17 Nov. 1918.

128. ECP, HP to ECP, 20 Nov. 1918; ECP to HP, 14 Jan. 1919.

129. For an account of Elsie and Herrick's relationship, see Hare, *A Woman's Quest for Science*, pp. 72–75. Also see Blake Nevius, *Robert Herrick* (Berkeley: University of California Press, 1962), pp. 298–303, 319. Elsie also served as a model for the female protagonist of the stories in *Wanderings* (1925). Of his novel, *The End of Desire*, Elsie wrote, "I suppose he thought putting in scraps of actual conversation . . . and accounts of such personal habits as hours of work and book bags would give a verisimilitude of life. He messes up his account of his own son in the same way he messes us up." She added, "Had Herrick any humor he could have got a lot of laughs at my expense" (ECP, ECP to John Parsons, 3 Apr. 1932). See also ECP, ECP to John Parsons, 2 Mar. 1932; and for correspondence involving Nevius's biography of Herrick, ECP, John Parsons to MacIlvaine, 12 Sept. 1960; to Lissa, 12 Sept. 1960; MacIlvaine to John, 6 Sept. 1960.

130. ECP, ECP to HP, 28 Apr. 1909.

131. "Herbert Parsons Dies of Injuries," sec. 1, p. 23, col. 3.

132. "Services for Parsons Here and in Lenox," *New York Times*, 19 Sept. 1925, p. 15, col. 4.

133. Hare, *A Woman's Quest for Science*, p. 66.

134. ECP, EC to HP, 19 Sept. 1896; Beinecke, ECP to Mabel Dodge Luhan, 13 Oct. 1925; Hare, *A Woman's Quest for Science*, p. 66.

5

The Closed Circle

Age-class, caste group, family, and race, each has its own closed circle—from unlikeness to exclusion or seclusion, from exclusion or seclusion to unlikeness—but each of these vicious circles the modern spirit has begun to invade and break down. In the spirit of our time fear of the unlike is waning.

—Elsie Clews Parsons[1]

The challenge to the conventional was at the heart of Parsons's work. She was concerned with opening up the possibilities of life by letting down the barriers to social passage. And it was through her writing that she tried to bring about change. By describing the conventions that kept people in rigid categories and by analyzing the social causes for them, Parsons aspired to loosen the knot of tradition. For her, the process of change required an examination and criticism of the accepted; or, as she expressed it, "Customs once generally questioned are apt to change or decay."[2] So she pulled at the conventional and pried into the spheres of social classification. She laid bare the underpinnings of society and hoped that the closed circle of tradition would yield to the wedge of inquiry.

In writing on the customs of contemporary society, her object was to reach a critical, thinking public, in addition to a more specialized, scholarly audience. Parsons published in magazines with wide circulation and broad appeal—the *Independent, Harper's Weekly, Scientific Monthly,* and the *Nation*—as well as in those aimed solely at the liberal and radical intelligentsia—the *New Review,* the *New Republic,* and the *Masses.* On occasion, her writings appeared in newspapers as well, such as the *New York Harold Tribune* and the *New York Times.* Parsons's books on what she called "social psychology" were directed toward a nonspecialized audience. These included *The Old-Fashioned Woman* (1913), *Religious Chastity* (1913), *Fear and Conventionality* (1914), *Social Freedom* (1915), and *Social Rule* (1916).

Parsons relied heavily on examples from other cultures to inform the discussion of contemporary society. As she said in the opening remarks to *Social Rule,* "To be enlightening, the sociological point of view of this study must be far reaching; it must include glimpses of many different societies." She assumed, therefore, that her reader had a certain grasp of ethnographical information, for this was, in her view, "indispensable to a liberal education." In her works on custom, convention, and social constraint, she was, nonetheless, predominantly concerned with her own society. This she stated very clearly: "Although I have tried to hold to a comparative point of view, I have assumed that for the time our interest is concentrated in our own culture." The character of the book, therefore, was "social rather than scientific."[3]

Parsons's usual style was to juxtapose examples of American customs with those of vastly different cultures. Usually this was done to emphasize the underlying similarities, though sometimes a stark contrast was made. Often she played on the ironic and the humorous elements as well. The closer to home she came with her work—to New York, Newport, and Washington society—the farther afield she ranged for supporting examples and the greater her delight in showing the shared ground of formality and etiquette. Her techniques of presentation varied. In a short essay intended for a popular audience, she often would begin with a quantity of examples from widely varying cultures to illustrate related issues. Toward the end of the article, she would give a crisp statement of her thesis, closing with several pointed questions that brought the otherwise esoteric examples from the remote cultures back to the United States. Another technique that she used on occasion was to begin an article with a vignette—sometimes based on a conversation in which she had participated—and then to tie this to specific issues in American society. In all her writings, Parsons conveyed the immediacy of the topic through examples taken from her own experience. Her point, though, always was critical examination of self. She would allow no complacent acceptance of the way things were. Her unrelenting comparison of middle- and upper-class Americans to the "primitives" and the "savages" of the world was intended to shock. This was to be a shock of recognition, which would ultimately provide a release from tradition. As Parsons said, "Primitive ideas are always grave and always troublesome—until recognized. Then they become on the one hand powerless to create situations, and on the other, enlivening."[4] She wanted those who accepted this as the best of all possible worlds to begin asking if it really was. She felt it was not and worked to change it.

Parsons emphasized that conventionalities, or the traditional ways of doing things, ran deep in human society. These were rationalized with ease, simply because that was the way things were done. It was the order of things. Tradition itself was rooted to deeper forces, to subliminal fears of difference and of change. To protect the social group from the one who in unlikeness challenged the correctness of their ways, and to secure order, society drew the lines of division. Through classification, differences were controlled, they were given order, they were made social. Thus, through the use of convention-alities and ceremonies, society could shore up the divisions of age, caste, class, race, and gender. And that order had ultimately to do with the protection of the society in its present form.[5]

This process of standardizing and stabilizing society demanded that individual expression be suppressed. It was not the wishes of one person, but the will of the group that was important for the survival of society. Uniformity yielded security. Parsons summarized, "Hence our insistence that the individual act invariably in conformity with his or her sex, age, class, caste, or nationality, with his or her set part in society. Hence our intolerance of effeminacy or mannishness, of pre-cociousness or immaturity, of the unladylike or the boorish, of inhos-pitality, of a lack of *esprit de corps* or patriotism."[6]

Still, there was a constant tension between the individual and the group. The former she equated with an expression of self without re-gard for convention, of inner identity without regard for collective classification. She referred to this as "personality." As a social being, the individual could not survive on its own. It was drawn to the group by what Parsons called the gregarious instinct. Society was forever as-sured of new members on which to work its will; and the constraints of the group crushed the wayward spirit. As Parsons said, "It is only as one of the group that you meet its other members concealing from them whatever in you is not characteristic of the group, whatever is erratic, changeable, changing, not open to classification, in short whatever is personal."[7]

The order of society, then, was based on social classification. Insti-tutions brought "together the like" while separating "the unlike." When a division in two such tidy categories was not practical, then the unlike was treated "as representatives of a class." A status was as-signed, "the status of sex, of guest or host, or superior or inferior rank, of wife or husband, of member of a group, a family group, an age group, an occupation group, [or] a local group."[8]

Through classification the social barriers were set in place, and the pathways of power were established. As a means of control, the dom-inant in a society established the ranking of others. Parsons stressed, "The classified individual may be held in subjection in ways the un-classified escapes." This included the abnormal who, once categorized, was "at the mercy of the normal."[9] Labeling was used most effectively against children, women, slaves, servants, immigrants—in short, against all those in a position of weakness. Parsons explained: "The preeminent function of social classification appears . . . to be social rule. In institutions where subjection is most desired, institutions like the Catholic Church or like a modern army, classification is most positive and most patent. Classification is nine-tenths of subjection. Indeed to rule over another successfully you have only to see to it that he keeps his place—his place as a male, her place as a female, his or her place as a junior, as a subject or servant or social 'inferior' of any kind, as an outcast or exile, a ghost or a god."[10]

Status vis-à-vis the opposite sex was one area in which the American vernacular had an abundance of labels. Following Parsons's argument, this itself would indicate the desire for control over such interaction. " 'Engaged,' 'attentive,' 'devoted,' 'a married man,' 'a man of family,' 'a grass widow,' 'a *good* woman,' 'a *bad* woman'—there is no end to such tags." Sexual relations were reduced through classification to either marriage or prostitution: "Prostitute or wife, the conjugal or the disorderly house, these are the alternatives."[11] Just as power could be gained from labeling, so could one assert power "by declassifying or demoting others." As Parsons said, "Adults may be called children . . . and a little boy or girl, 'only a baby.' " Men called "women" were verbally desexed; and women could be declassified as human by being labeled animal. She mentioned "dog," though the reader might mentally substitute the more graphic word, "bitch," which her publisher assuredly would have avoided, fighting, as one editor put it, the Puritan world.[12]

Employing a phrase created by Friedrich Nietzsche, Parsons called this urge to control others "the will to power." She explained in *Social Rule, a Study of the Will to Power* the use of the "popular catch-word" as a "mere verbal convenience." Parsons was at pains to differentiate between a causal and a descriptive use; her intent was the latter. The concept itself, she said, did not *explain* aspects of the human spirit. It was simply used to *describe* manifestations of human behavior. She wished to discuss behavior resulting from what Thomas Hobbes called a " 'general inclination of all mankind . . . a perpetual desire of power after power that ceaseth only in death.' "[13]

Parsons emphasized that the will to power was widespread: "There is an enormous amount of energy put to controlling or regulating human creatures, to keeping them in their place, to keeping them in order." The methods of exerting social control varied from separating people, to forcing them together, from encouraging procreation, to forbidding it, from "a rule of silence or of posture, hair-cutting, dieting, killing, torturing, especially whipping, mutilating, branding or smearing, clothing."[14] The outcome of all was the enforcement of order, the control of others.

One such social barrier that gave order to daily life was the separation of women from men. In *Social Freedom*, Parsons gave a comparative view to this division. "In general the separation has been practically contrived by the rule that woman's place is in the home, or a subdivision of it, and man's place, outside, in the world, in interests and occupations not open to women." The freedom of movement outside the home was variously restricted for women: "In certain New Guinea tribes during times of religious excitement the village is deserted by the women; they have to take to the woods. With us it is the woods, sometimes men say, which are no place for women. The streets of Seoul were once taboo to women by day; there are streets in New York once taboo to them at night. Once in England ladies went to the play wearing masks, today they sit in the House of Commons behind a grill. 'Through a lattice made of bamboo and a sort of silken net, they see and hear all that passes without being seen themselves,' writes a traveller of the accommodation made for ladies at Chinese banquets two or more centuries ago."[15]

Apart from the world of the men, safely inside their assigned boundaries, women were shielded from the dangers that lurked outside. This seclusion and protection rendered women dependent on others, fearful of the unknown, and cautious of anything that set them on their own. Parsons quipped: "Women hermits are extremely scarce. . . . Rarely indeed do women go off by themselves—into the corner of a ballroom, into the wilderness, to the play, to the sacred high places of the earth or to the Islands of the Blessed. Penelope stays at home." With woman's place firmly established, so also were her contacts limited: "Her acquaintances have been restricted to the family circle and to the segments of the other family circles it overlaps."[16]

The seclusion of women also afforded another protection, that of the men from undue exposure to female influence. Women were dangerous to men, especially to their activities of the hunt, war, and sacred worship. Parsons noted, "During their characteristic physiological processes, when they are most women, they are at all times a very menace."[17] This required them to be "In Quarantine," as a chapter in *The Old-Fashioned Woman* is titled. She quoted an "old couplet,"

Oh! menstruating woman thou 'rt a fiend
From whom all nature should be closely screened.

And then she compared the modern woman with her more traditional sisters: "Unlike the Australian woman who has not only to leave camp, but to encircle her mouth with red ochre and to warn off any young man who comes near her, unlike the negress of Surinam who has to call out '*Mi Kay! Mi Kay!*,' 'I am unclean! I am unclean!' to any one approaching her, a modern woman is supposed *not* to keep to herself if she thereby betrays her condition. She must be altogether secretive, and the better to deceive she must act normally in every way."[18]

So also in pregnancy did the old-fashioned woman try to appear unchanged. Parsons wrote, "My grandmother tells me that in her day women not uncommonly attempted to conceal their condition by lacing, and that in the latter part of pregnancy they rarely left the house, except perhaps for a short walk in the evening." In fact, they were instructed to behave so in the book, *Decency in Conversation amongst Women:* " 'May Gentlewomen—all the time of their going with child—wear long bellied, and strait laced garments.' "[19]

With the woman's sphere in the home, the men had the world outside; the streets and the businesses were theirs. Parsons drew examples from her own social class to describe the masculine realm: "The club-house is of course taboo to women. Some clubs they may not even walk past; to 'get at' even a husband or brother inside others, an English 'pub,' for example, or the Newport 'Reading Room,' or Casino, or even to send a message through to anyone, they have to lurk about door or sidewalk—and even such tempered proximity requires temerity."[20] Men saw their clubs as freedom from the constraints of female society. Parsons quoted a member of a New York club, " 'I could n't put my feet on the mantelpiece with women around' "; and she added, he ignored "the fact that the architecture of most New York clubs has made that feat at any rate unusual."[21] Such male groupings were not unique to the New Yorker: "New Caledonian and New Guinea husbands have private sleeping quarters and in American cities husbands are in the habit of rooming during the summer at their clubs. But even when they sleep at home, men make their club their headquarters for exercise, for drinking and gaming, for the entertainment of foreigners, for politics and ritual, for gossip and lounging. Englishmen are said to use it to sulk in."[22]

Outside the home and the club, where men and women were forced together, a certain division of space was maintained. In New York parks and on public transportation, the order was clear: "In Manhattan Island . . . park benches, ferry-boats, and cars are merely labelled 'men' or 'women.' Men are not expected to sit on the women's benches, but they may go on the women's side of the ferryboat.

Women, on the other hand, may sit on the unlabelled benches, but they may not go on the men's side of the boat."[23]

In the home, women faced the unavoidable differences of sex and age. To counter these, they erected barriers, thus, "carefully regulating their relations with their juniors and seniors and with the other sex."[24] At times, special precautions were taken to separate brothers and sisters, most certainly at play. Even the floor plan of the house reflected this division of spheres. While this was much more accentuated in other cultures, still the American home, provided the owners had sufficient funds, retained elements such as the "*boudoir* and 'study,' drawing-room and smoking room."[25]

Charged with keeping order in the home circle, women were the enforcers of conventionalities. As such, women "controlled" change within the family by acknowledging it with appropriate ceremonies. "How fond they are of ceremonialism! Of turning the child into a youth or maiden, the youth or maiden into a man or woman, of matchmaking, of mourning. Coming-out ceremonies, weddings and funerals all get their strongest support . . . from women."[26]

Initiation rites provided an exception to the usual direction by women. They were largely the concern of men, since quite often the initiates were "turning their backs on their mother only to turn their faces towards their father and their father's friends."[27] In "The Ceremonial of Growing Up," Parsons discussed initiation rites as a means of providing a ritually appointed time when change was recognized by all. Thus, growth was not accepted as gradual and incremental, but as something that was socially sanctioned. This was especially so with adolescence, which was "thought of as a crisis the better to ignore its earlier manifestations, and the better to concentrate and get through with the adaptations it compels." During the initiation ritual, the individual was imprinted with "the nature he or she is to bear for the rest of life."[28] In *Social Rule,* Parsons elaborated on the marking of the initiate: "So much is done to the initiates,—their hair 'is fussed with' or plucked out, their skin painted or scarified or tattooed, their teeth knocked out, their nails manicured, their sexual organs operated upon, their nose, lip, or ears bored, new clothes or ornaments put on." Proper moral standards for adult life were taught to the initiates. This was sometimes accompanied by physical abuse: "They may . . . be whipped or starved or segregated, sometimes with their fellows, sometimes in solitary confinement." They may go through ceremonial death and be reborn into their new status. All this, Parsons saw as a manifestation of the will to power: "Analysed, rationalised, or not, the desire to control a 'youngster' is a major motive to disciplining or

initiating him. Initiations may be considered indeed as great outbursts of the collective will over the individual and in particular of the
will of senior age-classes over junior."[29]

Rituals of initiation were imminently successful precisely because
they dealt with the collective, with the age class, for as Parsons said,
"Class membership . . . involves class conformity."[30] Just such an age
set was established among debutantes: "A girl usually makes her *début*
in a set. This set expresses its solidarity in different ways. In the
United States it shows itself through girls' lunches or 'sewing circles'
or 'teas,' where the 'buds' 'receive' with or 'assist' one another. They
have too their own passwords and pet phrases, their own standards
and ways of 'getting on together.' "[31] The girl joined this set between
the ages of seventeen and nineteen. Parsons remarked, "In certain
circles of our society a rigid line is drawn in a girl's life. . . . It deter-
mines her dressing, her hygiene, her occupations, her friends, her
name, her behavior, her point of view. As she steps across it she leaves
the nursery for the world."[32]

Parsons compared the custom of "coming-out" to similar rituals in
other cultures: "Our *débutantes* are apt to be older . . . than those elsewhere. Instead of a year or two 'abroad' or in a 'finishing school,' savage girls usually spend but a few weeks or months in a lonely hut or
in a bed or hammock or cage in a corner of the house or on the roof."
However, once the debutantes stepped out, their life was "everywhere
much the same." Great energy was lavished on looks, especially on
coiffure: "Her hair is curled or puffed or 'put up.' She begins to add to
it or to wear things in it. Chinese girls 'assume the hairpin.' In Thack-
eray's day, 'Lincoln green toxophilite' hats and feathers . . . were assumed." Her skin was cared for, perhaps tattooed, scarified, painted,
or powdered. The figure was altered through fasting or "banting,"
the latter a popular reducing diet consisting of lean meat and an ab-
stinence from fluids, starch, and sugar. The body was given a decorative touch: "Nose-, lip-, or ear-rings are generally hung at this time.
Sennar girls have a tooth knocked out. I have heard of New York girls
putting belladonna into their eyes before sallying from the dressing-
room into the ball-room." A change in name reflected the change in
their status. No longer were they addressed by their given name, now
they were a "Miss," and "their name appears for the first time on their
mother's visiting-card." They were expected to accompany their
mothers on the required social calls as they leave their cards.[33]

In addition to their concern with ceremonials, women also kept
watch on social intercourse, demanding that it follow a prescribed
format. They were "the foremost teachers of the proprieties, of

politeness, of good manners, of the amenities—all rules of conduct for life with others more or less unlike yourself and yet not to be avoided."[34] Good manners were like fortifications, a protection from personal intrusion. Parsons referred to Mrs. Abell, author of *Women in Her Various Relations*, for advice on the proper way to curtail a relationship. Mrs. Abell counseled, when one wished to distance oneself from an acquaintance, one should increase the ceremonious interaction; formality was the "most delicate way" to end a friendship.[35] Parsons discussed other equally formalized rules for interaction. The intent of all was to minimize the individual component and to maximize the conventional.

The rules of etiquette provided for a regulation of social life and assured the continuance of the social order. Certainly "calling" was one such formality that accomplished this. In *Fear and Conventionality*, Parsons spoke of this custom, which, in its elaborated form, was on the verge of disappearing: "I have had the good fortune to observe it in one of the few places where its practice is still vigorous, in Washington. Washington has not entered upon the decadent stage of calling, the stage of leaving cards or even mailing them. The Washington call must be made in person. Cards must be left, however, whether the hostess is seen or not."[36] These cards were never to be handed directly to the lady of the house, but rather were to be deposited on a table in the hall, or at hotels or apartment houses, in a box in the office. "A row of baskets is sometimes provided for these cards outside the door of the hotel parlour within which a row of ladies stand to 'receive.' " As Parsons observed, one experienced in making calls prided herself on her efficiency:

> From thirty to fifty calls may be made of an afternoon by the expert providing, as she puts it, she has luck, i. e. she does not find everyone in. She has of course drawn up her list with forethought and she is punctilious in timing each call. She keeps within a safe range of conversation in order not to be beguiled into exceeding her allotted time or into overdrawing upon the energy she needs for accomplishing her round. The fund of energy she starts with seems, however, at times to increase rather than lessen; each call done gives her, I take it, a stimulating sense of having acquired merit. At any rate at the end of the three hours, however tired she may be, her sense of accomplishment is vastly satisfying. And so for several months during the year the Washington resident pays her daily round of

calls, returning to the top of her list when she reaches the bottom of it, a being more gregarious or more impersonal it were hard to find.[37]

The custom of calling validated status through a complex order of who should call on whom first; the calling card was simply the marker of the contact. The barriers were set in place; "calling" kept them in good repair.

While women exercised their will within the home, still theirs was not the dominant position. As Parsons said, "From the institutional point of view . . . it is women who gratify men's will to power rather than men, women's."[38] Women, she said, had no institutionalized control over men, rather they were subject to the desires and dictates of men. The hierarchical order was man over woman, and elder over younger.

These two forces, the male and the elder, joined in the regulations of sexual interaction. The concern of the elders was for the control "over the sex life of their juniors, whether it [be] . . . in regulating sex impulse or in ignoring it." The elders determined when the young men and women would be allowed to meet, how they should court, and when they should marry. These arrangements were made for the convenience of the elders, who were inclined to be less than sympathetic with the desires of youth. As Parsons said, "Feeling but little the impulses of sex, the Elders deprecate them, belittle and degrade them. Courtship and marriage custom, the practice of periodic license or of prostitution are determined by the Elders to suit themselves, or at most, as compromises with the cravings of youth. The 'good of society' in sex relationships generally means the good of the Elders, of those to whom the intimacies of sex are distasteful and change in sex relations, vexatious." While the restraints were usually more stringent for women, the result was a lessening of freedom for both sexes. As Parsons said, "Whatever is a restriction upon the sex choices and sex activities of women is almost necessarily a restriction upon men."[39]

The concept of ownership was a key element in the control of human beings. Parsons saw this at the troubled center of American family life. She singled out the proprietary family as a perpetuation of archaic practices, of "parental consent of marriage, suits for seduction, for breach of promise, for the restitution of conjugal rights."[40] There was the assumption of paternal ownership and authority over children, especially over daughters. Manu's dictum was as applicable to the American family, as to the Hindu family for whom the god had declared: "By a girl, by a young woman, or even by an aged one, nothing must be done independently, even in her own house." Parsons observed, "Whatever the virtues of the proprietary family it does not encourage initiative, least of all female initiative."[41] In marriage, the principle of female ownership was transferred. In place of the father, it was the husband to whom the woman owed obedience and submission. And it was the husband who had the onerous task of suppressing her initiative and tethering her movements.

From ownership came both legal and psychological domination. Parsons linked this to marriage, "This aspect of proprietorship in living beings, proprietorship for the sake of malleability, figures in the conjugal relationship itself as well as in franker forms of slavery or of domestication. With your own you may do what you like."[42] Even among the matrilineal Pueblo Indian societies of the Southwest, specifically among the Zunis, there could be found a subservient attitude of women to men. Few women, Parsons explained, "are institutionally as independent" as they are. "Zuñi women marry and divorce more or less at pleasure. They own their own houses and gardens. Their offspring are reckoned of their clan. Their husband comes to live with them in their family group." Still, Parsons said, the Zuni women were in the role of man's caretaker: "Zuñi women 'look after' their husbands, look after them quite as meekly, I surmise, as a wife after a husband among peoples where descent is paternal and the wife, a chattel. I recall a little incident I once saw—an elderly Zuñi coming indoors from threshing and bidding his elderly wife bring him water to wash his hands. Her compliance was not an act of graciousness, it seemed to me, it was the carrying out of an order. She had the habit of doing what her husband told her."[43] In all societies, Parsons continued, wives performed services for their husbands that would not otherwise be fulfilled: "No slave or servant would care for you as well as a wife."

The husband's position of power over the wife allowed him control over her appearance as well as over her actions. She could be marked as his: "A man *does things to* his wife—he has her cut off her hair or like the Galla, part it, he has her blacken her teeth, he has her wear clothes befitting wedlock, clothes shabby or ornate . . . she is branded for him or cut, he has her forego ornaments or put them on." She was labeled "the wife of so-and-so or 'the hissing "missus" of too familiar husbands' [as] . . . notices to intruders to keep away."[44] The very act of procreation might also be claimed by the male, for, as Parsons said, "In patriarchal . . . cultures he *makes* her the mother of *his children*."[45]

The enforcement of this order was given divine sanction. In "The Supernatural Policing of Women," Parsons spoke of men's invention of spirits "to aid them in their mastery of the women." They banded together in secret societies and in theatrical display convinced the women that "their own systematic spirit impersonations [were] actual spirit apparitions." The social restraints on "savage woman," who "must neither pry nor roam" were enforced by husbands carrying magical amulets said to have power over women. Using an evolutionary framework that she elsewhere eschewed, Parsons saw an increase in the subjugation of women as the social organization grew more complex: "In developed tribal life and in early civilization supernatural reward or punishment is a more thoroughgoing affair than in savagery, and wifely subjection as well as the rest of the social order is thereby more systematically secured."[46]

As property of man, woman was appropriate for divine sacrifice. Still, while making an offering of the body, she herself could not occupy the same priestly class as men: "The chattel character of women both qualifies them as gifts for the gods and precludes them ascetic habits" and the position granted to men of "communicants with the gods." As the proprietary notion increased, there was a shift toward the emphasis on the chastity of women. In what Parsons referred to as "early culture periods," this shift was "held in check by the much more powerful tendency to give or yield exceptional privileges" to the spiritual leaders. However, when the differentiation was made between the religious leader and the political leader, religious chastity could be enforced. The priest was celibate, and the king had his wives. The result, Parsons said, was that "promiscuity even with the gods had to be stood in a corner by institutionalizing men."[47]

Religious chastity set the stage for secular chastity. As Parsons explained, "When marriage became frankly proprietary, women were bullied by both economic and religious sanctions into the observance of prematrimonial chastity and conjugal fidelity." Parsons continued, "This appreciation of chastity through religion has involved depreciation of marriage and of women. The early Christians rated virginity at 100, widowhood at 60, and marriage at 30. Marriage was held to be of brass, chastity of silver, and virginity of gold. Less concisely marriage is described as hell under a show of happiness, a matter of foul delight ending in filth."[48]

Marriage as an institution imposed by the elders to control sexual relations of their offspring required the maintenance of "conjugal segregation." Husbands and wives were themselves often the best enforcers of the taboos that set spouses apart from others. Referring specifically to Americans, Parsons noted the frequency with which they referred in conversation to their marital status. Women made constant reference to their husbands, and men felt compelled to refer to their wives. She wrote a poem "To a Married Man," in which she queried, why be so public about a private matter?

> Married, you say, but why?
> Why advertize a matter as personal
> As sleeping or excreting?
> Whatever makes you gay or wise or happy
> I welcome, but must a stranger
> Know the source?
>
> *Yes, because I love my wife*
> *And being proud of her*
> *I want the world to know*
> *She is my wife.*
>
> So marriage is a boast!
> Having an admirable woman
> You are an admirable man.
> I too would boast about a thing or two,
> But may not, lest I bore you.
> Is it fair?[49]

She further illustrated this compulsive reference to one's spouse with the story of an American woman, who, while traveling in France, found herself without any money. Unable to reach her banker and under threat of being ejected from the train, she sought aid from a compatriot. "He was quite willing to pay her fare; she was an American and a woman, but she was informed firmly and repeatedly that her knight was a married man. . . . Soon after I heard this anecdote I happened to repeat it to a Chicago lawyer who promptly joined in the laugh over the American man's timidity. 'Still, a married man travelling can't be too prudent,' he finished off." Parsons concluded that "circumspection towards women, in travel or elsewhere, or better still, indifference towards women, is the standardized attitude of American husbands."[50]

While indifferent to female psychology, American men were also sentimental about women. These two elements, indifference and sentimentality, fused together in chivalry, that Parsons saw as grounded in American society: "A democracy like the United States is the very stronghold of chivalry. Where else is there as much talk of being a 'thorough gentleman' or a 'perfect lady' . . . and where else is the charge of being 'common' or a *parvenu* or a *nouveau riche* so much resented? . . . And does not the American cherish chivalry because it gives him a sense of superiority and leaves him innocent of any sense of being undemocratic?"[51]

The standards of chivalry required that the stronger male protect the weaker female, the children, and the elderly. By so doing, he kept "them most rigorously and most subtly in their place." The polite response to such protection was appreciation, for one had been placed in an exalted position, and it was "plainly ungrateful and unreasonable . . . to wish to leave it." However, if those classified as the weaker decided to leave their assigned positions, the order was undone. Parsons noted, "As soon as there is any self-assertion, no matter how unconvincing, by the 'weaker,' the 'stronger' becomes demoralized, panic-struck. The one barrier he has counted on is threatened, he realizes, and threatened in the only way he fears—by implications of its superfluity. The merest hint that chivalry is not needed causes chivalry to fall to pieces."[52] With the coating of chivalry tarnished, a baser nature shone through. Power would be retained through "cruder means of self-defence," through calling on privileges of age, or class, to simple exclusiveness based on gender.

Chivalry led directly into the steel jaws of the double standard. Women were classified as sequestered or unsequestered, as inexperienced or experienced. Through such bifurcation—they were either good or bad—men were able to dispense with subtleties: "The personality of the woman a man feels that he is supporting, whether as wife or prostitute, may theoretically be disregarded and, along with her personality, her capacity for sexual response. Whether as a creature of sin or as an object of chivalry, a woman becomes a depersonalized, and, sexually, an unresponsive being."[53]

Once married, the woman who has become her husband's possession must establish her own worth and that of her husband's by entering the cycle of conspicuous consumption and conspicuous waste: "You must have things just as *good* as your neighbour, to keep your social position you must spend freely." Especially among "the capitalist class," the wife has been forbidden other outlets, so in "unending shopping and elaborate living," she expends her "feminine energy."[54] This "over-cultivated, leisure-class wife, self-cultivated because she has nothing to do" was married to "the under-cultivated and over-worked husband, unresponsive to anything but 'business,' largely because of the elaborate scale of expenditure set by the non-productive wife."[55] The wife, then, had become the consumer, and the husband the producer.[56]

In addition to the old-fashioned woman who achieved status through marriage and economic power indirectly through her husband's purse, there was a "new woman." Of her, Parsons said, "The *new woman* means the woman not yet classified, perhaps not classifiable, the woman *new* not only to men, but to herself. She is bent on finding out for herself, unwilling to live longer at second hand, dissatisfied with expressing her own will to power merely through ancient media, through children, servants, younger women, and uxorious men. She wants to be not only a masterless woman, one no longer classified as daughter or wife, she wants a share in the mastery men arrogate." There was a struggle in store for this new woman, since men, in the dominant position "will cede to women only what by ceding gives them an assurance of power . . . or they will cede only what they consider has ceased to give mastery."[57]

In fact, the struggle had been underway for years, and Parsons herself had been in the thick of it. She had worked to improve woman's position in terms of education, employment, and enfranchisement. She had fought for the legalization of birth control. She wanted women to have a choice and direction in their lives, not to be controlled by ideas and conventions that were not of their making.

As a way of breaking with the past and forging a new path, Parsons advocated college education for women. This, she said, had been "one of the first steps of the woman's movement of the nineteenth century." Viewed as "incompatible with family life," it had met with resistance. The first college women had been forced to turn "their backs on the family, but they were not so much traitors as outcasts."[58] They were labeled as selfish, choosing as they did to satisfy their own desires; and they were categorized as unwomanly. Indeed, the level of mental activity that they willingly undertook in the pursuit of their studies would likely, it was believed, render them less fertile. As Herbert Spencer cautioned in *The Principles of Biology*, "the overtaxing" of the brain had "a serious reaction on the physique" of women and resulted in a "diminution of reproductive power."[59] Finally, they were stigmatized as spinsters, since no man would wish to marry such a woman.

Parsons argued for the necessity of educating women, as a benefit to women themselves, to their families, and ultimately to society. Part of her reasoning was based on expediency: women were the caretakers of the family. If they were kept in ignorance, they would not be able to educate their children. As she said in *The Family*, "If women are to be fit wives and mothers they must have all, perhaps more, of the opportunities for personal development than men have. All the activities hitherto reserved to men must at least be open to them, and many of these activities, certain functions of citizenship for example, must be expected of them."[60]

Parsons spoke of "the nineteenth century's bloodless revolt of the daughters," which had, in part, achieved its goal. The doors of certain colleges had been opened to women. American family life had undergone a significant change, making college education at least compatible with the expectations for its daughters. As Parsons noted, "The age of marriage is considerably later than it was. Our grandmothers married in their teens, our mothers in their early twenties, and we between twenty-four and twenty-six. As the average of graduation from college is twenty-two, or even lower, we did not have to choose between marriage and college from the point of view at least of life's time schedule." Life was freer "in endless ways" for the young woman. For the unmarried, at least, attitude toward their employment was changing. "Not many mothers could any longer be found who . . . would consider a daughter's proposal to work for a man indecent or caution her to always carry a parcel and an umbrella as a safeguard."[61]

The outcast and exile of the family in the nineteenth century, the college-educated daughter, had been "taken back into the bosom of a penitent family" in the twentieth century. But, Parsons asked, what of the changes in her position? "Her economic status is just the same as that of the non-collegiate wife. Her daily round of occupations is very much like that of every other housewife. Her household may be run a little more systematically, but it is run in the traditional way. She too is the vicarious consumer of her husband's wealth, in Professor Veblen's lively terms, the foremost illustration of his power for conspicuous waste."[62] Women had gained a new freedom, but the stacking of the deck was still the same.

Another pariah had taken the place of the college-educated female. She was the professional woman. The same aspersions were hurled at her, but they were intensified. She was the ultimate of the unwomanly woman. And the harassment for those who succeeded in their profession was unceasing. Parsons recalled the treatment of Dr. Hannah Myers Longshore, the first woman physician in Philadelphia. A druggist, who refused to fill her prescription, told her "to go home 'to look after her house and darn her husband's stockings.' " A woman lawyer, seeking admission to her state bar, was remonstrated by an official of the court who said, " 'The constitution of the family organisation which is founded in the divine ordinance as well as in the nature of things, indicates the domestic sphere as that which properly belongs to the domain and functions of womankind."[63]

If a woman insisted on the pursuit of postgraduate training, not only did she meet scorn in the outside world, but also inner conflict as well: "She comes to a parting of the ways, matrimony on the one hand, her profession on the other. Prejudice against married women in schools, in colleges, in government service, in almost any kind of work in fact, her suitor's traditions, the exigencies of his own work, her own traditions or her moral or intellectual faithfulness, one or another insists on a sharp cut answer as to whether she will 'run with Artemis / Or yield the breast to Aphrodite.' "[64]

The advances in woman's education yielded frustration. Allowed to pursue advanced study, she was still limited to the home sphere. Should she chose a career, she was denied a family. As Parsons said, the modern woman "has been educated for a life she is not allowed to live, taught to seek self-expression and then denied it because of the narrow limits within which love and maternity are open to her, limits incompatible with her education."[65] Yet there were those who were concerned about the falling birth rate of "the native born," a euphemism for the Anglo-Saxon population. Parsons referred to them as "the race-suicide croakers," who bemoaned the fall in the birth rate, but would do nothing to challenge the obstacles set in the path of the young woman. Indeed, they manned the barriers to woman's progress.

In "Penalizing Marriage and Child-Bearing," Parsons expanded on her position. She stressed the urgent need to recognize the woman who had pursued advanced education. Not only, Parsons asserted, should employment opportunities be made available for her, but there should also be the flexibility to allow her time for the care of her family. Old attitudes toward the pregnant woman and the nursing mother needed to be changed. The practice of confinement, which required "a woman for some months before her child is born to live in retirement," must be viewed for what it was, "a serious handicap to the productive activity." The taboos against the nursing mother, which Parsons said were less stringent than those against the pregnant woman, needed to be set aside. As she said, "Moderate work is not injurious to suckling; but the nursing mother cannot perform this function well if she is under the strain of accommodating her nursing to her work. Her work must be accommodated to her nursing, and this means that provision must be made for nursing at convenient times and places in connection with her work."[66]

Rather than encouraging such efforts on the part of married women, there had been a punitive attitude. A married woman was forbidden employment, and this was often stipulated in the policies of place of business. If, indeed, she had been able to obtain a position, there was no allowance made for maternity leave or child care. Parsons referred to "our wasteful competitive system of production," which allowed for no such flexibility, but rather required adjustment by the worker to the demands of the job. "A whole day's work or no work are the alternatives."[67] Quite clearly, she said, women were being punished for having chosen to marry and bear children.

Yet, in spite of the constant harassment directed toward women who had elected to combine family and career, and the barriers against their employment in the work place, still there had been significant changes in the life of the new woman. In "Feminism and Sex Ethics," Parsons attributed much of this "to progress in the practice of medicine," as well as to economic factors that encouraged " 'the spacing of babies,' late marriage, childless marriage, [and] persistent celibacy."[68] The development of more effective birth control and the changes in the economy that fostered such medical advances had made possible a separation of mating from parenthood. In "New Morals for Old, Changes in Sex Relations," Parsons predicted, "Birth control makes possible such clear-cut distinctions between mating and parenthood that it might be expected to produce radical changes in theories of sex attitude or relationship, forcing the discard of many an argument for personal suppression for the good of children or the honor of the family, and forcing redefinition of concepts of honor and sincerity between the sexes."[69] She saw this as a crucial advance toward freeing women from the drain of excessive childbearing. The deep-rooted idea "that women must bear children because they can't help themselves" was being supplanted. Along with this change came the possibility of a new relationship between a man and a woman, based not on dependence and obligation, but rather on reciprocity. Parsons wrote, "Desire for responsiveness replaces the desire for proprietorship. Love-making becomes mutual, a matter of mutual satisfaction, of mutual devotion."[70]

Parsons had been vocal and ardent on the issue of birth control. With energy, she worked for the cause of Margaret Sanger, who had been arrested for publicly advocating the use of birth control. At the request of the Birth Control League, she elicited support for Sanger from New York women. These women had been carefully selected: they were liberal in political views, as well as "mothers of two or more children and members of fairly well-known New York families." The result of this effort, Parsons referred to as " 'the world's worst failure.' " The women had been asked to sign the following statement:

1. We approve of Mrs. Sanger's course in publishing birth control articles.
2. We believe that such information should be readily accessible.
3. We have imparted birth control information.
4. We have practised birth control.[71]

In a letter to the *New Republic,* Parsons wrote, "Out of about fifty women who were selected as meeting the aforesaid requirements . . . six women agreed to sign the first three articles, and three women all four articles." The others refused to sign for several reasons. Two or three women said they were not informed enough about the issue. Others deferred to the medical profession, without cognizance that, under the New York State law, even a physician was culpable if found disseminating information on birth control. These women failed to consider also "that the discretion of the doctor is largely influenced either by his patient's income or by her capacity for nagging." For Parsons, the more direct refusal was "particularly interesting."

> "I'm just not the person for that sort of thing. . . . " "You're going to publish it in the newspapers! I couldn't stand that! . . . " "I consulted with my son and he objected very much to the publicity. . . . " "My husband says until he gets this lawsuit off his hands I must do nothing conspicuous. . . . " "My husband says it would be improper for me as the wife of a judge to sign. . . . " "My husband laughed when I read him the statement."[72]

Parsons concluded the letter by contrasting the refusal of these women to make a public statement concerning birth control with the behavior of ex-convicts of Sing Sing Prison who, in an effort to effect prison reform, sat on a stage in Carnegie Hall and spoke to the audience of their experiences. "The most effectual way they could bear witness was to lay bare their own lives. To save other men they had to testify against themselves." Parsons queried, "Is the character of Sing Sing prison indeed more socializing . . . than the character of New York homes? Or is it that men are more self-sacrificing than women?"[73]

The question with the slice at women was answered by Parsons herself on several occasions. She was not easy on her own sex. Indeed, she was intensely critical. In "Friendship, a Social Category," Parsons commented, "But even at its meekest moments friendship is well aware that ranged against it are all the social conservatives—the very young, the old, the priesthood, and, if I may be pardoned so sweeping a generalization, women." She referred to a remark made by a man of the Koita tribe of New Guinea "that girls were 'no good for *henamo,*'" a ceremonial friendship established at birth. Parsons added, "That women are comparatively poor friends is, I believe, world-wide opinion."[74]

Parsons's reservations about the nature of women carried over to her work in the woman's suffrage movement. In an article in *Harper's Weekly,* she addressed the issue of the enfranchisement of women. Those who opposed woman's suffrage pointed to the tendency of women to interact on a personal level, indeed, to interfere, direct, and control. Those who were supporters argued that this "'personal' attitude" of women would disappear when they were given the vote. In Parsons's view, the desire for control was part of woman's character. She chose direct and blunt language to describe their social conservatism. They were connected with the perpetuation of customs and conventionalities through a "desire to run other people's lives for them, to have them meet the changes in their life not as they occur and as they, the affected, like, but as *you* like and when *you* like." She concluded that, if women, indeed, were more concerned with the ceremonial than men, as she had proposed, it would be "evidence that they are more given to *managing* others." Parsons opined that there was every reason to expect that women would transfer this desire for control to politics, that they would be concerned with the personal life and moral conduct of candidates, and that they would try personally to influence political issues. She queried, "Why then enfranchise women? Why not continue to keep them out of the way of doing harm? Because you can't." The enfranchisement of women was, as her article was entitled, "The Lesser Evil."[75]

Custom and conventionality Parsons saw as an anchor to woman's progress. With women tied to the home, afraid of venturing out alone, their movements were circumscribed, and instead of rebelling, they acquiesced. Even the suffragist, as Parsons remarked, ignored this issue: "Anxious beyond measure for the vote, she is wholly unperturbed by the constraints of her daily life. Loath to be wholly dependent upon men in the limited number of matters which make up government, she is willing enough to be dependent upon them and upon women too in those endless details of daily life any woman might be expected to determine for herself."[76] Parsons illustrated this by recalling her experience at a political convention in Saratoga, New York, where several women were lobbying for suffrage. "One evening one of them wanted to go with a man to a dance, but she would not go, I overheard her declare, unless another woman went with them. The following afternoon another suffragist who had started to motor to New York took the train at Albany because . . . one of the two men motoring with her had to remain in Albany. 'I couldn't think of getting into New York after midnight with only one man.' " According to Parsons, until woman was able to stand strong, alone and on her own, then all the other changes—in suffrage, in property rights, in the right of guardianship—would simply be cosmetic. "The conventionalities of their daily life" must need be changed.[77]

Applying her critical edge to society, Parsons had dissected the customs and conventions, especially of American society. She had cut away the finery to expose the naked flesh. Her hope was to help free the individual from the constraints of the traditional, to unleash the personality from the hold of the collective will. As one who viewed feminism as a form of humanism, she saw benefits for all in such loosening of the bonds of tradition. Men, as well as women, had been cut off from self-expression and held in rigid confinement. She spoke of how poetry, music, and novels were viewed as inappropriate pursuits for men. "A Wisconsin Congressman of my acquaintance," she remarked, "considers it expedient to keep his talent as a pianist a secret from his constituents." In employment, a man was allowed less flexibility than a woman, for if he held a job traditionally associated with women, he was scorned. For instance, a male nurse occupied a lower social position than a female nurse. Parsons added, "There would be even more prejudice against a man kindergartner in the New York Department of Education than against a woman professor in Columbia University."[78]

Parsons intimated that change in social order would come about only through economic forces, though she was less than clear as to how this was to happen. She had little hope for what she called "deliberation," or a rational, planned approach to change. People had to be made to feel uncomfortable enough to adopt new ways, and discomfort was most readily felt in the pocketbook. As she wrote in "New Morals for Old, Changes in Sex Relations," "Social changes . . . are rarely due to deliberation. . . . In our society they are due mainly to economic causes. Housing congestion in New York will in time affect birth-control legislation in Albany; and fear of an overpopulated world will drive church as well as state into a new attitue toward multiplying to the glory of God."[79]

Women, Parsons argued, needed to become economically independent of men. Through economic equality, they could achieve social equality. Specifically, to obtain change in women's status, Parsons suggested a "kind of social experiment and organization which would increase through education the earning capacity of women, raise through unionization their wages or salaries, and insure them through forms of maternity insurance against the economic risks of child-bearing." Maternity insurance might be part of a dowry, or a form of job benefit, or a wedding gift. She quipped, "I recommend to the determinedly chivalrous American to give his bride instead of a pearl necklace or an engagement ring a paid-up maternity policy thereby ensuring her against being economically dependent upon him during periods of child-bearing."[80]

Parsons's work on social psychology was unevenly received. One critic took her to task for offering no more than a criticism of the traditional in *Fear and Conventionality*. The reviewer wrote, "If, as the author insists, human nature is much the same in all countries and all ages, and if conventions are rooted in fundamental human instincts, it surely follows that, no matter how society may change, it will always have conventions."[81] Thus, according to the reviewer, Parsons had avoided "the crucial question." In her critique of Parsons's work, Signe Toksvig remarked, "It is evident that . . . she has only begun to think about the new social order, and that her whole well equipped attention has been focused on the analysis of the old." Toskvig assessed Parsons's "outstanding contribution" as the ability to make us see that social progress, when based on inequalities of sex and age, is simply a link with the traditional, and thus is no progress at all.[82] Another critic found in her work on *The Old-Fashioned Woman* "the gift of making us 'see ourselves as others see us.'" The reviewer continued, "She discusses the social customs of New York and London with the same air of complete detachment with which she handles the superstitions of the Paraguayan Abipones or the traditions of the Kayans and Kenyahs of Sarawak. Indeed, the reader of this interesting volume is not infrequently forced to the conclusion that Mrs. Parsons finds little to choose between the habits of the Figian Islanders and the habits of the Islanders of Manhattan."[83] In his review of *Fear and Conventionality* for the *American Anthropologist*, Pliny Earle Goddard also remarked on the comparisons that Parsons made between American society and "the so-called barbarous peoples." He wrote, "The ethnological readers of the book, too, will be surprised to find that the customs of New York and Washington after all are not radically different from those of Australia." Indeed, he suggested, that perhaps in the future "Parsons's book may be a source of ethnological information concerning the inhabitants of the United States of the twentieth century."[84]

It was precisely the cross-cultural perspective that Parsons herself valued in her work. Years later, after she was thoroughly immersed in ethnographic writings, she remarked on, as she called them, her "popular" books: "I doubt if I could write them now, but at the time they had a sort of pioneer quality in regard to spreading a comparative point of view."[85]

In her work, Parsons compiled the evidence for the power of convention. In her life, she fought it, determined to go where she would go. But it was in her dreams for a new age that she saw its undoing. The snake of tradition would let loose its tail. The fear of the unlike was intimately bound to a fear of change, and "that fear whether of change wrought by life or of change threatened by the stranger, that great fear, is passing. With it are bound to go the devices of self-protection it prompted—ceremonial, conventionalities, and segregation."[86]

NOTES

1. Parsons, "Feminism and Conventionality," in *Women in Public Life: The Annals of the American Academy of Political and Social Science* 56 (1914): 53.

2. Parsons, *Fear and Conventionality* (New York: G. P. Putnam's Sons, 1914), p. xiv.

3. Parsons, *Social Rule* (New York: G. P. Putnam's Sons, The Knickerbocker Press, 1916), p. 11.

4. Parsons, *The Old-Fashioned Woman* (New York: G. P. Putnam's Sons, 1913), p. v.

5. Parsons, "Feminism and Conventionality," pp. 47–53.

6. Parsons, *Fear and Conventionality*, p. viii.

7. Ibid., p. ix.

8. Ibid.

9. Parsons, *Social Rule*, pp. 2, 3.

10. Ibid., pp. 4–5.

11. Parsons, "Sex," in Harold E. Stearns, ed., *Civilization in the United States, an Inquiry by Thirty Americans* (New York: Harcourt, Brace, 1922), pp. 313, 316.

12. See Parsons, *Social Rule*, pp. 5–7, for a discussion of declassification.

13. Ibid., p. 2, n. 1.

14. Ibid., pp. 8, 9.

15. Parsons, *Social Freedom* (New York: G.P. Putnam's Sons, 1915), pp. 24–25.

16. Parsons, "Feminism and Conventionality," p. 49.

17. Parsons, *Old-Fashioned Woman*, p. 91.

18. Ibid., p. 98.

19. Ibid., p. 83.

20. Ibid., p. 12.

21. Ibid., p. 118.

22. Ibid., p. 119.

23. Ibid., p. 126.

24. Parsons, "Feminism and Conventionality," p. 49.

25. Parsons, *Old-Fashioned Woman,* pp. 12, 22.

26. Parsons, "The Lesser Evil," *Harper's Weekly,* 26 Feb. 1916, p. 215.

27. Parsons, "Feminism and Conventionality," p. 52.

28. Parsons, "The Ceremonial of Growing Up," *School and Society* 2 (1915): 408–9.

29. Parsons, *Social Rule,* pp. 25, 27.

30. Ibid., p. 29.

31. Parsons, *Old-Fashioned Woman,* p. 28.

32. Ibid., p. 24.

33. Ibid., pp. 24–25, 29.

34. Parsons, "Feminism and Conventionality," p. 50.

35. Parsons, *Fear and Conventionality,* p. 75.

36. Ibid., p. 104.

37. Ibid., pp. 105–6.

38. Parsons, *Social Rule,* p. 52.

39. Ibid., pp. 34, 36, 40.

40. Parsons, "Feminism and Sex Ethics," *International Journal of Ethics* 26 (1916): 463.

41. Parsons, "Higher Education of Women and the Family," *American Journal of Sociology* 14 (1909): 758.

42. Parsons, *Social Rule,* pp. 35–36.

43. Ibid., pp. 44–45.

44. Parsons, *Fear and Conventionality,* p. 143.

45. Parsons, *Social Rule,* p. 46, her emphasis.

46. Parsons, "The Supernatural Policing of Women," *The Independent* 72 (8 Feb. 1912): 307, 309.

47. Parsons, *Religious Chastity, an Ethnological Study* (New York: Macaulay Co., 1913), pp. ix, 276–77, 123.

48. Ibid., pp. 278, 279.

49. ECP, unpublished poem.

50. Parsons, "Sex," p. 316.

51. Parsons, *Fear and Conventionality,* p. 74.

52. Ibid., p. 76.

53. Parsons, "Sex," p. 317.

54. Parsons, *Social Rule,* pp. 77, 78, n. 1.

55. Parsons, "Sex Morality and the Taboo of Direct Reference," *The Independent* 61 (1906): 392.

56. Parsons, "New Morals for Old, Changes in Sex Relations," *The Nation* 118 (1924): 552.

57. Parsons, *Social Rule,* p. 56.

58. Parsons, "Higher Education," p. 759.

59. Herbert Spencer, *The Principles of Biology* (New York: D. Appleton, 1874), vol 2, p. 486. For an examination of these attitudes toward the education of women, see Margaret W. Rossiter, *Women Scientists in America* (Baltimore: The Johns Hopkins University Press, 1982), especially Chapter 1, "Women's Colleges: The Entering Wedge," pp. 1–28.

60. Parsons, *The Family* (New York: G. P. Putnam's Sons, 1906), p. 346.

61. Parsons, "Higher Education," p. 760.

62. Ibid., pp. 761–62.

63. Parsons, *Old-Fashioned Woman*, p. 134.

64. Parsons, "Higher Education," p. 762.

65. Parsons, "Facing Race Suicide," *The Masses* 6, no. 9 (June 1915): 15.

66. Parsons, "Penalizing Marriage and Child-Bearing," *The Independent* 60 (18 Jan. 1906): 147.

67. Parsons, "Higher Education," p. 763.

68. Parsons, "Feminism and Sex Ethics," p. 463.

69. Parsons, "New Morals for Old," p. 552.

70. Parsons, "Penalizing Marriage," p. 147; "Feminism and Sex Ethics," p. 463.

71. Parsons, "Wives and Birth Control," *New Republic* 6, no. 72 (18 Mar. 1916): 187.

72. Ibid., p. 188.

73. Ibid.

74. Parsons, "Friendship, a Social Category," *American Journal of Sociology* 21 (1915): 233.

75. Parsons, "The Lesser Evil," p. 215.

76. Parsons, "Feminism and Conventionality," p. 48.

77. Ibid., p. 48.

78. Parsons, "Feminism and the Family," *International Journal of Ethics* 28 (1917): 52; *Old-Fashioned Woman*, p. 145.

79. Parsons, "New Morals for Old," pp. 551–53.

80. Parsons, "Feminism and the Family," pp. 54, 56.

81. Anonymous, review of *Fear and Conventionality, The Outlook,* 10 Feb. 1915, p. 348. Parsons's books on social psychology did not have a ready market. They were too popular for many scholars, and too weighty for the lay audience. See Peter Hare, *A Woman's Quest for Science* (Buffalo, N.Y.: Prometheus Books, 1985), p. 20.

82. Signe Toskvig, "Elsie Clews Parsons," *New Republic,* 26 Nov. 1919, pp. 17–20.

83. Anonymous, review of *Old-Fashioned Woman, The Outlook,* 30 Aug. 1913, p. 1011.

84. Goddard, review of *Fear and Conventionality, AA* 17 (1915): 343.

85. UM, ECP to Leslie White, 4 May 1931.

86. Parsons, "Feminism and Conventionality," p. 53.

Elsie, 1902 (courtesy of the American Philosophical Society).

Herbert, Lissa, and John Parsons at Stonover Farm, 1904 (courtesy of the American Philosophical Society).

The Taft Tour of the Philippines, 1905. *Back row, left to right:* Representative Herbert Parsons, Captain James K. Thompson, Amy McMillan, Representative Frederick H. Gillett, Elsie Clews Parsons, Senator Francis G. Newlands. *Middle row:* Mabel T. Boardman, Secretary William Howard Taft, Edith McAllister Newlands. *Front row:* Representative Nicholas Longworth, Miss Alice Roosevelt, Colonel Clarence R. Edwards (courtesy of the American Philosophical Society).

Elsie in her bathing suit, the Bahamas, 1911 (courtesy of the American Philosophical Society).

Elsie in her fieldwork garb in the Southwest, circa 1915 (courtesty of Fanny
Parsons Culleton).

Elsie in her riding habit, ready for fieldwork in the Southest, circa 1915 (courtesy of Fanny Parsons Culleton).

Alfred Louis Kroeber, 1911 (courtesy of the University Archives, University of California, Berkeley).

Elsie in her riding habit in the Southwest, circa 1915
(courtesy of the American Philosophical Society).

Elsie on horseback, circa 1915 (courtesy of the American Philosophical Society).

Elsie in the Southwest, circa 1920 (courtesy of the American Philosophical Society).

Elsie dressed for fieldwork
in Mexico, circa 1930
(courtesy of Fanny Parsons
Culleton).

Gathering of anthropologists at the Parsons' Lounsberry residence, circa 1925. *Left to right:* Franz Boas, Elsie Clews Parsons, Esther S. Goldfrank, Ruth Benedict, unknown, Margaret Mead, Gladys Reichard, and Pliny Earle Goddard (courtesy of the American Philosophical Society).

Franz Boas. The inscription reads: "Elsie Clews Parsons, Fellow in the struggle for freedom from prejudice, Franz Boas" (courtesy of the Rye Historical Society).

6

The Heretics

"The loss of sympathy came hard to him as to others." This Elsie wrote of the pacifist and essayist Randolph Bourne. The same could well have been said of her and her cohorts who worked for peace and equality and for the creation of a new world. Elsie and her liberal and radical friends believed in the strength of their ideas. They were on the swell of the Progressive Era, a time when many were convinced a positive change could be made in the social and economic order. They rode the crest of the wave, all the while attempting to stir those who had sunk to complacent depths. Through reason and articulation of thought—through writing articles, pressuring politicians, appealing to the masses—right would prevail. When it did not, when the Progressive wave crashed in the trenches of Europe, and the vision of peace was bespattered with blood, they went their separate ways. To be sure, they were still linked by the ties of friendship and intellectual sympathies, but they were no longer electrified by the imminent creation of a new social order.

Still, before the wave crashed, they were bound to the new age. Walter Lippmann spoke of this in *Drift and Mastery:* "Our time . . . believes in change. The adjective 'progressive' is what we like, and the word 'new,' be it the New Nationalism of Roosevelt, the New Freedom of Wilson, or the New Socialism of the syndicalists. . . . In the emerging morality the husband is not regarded as the proprietor of his wife, nor the parents as autocrats over the children. We are met by women who are 'emancipated'; for what we hardly know. We are not stifled by a classical tradition in art: in fact, artists to-day are somewhat stunned by the rarefied atmosphere of their freedom. . . . The battle, in short, does not lie against crusted prejudice but against the chaos of a new freedom."[1]

The turbulence of the new freedom was felt by all, by those who feared it and those who embraced it. Reflected in literature, art, and politics, it was given voice in the liberal and radical press, in the *New Republic,* the *Masses,* the *Dial,* the *Seven Arts.* While Elsie's wartime "propaganda," as she referred to her articles, appeared in all of these, she published most frequently in the *New Republic*. Founded in 1914, and intended as the "apogee of progressivism,"[2] this magazine had initially been the lodestone for the liberal intelligentsia. The group of writers who sustained it was known as the New Republic crowd, and Elsie was part of this group. To these people—pacifist and essayist Randolph Bourne, playwright and essayist Clarence Day, historical novelist Frances Hackett, journalist Walter Lippmann, feminist and essayist Signe Toksvig—Elsie was linked through bonds of friendship and shared concerns. All of them were intensely caught up in their aspirations for change. Theirs was not an idle enterprise. They drew together around the causes of women suffrage, pacifism, freedom of expression, and liberation of sexual mores. In their journalistic articles, they expressed the concerns of the new age, and their words gave a measured pulse beat to a passionate period.[3]

It was in Greenwich Village that the liberal and radical intelligentsia established their center. "The heyday of the Village," Henry May noted, " . . . began in 1913, when Henrietta Rodman moved the Liberal Club from uptown to MacDougal Street and Polly Holiday, an anarchist from Evanston, began to run her restaurant on the floor below it."[4] In his description, William O'Neill fleshed out the picture: "Women bobbed their hair, wore sandals, peasant skirts, and worse. Men had soft-collared shirts and sometimes went without a hat, leaving themselves practically naked. They voted Socialist, if at all, admired revolutionaries, painted their apartments black. Villagers practiced free speech, free love, and contraception. They liked to eat at Polly Holiday's famous restaurant, where Hippolyte Havel might call them 'bourgeois pigs' while waiting on their table. Afterward they would go upstairs to the Liberal Club where all points of view found expression."[5]

The social rebels who gravitated to the village shared in a certain intellectual orientation and vision for the world. Along with a rejection of the traditional in mores and in religion, they embraced Henry James's notions of innovation, John Dewey's social reconstructionism, and Thorstein Veblen's skepticism. Armed with Henrik Ibsen, Friedrich Nietzsche, and George Bernard Shaw, they honed their contempt for nineteenth-century morality. Fyodor Dostoevsky was a source of renewal for "their religious instincts," while Sigmund Freud convinced them of their need for sexual expression. Politically, they identified with socialism. Henry May summarized, "All these influences had combined to produce a new kind of radicalism, passionate yet somewhat imprecise. The Young Intellectuals agreed on at least one point: they were uninterested in any plan for social improvement which was not also a program for spiritual and artistic liberation."[6]

An intellectual enclave with a distinctive personality, the village still was part of New York City with its diversity of immigrant groups and disparity of income. Rejecting their own past, the new inhabitants of Greenwich Village identified with the poor and the oppressed. They embraced the problems of the foreign-born and championed the causes of the working class. In *The New Radicalism in America,* Christopher Lasch referred to this as the "radical reversal of perspective," an attempt "to see society from the bottom up, or . . . from outside in."[7] Yet, while throwing their support to the poor, their eye was caught by the glitter of affluence. "Wealth, unabashed and ostentatious, was all around. The Young Intellectual could see, of course, the Fifth Avenue mansions and the parade of limousines. He could see, as in Chicago, the magnificence of conventional patronage of the arts. . . . But he might also run into a different kind of philanthropist, the rich radical, the hostess who gave socialist teas, the venturesome backer of avant-garde and radical magazines."[8] It was this combination of intellect, creativity, and wealth, along with a certain unfettered optimism that energized the new age. And it was precisely in this milieu that Elsie and her liberal and radical friends came together.

A progressive endeavor sponsored by the New Republic crowd, as well as by others, was the founding of the New School for Social Research in the spring of 1919. As Alvin Johnson recalled, "I went over to the school the evening of the opening. The long, narrow reception room was jammed. I saw there about every liberal I knew, and a lot I had heard of. Miss Smith was writing down registrations in hectic haste. . . . From time to time she would jump up, wave a bill over her head, and cry, 'Who gave me this twenty-dollar bill?' " Students and instructors alike were drawn to this experiment in education that emphasized "free and untrammeled teaching." Elsie taught a course on "Sex in Ethnology" in the opening term, and one of her students was Ruth Benedict. As described in the *New School Bulletin,* the course included " 'surveys of a number of societies presenting a distinctive distribution of functions between the sexes, and of topical analyses of the division of labor between men and women.' " Anthropology and the liberal milieu of the New School were to Benedict's liking, for she continued the next term with Alexander Goldenweiser. With both Parsons's and Goldenweiser's encouragement, she went on to study with Franz Boas at Columbia.[9]

There was an intensity of purpose in this age, and much of it was conveyed in the correspondence of Elsie Clews Parsons and Randolph Bourne. Their friendship was one of kindred intellects. Bourne expressed this affinity when he wrote Elsie, "You are the only other renegade Anglo-Saxon I know besides myself."[10] When compiling a posthumous collection of his letters, Alyse Gregory, suffragist and close confidant of Bourne, wrote Elsie, "You were the only woman Randolph knew who gave him the sort of intellectual stimulus he so needed."[11] This friendship must have been especially dear to Bourne, since he perceived himself barred from closeness with women. With his head permanently misshapen from a difficult birth and his torso twisted from spinal tuberculosis suffered at the age of four, Bourne keenly felt his disabilities. Of this he wrote, "The doors of the deformed man are always locked, and the key is on the outside. He may have treasures of charm inside, but they will never be revealed unless the person outside cooperates with him in unlocking the door. A friend becomes, to a much greater degree than with the ordinary man, the indispensable means of discovering one's own personality. One only exists, so to speak, with friends."[12]

Randolph Bourne (1886–1918) fused his undergraduate work at Columbia in literature and the social sciences into what he labeled literary radicalism.[13] He wrote for the *New Republic*, the *Dial*, the *Masses*, and the *Seven Arts*. Incisive and acerbic, his essays prodded the complacent. He made it uncomfortable for those who accepted the status quo, especially for liberals, who became, in his view, apologists for the U.S. entry into the war. As Parsons wrote on his death, "He was a critic of great ability in a community not only possessed of but few critics but unaware of the lack. Intolerant of intellectual sham and impatient of compromise Randolph Bourne did not buffer the facts for either friend or enemy—and he had both friends and enemies."[14] Goldenweiser esteemed Bourne as "the apostle of the intellectual class in America."[15] Lasch's definition of an intellectual fit Bourne: he was one "for whom thinking fulfills at once the function of work and play."[16] What was written of Randolph could equally be said of Elsie. They both were a "mingling of passionate resolve and critical inquiry which was the very spirit of America" during the Progressive Era.[17]

For his part, Bourne found Elsie spiritedly alive. He wrote a friend about her, comparing the time spent with her to his experience in a colony of intellectuals at Dublin, New Hampshire: "Did I tell you about my reminiscence of Dublin in the shape of a week-end at Lenox? I was almost wheedled from Dublin by these open hills and wind-swept moors. And my hostess, Elsie Clews Parsons, has severely wrested Miss Lowell from my bright foreground. After all I am an ethnologist, and she is a so clever and stimulating one that she sets one's thoughts tumbling all over each other. And such a fine adventurousness and command of life as she radiates. Do you know her? If you are interested in rare persons, there she is."[18] Randolph was a frequent guest at Stonover Farm in Lenox. On one occasion, Elsie asked him for a visit after the older children had returned to school: "So between a pleasantly quiet house and the cabin we ought to have a nice time together—even if I sometimes write in one and you in the other." Another time, she enticed him with the promise that "the Berkshire air is an asset in solving problems, personal or impersonal. At least it has often so proved to me."[19] Indeed, Bourne found it thus: "O, those Berkshire hills, and the soft air of that flying Sunday afternoon! That ride was one of the most delicious of all my experiences. I'm so grateful that you thought of lugging me along." The visits were productive as well. On his return to New York, Bourne wrote Elsie, "My work was wonderful. Your house is the great, good place indeed. And I like so much the air of seeming satisfied, or at least not seeming dissatisfied that the mood is continuing with me back in New York. This much did you do for me." In another letter, he expressed his need for Elsie's company, "I want to be a prophet, but it is so very hard to keep my mind on it unless people like you are around."[20]

Elsie and Randolph concurred, there was no intellectual center in the United States. Elsie wrote him, "As for your disappointment in not finding social, you call them intellectual—but to either of us, I guess that's just the same—centres for yourself, I can't tell you how often I've had the same disappointment. . . . I go to gatherings of two or three only for the individual I may be lucky enough to chance on."[21] The Heretics provided for this. This was a select group of intellectuals who gathered each month for dinner, a speaker, and discussion.[22] For Elsie, the Heretics meeting made possible "worthwhile" contact. She intended to try one other gathering: "I'm going to the Liberal Club too, this winter. The one night I've been in town for the last few weeks Dr. Lowie dined with me and suggested the Liberal Club, saying it was more 'representative' than the Heretics."[23] Elsie was among the first members of another group, the Supper Club, which gathered once a month on a Sunday evening for a dinner and informal discussions on questions of urgent interest.[24]

These gatherings of liberals and radicals that thrived in Greenwich Village apparently inspired an off-shoot, the Civic Club. With great delight, Bourne wrote Elsie, "If you haven't heard this tale, I really should be there to tell you in person. It is too good. The Civic Club . . . is making a desperate bid for respectability. It is to be as different as possible from the vulgar and licentious Liberal Club. It must have nothing to do with Greenwich Village. Its quarters must not be below 31st St. Its qualifications must be broad enough to let in honest conservatives. To be a member you must . . . 'have an interest in human welfare, expressed in concerted effort for the amelioration of society.' It would seem that this was broad enough to admit almost anybody but idiots and human monsters." For "the sake of conjugal harmony," a special provision had been made for spouses to become automatic members should their mate so request. As Bourne related it, "In other words, spouses are not . . . subjected to the test of 'interest in human welfare,' but tag on as being of one flesh with their mates." He related an incident involving Leonard Abbott of the Ferrer School (an experimental school in New York named after an anarchist leader) and the labor activist John Reed: "The best joke of all I have forgotten: After this tagging-on spouse rule was adopted, two unrespectables, Leonard Abbott . . . and John Reed, presented themselves for membership. They asked that their temporary wives be automatically made members too. What more chaste and perfect than such a demand? The membership committee . . . turned them down!. . . . Leonard Abbott and John Reed, two as civically-minded persons as the club contains, could not enter because taking the constitution at its face value, they wished their spouses to tag along."[25]

Elsie's article in the *New Republic*, "Must We Have Her?," had appeared, as Bourne told her, "at a supremely dramatic moment, only a day or two after . . . [the] new Civic Club had adopted its anti–Social Freedom constitution." Elsie had addressed what she called "the tagging-on phenomenon," which required both husbands and wives to be invited to social gatherings. She reasoned, "A husband or a wife is a personal taste, a private taste. To force your predilections on others is generally accounted in bad taste. In this case you not only obtrude your matrimonial taste on others, you obtrude it crassly and irresponsibly. You do not even sit next to your husband or wife at the dinner table or talk to him or her in the entr'acte." There were certain situations, Elsie conceded, for which the couple should be extended a joint invitation. These included large social functions, such as "a very large ball or a fashionable wedding, or an all-inclusive garden party." For these gatherings, the couple was viewed as a representative of their family. "And as long as the form of social intercourse is purely ceremonial," Elsie remarked, "this attitude seems fairly justifiable.

For in connection with a ceremonial the individual does not count as a personality but as a representative of an institution, of the family, let us say, or of marriage." However, when invitations were extended not on institutional grounds, but on personal choice—for a dinner party, a group discussion, a game of tennis, or a yachting party—the individual alone, Elsie urged, should be considered. She concluded, "For an institutional sanction or propaganda an institutional method of selection is proper enough; but for personal relations only a personal method of selection can succeed. Ceremonial forms of intercourse are becoming archaic, they are passing rapidly, extraordinarily rapidly, out of modern life. Most of us like this change or affect to like it."[26]

The founders of the Civic Club, who had so solicitously made provision for the inclusion of spouses, received a "colossal jar" by Elsie's article. It was the general consensus, Bourne related, that the stipulation for inclusion was "a kindly measure destined to give the stupid and patient wife married to the high-brow, an opportunity to mingle socially and improve herself intellectually with her husband's brilliant circle." He queried, "Would you take away ... her only chance ... of spiritual growth?" and added, "They really think you are rather heartless."[27]

In a letter to a friend, Bourne recounted an incident that illustrated another ramification of the inclusion of spouses: "E.C.P. told me a good story about a Barnard girl ... [who] thirsted for intellectual discussion, and would accost young men in her courses with an opening 'Lovely weather we're having' or something like that. The man would reply, 'Yes, MY WIFE thinks it charming' or some other crusher; showing the non-existence of any conception of social freedom in graduate schools." From his own observation at Columbia, Bourne was familiar with this situation. He remarked, "A big reform is needed. What E.C.P. calls 'Tagging-on spouse problem' should be handled without mercy." The young woman invited Elsie to talk to Barnard students on the necessity for intellectual discussion in graduate school. As Bourne said, Elsie had also "been shooting them up morally at Bryn Mawr."[28]

In June, 1916, Elsie was asked to deliver an address at Barnard. Candidly, in response to the invitation, Elsie explained her position toward politics and education: "I am for practical & definite pacifism in nursery & school & for democratic tolerance of all nationalities as against the melting pot-propaganda." She continued, "I am a bad speaker & so must read. Nor am I up to making a graceful ceremonial address. For these reasons & because my brand of Americanism is not in much favor, I believe, in school circles, please feel entirely at liberty to withdraw your invitation."[29] Indeed, this was the result. Elsie wrote Bourne, "So they'll lose a few Zuñi anecdotes and a few references to Anglo Saxon arrogance."[30]

Through her opposition to the war, Elsie had become marked as a radical. This came as a surprise only to her father. In June, 1917, Henry Clews wrote to her, "A Times reporter has just been in to see me and said he was ordered by his paper to interview me in relation to a report that Mrs. Parsons had become a member of the People's council organization, which has for its purpose 'a deplorable effort to promote peace.' I took this down from him word for word as he uttered it. He said that the report came to the Times from some important high official in Washington. I denied having any knowledge of the matter and could not, therefore, give him any information." Her father warned Elsie that "the Washington authorities" were intent on suppressing opposition to the war: "I thought you ought to know of this and I advise that you keep yourself aloof from such movements as the time has not arrived for them." He spoke of "the marvelous success of the Liberty Loan and the subscriptions to the Red Cross" and saw this as an expression of "the unanimity of sentiment among the people in this country to back the Government at any cost in life and property to bring about a permanent peace."[31]

Elsie was alone among her family in her opposition to the war. Her husband was serving in France, and her children were enthusiastic supporters of the war. In April, 1917, John wrote his father a letter from St. Paul's School that began, *"Don't show Mother this."* He continued, "We have military training . . . twice a week . . . from . . . half hour to an hour. It is compulsory. . . . You ought to let Mother live in peaceful ignorance about this. I like it also and I will not have Mother trotting up hear [*sic*] and making a row."[32] By the following November, the excitement of the training had waned. John wrote his father, "I spent last Friday sitting on a rock with a wooden gun in my hand supposedly guarding a picket line, but in reality doing nothing but bore myself to death."[33]

Elsie's mark as a radical became official in January, 1919, when a front page article in the *New York Times* announced, "LISTS AMERICANS AS PACIFISTS, Senate Committee Puts Sixty-two Well-Known Men and Women into Record. . . . Roster Furnished by Military Intelligence Service. . . . Special to the New York Times. Washington, Jan. 24.—There was placed today in the record of the Senate Committee which is investigating German propaganda the names of sixty-two men and women who have been recorded as active in movements which did not help the United States when the country was fighting the Central Powers." The organizations included "the most prominent of the so-called pacifist and radical movements in this country." Among those individuals named were "clergymen, professors, lawyers, writers, Socialists, labor leaders, architects, an I. W. W. agitator, and one former publisher of a New York newspaper." The Senate Committee on German Propaganda had learned of the existence of this list when a representative of the Military Intelligence Service, Archibald E. Stevenson, had given testimony on "Bolshevist, socialistic, and other radical movements in the United States." Mr. Stevenson referred to it as a " 'Who's Who in Pacifism and Radicalism.' " Among others listed were Jane Addams, Kuno Francke, Elizabeth Gurley Flynn, Rabbi Judah L. Magnes, the Reverend Norman M. Thomas, L. Hollingsworth Wood, and Eugene V. Debs. Elsie's name appeared with the following information: "Elsie CLEWS PARSONS (Mrs. Herbert) of New York. People's Council of America. American League to Limit Armaments."[34]

Parsons's position on the war was quite simple. She was a pacifist, and as such, she was opposed to the use of force. In a letter to the editor of the *New York Tribune,* Elsie wrote, "One may be a nonresistant in war because of a very passionate resistance against adding to the pain and suffering of the world." The philosophy of non-resistance derived from a "desire to lessen suffering; it is an expression of desire and of faith born of desire."[35] In a letter to the *New York Times,* she argued that "the feud theory of war" led directly to one side arming in response to the aggression of another: " 'You did it to me and so I do it back to you . . . it would be ignoble in fact if I did not retaliate.' " Notwithstanding the rhetoric about arming for peace, this principle, Parsons said, was the basis for the military build up in the United States.[36]

L. Hollingsworth Wood, secretary of the American League to Limit Armaments, wrote Parsons, "I noticed your very interesting letter in the New York Times of yesterday." He invited her to work with his organization, either in making speeches, working on publicity, or writing. The league, based at Columbia University and headed by a council of fifteen, collaborated with labor and peace societies, though Wood noted that the latter had "been so timid in the past that we want an organization which will speak out more defiantly to our militaristic friends."[37] Elsie agreed to write articles for newspapers and offered to send on "the pacifist papers, 'Towards Keeping the Peace,' " which was a collection of her essays on the war.[38]

Elsie's work came to the attention of Elizabeth Gurley Flynn of the Industrial Workers of the World, who along with one hundred and sixty-six Wobblies had been charged with violation of the Espionage Act. She wrote Elsie, "I would very much like to meet you and talk to you about some aspects of our cases which I feel would interest you, and am emboldened to write by your evident interest at the Heretics' dinner." She continued, "Miss Rodman, Mrs. Cothran and other mutual friends said you are not at all a formal person and I could address you directly and without ceremony."[39] Elsie responded with frankness, "No, I am not a formal person, but I have other limitations. In so far as I understand the I. W. W. movement I have not been altogether sympathetic with it. Sabotage, for example, does not appeal to me. (I am not referring of course to newspaper lies, but to the theory itself of sabotage) and labor sabotage appeals but little more than capitalistic or international sabotage." Elsie explained that her interest in Flynn's presentation at the Heretics "was primarily an interest in war psychology." She was not in accord with the position of William Heywood, leader of the IWW, that war was "peculiar to a capitalistic economy." Rather she was certain that "labor throughout the world is just as much involved in responsibility for the maintenance of this war as capitalism or as such intelligentsia as was present with us the other night." Still, she did view labor as "less responsible for provoking war since capitalism controls the organization of opinion & for the plutocracies war begins as a game." Elsie assured Flynn that she would enjoy visiting with her, and added, "If you could spare the time from your case I wish you would come out here [to Harrison] to spend a night. My schoolchildren motor out here in the afternoon and they could pick you up where ever was convenient for you. They get in to town in the morning by nine. Would next Monday be possible for you?"[40] Flynn responded that she would not be able to accept Parsons's "kind invitation." She had received a notice to appear in Chicago for arraignment on Saturday, December 15. Expressing the hope that this was only a formal matter, and that she would be back in New York the following week, she promised Parsons that she would write again on her return.[41]

By 1917, there was a bifurcation of the Progressive movement between those who supported U.S. involvement in the "war to end all wars" and those who remained committed to pacifist principles. This split was played out in the *New Republic;* and in the end, with liberal patina tarnished, it endorsed the U.S. involvement in the European conflict. A very personal view of this shift in *New Republic* policy was conveyed by Bourne in his letter to Elsie, dated May 28, 1917. He had been discussing the draft and the position of the young men who opposed the war, yet, at the same time, who did not want to be punished for resisting conscription. Then he turned to censorship of the press, and asked Elsie, "Can you believe it? A complete suppression of speculation, criticism." He continued, "The only relief is the amusing predicament the N[ew] R[epublic] must find itself in," that of risking censure for violating the government insurgency laws. Bourne continued, "It merely goes to show how powerless the individual is when he gets into a great 'culture-pattern' like the running of a war. . . . Once the machine is set going no one can control it." Herbert Croly and Walter Lippmann had been "obsessed," Bourne said, "with the idea of themselves controlling the war-technique in a democratic manner." They would keep life in balance, guard against excesses, protect "women and children in labor, [raise] a democratic army of conscripts—everything polite, well-bred, humane, enlightened." Now, however, they were "slightly aghast at the terrible forces they have unloosed," and Bourne expected that soon "futile walrus tears" would flow over "the 'mistakes' of the Government, the 'unwise' censorship . . . all of which was completely implicit in the whole affair and was foreseen by every pacifist from the beginning." He concluded, "I am acquiring a feeling of cold anger against the whole crowd, and I haven't been near the place for weeks."[42]

The pacifists turned angrily against those liberals who they felt had betrayed the cause of peace. Bourne wrote Elsie of one such encounter, a dinner with two committed pacifists and with Lippmann: "We three formed a strong coalition against W[alter] L[ippmann], and I never saw a man become so progressively depressed. His intellect finally seemed to choke up, and he refused to meet anything that was said. He told me later that he was not half as sure that he was right as I was that he was wrong. I pointed out that this humility went ill with the confident dogmatism of the New Republic about 'willing American participation' and the sure glories of the League of Peace."[43] Still another outspoken opponent of the war and editor of the *Dial*, Thorstein Veblen, viewed the liberals support of governmental policy as a "disguised return to the status quo—the old system improved with modern furnishings like the League of Nations." As Bourne reported Veblen's view, "They didn't really want to make the world safe for democracy; they only wanted to make it safe for diplomacy."[44]

The pacifists found other outlets for their views. They published in the *Masses*, the *Dial*, and the *Seven Arts*. Each was threatened with legal action on the part of the government for violation of censorship statutes. Max Eastman described by his biographers as "a lone wolf [who] . . . could not run in packs, no matter how small or distinguished," became editor of the *Masses* in 1912.[45] Along with Floyd

Dell, Eastman worked toward the creation of "a free magazine" that was described as "Owned and Published Co-operatively by Its Editors. It has no Dividends to Pay, and nobody is trying to make Money out of it. A Revolutionary and not a Reform Magazine; a Magazine with a Sense of Humor and no Respect for the Respectable; Frank; Arrogant; Impertinent; searching for the True Causes; a Magazine directed against Rigidity and Dogma wherever it is found; Printing what is too Naked or True for a Money-making Press; a Magazine whose final Policy is to do as it Pleases and Conciliate Nobody."[46] Even the contributors to the magazine felt themselves part of the endeavor. Of independent minds and unpaid for their writing, they were entitled to the solicitous treatment accorded them by Eastman. They were, after all, the shining lights of the left. A partial listing of them included Sherwood Anderson, Mabel Dodge, Vachel Lindsay, William Carlos Williams, Randolph Bourne, Bertrand Russell, and Maxim Gorky as well as Elsie Clews Parsons. The editorial board and the contributors together had a feeling of creating a new social order. As O'Neill opined, "The *Masses* was not so much a publishing venture as a movement, even for some a way of life."[47] True to its promise of being a magazine with "no Respect for the Respectable," the *Masses* treated religion and sex in a manner that offended a great many. As a result, it was banned from sale at New York subway news stands. Eastman and the editorial board sued. Attempting to assemble twenty prominent citizens who supported the *Masses*, Eastman wrote Parsons that a hearing was to be held before "Senator Thompson's Legislature Committee upon the right of Ward & Gow to exclude The Masses from the Subway and Elevated Stands."[48]

Elsie also published in the *Dial,* which in 1918 had been moved from Chicago to New York. Along with the move came the Reconstruction Board of John Dewey and Thorstein Veblen.[49] There was a good deal of "lively squabble over authority" between the editors and the associate editors.[50] At the center of it was Bourne. Assured of a position on the magazine, Bourne brought with him the financial contributions of Scofield Thayer.[51] Still, Thayer could not protect Bourne from the self-editing of the magazine. As Bourne reported, "They censor all my reviews at the 'Dial' now, for fear my dark obscure cynicisms will get us all into trouble." In the struggle for power, Bourne said, "Dewey seems convinced that these wild young pacifists intend to run away with the paper."[52]

Bourne's energy and financial need for a journalistic outlet led him to other ventures. In September, 1917, the *Seven Arts* had gone down with the ominous threat of the Seditious Act. As he wrote Elsie, "If you have seen the Tribune lately, you have read of the staggering blow that has come to the Seven Arts, its patriotic patron having become scared and dropped it." Four months earlier, Bourne had approached Elsie for support of a new publication to be called the *Promise*, which he and Van Wyck Brooks were planning. Playfully, he asked, "Do you not know some kindly capitalist who would give fifty or a hundred thousand dollars to start it?" Their intent was "to do what . . . both the 'Seven Arts' and the 'New Republic' ought to be doing—express new growing forces of the American intelligentsia." Bourne continued, "The 'New Republic' is off to make the ruling class liberal, and is vitiated by its dress-suit atmosphere. The 'Seven Arts' has its Freudian religion and doesn't touch the reformed Puritan strata like Brooks and myself." He envisioned articles on a regular basis from Parsons, "Max Eastman and Ridgely Torrence and Floyd Dell and Lee Simonson and Dreiser and Harold Stearns and the other pro-democratic, pro-hyphenate, pro-Negro, anti-Puritan, anti-English Americans." Apparently Elsie did not encourage such an undertaking, since Bourne wrote her, "You did not seem very powerful when I spoke of starting a new paper," and then added, "but, after all you do consort with the capitalist class, and you might help us speculate as to where we could lay hands on some money to keep the paper going."[53]

In 1917, Elsie reflected on the imminent change in political mood: "The time is not distant, perhaps it is at hand, when, progressives having ceased to pay further attention to conservatives, everybody will call himself a progressive." The outcast will then be "the skeptic of progress." She observed, "Even to-day you are found much more aggravating when you say you do not believe in social progress than when you say you do not believe in God. Social progress has become . . . a certitude." Science had replaced religion as the "modern faith."[54] Even the war was in the Progressive spirit, for, as Elsie remarked, "We hear, [it] is being fought for liberty, for freedom from German rule, for the independence of small nations, to set the world free."[55] It was a "War for Democracy." With so many attaching themselves to the Progressive label, there were those few who felt the need to move further to the left. This was, as Henry May referred to it, the "radical rebellion within progressivism."[56] On the position of the radical, Elsie observed, "The ornamental radical is not only tolerated, he is even welcome, for he flatters the spirit of the practical man, giving him not only a sense of superiority in common sense, but a sense of tolerance. The practical American likes to think of himself as tolerant. The American, practical or theoretical, regales himself on catchwords and of all his catchwords 'liberty' is one of the most precious."[57]

Bourne remarked on a singular result of so many aligning themselves with the liberal movement. He wrote Elsie, "I think we must say farewell to Henrietta. She is discovering that there are so many radicals to-day that to be radical is to be conventional. Back to the old homely virtues for her, the dutiful wife, the monogamic home, the twain who have become one flesh. . . . Henrietta is a perfect barometer of the swing of ephemeral vanguardism."[58] Elsie admitted to Bourne that she had a tendency to become "a bit snobbish" when trying "to describe the . . . Henrietta types." It was simply too "easy to put them down as *bourgeois,* and let it go at that." What made this type radical was not the desire "for clear thinking and simple living," but rather a narrowness that grew out of "the lack of certain cultural experiences." In the same way, she said, people become conservative: "To have an interesting flavor," either conservatism or radicalism must be first the result of personal experience.[59]

The optimism for change and the aspiration to shape new souls ebbed in 1917. The pacifists were embittered by their loss. They turned from the fray to look inward with a realization that the fresh new age had ended in defeat. Many of the radical thinkers, tired and worn with spent emotion, left the struggle. Elsie was one who did so. In notes for "A Confession of Faith," which was to be part of the manuscript, "Towards Keeping the Peace," she wrote that it was "hard to realize the bitterness, the resentment, the sense of outrage that the unquestioning acceptance of militarism [had] aroused." It was, she said, "not the downfall of civilization in [the] first weeks of war, but [rather] a betrayal of the spiritual life" that was the source of her bitterness. The insistence by others "on war psychology aroused opposition & then, when seen to be fruitless, ironical apathy & a spirit of self-defense." There was a "sense of the immediate futility" of effort against a war that had "already taken on an historical perspective." She concluded, "I doubt if any critics of Germany were as bitter as pacifists of this type were against militarist converts."[60]

Disheartened by the failure of the pacifist movement to keep the United States from entering the war, and cynical about active involvement in political affairs, Elsie withdrew. She turned away from the new age and the Progressive, to the old and the traditional. She left contemporary American life behind and journeyed to the pueblos of the Southwest, to the Sea Islands of the Carolinas, and to the villages of Mexico. This was a conscious choice for her. The world would not change, so she turned her back on it and followed her own paths. In 1917, she wrote Herbert regarding the British attempts to draw the United States into the war, and she concluded, "It may seem a queer taste, but Negroes and Indians for me. The rest of the world grows duller and duller. But for you and the children, I would certainly spend little time in this part of it." To anthropologist Alfred Kroeber, she expressed a similar sentiment, "Life for a militant pacifist has been rather trying these past months and if I hadn't had my Zuñi notes to write up & no end of Negro folk-tales to edit I'd be worse off than I am."[61]

Elsie let it be known that her scientific work precluded involvement in political causes.[62] Only for the trial of Margaret Sanger on charges of distributing birth control information did she leave her self-imposed exile. For this, she contacted people in an attempt to gain support for Sanger; and she delivered speeches—one to a gathering of over three hundred people in Chicago, and another at the dinner held to honor Sanger on the night before she was to appear in court for sentencing. Elsie wrote to Bourne, "The last time you called me up I was destitute. What a fool I was to try to withstand New York for over a month. The Sanger case finished me; so much so that I had begun to take people seriously in my old style."[63] She felt more at peace in the Southwest, for, as she wrote Herbert, "Living among Americans, white I mean, not Indians, who have never heard of the Balkans and ask you if the Teutons are the English, the war seems somewhat remote." The next month, from Zuni, she remarked, "The only reference to your war I heard during the 20 days was, 'Haven't they finished killing each other off yet?' It was said of course by a Zuñi."[64]

Her friends who had shared the hope for a changed world did not allow Elsie to leave them without protest. They challenged her to come back to them from the recesses of her study, or the far-reaches of her fieldtrips, to write again with passion about the problems of modern America. Bourne was one who questioned her retreat. He urged her to publish some of her pamphlets and articles on militarism as an anthology: "They are too good and pertinent to let die, and you could get by with some of your war psychology too that the N[ew] R[epublic] did not print. Don't say that you are going to publish nothing but technical scientific stuff now. . . . We need your point of view turned on all these modern problems. I wish you could be persuaded to think of it."[65] Nonetheless, Elsie remained at Stonover Farm in Lenox, as she said, out of touch with the world. She concentrated on her translation of Portuguese-Creole tales and depended on

Bourne to keep her informed. She nurtured a sort of suspended animation. As she explained, "I've been illustrating how you can be living and not living, present and absent, so immersed I've been in the Portuguese folk-tales."[66] Bourne found life dull without Elsie. He wrote, complaining, "You haven't written me this summer, and I hope it is because you are still doing fieldwork in some strange region or writing your folk-lore journal."[67]

For her part, Elsie had developed a new ideal, which she could not always practice but which brought her a certain détente with the world. To Bourne, she remarked, "How much you expect of things *as they are!* Is that youth or immaturity? I have found less expectations of things ahead, for myself and for the world; but each moment I take what's in it and don't grumble."[68]

The intensity of Bourne's critical flame also burned low. In 1918, he wrote Elsie, "The war has practically passed out of my consciousness, and, like you, I read the papers almost without emotion." But the pull of their friendship had not diminished. He continued, "I wonder where you are now. Lenox does not seem far away; I wish it were near enough to run up for tea."[69] Bourne was reflecting on his life: "I started a novel, autobiographic about my childhood. It turned out incredibly bad, after 15,000 words or so, but I may start on a new tack. I feel more like a literary man this summer than usual. I should have been more successful in the past if I had seen that this was my doom."[70]

Elsie's good friend, Clarence Day, expressed his displeasure with Elsie's absence through verse and humor. When she left to collect folktales in South Carolina, Day wrote:

> I hate to be forsaken
>   My heart dislikes to break.
> But Elsie's gone to Aiken
>   And left me here to ache.[71]

Of her Southwest work, he complained, "You never say anything much to me anyway—except about Zuni when I turn in desperation to them and unlock you on that side if I can't from others—so I end with my head as full of Zunis as it once was of hair and have to comb them out all the evening."[72]

All of her friends noted the change in Elsie's writing. Bourne expressed his reservations about this, as well as about the import of her subject matter. Thanking her for an article, he commented, "Is it a little too packed with data, do you think? I like you best when you are talking yourself, and there was not enough of you playing around the subject."[73] Day humorously decried the direction her thought had taken. On receipt of "The Teleological Dimension," her critique of cultural evolutionary theory, Day wrote, "Elsie what *do* you mean by saying that the spread of ethnological knowledge will undermine the theory of lowly cultural beginnings? Did the missing link know how to play the piano?" In a postscript he added, "What I mean is—however irregular and ebb-and-flowing the cultural movement has been, and however far below the apex we may conceivably be at this moment, the beginnings were on the whole lowly, weren't they? There has been on the whole an advance? Eh? Good God! If I get out of touch with you for more than a month or so I always find myself behind the times."[74] Signe Toksvig was more blunt. She wrote Elsie that she should not "continue to bury" herself in the United States, that in England she would have "far more intelligent appreciation" of her work. She continued, "You'd be forced to write there; people would demand it: it would be forbidden that you should concern yourself with noting down the difference between Tsola and Tsóla! (a very small squirrel & a tiny squirrel)." Toksvig added that it should be Parsons's "exclusive business to think about human absurdities and to publish" her thoughts on the subject. "There is enough for a life work."[75]

With great fondness for Elsie, Day parodied the exotic customs about which she wrote. On receipt of her article concerning adoption into the Hopi tribe through ritual headwashing, he wrote, "Elsie! Wait! If there's going to be all this adopting of you into Indian tribes I'm coming right up. I'm an Indian. I've never told you but I used to be a regular Mopi before I met you, and I want to adopt you into my present tribe which is much better but the name is secret. I'll be there Monday. Please have your hair ready—We don't wash it in my tribe, we just cut a lock of it off. That's why mine's almost gone. I am bringing a bowl of chop-suey and two ceremonial kisses." He said there was "a vacancy" in her "list of relatives by adoption." She had "a father mother aunt etc but no uncle." He continued, "Put me down on your card as uncle, at once. As to the ritual song, I am practising hard but may need your help. It's a combination of Home Sweet Home and the Star Spangled B[anner] and I do wish you'd learn them. Your name in my tribe will be Gr-row-wow-but-but, which literally translated means The Biting Why-teller." He added, "Your Sichumovi ms is full of interest and fun," and closed "Your affect[ionate] uncle."[76]

In only a slightly more serious vein, Day created "Portrait of a Lady," an account of Elsie's fieldwork in the Sea Islands of South Carolina. He reminded her, "Elsie dear. You remember that account I wrote of your Sea Island trip. You said it wouldn't interest anybody.

Haha! One on you! The New Republic wants to publish it. . . . They want to print it just as I wrote it, referring to you as 'Elsie,' but not giving your last name; so it will be anonymous to those who don't know of you."[77] On receipt of her telegram that gave him permission to publish the article, Day responded, "I'd have been delighted . . . if only you hadn't used that word 'copy.' " He suggested that perhaps she had used "it in some good sense." However, if not, he said, "I'd bury that Sea Island letter and the New Repub[lic] along with it, before I'd use you as 'copy.' It would make me squirm the rest of my life." He continued, "Of course the Sea Island letter is only a glimpse of you—a very imperfect portrayal. (. . . I wanted a whole set of pictures that would let me paint some of your other sides if I only could.) But in its incomplete way it does give a taste of your flavor, and I think and hope it is an authentic taste, and that's why I want to share it."[78]

In his humorous and satirical "Portrait of a Lady," Day described Elsie as constantly searching for and journeying to some corner of the continent that interested her. He wrote, "In between, she lives with the rest of us—she has to—and conforms to our ways, or to most of them anyhow, just as Stefansson does with the Eskimos: she wears the usual tribal adornments, and bead-work, and skins, and she sleeps and eats in the family's big stone igloo near Fifth Avenue. An unobservant citizen might almost suppose she was one of us. But every now and then her neglect of some small ceremonial sets the whole tribe to chattering about her, and eying her closely, and nodding their hairy coiffures or their tall shiny hats, whispering around their lodge-fires, evenings, that Elsie is queer." He wrote of her sojourn on the Sea Islands, of her misadventures as the guest of a white family who guarded her from the black inhabitants of the island, of meeting up with Mr. Jack who was "chock-full of folk-lore," and with James Bone who had "a cart as well as a horse. They all got in this cart and went cruising away into the interior. It was raining like hell, I forgot to say, but they didn't much mind. . . . It was dark now . . . and Mr. Jack and James Bone were tired. The expedition conferred. James Bone said they could go to some friends . . . who had a large house with five rooms in it. So they steered for this landmark. But when they arrived, very late, all the five rooms were found to be full. . . . But James Bone was insistent. He went indoors and stirred them up with a great deal of talk and excitement. . . . [They] somehow packed themselves into three rooms, and gave up the two best to Elsie, who promptly retired." Here Elsie stayed in complete comfort, for "she could smoke all she wished, she had a fireplace, and the cooking was good."[79] She filled her notebook with tales and then, along with Mr. Jack, put to sea again in search of another island and its inhabitants.

In spite of her friend's teasing and remonstrances, Elsie had selected her enterprise, and her choice was anthropology. Her solution to the weariness she felt with the world was physical withdrawal. She simply left—to do fieldwork, to explore the customs and lifeways of others, to luxuriate in the freedom this brought to her, to do science. This withdrawal from her own society was part of a change in Parsons's life plan. In a real sense, her work in anthropology would be a reversal of her earlier work in sociology. She had relinquished her involvement in political movements; she was no longer tied to change in social order. Her work would not be directed toward the elucidation of broad, general statements about society, as it had been in her earlier publications. She turned from the general to the minute, to the mosaic of social data, as Gladys Reichard described Parsons's work. However, embedded in this mosaic, there would still be the critique of social custom, though it would be softer and less harsh than that directed against American society, for, as Franz Boas said of her, she was "intolerant towards ourselves, [and] tolerant towards others."[80]

NOTES

1. Walter Lippmann, *Drift and Mastery* (orig. publ. 1914; Englewood Cliffs, N.J.: Prentice-Hall, 1961), pp. 16–17.

2. Eric J. Sandeen, *The Letters of Randolph Bourne* (New York: Whitson Publishing Co., 1981), p. 269.

3. For a discussion of the *New Republic* crowd and Greenwich Village, see John Adam Moreau, *Randolph Bourne* (Washington, D.C.: Public Affairs Press, 1966).

4. Henry May, *The End of American Innocence* (New York: Alfred A. Knopf, 1959), p. 284. The Liberal Club had been founded by the Reverend Percy Grant to foster reform and to promote liberal discussion. The group divided, with the more radical members following Henrietta Rodman to Greenwich Village. See Sandeen, *Letters,* p. 282, n. 2.

5. William O'Neill, *The Last Romantic* (New York: Oxford University Press, 1978), p. 28. For another view of Greenwich Village at this time, see Moreau, *Randolph Bourne,* pp. 96–97; and for the intellectual milieu of the times, see Arthur Frank Wertheim, *The New York Little Renaissance* (New York: New York University Press, 1976).

6. May, *End of American Innocence,* pp. 303–4.

7. Christopher Lasch, *The New Radicalism in America* (New York: Alfred A. Knopf, 1965), p. xv.

8. May, *End of American Innocence*, p. 282.

9. Alvin Johnson, *Pioneer's Progress* (New York: The Viking Press, 1952), pp. 278, 275. Judith Modell, *Ruth Benedict* (Philadelphia: University of Pennsylvania Press, 1983), p. 111, quoting *New School Bulletin 1919*, p. 5. Margaret M. Caffrey, *Ruth Benedict* (Austin: University of Texas Press, 1989), pp. 95–97.

10. ECP, Bourne to ECP, 4 July. For a discussion of Bourne's and Parsons's friendship, see Bruce Clayton, *Forgotten Prophet, The Life of Randolph Bourne* (Baton Rouge: Louisiana State University Press, 1984).

11. ECP, Gregory to ECP, 21 Sept. 1923.

12. Bourne, "The Handicapped," *Atlantic Monthly* 108 (Sept. 1911): 321.

13. Sandeen, *Letters*, p. 8.

14. ECP, copy of letter to the *Evening Post*, dated 25 Dec. 1918. Elsie sent a copy of this letter to Herbert, saying, "Randolph Bourne died this week of pneumonia. The newspaper notices were so inadequate I felt like writing the enclosed" (ECP, ECP to HP, 25 Dec. 1918).

15. ECP, Goldenweiser to ECP, 12 Mar. 1920.

16. Lasch, *The New Radicalism*, p. ix. See also Sandeen, *Letters*, p. 5.

17. Louis Mumford, "The Image of Randolph Bourne," *New Republic* 64 (24 Sept. 1930): 151.

18. Sandeen, *Letters*, p. 344. Sandeen is quoting a letter from Bourne to Elizabeth Sheply Sergeant, 15 Nov. 1915. He had been staying in Dublin, New Hampshire, in a colony of intellectuals. See pp. 318 and 322 for Bourne's description of Dublin. Amy Lowell was "an American poet and an eccentric member of the famous Lowell family" (p. 317, n. 3).

19. Bourne Papers, ECP to Bourne, 22 Sept. 1916; n.d. [fall 1915?].

20. ECP, Bourne to ECP, 2 June 1916; 25 Oct. 1911; 3 Aug. 1916.

21. Bourne Papers, ECP to Bourne, 28 Oct. 1915.

22. A typewritten list included among the Parsons Papers listed the following members of the Heretics: Randolf [*sic*] Bourne; Evans Clark; Henderson Deady; Herman Defrem; Adolf Elwyn; Pliny Goddard; Alexander Goldenweiser; Alyse Gregory; Alcan Hirsch; Harry Hollingsworth; Leta Hollingsworth; Charlotte Howell; Herschel Jones; Edward Kasner; Arthur Kellogg; Freda Kirchwey; Alfred Kuttner; Margaret Lane; Winthrop Lane; David Mitchell; William Montague; Helen Parkhurst; Maurice Parmelee; Elsie Clews Parsons; Henrietta Rodman; Benoy Sarkar; Salwyn Shapiro; Theodore Schroeder; Inis Weed.

23. Bourne Papers, ECP to Bourne, 28 Oct. 1915. The Liberal Club was located in a loft on McDougal Street in Greenwich Village. See David Kennedy, *Birth Control in America, the Career of Margaret Sanger* (New Haven: Yale University Press, 1970), p. 8.

24. ECP, Organizers of the Supper Club (Alice Carpenter, Alice Duer Miller, Walter Lippmann, Rose Pastor Stokes, and Ernest Poole) wrote a letter of invitation for membership to Herbert Parsons, 31 Jan. 1916. Members of the Supper Club were listed as follows: Mrs. Mary Heaton Vorse, Mr. Max Eastman, Mrs. Borden Harriman, Mrs. Elsie Clews Parsons, Mrs. Ernest

Poole, Mr. Francis K. Hackett, Mrs. Frank Cothren, Mrs. Ogden Mills Reid, Mr. J. G. Phelps Stokes, Mrs. Norman de R. Whitehouse, Miss Ida Rauh, Mrs. Rose Pastor Stokes, Mr. San A. Lewisohn, Mr. Henry Wise Miller, Miss Mary E. Coffin.

25. ECP, Bourne to ECP, 15 June [1916]. On the Ferrer School, see Sandeen, *Letters*, p. 227, n. 8.

26. Parsons, "Must We Have Her?," *New Republic*, 10 June 1916, pp. 145–46.

27. ECP, Bourne to ECP, 15 June [1916].

28. Sandeen, *Letters*, p. 366, quoting Bourne to Dorothy Teall, 21 Apr. 1916.

29. ECP, ECP to W. P. Montague, [June 1916?].

30. Bourne Papers, ECP to Bourne, 14 June 1916.

31. ECP, Henry Clews to ECP, 22 June 1917.

32. ECP, John Parsons to HP, 23 Apr. 1917.

33. ECP, John Parsons to HP, 18 Nov. 1918.

34. *New York Times*, 25 Jan. 1919, p. 1, col. 4, p. 4, col 6.

35. Parsons, Letter to editor, *New York Tribune*, 22 Jan. 1918, p. 8, col. 4.

36. Letter to editor, *New York Times*, 10 Jan. 1915, sec. 3, p. 2, col. 6.

37. ECP, L. Hollingsworth Wood to ECP, 11 Jan. 1915. Among the leaders of the group were Nicholas Murray Butler, George Foster Peabody, and Abraham Jacobi, who was Franz Boas's uncle.

38. ECP, L. Hollingsworth Wood to ECP, 16 Jan. 1915.

39. ECP, Elizabeth Gurley Flynn to ECP, 6 Dec. 1917.

40. ECP, ECP to Elizabeth Gurley Flynn, 10 Dec. 1917.

41. ECP, Elizabeth Gurley Flynn to ECP, 13 Dec. 1917.

42. ECP Bourne to ECP, 28 May [1917]. For information on the *New Republic*, see David W. Noble, *The Paradox of Progressive Thought* (Minneapolis: University of Minnesota Press, 1958), pp. 34–77.

43. ECP, Bourne to ECP, 9 May 1917.

44. ECP, Bourne to ECP, 4 Feb. 1918.

45. O'Neill, *Last Romantic*, p. xvii.

46. *The Masses* 5, no. 1 (Oct. 1913): 2.

47. O'Neill, *Last Romantic*, p. 34.

48. ECP, Eastman to ECP, 26 June 1916.

49. Sandeen, *Letters*, p. 351.

50. ECP, Bourne to ECP, 29 July 1918.

51. Sandeen, *Letters*, p. 352.

52. ECP, Bourne to ECP, 12 Sept. 1918; 29 July 1918.

53. ECP, Bourne to ECP, 1 Sept. 1917; 9 May 1917; 1 Sept. 1917.

54. Parsons, "The Teleological Delusion," *Journal of Philosophy, Psychology and Scientific Method* 14 (Aug. 1917): 465; "The Wonder," *New Republic*, 10 Nov. 1917, p. 56.

55. Parsons, "Patterns for Peace or War," *Scientific Monthly* 5 (Sept. 1917): 231.

56. May, *End of American Innocence*, p. 28.

57. Parsons, "Patterns for Peace or War," p. 231.

58. ECP, Bourne to ECP, 15 June [1916].

59. Bourne Papers, ECP to Bourne, 24 June 1916.

60. ECP, unpublished manuscript, "A Confession of Faith."

61. ECP, ECP to HP, 21 Nov. 1917; Alfred Louis Kroeber Papers, ECP to Kroeber, 11 May 1917.

62. ECP, Louis Lochner to ECP, 22 June 1917.

63. Bourne Papers, ECP to Bourne, 5 Feb. 1916.

64. ECP, ECP to HP, 16 Feb. 1918; 9 Mar. 1918.

65. ECP, Bourne to ECP, nd.

66. Bourne Papers, ECP to Bourne, 22 May 1917; 22 Sept. 1916.

67. ECP, Bourne to ECP, 7 Sept. 1916.

68. Bourne Papers, ECP to Bourne, 28 Oct. 1915.

69. ECP, Bourne to ECP, 29 July 1918.

70. ECP, Bourne to ECP, 29 July 1918.

71. ECP, Day to ECP [1920].

72. ECP, Day to ECP, 21 Dec. 1917.

73. ECP, Bourne to ECP, 9 Sept. 1915.

74. ECP, Day to ECP, 14 Sept. [1917].

75. ECP, Toskvig to ECP, 26 Aug. 1923.

76. ECP, Day to ECP, 4 Aug. 1920.

77. ECP, Day to ECP, 29 June 1919.

78. ECP, Day to ECP, Thursday [1919].

79. Clarence Day, "Portrait of a Lady," *New Republic*, 23 July 1919, pp. 387, 388, 389.

80. Boas, "Elsie Clews Parsons, Late President of the American Anthropological Association," *Scientific Monthly* 54 (May 1942): 483.

7

Observations of Other Worlds

In February of 1940, on receipt of *Pueblo Indian Religion*, Judge Learned Hand wrote a note of thanks to Elsie Clews Parsons. Couched in this discursive, slightly strange note is the following observation on her predilection for observation: "I think she took up anthropology because she was always disposed to look at folks from a little distance anyway. Why was she so disposed? Ah, that you never found out. Maybe you couldn't; probably she doesn't know. But that is a strong trait in her. People say it is because she doesn't care; but that isn't quite it. You know as much as that."[1]

Long before she was involved in anthropology or folklore, Elsie Clews was by choice an observer. In one of her first letters to Herbert, she had written, "It is so much easier to be a looker on than an actor and I always return to my vantage point of observation after brief desertions therefrom the more convinced of this truth." "Why was she so disposed?" Judge Hand had asked in 1940. In 1896, she had answered the question. She had just spoken of her view of death and its finality. She added, "It is a very bitter point of view and one to be ignored as much as possible." Elsie's solution to unpleasant things that could not be altered was just that, to ignore them. Playfully she wrote, at the age of twenty-two, "Do you know I am getting more and more cowardly in my old age and the things I wish to ignore accumulate." Penned in her young hand, Elsie had marked a course for her life, one from which she temporarily deviated. Under Herbert's influence, she laid aside her role of observer: "It seems to me that I am learning much just now chiefly through unlearning much. In the first place, I have turned my back on my old part of looker on. . . . You can't know what a vital change the dismissal of it means for your friend who is so set in her ways."[2] This was not to last, for she soon reverted to her customary stance. In "The Imaginary Mistress," a thinly veiled autobiographical account, Elsie described the protagonist—herself—as "an intellectual woman . . . possessed of an extraordinary facility . . .

for detaching herself from her experience, for viewing it and even acting upon it impersonally." Noting this aspect of Elsie's personality, Antonio Luhan, a Taos Indian, remarked that she was "as deep as a well." Elsie said, "He may not know that it is not merely because I have to be [this for the requisite secrecy of her fieldwork] but because I like to be. I like the cool feeling of it."[3]

Initially Elsie's fieldtrips grew out of her travels. At one point she became impatient traveling as a tourist, and determined she would no longer do so. She also grew impatient traveling with others, and decided she would travel alone. But there was an overlap in these two sorts of journeying. She began her trips to the Caribbean in 1911, accompanied by her friend, Kirk Brice. She was still traveling for pleasure and adventure, though her interest in the folklore of this area began at this time. Of her trip to Nassau in the Bahamas, she wrote Herbert, "Both afternoons and evenings we have sailed away & had beach suppers. Today we are off for overnight. There are strings of little islands, pretty beaches & warm and friendly water. Some say sharks & some say none; but I am not taking chances. . . . Sailing and swimming are all one feels like doing." She told Herbert, "Our presence will be advertized from the odds and ends of acquaintances we have met to N. Y. C., Washington, Newport, Boston." In another letter, she added, " 'Poor Herbert'—the men are saying—with Kirk."[4]

Elsie returned to the Caribbean the next year for "the Pirate Cruise," an adventure masterminded by John T. McCutcheon. Elsie, McCutcheon, Brice, and Katherine Dexter set sail for Nassau. En route, Elsie, John, and Kirk took a detour to the Andros Islands in a small boat, at Elsie's suggestion. By moonlight, they sailed over "the tumbling, sinister white waters of a reef," waded to shore equipped only with a flashlight, and slept on the beach. In the morning, they set sail for Nassau, only to meet the Tongue of Ocean, a treacherous stretch of current and wind. With their craft swamped and all hands bailing frantically, they managed to land at Mastic Point. The inhabitants declared, " 'It was an act of God. . . . No boat can cross the reef!' " Their chartered ship, the *Heather,* came to their rescue, but Elsie, "still game and venturesome," decided to sail to Nassau on the local schooner, the *Sundog.* McCutcheon, who wrote about this in *Drawn from Memory,* accompanied her. They fell asleep on the deck "between the charcoal brazier and a heap of conch shells . . . with the helmsman's song as lullaby and the creaking shrouds and swaying masts outlined against a brilliant tropic sky." The four of them sailed on to "the mountainous shore of northern Haiti," where they observed the mid-Lenten festivities. McCutcheon notes, "The evident hostility of the people made us uncomfortable, so we soon returned to the *Heather*."⁵

It was in her 1914 European travels with Grant La Farge that Elsie determined she could no longer travel as a tourist. She wrote Herbert from Messina, Sicily, of the trip to Pompeii and Paestum." "From the start the motor put me in an awful temper . . . so I didn't enjoy the trip and I fear I spoiled much of Grant's enjoyment. . . . As a matter of fact I'm spoiled for a tourist." She referred to her trip with Herbert to northern Europe in 1902, and said that since then "I've so entirely changed my way of enjoying things and I know quite well I can't expect other people to enjoy doing things the way I do. I'd much better travel alone." In Gibraltar, Elsie grew impatient with the organized tours, especially one that went through tunnels in the face of a rock, "Of such herding I am more intolerant, I find, than ever, and I fell to thinking with regret of the last fortress I had scaled, a ruin holding mesa above the Jemez River."⁶ The freedom and expanse of the Southwest exerted a hold over Elsie. Her memories of the pueblos and the mesas had become a standard for measuring other experiences.

Elsie's interest in the Southwest was first awakened in the months before her marriage when she had planned a honeymoon trip aboard the Santa Fe railroad for the Indian country of New Mexico and Arizona. It was not until August, 1910, that Herbert and Elsie briefly visited the Southwest, while on a more extensive journey to national parks in the West. As she related in her manuscript, "In the Southwest," Herbert, as a member of the Committee on Public Lands, made a visit to the Grand Canyon with a forester who was not inclined to have Elsie join them. Instead, Elsie traveled to Santa Fe where she intended to rent a horse and explore the country. She presented her letters of introduction to the federal officials of the Department of the Interior. As she wrote, "They were nice fellows but one had never been on a horse . . . and the other kept advising me that the country was very rough indeed." She attempted to rent a horse on her own, but this also did not work. Revising her plans, Elsie caught the train to Española. On the train, she met a woman who said she "could supply me with a pony that would out match any livery stable horse." This woman was Clara True, who invited Elsie to stay at her Pajarito Ranch, adjacent to the Pueblo of San Ildefonso.

Pony and Indian boy as guide were quickly supplied, the pony had spirit, and we galloped across the valley with a dash that was a little overthrilling—I had ridden all my life but this was the

first time I had ridden cross saddle. . . . There was a scramble up
the canyon by steep cross-cuts known to the boy and then across
the tablelands a long stretch of delightful, easy riding—by this
time I was more at home in the Mexican saddle and my knees
began to have a grip in them. . . . At the ruins . . . I wandered in
and out of the skeleton of that partly excavated town in the edge
of the mesa . . . and as I examined the wall niches and hearths,
the lintels and passages I tried to reconstruct the past as one always does in ruins that allure. . . . Presently I was beset by that
infantile impulse to dig which sublimated a bit . . . turns people
into archaeologists.

Learning of Elsie's desire to excavate, True directed her toward a
square house ruin on her property and sent her off with Pedro Baca,
a Santa Clara Indian, to assist her, and a pack burro to carry the
equipment. Setting up camp for the night, Elsie selected a cave that,
as she described, provided a "frame on the moonlit talus below and
the pines beyond." She reflected that "one was fortunate indeed to
live for a time in a world of such beauty." In the course of excavating
a ceremonial mound, Elsie found herself intrigued not so much by
the artifacts that she unearthed or the shape of the chamber that
was revealed, but rather by the reactions of Pedro Baca, by what he
said and what he refused to say. Communicative about the mundane,
he would respond to any question about a ceremonial object with
" 'Don't know.' " As she wrote, "I am more curious about what he
would not tell me and why he would not tell than about any particular
of the excavation." She added, "If ever I come to work seriously in this
country I suspect that it will not be as archaeologist, but as a student
of the culture of today. It is interesting to reconstruct the culture of
the ancient town builders, but it is still more interesting to study the
minds and ways of their descendants."[7]

During the course of the year, Elsie systematically pursued her interest in the Southwest. In a notebook labeled "American Ethnology
SW," she included information on "Bibliographical Notes, Addresses,
Plans, Problems." On the page marked "Plans," she had written,
"Make close topographical study elevations. *Water supply.* Chart all
bluff rock formations for artificial cave dwellings & sandstone (long
lodges over precipitous slopes or vertical wall for cliff-dwellings)." She
made a list of things she needed to learn: sketching in water colors,
Spanish, cooking, crosssaddle riding, fauna and flora of the South-
west, and masonry. She wrote, "Cultivate Holmes W. H. Chief of
Am[erican] B[ureau] of E[thnology]. Also Hodge. Boas, Nat[ural]

H[istory] M[useum] Goddard. *Spinden.* Learn Anthropological measuring. Practice with pistol, with compass." Tucked in the leaves of the notebook, Elsie had slipped a letter from Frederick Hodge, dated October 31, 1910, relating to her query about an archaeological map of the Southwest, of which the bureau had none.[8]

Elsie laid plans for her return the following year. She obtained information from the School of American Archaeology, in Santa Fe, New Mexico, pertaining to work in progress during 1912, as well as to the U.S. regulations for the excavation of ruins. She sent inquiries about excavating "Pu-Ye Cliff, at Pajarito Cliff . . . in Jemez Forest." A colleague of Herbert's from the Republican National Committee, Charles D. Hilles, requested permission for her from a representative of the Department of the Interior. He was informed quite tactfully that following the act of June 8, 1906, excavation was limited to "reputable museums, universities, colleges, and other recognized scientific or educational institutions." The official requested that "Mrs. Parsons [explain] the reasons actuating her in asking this permit, complying with Paragraph 5 of the rules as nearly as she can," and that with this information, he would seek recommendations from the Smithsonian for her excavations. Hilles wrote Parsons of the results. Since a request for permission to excavate was subject to the regulations of three departments, he saw little hope of a waiver. He concluded, "I doubt if anything can be done, except for you to make formal application, which must be referred to the Smithsonian Institution for recommendation."[9]

As part of her list of plans for the study of the ethnology of the Southwest, Elsie had noted, "Visit museum collections—National Museum, Amer. Mus. Nat. Hist., Field Columbian Mus." Prior to her trip to the Southwest in September, 1912, she contacted Henry Fairfield Osborn of the American Museum of Natural History, who in turn wrote to the director, Frederic A. Lucas, "Mrs. Herbert Parsons leaves on Friday, for . . . New Mexico to visit an Apache dance. . . . She will be glad to observe or collect for us. Are any of our Indian men in the Museum? Will you kindly arrange for Mrs. Parsons to see our Apache material."[10] In this way, Elsie met one of the museum's "Indian men," Pliny Earle Goddard. As Lucas reported to Osborn, "Dr. Goddard met Mrs. Parsons and showed her our collections; gave her letters of introduction to the Agency physician and the best interpreter." Goddard also provided Elsie with a letter of introduction to the archaeologist, N. C. Nelson, as well as a catalogue of the Spinden collection from the Rio Grande so that she might know where the lacunae lay in the holdings.[11]

Goddard conveyed to Elsie "by messenger" a copy of *Jicarilla Texts,* along with "a short popular account of the pottery of the Rio Grande Valley by Dr. Spinden." Counseling Elsie on her plans to film the Apache dances, Goddard wrote, "I have consulted Mr. Chapman, curator of ornithology, who has a great deal of experience with moving picture cameras. He said that one without previous experience could not hope to get good films. Had there been sufficient time, you could have practiced a little with the camera and probably been able to secure pictures." Goddard encouraged Elsie "to visit Mr. Nelson's work in the Galisteo Valley." He added, "Mrs. Nelson is with him and I think they will be able to make you comfortable should you care to stay some days." Goddard wrote to Nels C. Nelson, "This is to introduce to you Mrs. Herbert E. Parsons of New York City who is much interested in the ethnology and archaeology of the Southwest. Kindly give her every opportunity to see your work and the ruins of Galisteo Valley." He also sent a letter of introduction to Edward Ladd, who, as he said, was "the best educated and influential Jicarilla Apache." Goddard advised Elsie, "If you find him at the feast he will be able to give you a great deal of information about the dance and I think will be inclined to do so."[12]

Elsie's trip was exhilarating. She wrote Herbert of "the glory of this place," and longed to share it all with him. As she said, "I do wish you could see and feel it." Of her trip on horseback to the Apache dances, she wrote, "I hope your work was as enjoyable, but not as hard as mine. I could not have stood it outside of New Mexico. We rode about 230 miles, including 36 the afternoon I arrived here from Santa Fe. The same horses and a pack animal's gait. Too cold at night for me ever to sleep sound, & never any time to rest at the mid day's stop. At the end of our 30 miles yesterday morning under an unmitigated sun & with weary horses, I was all in, but today I have rested up, and the sun burn pains in my face have gone."[13]

With the help of traveling companion Clara True, Elsie began "ethnological pursuits of evenings around the camp fire." She also began gathering artifacts for the American Museum of Natural History, a yield that was not too rich, for as she said, "So far my collecting for the Museum consists of the washed up drum cast after last year's feast into the lake." Elsie continued, "The Apache encampment was most interesting. Scattered tepees over a rolling pasture land. It was a sort of stage box to which all day long all kinds of visitors came. Santa Clara Indian friends, Indians from other pueblos with pottery or fruit to peddle. Apaches to sell horses . . . ranching white men, &

strange-looking white women from Dulce, the Apache settlement. But what brought us most visitors were our 4 beaver skins. The Indians braid their hair with beaver fur, and word going abroad that we had it, they came to look at it, hankering like a Fifth Ave. shopper." There were foot races, but very little dancing. As Elsie said, "We saw nothing ceremonial." The Apaches told them that "they were too poor this year to pay for ceremonies." Elsie added, "They may also have been too drunk the night the ceremony was due. And so we brought back the beaver skins wh[ich] C[lara] T[rue] had taken as an admission bribe."[14]

Elsie wrote Goddard about the Apache dance at Laguna Piedra, during which the ceremonial drum is thrown into the lake: "One of these old drums, the hollowed out section of a cottonwood tree (?), had been washed up, & we secured it. The Apaches themselves would of course not touch it; nor would the Santa Clara Indian who told us about it." She asked Goddard if he wanted it for the museum collection. It was, she said, "quite bare of any decoration and . . . rather bulky, standing about three feet high." She stressed that sending it would be "somewhat troublesome," and that she would not do so unless, as she said, "you *really* want it." Of her ethnological work, she reported, "I made some excellent relations in Santa Clara, but I needed a little more time (I was away only three weeks) to get any ceremonial things. However, I think Miss True will get some for us this winter. She has unequalled opportunities."[15]

Goddard responded to Elsie's letter thanking her for the information about the Apache drum, and, as he said, "to the fact that it is thrown into the lake of which I was not aware." He was most interested in receiving the drum for the museum's collection, on the condition that "it is not too difficult for Miss True to get it to the station." Goddard encouraged Elsie in her interests: "I believe there are problems in the Southwest and perhaps other wheres [*sic*] in North America that you are better prepared to investigate and present than anyone else because of your special work in the sociological field. I am particularly glad that you are interested in the practices among the Pueblos of the Rio Grande Valley and hope you will be able to secure the required material."[16]

The following year in 1913, Elsie was en route to the Southwest when she unexpectedly met up with her friends from "the Pirate's Cruise," Kirk Brice and John McCutcheon, who were on their way to join an Apache deer hunt in Arizona. Elsie was anxious to visit Acoma, for, as she said, it was reputedly "the most beautifully placed pueblo of them all . . . on a high almost entirely sheer mesa." Though there was no scheduled stop, she recounted to Herbert that John Mc-Cutcheon, "powerful man that he is, got no. 3 California Limited stopped for me."[17] In her manuscript entitled "In the Southwest," she wrote of this experience:

A few years ago The Atchison, Topeka and Santa Fe Railroad straightened out a curve and moved its Laguna station three miles to the west of the pueblo. A town, New Laguna people call it, is now growing up around the station; but the noonday that the California Limited made an unscheduled stop at Laguna to my advantage, there was nothing alongside the railway but sage and greasewood, station building and the section house. . . . To make that trip of sixteen miles down the southern valley plain I found an Overland car which by good luck had just been driven in to the station by its demonstrator-agent, Mr. Clack, once of the Panhandle of Texas now of Gallup. With Mr. Clack was a Mexican acquaintance who at Acoma introduced Mr. Clack as his cousin, and me as the wife of Mr. Clack, to take off for the Indians the edge of unfamiliarity.

In exchange for this courtesy I told the men the little I knew of the mesa-built town; of the feat of its capture by the Spaniards and of how, years later, the Franciscan friar escaped to Zuñi, his robe turning parachute when they threw him off the cliff, a legend of truly medieval flavor.[18]

Elsie found Acoma to be "rewarding from both a scenic & an ethnological point of view." Mr. Clack she regarded as her "knight errant . . . as unexpected a treasure as any I ever found." On parting, he said to her, " 'You's the most romantic woman I ever met.' "[19]

Elsie returned to the Southwest in August, 1915. Detailing the plans for her trip, she wrote Herbert, "My first post office address will be Gallup, New Mexico. I'll outfit there. I've written Clara True to join me or send me on one of good Santa Clara men. Also Goddard has written about me to Kroeber, the man working at Zuñi for the Museum. I'll be in time for the 'dances' at Hopi."[20]

Elsie arrived too late to meet Alfred Kroeber. He wrote to her, "Dr. Goddard's note telling me of your visit finds me with my suitcase packed, but I hope our meeting is only deferred." He suggested that she meet "Mr. Kelsey, who is boss among the Americans at Zuni. . . . His hospitality is somewhat curbed by his cook; but a friendly word will go far with the lovely old lady, and may prove of service if you wish the most orthodox accommodations obtainable." His interpreters, he said, would "prove of little service." One was "too young and timid," another too intent on impressing the people for whom he worked, and still another was a witch and, Kroeber warned, "would get you in bad with everyone else." He strongly urged Elsie, should she intend to stay in Zuni "for more than a day . . . to lay your plans before [Margaret Lewis, the governor's wife] . . . and ask her advice how to carry them out." He closed, assuring Elsie that "if you take to [the Zunis] as I did, you will think your trip worth while."[21]

Her fieldwork went well. She wrote Herbert, "This place is a huge success—so I'm staying here all my time & not going on to the Hopi country." She had followed Kroeber's advice, the result being that she was especially pleased with her accommodations, "I'm staying in the Zuni Governor's house, the house Kroeber of the Nat. Hist. Mus. lived in. The woman is an extremely well educated Cherokee, once a schoolteacher here & she is a great help."[22]

This connection with the governor's wife would be crucial for Elsie's fieldwork. Margaret Lewis had come to Zuni from Oklahoma in 1900 to teach school. Elsie described her as "one of those Cherokee who are descended from three races at least. Her language, dress, and more superficial ways of life appertained to one culture; her ease and grace and suavity were to another; her hair and coloring, perhaps her grit, were Indian." Margaret Lewis's life in Zuni was lonely at first. As Elsie wrote,

I suspect she was snubbed by the few White people of the place. I have heard her say that nothing in the world would make her marry a white man. At any rate she learned to speak Zuni and in three or four years she married Lewis, one of her pupils. After a term of living with his parents until the way they spoiled and fed the babies became intolerable, she got them to build her a house on the north side, on new land rendered irrigable by the reservoir at Black Rock. Here she lived according to ways half White, half Zuni. Sometimes the family slept in bedsteads, sometimes on quilts on the floor. They always ate around a table, but the dishes were often native, sometimes contributed by the children's grandmother. When she had the money, Margaret preferred to buy things, much inferior things, from the store. . . . Her clan at home among the Cherokee, she had told the people, was Wolf. There being no Wolf clan proper at Zuni she was assimilated with the Coyote clan, her children belonging . . . , of course, to that clan. To all the native amenities of intercourse she was compliant, so that people felt at home with her and . . .

her house was frequented as much as any house in town. In those gubernatorial days in particular . . . there were many visitors.[23]

Margaret Lewis was an exceedingly competent woman, and there were those who said that her husband " 'wouldn't be governor but for her.' " Elsie witnessed her helping to solve a dispute over farming land that involved a Zuni whose pasture land had been encroached upon by Mexicans. The aggrieved Zuni and the Indian agent came to the Lewis's home. In fact, they settled themselves in Elsie's room, directly in front of the fireplace so that the agent was "conveniently placed to spit into it." Ostensibly the interpreter, Margaret Lewis acted as mediator. Elsie recalled, "Presently when the baby began to cry she asked the Governor to take it out to quiet it. The Governor had ingratiating ways with the baby, and besides he could be spared more readily than the interpreter who quite obviously was more than mere interpreter. In fact, while Lewis looked after the baby, Margaret transacted the business of the meeting, to the satisfaction alike of farmer and agent."[24]

Elsie surmised that in council meetings and on formal occasions, the governor acted on his own. However, much of the tribal business was transacted informally at the Lewis's home. She recalled, "One or another of the officers was always dropping in at the house, and sometimes a *shiwanni* [a priest], it was on these visits that her judgment and advice would be given."[25] When the governor and Margaret divorced, Elsie wondered how the council would manage without her advice. Elsie found the answer on one of her visits to Zuni: "Margaret said that they did not even try to get on, they kept coming to her to interpret and counsel just as if Lewis were still in the house. It flattered her, I think, yet as she had now gone back to teaching to maintain the family, she felt that the dependence of the politicians on her was importunate and excessive. . . . So one night she flatly told the little gathering of officers and priests that she could no longer take the responsibility they imposed upon her. 'But we have got used to you,' they urged, always a cogent reason for any policy in native eyes. She was firm. As is their way, they went on nagging. Finally a priest left the room to return shortly with the governor's cane—Lewis had removed the cane, of course, to his mother's house."[26] This was the official cane, silver topped and hung by a ribbon to the wall of the governor's house. On it was displayed an inscription dated 1863 from President Abraham Lincoln.[27] Other priests were called, and Margaret was installed as an officer of the council with "the rite of breathing from the cane."

After Elsie's departure from Zuni, Margaret Lewis wrote to her about the events of the pueblo. In her notebook labeled "Zuñi 1915, Ceremonialism, Shalako, Kewekewe," Elsie wrote, "Oct. 27. M. Lewis writes 'The Zuñis are working like bees, getting their corn, beans, 7 houses finished for Shalako [a winter ceremonial].' Also that Shalako was to be from Dec. 3–10." With this information, Elsie was able to plan her return trip in time for Shalako. In later years, Margaret would keep a calendar of ceremonial events for Elsie, with detailed daily entries. Elsie would also send her lists of questions that she needed answered to finish her writing. Margaret Lewis never failed in her diligence. She was as a partner in Elsie's work, for she shared her interest in the traditional ways of the Zuni. As she had told Elsie, she wanted the Zunis to maintain their ancient customs and their religious beliefs.[28]

The Lewis home became the center for anthropologists at Zuni, and Margaret Lewis apparently enjoyed the contacts. She kept Elsie informed about the anthropologists who were staying with her—about Kroeber's departure and Leslie Spier's continued presence, about Goddard, of whom she was very fond, and of Robert Lowie.[29] Years later, Lewis would reflect on her friendship with Elsie: "She was a real friend of my husband and me. We always wrote each other. She had four children, as I have, and they were born at the same times when mine were. We joked about it. Although she was very talkative, we enjoyed having her with us and she was also glad for that."[30]

Elsie had boarded the train in high spirits after her first trip to Zuni. She wrote Herbert en route, "I've had a hard but accomplishful jaunt." Rather than going directly home, she had decided to pass through New York, as she said, "to see Goddard & Kroeber & get some books I need to complete my articles, the fruit of the last two weeks of field work." From her August research in 1915, Elsie had found a place to which she could return in the future, one that met the exigencies of her life. As she expressed it, "In Zuñi, I shall have a great opportunity for brief periods of fieldwork, the thing I've been hankering for for years."[31]

Elsie did return again and again to the Southwest. Her fieldwork was planned both around the schedule of the Indians and that of her family. To Herbert's request that she postpone her departure, she dashed off a telegram, "Impossible to leave this Sunday. I am only going to South West to do necessary piece of work would not take that railway journey for any possible pleasure looking forward to seeing you on twenty-seventh." Leaving on another fieldtrip, she wrote, "It is a sort of shabby trick leaving you alone this time of year at Harrison, the spring is more cheerful; but it was so much the best time to leave

as far as the little boys were concerned, & a pretty good time, though
not the best which would interfere with the holiday season, as far as
my work was concerned, that I decided to go. If you have visitors out
or stay in town now and then perhaps you wont be so lonely after all
& I'll be back before you know it."[32]

Elsie had established two separate spheres, one at home and one in
the Southwest. She moved between them with an ease and fluidity of
which she spoke, "It is always a bit surprising to me how one can step
out into the world of adventure and then step back home to find it
just as one left it, only more so. The little boys even remembered the
page we had left off reading 'Alice in the Looking Glass.' "[33]

Her departures were always amply papered with lists of instructions. For medical emergencies, she advised, "Remember for any sign
of serious indigestion salt & water to induce vomiting & a large dose
of caster oil. For a cut, bichloride tablets. (You had much better get
them.) Take some whiskey too. Dont ask them if they are cold, just
feel their hands, particularly Lissa's." During her absence, her children were in the care of Mary Carmody, whom Elsie had met when
the latter was a maternity nurse for immigrant women. Miss Carmody
was conscientious and loving in the care of the children, and she
wrote frequent letters to Elsie keeping her informed about their
health. So much faith did Elsie place in the children's nurse that she
revised her will to have Miss Carmody listed as the guardian of John,
Herbert, and Mac (Lissa to remain under the guardianship of her
grandmother). With life planned for the care of her four children, she
departed, always careful to leave explicit information as to where she
could be reached. For her August fieldtrip in 1915, she added, after
the news of her work in Zuni, "Do let me know if anything goes
wrong, for it's the sort of situation where I'd like to come home if at
all needed."[34]

The children themselves were only tangentially connected with her
world of work. Wrote John to his mother, "Would you like me to make
anything particular [in work-shop] for you to give to the Zunis?" And
Mac wrote his father from boarding school, "Has Mother gone back
to her Indians yet?" In a piece entitled "Solidarity," Elsie recorded her
son's interest in her work: "One of our hosts down East wanted a book
about Indians. 'Send him that book you wrote, Mother. . . . Not interest him? Sure it will. There's some good stories in it and he can remember us by it."[35]

When her mother departed, Lissa assumed certain responsibility
for the care of her brothers. Still a child herself, at the age of thirteen,
she wrote her father the following note: "Did Mother get off all

right. . . . How are the little boys. I hope they are all right. John's cold is much better. He takes his inhaling and medicine very regularly and well like a good little boy should!?! Give my love and kisses to the babies and to you."[36] Of her mother's fieldtrips, Lissa recalled the drama of Elsie's return:

> She started going on them when I got into my teens. . . . She would come back to New York after one of them—looking, really, as my grandma said, perfectly dreadful, "scandalous," my grandmother said—because she wore khaki clothes and she had an old felt hat and she had been touching up her hair and of course it hadn't been touched up while she'd been away, so she wore a bandanna tied around it, and there [were] these saddle bags full of manuscripts. And she had string bags full of manuscripts. "Disreputable" was the word my grandmother would use, referring to the luggage. She would say, "Your mother is here, and that disreputable looking luggage in the front marble hall belongs to her."[37]

Apparently Elsie began planning secretive returns to her New York apartment. Lissa continued, "The two maids were there all the time, and they were under instructions never to let any of her friends . . . and . . . us know when she was returning from one of those trips. This absolutely fascinated me." But there were three people who knew: one who did her face; one, her nails; and one, her hair. "They were always informed beforehand, and they greeted her on the doorstep and whisked her in. And when she announced that she was back, she was all fixed up. And when mother was fixed up she was very beautiful."[38]

Through the years, her family continued to worry about her fieldtrips, so she resorted to subterfuge. As Ralph Beals recalled, "When she went off to Mexico or some similar trip, her family always raised objections—she was getting too old to be trusted alone!—so she would unobtrusively slip off . . . taking only an overnight bag and having stashed away other items she wished to take . . . —and simply take off, leaving no word where she was going. Some weeks later she would write and tell her family where she was and how long she intended to stay there, forbidding them to bother her except in extreme emergencies."[39]

Once in the field, Elsie settled in as well as she was able. As Beals remarked, "Elsie did not by the remotest flight of imagination 'go native.' . . . She lived as comfortably as circumstances allowed and in Mexico this meant living in whatever hotel or inn was available."

When there were no such accommodations, she willingly adapted, as she had done in Zuni.

In dress, Beals recalled, "Elsie cared very little for the local style or opinions." He described her presentation of self in the field: "She wore rather plain serviceable dresses and always wore a sort of shawl over her head, fastened back from her face by two clips or pins, giving on the whole a rather Egyptian effect. Inasmuch as she could not affect the styles and behavior of the locals, she tended to ignore them, on the grounds that whatever she did she would be conspicuous." In Mexico, because of her manner of dress, Parsons was taken for a gypsy, a *Húngara,* and asked, on occasion, to tell fortunes. To the people, she created a rather strange apparition. In Tepic, Beals remembered walking with Elsie in a middle-class neighborhood, "where a young man was showing off his new camera to a group of admiring girls and boys of his age. When he saw Elsie he called to the others to look while he moved into the street and snapped two or three pictures of her." Elsie, Beals said, "was about as furious as I ever saw her, yet could say nothing really for she had been . . . doing the same thing to others."[40] Margaret Lewis, too, commented on Elsie's style of dress: "She was a very rich lady, but you could not guess it. . . . She always dressed in sloppy dresses. One summer she brought white shoes with her. I thought that was funny and I told her so. She became mad, so I explained that when the rains come she would realize her mistake. I told her that anyone who comes to Zuni should know that it is not New York City. The roads are muddy here."[41]

Elsie was ready, Beals emphasized, to participate in all events: "She visited people in their homes or at work, tried to make friends and often did, spent long hours with them and often helped in household crises, usually with money." In appraising her abilities as a field-worker, Beals recalled an incident at Mitla when a large black dog had knocked over a baker's cooling trays in an attempt to get at freshly baked buns: "There was a . . . commotion heard over much of the town. Elsie promptly investigated to learn that this was what one could expect from a black dog, unfit to carry the soul across the river at death, in fact a creature of the devil." Beals concluded that this illustrated Elsie's attentiveness to the unusual and her keenness to search for "explanation and reactions." She was, Beals said, "a good ethnographer, constantly sensitive to her environment and alert to any way of getting to the thoughts and feelings of others."[42]

For Elsie, fieldwork, which had started as a reaction to the tedium of traveling as a tourist, became a central focus. In this, she could engage her mind, spirit, and intellect. She did so with total immersion.

Of Parsons's fieldwork, Gladys Reichard remarked, "Her success with natives, hosts of whom count themselves her friends, was due to an innate simplicity. She used to say that her idea of complete comfort was to have *at the same time* a cigarette, a cup of coffee, and an open fire. And characteristically she added quietly, 'You know it is very hard to get all three together. It is easier among Indians than among ourselves.' "[43]

Her work in the Southwest would continue, and she would return to the Caribbean to collect folktales. This new course for her life brought new connections. Through Goddard of the American Museum of Natural History, she had met Robert Lowie, who at that time was also on the staff of the museum; Alfred Louis Kroeber of the University of California, Berkeley; and the central figure in American anthropology, Franz Boas of Columbia University.[44] These men became her link to a new way of life, that of anthropologist.

NOTES

1. ECP, Judge Learned Hand to ECP, 9 Feb. 1940.

2. ECP, EC to HP, 19 Sept. 1896; 2 Aug. 1898.

3. Peter Hare, *A Woman's Quest for Science* (Buffalo, N.Y.: Prometheus Books, 1985), p. 67; Beinecke, ECP to Mabel Dodge Luhan, 10 Oct. 1922.

4. ECP, ECP to HP, Feb. 1911; 27 Feb. 1911.

5. John T. McCutcheon, *Drawn from Memory* (New York: Bobbs-Merrill Company, 1950), pp. 253, 254, 257.

6. ECP, ECP to HP, 27 Apr. 1914; 20 Apr. 1914.

7. Hare, *A Woman's Quest for Science*, pp. 127–29, quoting ECP's "The Accident of the Forester," in the unpublished manuscript, "In the Southwest." Elsie eventually acquired Pajarito Ranch from Clara True through a drawn-out settlement of a loan on which True defaulted.

8. ECP, Notebook on "American Ethnology SW"; Hodge to ECP, 31 Oct. 1910.

9. ECP, ECP to Lewis Sawyer, Secretary of Agriculture, 5 Sept. 1912; Lewis Sawyer to Charles D. Hilles, 5 Sept. 1912; Charles D. Hilles to ECP, 9 Sept. 1912.

10. American Museum of Natural History, Osborn to Lucas, 4 Sept. 1912.

11. American Museum of Natural History, Lucas to Osborn, Sept. 1912.

12. American Museum of Natural History, Goddard to ECP, 6 Sept. 1912; Goddard to N. C. Nelson, 6 Sept. 1912; Goddard to ECP, 6 Sept. 1912.

13. ECP, ECP to HP, 12 Sept. 1912; 18 Sept. 1912.

14. ECP, ECP to HP, 18 Sept. 1912.

15. American Museum of Natural History, ECP to Goddard, 1 Oct. 1912.

16. American Museum of Natural History, Goddard to ECP, 7 Oct. 1912.

17. ECP, ECP to HP, 1 Oct. 1913.

18. ECP, "Laguna Lodging House," chapter from "In the Southwest," p. 1.

19. ECP, ECP to HP, 1 Oct. 1913.

20. ECP, ECP to HP, 7 Aug. 1915.

21. ECP, Kroeber to ECP, 10 August 1915.

22. ECP, ECP to HP, 15 Aug. 1915.

23. ECP, "The Governor of Zuñi," from "In the Southwest," pp. 6–7.

24. Ibid., pp. 5–6.

25. Ibid., p. 6.

26. Ibid., p. 9.

27. Ibid., p. 1.

28. ECP, Margaret Lewis to ECP, 30 July [no year].

29. ECP, Margaret Lewis to ECP, 21 Aug. [no year].

30. Triloki Nath Pandey, "Anthropologists at Zuni," *Proceedings of the American Philosophical Society* 116, no. 4 (Aug. 1972): 329.

31. ECP, ECP to HP, 31 Aug. 1915.

32. ECP, ECP to HP, 29 Nov. 1915; 16 Nov. 1920.

33. ECP, ECP to HP, 21 Mar. 1918.

34. ECP, ECP to HP, 9 Sept. [no year]; 27 June 1910; 15 Aug. 1915.

35. ECP, John Parsons to ECP, 26 Feb. 1918; Mac to HP, 27 June 1920; "Solidarity," ellipses in original. Elsie did take the boys on some trips with her. In July, 1923, Herbert and McIlvaine joined her in Taos, where they all stayed at Mabel Dodge Luhan's house; and in 1925, she took them to Guatemala over the Christmas break so that they might "see something of Latin America and hear some Spanish." See ECP, letter with no addressee, 6 July 1923; ECP to Dean Mendell, St. Paul's Academy, 5 Dec. 1925.

36. ECP, Lissa to HP, 11 Apr. 1914.

37. Elsie (Lissa) Parsons Kennedy, "The Reminiscences of Mr. and Mrs. John D. Kennedy" (Oral History Research Office, Columbia University, 1966), pp. 21–22.

38. Ibid., p. 22.

39. NAA, Beals to Hare, 31 July 1978.

40. NAA, Beals to Hare, 31 July 1978; Parsons, "Curanderos in Oaxaca, Mexico," *Scientific Monthly* 32 (1931): 64, n. 4.

41. Pandey, "Anthropologists at Zuni," p. 329. It was not just in the field that Elsie was eccentric in her dress. Her granddaughter, Fanny Parsons Culleton, recalls, "She always wore the most extraordinary clothes. . . . She always wore long stockings that were woolen and sandals and a long skirt and beads and a silk blouse with . . . long sleeves. And a cape, or a shawl sometimes, and when she went outside, a turban. Well, this . . . was back in the 30s, this was totally out." (Fanny Parsons Culleton, interview by Rosemary Lévy Zumwalt, 6 July 1988.) Natalie Woodbury recalled a time when Parsons came to Barnard to give a talk in Gladys Reichard's seminar. When Reichard asked Woodbury to meet Parsons at the front of Mill Bank Hall, Woodbury queried, "How will I know her?" and Reichard responded, "You'll have no trouble." (Discussant remarks at Feminist Perspectives on Elsie Clews Parsons and Her Works, AAA Meeting, Phoenix, Arizona, November, 1988.)

42. ECP, Beals to Hare, 31 July 1978.

43. Gladys E. Reichard, "Elsie Clews Parsons," *JAF* 56 (1943): 48.

44. For information on how Parsons met these leading anthropologists and began work in anthropology, see the following letters of the UCA: Gladys Reichard to Alfred Kroeber, 23 Mar. 1942; Kroeber to Reichard, 26 May 1942; Reichard to Robert Lowie, 6 Apr. 1942; and Lowie to Reichard, 10 Apr. 1942.

8

The Scientists

"We miss you very much in our narrow circle," Franz Boas wrote to Elsie. He continued with news of his students. "Ruth Bunzel is doing remarkably well. She is ambitious to learn the Zuni language and I have some hopes of getting money for her to go south from Columbia." Ruth Benedict was to go to Europe, and Gladys Reichard had not yet heard about her fellowship. "Margaret Mead sends encouraging reports. I believe she is getting a good deal that will clinch the point that fundamental individual natures depend upon cultural setting more than upon hereditary or innate characteristics." He included information about the visiting anthropologists, "We have had quite a number of European visitors: Malinowski is in Berkeley now, but will be here in May; . . . Mauss of Paris is expected—May; Pelliot, the French Sinologist, is very much of a scientist."[1]

The "narrow circle" to which Boas had referred was the Columbia group of anthropologists. Trained by Boas, they maintained their association one with another through shared interests, frequent correspondence, and, when in New York, by attendance at "Tuesday lunch." Each week during the school year, the anthropologists would meet for a discussion of recently published books and current research. They would convene, Esther Goldfrank recalled, "at the Hotel Endicott on Colulmbus Avenue and 81 St., a location convenient to the American Museum of Natural History, to which the 'regulars'— Pliny Earle Goddard, Robert Lowie, Nils Nelson, and Leslie Spier— were attached." Erna Gunther and Gladys Reichard, both students of Boas's, and Goldfrank, Boas's secretary, joined the group. Goldfrank remarked that "Elsie Clews Parsons came whenever she could get her 'mother's car.' " She added, "Of course, when they were in town, Kroeber . . . and Edward Sapir . . . were 'regular irregulars.' In large part, the luncheon talk concerned field-work, past and projected, and publication problems."[2]

After one such gathering in June of 1918, Alfred Kroeber wrote Elsie, "You are author again. Boas brought it to lunch today. It was the last gathering of the season, and all of us were jovial."[3] Lowie reported to Kroeber in 1919, "Our Tuesday lunches vary in interest. Mrs. Parsons, Goddard, Boas, Nelson and myself practically always attend, Spier often . . . Goldie hardly ever; Schleiter sometimes turns up about the time the rest of us are ready to quit."[4] Disappointed in not having seen her, Boas wrote Elsie in June of 1924, "I had hoped to see you to-day at lunch. We are going to meet once more next week. I trust I may see you once more before we sail [for Europe]. There are several things that I should like to discuss with you."[5]

With all this, with the exchange of ideas, of suggestions, of field experiences, and future plans, came the intermingling of personalities. For Elsie, this was crucial. She had found the social and intellectual circle for which she had so long sought. Years later, after her first introduction to the group, she explained her feelings about the department to Lowie. In an exchange of letters, Elsie and Lowie discussed the situation at Columbia. Boas had retired, the search was on for his replacement, and tensions ran high over those singled out for consideration. Ruth Benedict, Ralph Linton, and W. Lloyd Warner were the three candidates. Boas supported Benedict, while others divided over Linton or Warner. Elsie was alarmed over the possible choice of Warner, who had not been trained in the Boas tradition, but had done graduate work at the University of Chicago where he had been influenced by A. R. Radcliffe-Brown. She wrote Lowie what she later referred to as "my emotional note," and Lowie responded: "If the authorities at Columbia call Warner there, it obviously means that they do not care to perpetuate Boas's brand of anthropology and are bent on a new deal altogether. I profoundly sympathize with Boas's distress over this situation; but I cannot regard it as catastrophic. Aren't you for once taking an *institutional* point of view? Columbia is not the world, and Boas's great life work is not nullified if its effects persist in the literature and in other academic centers."[6] Lowie had singled out one of Parsons's aversions, and she admitted, "It *was* being institutional, both institutional and personal for such are my relations to Columbia and the Department." In a draft of her response to Lowie, she continued, "The Department is my immediate world in anthropology and I would regret being cut off from it in a Warner-Benedict plunge into the Radcliffe-Brown morass." She thought better of her pointed reference to Ruth Benedict and to W. Lloyd Warner, for in the final copy of this letter she simply indicated her concern over losing her connection with the department due to a "sink into the Radcliffe-Brown morass."[7] She added that this "would be catastrophic for anthropology." Her concern, she assured Lowie, had been for the future of anthropology, and not for Boas personally.

In the draft of the letter, she wrote, "He has such a blind spot about people that he cant foresee a mess or see through designfulness. We all know this and despair of doing anything before the crash."[8] In the final copy, she had scratched out the last sentence and had written instead, "Along such lines it is difficult if not impossible to be of service to him."

Elsie Clews Parsons had met Franz Boas when he was firmly established as the leading anthropologist in the United States. He was not quite of the age to be called "Papa Franz" by his women students, and "the Old Man" by his men students, but he was close to that age. Solidly situated at Columbia University, yet ever striving for improvements in anthropology, Boas was the master. Clearly, Elsie had known of Boas during her graduate work in sociology at Columbia, as well as during her tenure as Hartley House Fellow and as an instructor at Barnard College. It was not until 1915 that she began a correspondence with him that soon took on the warm glow of friendship. Built on a feeling of mutual respect and an appreciation for intellectual honesty, their friendship was one of sincere affection one for the other. As Elsie became more immersed in anthropological inquiry, she shared with Boas his concern for fostering research in anthropology and folklore. Together they would form a powerful blend of intellect, dedication, and energy.

Though Elsie was never literally a student of Boas's, still, in the early years, he could well have been viewed as her mentor in anthropology. With the passing of years, they were as colleagues and close friends. While their letters came to reflect a discourse among equals, in the salutation there remained an imbalance. Elsie always began her letters "Dear Professor Boas," while he would write "Dear Elsie," or "My dear Elsie."

Elsie had already begun her fieldwork in the Southwest when Boas encouraged her to pursue still another area, the collection of folktales from the Caribbean. Not only did Boas suggest the area of work, but he also obtained professional status for her. At the 1915 meeting of the American Folklore Society, she was appointed to the editorial board of the *Journal of American Folklore* to help with the publication of Negro folklore.[9]

For her second trip to Zuni, planned to coincide with the winter solstice ceremony of Shalako, Elsie had invited Boas to accompany her. In a rather formal style, he declined, "My dear Mrs. Parsons, It is very good of you to invite me seriously to join you in your trip. It is a sore temptation for a trip to the interesting Southwest in your company would be a treat. But . . . I must stick to my work."[10]

Four years later, Boas agreed to a joint fieldwork trip to Laguna, where he studied the language, and Elsie, the kinship. En route to New Mexico, Elsie wrote Herbert, "My companion seems compatible in his travelling habits—unobtrusive personal ways & not attaching over much importance to necessary adjustments. He is down spirited over starvation in Germany and the prospect of an unsettled Europe; but I have hopes that once in N. M. he will forget about it, although he has ordered the Times sent on."[11] Boas was pleased with the work. On his return, he wrote Elsie, "I enjoyed the work in Laguna very much indeed and am grateful to you for the opportunity that you have given me to see the Indians of the Southwest." He admitted to a changed perspective, "Two years ago, I had not the courage of undertaking any new work, but I feel differently now. Since my body has held together these years I no longer feel that I have to think only of closing up what I have done in former years." Boas said that he felt they had been "pretty good cohorts" in their work, and he added, "I trust you may have the same feeling."[12]

Elsie made it possible for Boas to return to the Southwest the following summer. He wrote to her: "I do not know whether you appreciate how much the two summer trips that I owe to you have meant to me. Ever since I left the Museum in 1905 it has been a struggle for me to find opportunity for work in the field and after my various attacks of illness in 1915 and 1916 I had given up my mind to try to work at what I had done and thought in past years. It is not saying too much if I say that the new work has made me younger and restored a good deal of my energy and enterprise, and for that I thank you."[13] In 1921, they went again to the Southwest. Boas worked at Cochiti, and Elsie at Jemez. Of this, she wrote Herbert, "Dr. Boas is to let me know soon when he goes to Cochiti where I may pay a visit. It is about five hours on horseback."[14]

From his work at Laguna and Cochiti, Boas wrote *Keresan Texts*. He asked Elsie if he might dedicate it to her, and she responded, "I am delighted with your wish to dedicate to me the keres texts—who would not be?—and with the expression you give it. . . . As I used to tell you I do like compliments from friends and from boys, and I don't worry over whether or not I deserve them."[15]

This newfound energy for fieldwork remained with Boas. In June, 1927, he wrote Elsie from Denver, Colorado, on his way to Portland, Oregon: "It seems to me often very curious that after years of retirement I am again so in the midst of anthropological activities. The change is very largely due to your insistence. I had so fully made up my mind that I wanted to close off my work and I thought so definitely that I could not do any more, that it was quite a change of heart and I finally accepted your invitation to go to the southwest with you, and the stimulus received then has been permanent—not withstanding all the sadness that has come over my life since."[16]

This sadness in his life, Boas shared with Elsie, just as he did his pleasures. In October of 1924, he wrote, "My daughter Gertrud passed away last night after a week's illness—infantile paralysis. Please don't answer."[17] The next year Boas's son was killed in an accident. Elsie wrote Herbert, "You will hear sometime from Dr. Boas who wants your advice in agitating against dangerous [railroad] crossing. That way, in Michigan, his son was killed, and as usual his emotion wants expression in righteous action."[18] Four years later, his wife died. He acknowledged Elsie's attempt to help ease his sorrow, "Thank you very much for your invitation. It is just you who think of the right thing at the right time. I should accept without hesitation— but we each have our own way of meeting fate. There is a German saying, 'Ein gutes Pferd fällt in den Sielen,' a good horse dies in harness—and suffers in harness. Just now I shall feel that I want to stick to my guns. You have met fate your way and so shall I."[19]

The nature of their correspondence took on the quality of good friends conversing. Elsie wrote Boas, thanking him for the translation of her article into German, and noted, "My German is improving as I have an Austrian in the household who is worthless as a waitress but who is enlarging the vocabulary of the little boys and me." She continued with news of her son. "A handsome silver cup adorns the mantel piece, won by Mac in an essay competition, his subject being Indian life which he chose out of a list of twenty & wrote five hours on. I infer that Schulz ('Jack in the Rockies,'etc.) and I were his authorities, and the mixture is sort of funny. He realized that he 'left out the religion,' not time for it." Boas replied, "I am glad you wrote me of Mac's good work. There is no greater joy than to watch the development of the young."[20]

Boas shared his hopes and his despairs with Elsie in a way that he did with no one else. Problems with his health plagued him, and he worried about his ability to continue with his work. As he grew older, he devoted himself almost entirely to social issues, especially those relating to the persecution of the Jews in Germany. He confided to Elsie, "I feel very much depressed. A couple of weeks ago my heart showed again evidence of weakness and the enforced lack of movement and general laziness opposes me. I suppose I'll have to get accustomed to the idea that the days of my usefulness are over although I still feel the strong urge to participate in the struggles of the day and carry on the fight for what I consider right."[21] Attempting to counsel him, Elsie told Boas that for herself she always linked depression to a physical cause, and this rationale helped her to overcome it. He still had so much to contribute to the world, she emphasized, and for that reason he should conserve his strength. She queried, "Why not . . . ignore the 'fight' part which is surely telling on the heart. Thinkers are more 'valuable men,' as the Zuñi would say, than fighters."[22] Boas, however, could not resign himself to an acceptance of the limitations placed on him by his health. He queried, "Can a leopard ever change its spots?" and continued with a description of himself and his attitude toward work, "I remember very distinctly my feelings when I was young; on the one hand the intense desire to learn and to understand; on the other the dissatisfaction with a pure concentration upon knowledge and the intense desire for action which took more and more the form of a desire for action where I felt I could be of use." This, he said, had never left him. Indeed, he felt even more compelled to action, though he deemed the effort to be "almost hopeless." As he said, "Now I cannot keep out of the fight between individualism and the attempt to subjugate all reason to an emotionally fomented group consciousness."[23]

Boas felt intensely and personally involved. Beleaguered European Jews wrote "frantic appeals for help" to him. He located positions in colleges and universities for some who were scholars; and he raised funds to support students. He wrote Elsie, "Out west we find a great many families ready to take students in free. I am trying to work this through the International Student Service and through the Coordinating Committee. I am trying now also to get help for younger people who are being thrown out of schools. I cannot sit entirely still under these circumstances without trying to do something, at least, as long as I see that I can be of some help."[24]

While closely aligned in their political views, Boas and Elsie diverged in their views of Norman Thomas, the Socialist candidate for president in 1940. Elsie published a statement in the *New Republic* that declared, "In view of international relations, I shall vote for Norman Thomas." He was, she said, the only presidential candidate who understood how to "get on with people you disagree with or dislike," and who viewed war as "a cultural set back." Boas asked Elsie if she really believed what she had written, and added, "I am so absolutely disgusted with the behavior of the Socialists towards communists, the New Leader and Norman Thomas himself, that this year for once I am not going to vote Socialist ticket."[25]

They corresponded about their work, and, in Boas's case, about his desire for work. He wrote, "I am glad when I am at work. When I have nothing to do I feel sometimes as though I could not stand up under the load." Of Elsie's research, he commented, "I am glad to know that you are in the field, probably busy every minute and getting interesting material. It is the best we can do."[26]

Elsie made available funds for Boas to return to the Northwest in 1931. He wrote, "I thank you very much for your continued help in my work. I wish I knew how to reciprocate sometime! I am leaving on the 15th and hope to spend the time until June 10th at Fort Rupert." He told her of his plans for the trip. He was taking along a whole manuscript with the intent of finishing it. As he said, "I want to get through this work which has been hanging on for over 35 years." And then he intended to complete his work on the Cochiti and the Salish. Finally, after all this, Boas said, he wanted to turn the work "over to younger minds."[27]

On his return, Boas told her about his fieldwork and his reaction to his return to Fort Rupert after so many years, "The stay out west was quite interesting, in a way sad in so far I was conscious that it is the last time I could go there. I have tried my best to fill the gaps and get whatever was needed, but of course it will not be complete anyway." He had taken an assistant with him, whom he referred to as "Julia, the little Russian girl." As he told Elsie, "She made good friends with the people, worked with it, [and] wrote love letters for the girls. . . . I had Julia observe in detail the laying out of their complicated patterns & I collected many pictures of dances to study dance styles; I had Julia learn dancing and I collected all 150 songs of all kinds and ovations, so that I have good material for the study of all art styles—one of the things I wanted." Boas had been concerned about checking on the material that had come to him through George Hunt. As he said, "You know that all I got during this last 20 years came from him so I had to make sure. On the whole everything seems to be right. Then I wanted to check his Kwakiutl style and see in how far there is a uniform style of storytelling." With all this, there was for Boas the emotional reactions to the changes that had taken place: "The degradation of the Indians, since I have been out there is terrible, but from an ethnological point of view it brings out a number of most interesting points. All their old beautiful camps are gone, but in their feast they act as if they own them. They tell so & so that he is to eat out of the wolf dish & pretend to send it to him, but there is no dish. The outer impression is that of a poor white village, but the life has all the old flavor."[28]

Boas referred to his problems writing up the Kwakiutl material, "I have been working particularly on the more intimate material as exhibited in conversations to which I listened, and which I had later reenacted. What troubles me most in all the material is the lack of any real inner excitement." He puzzled over this and concluded, "Still I think I can understand the situation in which by rigid prescription of behavior a feeling of awe is developed in the audience although the subject matter of their awe is so vague that it can hardly be described."[29]

In addition to funding several of Boas's fieldtrips, Elsie played the role, in Esther Goldfrank's words, of "Department angel."[30] She contributed to what she designated as Boas's "secretarial fund." Pliny Earle Goddard had first approached Elsie when in 1915 he collected money as a contribution to Boas's research. In 1925, Boas wrote of his reaction to these efforts: "Goddard tells me that he has collected funds for assistance for my scientific work and I feel certain that he has asked you and that, as usual, you responded. . . . He has done this once before in [19]15. At that time I thought I had only a couple of years to live and I felt differently about it. Later on, when I had regained strength, I always felt half ashamed on account of my yielding and that is the way I feel now." He was "grateful, deeply grateful," but he was sure Elsie would understand when he said "frankly . . . I do not like it." Had he known of Goddard's plan, he would "have forbidden it." However, Boas was caught. He needed the funds to carry out his work, and this he felt compelled to do. As he said, quite simply, "I feel that it should be foolish on my part to decline, because I do believe that my work is worth doing."[31] Elsie continued with her contributions to Boas's work, usually on a biannual basis. Boas would write her letters of thanks that detailed the work he had accomplished. She responded to one such letter, "What a hell of a lot of work you get done, to use a phrase from American folklore. I am so happy to be able to contribute to it in the smallest degree."[32]

With mutual trust and respect, Boas and Parsons acted as literary executors, one for the other. Elsie had, in an undated note, designated "Dr. Boas (next Dr. Kroeber) my 'literary executor.' " In June of 1924, Boas wrote, "I wanted to ask you, if you would permit me to state in my will that all my unpublished Manuscripts should be turned over to you, without any obligation on your part, but in the hope that you would try to put them in the hands of people who might use them to best advantage, either for publication or for study."[33] She responded, "I feel deeply appreciative of being named as your literary executor. It is a trust of the highest honor." She added, "I am not so sure, however, that you wont be mine."[34]

In 1938 Robert Lowie published his *History of Ethnological Theory.* On receipt of her copy, Elsie wrote him, "The Christmas present was here on my return and I read the Boas chapter at once and was very much pleased with it." She found it to be "a very just and discerning appraisal," and she thought that Boas would like it. Elsie promised to tell Lowie of Boas's reaction when she next saw "the Columbia crowd." This she did: "I saw Boas at lunch. I couldnt get much out of him except that he thought anthropology in the U. S. A. would be about where it is today even if he hadn't come along, historical methods were in the air, and so the chapter on F. B. seemed exaggerated. I really think he doesn't like to be written up, in any terms; it makes him uneasy. He likes the chapter on Tylor."[35]

Elsie did remark on a certain omission, that Lowie had overlooked the way in which Boas "followed up the work of students, seeing to it that they got their material written out and printed; also his interest in getting them positions, etc." She pondered, "I wonder if he was not outstanding along these lines, at least at a time when other professors did not take as much trouble about their students, and perhaps this attitude was a factor in building up his so-called 'school.' " On further reflection, she raised another critical point, "You do not mention his ardor in combating the scientific fallacies which bolster up social injustices. This has been more marked, of course, in recent years but it was always there and is an essential part of his make-up." She told of a photograph of himself that Boas had given her "a year or two ago" and had signed, "Elsie Clews Parsons, fellow in the struggle for freedom from prejudice." She added, "I began that way and he ends that way. I suppose somewhere our trails crossed."[36]

The narrow circle to which Boas had referred was called "the gang" by Pliny Earle Goddard. On December 28, 1916, Goddard sent Kroeber a telegram: "The gang is here and missing your psychological point of view Franz Boas Elsie Blew [*sic*] Parsons Michelson Laufer Spier Mechling Spinden Mousen Hagar MacCurdy Parmelee Tozzer Dizon [*sic*] Edward K Putnam Oetterking Judd H Newell Wardle Nelson Helen Boas Lowie The Aitkens Marie Boas at Hotel Majestic."[37] The occasion for this gathering was a joint meeting of the American Anthropological Association, the American Folklore Society, and Section H of the American Association for the Advancement of Science, held at the American Museum of Natural History in December, 1916. By this time, Elsie was well situated in the circle of anthropologists. She had been appointed assistant editor of the *Journal of American Folklore* in 1915, and she had been conducting fieldwork in the Southwest for four years, as well as collecting Negro folklore in the Caribbean and in the United States. Her articles had appeared in the *Journal of American Folklore* and the *American Anthropologist,* and her books were favorably reviewed in these same journals. Elsie's identity now was as an anthropologist; her commitment to the discipline was total. She brought to anthropology the same intent of purpose that earlier she had directed toward sociology and movements for social change. Her friendship with certain anthropologists took on a depth and an intensity to match her intellectual attachment to the discipline.

Her first acquaintance in the anthropological circle had been with Pliny Earle Goddard. In his position as curator at the American Museum of Natural History, Goddard had been helpful in Elsie's early southwestern work. Theirs was a friendship that flourished, and the intimacy that developed was reflected in Goddard's letters to Elsie. In November, 1913, he wrote, "I haven't forgotten my ethnological quest of finding out what you think about human mating and why you came to think it when most people do not dare to ask."[38] Goddard desired more contact with Elsie. He was encouraged by their relationship, for there was "so little barrier to a free exchange of thought and feeling."[39] He wrote invitingly, "The cigarettes are waiting, so am I. . . . Really I would like to talk over my lectures with you. Do come in."[40] As the new editor of the *American Anthropologist*, he asked her to discuss "Dr. Lowie's paper on ceremonies." Goddard had plans for Elsie. He declared, "You are going to help me make the Anthropologist more than a mere record of fieldwork accomplished. When I said the other night *we* had the journal to play with I was not using an editorial plural."[41] For her part, Elsie included Goddard among her circle of friends. She invited him out to Lenox to spend a few days. Of this she wrote Herbert, "Goddard enjoyed his visit, I think. I took him up Bald Summit, as Hawthorne called it."[42]

To assist Elsie with her work in the Southwest, Goddard had written a letter of introduction to Alfred Louis Kroeber in August, 1915. Kroeber was in Zuni conducting research under the auspices of the American Museum of Natural History, with funds Goddard had obtained for him.[43] Kroeber had left Zuni before Elsie arrived, so they did not meet at this time. However, they had ample opportunity to meet during Kroeber's sabbatical leave (1915 through 1916) from the University of California. Then from August 1, 1917, to June 30, 1918, Kroeber took Lowie's position at the American Museum of Natural History, while Lowie taught at the University of California.[44]

Elsie made overtures of friendship to Kroeber. In February, 1916, she wrote, "If you have any wish to be nice you will invite yourself by telephone to tea some day this week after Tuesday. I will try not to ask you about Zuñi derivations."[45] And in June of the same year, she wrote him from Stonover Farm about her cabin, which served as her study, "I'd like you to see the place I found & made two years ago. But Zuñi is probably too close at hand for you to come up, say the week after next."[46] On June 11, 1916, his fortieth birthday, Kroeber responded to her invitation with a personal reflection on inner changes: "Six months ago, when I settled down to the first chance to work since kid days, so great a contentment came over me that I forgave all my enemies, pulled the chip off my shoulder, and really thought that so far as I was concerned the spear was already been beaten into a pruning hook. It was a pleasant dream, and the New York winter a very happy one. But the sword is again where it belongs—to stay." His assessment of life included a defiant look to the future. "As I am forty today, I may still if fate wills it, and in spite of all the waste of the past, take and give a few blows before they roll me over into the ditch or I retire into the sheath of the old age class. So be it: I'm ready." Kroeber ended the letter on a positive slant, "It's a nice world and nice to have friends in it. If you can remain gracious through all my blatancy and contradicting, I shall look forward with pleasure to accepting your next invitation to Lenox—in a year or in five."[47]

As the months passed, Kroeber's relationship with Elsie became more friendly, even playful at times. The opening salutations of his 1916 letters reflected this change. The "Dear Mrs. Parsons" soon disappeared to be replaced in August by "Dear E. C. P.," in September by "Dear Propagandist," and in October by "Dear Accusatrix." To these forms of address, Elsie reponded, "As long as you are nice enough to send me reprints and correct my Zuñi you may call me whatever bad names you like—psychologist or even moralist."[48] With a friendship that deepened, Kroeber would begin "Elsie dear" (18 December 1918) or "Very dear Elsie" (6 August 1918). Frequently there was no opening form of address, rather Kroeber would begin with a remark as if in reply to something Elsie had just said. Later, as they drew apart after a time of intense closeness, Kroeber marked the distance with the saluation, "Elsie, old pal" (19 January 1919) and "Witch dear" (22 February 1919). Finally, in his last letter to her, Kroeber went almost full circle. In 1939, she had become "Dear Elsie" again.

Elsie and Kroeber shared their work and commented on each other's writings. She wrote to Kroeber, "As for squeezing you dry, I doubt my capacity and admit my inclination." Playfully, she added, "Nevertheless you ought to be ashamed of your implication, since you know quite well I've offered more than you are willing to take and more than three fourths of the way I cant go." She sent him a copy of an article on Zuni that was to be published in the *Journal of American*

Folklore and wrote, "Keep it and when you find mistakes or gaps now or later at Zuñi do be good & notify me." They were linked through their research on Zuni. In May, 1917, Elsie wrote Kroeber, "Did Margaret Lewis write you I was at Zuñi in January & of our trip to Acoma? You suggested Acoma. You may remember. I doubt if it is as fruitful as you surmised. I only scraped it a bit, of course, but its ceremonial life seemed more disintegrated than I had expected."[49] She enclosed a copy of a song that she had recorded at Zuni, composed in honor of Kroeber. It was, she said, "no doubt the greatest compliment ever paid you." She added, "Lewis sang it, & dictated it & [Margaret A. Lewis] translated. No doubt like all my Zuñi it's very faulty, but you can correct it for yourself."

> South Fathers South Clouds
> rain touches [i.e. falls] Road catching up
> [Kroeber] appeared   You oriole
>   learn
> talk   Pima   Pima   Santo
> Domingo   Santo Domingo
> [Kroeber speaks]
> "Your tale is pretty and your way of living."
> Ground wet till [spring]
> ahaea   ahaee
> aha a   ahaa a
> ihi i   ihii i

The Zunis had nicknamed Kroeber "oriole," since the khaki clothes he wore were the same coloring as the bird of that name.[50]

For his part, Kroeber offered a familiar assessment of Elsie. He wrote: "Scientific work *is* fun; but I wonder whether you will be long satisfied with it. Once one has stirred reactions in large numbers of human beings, I doubt if anything of less intensity yields permanent content. Perhaps you are resting while a new line of attack germinates. At any rate, with three good books at your belt, you should have some better ones in you."[51] In June, 1917, he responded enthusiastically, "I liked your manuscript very much. If you've written better, I don't remember them; and it makes a lot of things clear that heretofore left me wondering what you were driving at."[52] Dismissing his ideas as old and "all half baked," he said, "You write provocative books that are distinctly good, and very clever unethnological articles on ethnological subjects, but I'd be sorry if I wasn't at least as much interested in you as in your formulations, and I am ready to discuss either with anybody." Acknowledging that Elsie would not make known such personal reactions, he pointedly queried, "But isn't that a suppression?" As he knew Elsie would, he answered, "I'm quite sure you look upon it as a question of taste, but is it a natural taste? If so, you strike me as a remarkably anomalous person. I try to rule personality out of the understanding of culture, but what is left in life if we eliminate personality? I'm rather confident you don't eliminate it, ultimately. But aren't you whittling it down pretty slender with cultivated restraint? Or is it just that I'm not as subtle a person as I have business to be?"[53]

Shades of adoration emerged in his letters. In August, 1918, he wrote, "Very dear Elsie! I like to say it, so break rules. It's hard to picture you at Newport. I almost wish there'd be a chance to pop in there." He closed with, "Elsie, it's pleasant even to be away from you. I'm not a bit piney." Anticipating the separation when he returned to the West Coast, he added, "But I admit the end of September will look different; and after the first month of reestablishment has rolled off, I expect loneliness. You may be surprised at the sentimental letters I can write. I like it better this way." In another he wrote, "This evening with you would be pleasant to live and to remember."[54]

Elsie wrote to Herbert, who was stationed in France at the time, about some of her activities with Kroeber. She told about going to see the Copear French theater's *Brothers Karamazov,* "Beautifully staged and well-acted—past midnight à la Parisien." From their home in Harrison, New York, she wrote, "Kroeber came yesterday to play tennis, but instead of playing we strolled to the water." "Kroeber," she said, "regrets that you are not here to know, but I doubt if you would make much out of each other."[55]

Kroeber was not alone in his desire to be near Elsie. His good friend and colleague, Pliny Earle Goddard, anticipated the pleasure of her company. He wrote, "I am glad my trip with you is to be the last of the series rather than the first. By that time you will appreciate a playmate I hope." He acknowledged Kroeber as one who wished to be a presence in Elsie's life. "He wanted you very much last summer. He should have known that there are others; but Kroeber looks upon you as a goddess unfettered by human ties."[56]

A competition slowly escalated between Goddard and Kroeber. Vying for some sign of Elsie's favor in June of 1918, Kroeber expressed a wish to receive a letter before Goddard. Then he felt contrite, "I don't know whether it was something devilish or meanness that made me want to be the one to get the first letter. Most likely a shred of proprietary sense. And I feel cheap and won't do it again."[57]

With her usual care for privacy in personal matters, Elsie insisted on discretion. In response to her query about what his sister might have revealed to Goddard, Kroeber responded, "Pussy is never discreet, but as the concern over what Goddard might take in has always been mine to the lesser extent, I really didn't notice what she blabbed. I thought I had been very careful to give her nothing but the noncommital externals." Whatever tension had arisen because of the sensitive crossings of the heart, Kroeber was certain would be dissipated. As he wrote, "The three of us shan't be together anymore for some time (unless you go out of your way to bring it about) so it doesn't matter."[58]

For Kroeber, Elsie must have been a puzzle. She clearly enjoyed being with him, but she had definite limits, and of these he soon became aware. She had arranged for Kroeber to take a house in Lenox for the summer of 1918. At the same time, she firmly let him know when he presumed too much of her. She would be unfettered. Attachments for Elsie had never meant a lessening of freedom. She continued to see her dear friend of many years, Grant La Farge. Of this, she wrote Herbert from Stonover Farm, "Grant was here last weekend and Kroeber is coming this week." There was pleasure in this variety, for, as she added, "The two men are as different as two can be and comparisons amuse me."[59] The message implicit in these contiguous invitations was not lost on Kroeber. He wrote, "If you get the house, I'll be happy to tumble into it; and whatever loneliness comes with it, will be good medicine. . . . I'm going to Boas on the 27th and about the 5th will arrive in Lenox if you still want me, to stay as long as I can. I'm chastened you see, and the pride is out of me for a time. You can guess who did it." Still, Kroeber wavered over his decision to come to Lenox. He apologized for being "hang-backy," but said he felt pushed in one way and pulled in another. "I'd like to come and I'd like to go when and where is your say. . . . Be patient with me: I may learn slowly."[60]

One month later, Kroeber had regained his buoyancy. He playfully alluded to his ranking in Elsie's eyes, "On account of a nameless Englishman, I'm at least number 2—or perhaps 20—on your score card; but you're number 1, and a big black one at that, on mine." With the passing of time, he had become "satisfied, both at trial and failure." He continued, "And as to what the future may bring, I really don't know, don't want to know, and am entirely serene about. That I have to thank you for." Elsie puzzled over his allusion to ranking, and Kroeber explained, "I fear you're not on to score cards. Too uncompetitive. One doesn't score values, but hits, runs, and outs. I'll never wholly lose interest in those. But I'm not thinking too much. Really. I do say everything I want when I'm with you, except the rare times when I get no encouragement to go through to the end. When I'm away, there is sometimes a holding back; but the reason only—paper."[61]

Elsie and Kroeber were to go to Zuni together for fieldwork in September, 1918. Elsie enforced "injunctions against talk," and Kroeber agreed to tell people he "was going for a collection and final vacation" before his return to teaching. He anticipated one sticking point, "Goddard will hint or ask of course, but I'll refer him point blank to you."[62]

The final preparations for the trip were made through the mail, since Kroeber had left for California at the end of August. This resumption of teaching and of museum work he found depressing. "The truth is, to put the neck back in the yoke even for a moment does rouse a resentment." Elsie had sensed his displeasure and had assumed a connection with her request for secrecy regarding the trip to Zuni. She begged his patience. He responded, "Humoring you is mild as against what I want to do, and do cheerfully, no, with fun, ordinarily. I suppose the privacy chafes me because it is so contrary to all my usual loquacious habits—confiding difficulties to people, for instance, as a method of working them out for myself. You've no idea how many times I've had to pull myself up hard to leave you out of the Zuni trip, and the constant sense of uneasiness that pervades me lest I blab you in." Kroeber expressed a sense of relief that Elsie did not want the trip "kept confidential after it's over." And he apologized for having to send a telegram that might have, as he said, "broken your method." Elsie was not pleased on the receipt of the telegram and expressed her displeasure to Kroeber. He responded, "Honestly, Elsie, I learn your tactics awfully hard." He did acquiesce, "You're no doubt the wisest, and circumstances have made you experienced." However, Kroeber had not grown accustomed to the machinations. For his part, he said, "If they talk idly, it's idle. Talk goes on anyway." Four hours later, he wrote her another letter, beginning exuberantly, "Partner dear: Forget everything except the proposal to avoid Labor Day in Chicago." He had just made a long trip to recover a twenty-blade knife, as he explained, "and came back a new man after the eight miles. I should have hiked first and then written. It seems to be a desire that I must do something—work, make love, dispute."[63]

One reaction that Kroeber had fully anticipated was that of Goddard. Kroeber wrote Elsie, "Goddard ran true to dope. When Zuni came up, his mind began to brew. While he gathered himself, I filled in about New York in September being an anticlimax, and the like. Then he shot his question in the very words: 'Are you going to Zuni alone?' I parried, 'I knew you would ask that and you know I can't answer.' He laughed, flushed, looked sick—and away—and said, 'Well, it will be a climax.'[64]

Kroeber had left his research materials on Zuni with Elsie. For the trip, he requested, "Please don't fill up your suitcase with my Zuni notebooks, but put them where most convenient and let me have to get at on the train only some three or four that seem wholly devoted to language." He reminded Elsie that on "this last lap of my 'last' vacation," he would work only on language and some buying for the museum. He added, "I mean to have all that is given me of one thing eminently proper to a vacation; and science is to be left in its place."[65]

En route to Zuni, Elsie wrote to Herbert about the trip, which she found "somewhat less tedious trip than usual." She continued, "It is cool, no steam heat, no passenger chatter & Dr. Kroeber is along for company." She explained that Kroeber would be collecting tales, "put up to it by me, & also Museum things for his Cal. museum." In vain she had "tried to persuade him to go first to Hopi for a week," but these plans were not to his liking. She added, "If I go, it will be after he leaves Zuñi in a couple of weeks or so." Reflecting on this new mode of travel, she wrote, "This is the first time I've had any outside companionship in this country & I'm rather curious to see how it will work. I have some doubts, although of course Kroeber is an older resident of Zuñi than I am. But as you know I am a crank in travel."[66]

Of their fieldwork in Zuni, Elsie also wrote Herbert. She remarked on Kroeber's expertise in the Zuni language. However, her own research was not progressing: "Unfortunately we are short on interpreters & so I dont get my usual amount of work done which depresses me from time to time." Still, she was able to "compare facts and impressions" with Kroeber, and she was gratified to know that the language was being recorded by him. Several days later she told Herbert of the continued search for an interpreter: "I have a 'witch' in view, but he may scare off." She spent her time "going about from house to house with Kroeber, 'trading' i.e. buying for his California museum." She found this "a good way to enlarge my limited acquaintances." On her way home from Zuni, Elsie wrote Herbert that "the partnership in work with Kroeber" had proven "helpful and agreable." Kroeber had gathered enough information on the Zuni language to prepare a grammar; and she had added to her "knowledge of the religious life." She would be kept busy "well into the winter" writing up her notes, and she looked forward to "the leisure of Louns-berry" to accomplish this. She explained that Kroeber had returned to the University of California.[67]

In spite of the cheerful letters to Herbert, the trip to Zuni was not a total success. On a personal level, it ended in disaster. From Berke-ley, Kroeber wrote, "Elsie, what you said on the last 24 hours sent me off with a sense of Zuni having been wasted. It was for you—I hadn't suspected it because I was content. . . . It was that that threw you into robbing expeditions and the like, naturally enough, that derailed me." Kroeber apologized for not having anticipated the problems. "I take the blame: I ought to have known. You did though I don't think through greater experience." He ended his letter, "Well, Elsie, old partner, good luck to you, and such peace as your soul wants, and my thanks for a filled half year."[68]

Shortly after returning from Zuni, Kroeber received a letter from Goddard, which conveyed "a vigor of enthusiasm about Zuni lan-guage that cloaked," as Kroeber said, "the silence of his realer emo-tions. I told him he was still jealous." Kroeber added, "You can make him happy if your principles let you." The two men were making the attempt to mend the rupture in their friendship. With a salutation, "Very nice Elsie," Kroeber wrote: "Goddard and I are going to save for ourselves what we can out of the wreck. There is no further at-tempt at anything three cornered; and any bitterness is to be dragged out into daylight. I feel very much better. And I wish you too success in sheathing the sword. I don't believe any is lifted against you."[69]

As the months passed, Kroeber gained a perspective on his time with Elsie. In response to a letter from her in which she spoke of feel-ing "melancholy," Kroeber wrote: "I do look back with a great pleas-antness on the flowers along the Hackensack, and the garden walk at Harrison, and the music room, and the cool dinners on the porch, and Lenox lying spread before us on the bald hill, and the many houred cabin, and the last paddle up the Housatonic to the little fire in the dusk; and I am grateful and will never forget them; and if Zuni fell below par, the fault is all mine. And I do wish I could make it all up to you; but it doesn't seem for such things to be."[70]

Elsie and Kroeber had planned a joint project on Pueblo ceremo-nial organization. The challenge lay in combining their varying ap-proaches, as Kroeber said, "to reconcile into one work a tendency to tie up and a tendency to drive wedges, an interest in time relations and one in classifying with a sharpness attainable only by elimination of the time factor." The effort to surmount such differences, he thought, would be salutary for both. Still, he saw "clearly the central problem of binding our two personalities into one team. We may not do it; I may be the first to bolt; but I think it's worth trying." Anxious to begin the project, Elsie prodded Kroeber, and he begged patience, "Please remember that I have many impressions of the southwest, but little knowledge—very little, compared with you."[71] Two years later, in 1920, Kroeber was still asking Elsie to "be patient." He had other pressures that drew him away from his research. "After all, Elsie, you are new at this work and have two or three good sized careers already behind you—sociology, propaganda, maternity—so that ethnology isn't yet much more than an excursion. But I've had nothing else in my life than ethnology and if I don't play very right shall have nothing else. Therefore it is that other things just now take precedence: above all the economic margin that brings freedom."[72]

Kroeber would fluctuate between a guarded optimism and despair over their "joint venture." As he said, "We insist on weighing too differently." He suggested another approach: "Let's both attack the problem, but separately, and see how near our tunnels come to meeting in the bowels of the mountain. . . . I suggest that we finish our jobs simultaneously, each with full knowledge of the other but without direct refutation, and print them under one cover, as separate papers, but with a paragraph of joint introduction." He saw this as a way to work jointly on a project, yet avoid the "compromise and strain."[73] Elsie and Kroeber did not attain even this degree of cooperation. The joint venture in research did not materialize.

Resigning himself to the divergence of their approaches, both in personal matters and in research, Kroeber attempted to establish again a friendly exchange. He queried, "Tell me something of yourself—your writing . . . your new friends, Lissa and John, Herbert's return, the latest Russian music, a garden close if you have found one—anything to assure me that Elsie is still willing to be a person and a very feminine one to me." She resumed her correspondence, and he wrote: "It's pleasant to get your letters and the gossip in them, and it makes me feel poor not to reciprocate. We too have our gatherings—more irregular—but there's mighty little science in them even if the basis is anthropological work; and the personal is to the fore. My penchant you know, and it's grown nearly to the extent of Goddard's." He closed his letter with a hint of yearning for times past. "Elsie, you have been a lovely witch and will always be a splendid brother in arms, but I prize the witch even more and regret her." Kroeber's feeling of competitiveness still remained for Goddard. He wrote, "Regards to Goddard—and I do *not* promise not to be jealous." Referring to Elsie's and Boas's joint fieldwork at Laguna, he queried, "Can you make a good corn bread? a smooth custard? an Irish stew? a French pancake? Goddard reports you cooked one meal for the old man." He vowed, "If ever we go again to Zuni, Hopi, or camp, I'll cook more than that for you, and the rest you'll cook for me—instead of robbing shrines at dusk and eating cold stuff in the dark."[74]

Kroeber and Elsie met again, but the pleasures of their earlier times would not return. After one such unhappy reunion in New York, Kroeber wrote, "It opened as a depressing visit—worse than your dullness of autumn. That it ended differently, you must lay largely to yourself. You like me best with people; I like you ever so much more in New York or Lenox or Cambridge than at Zuni."[75]

Kroeber was able to travel back to California with a feeling of resolution. The question he had been asking himself for years about the university—"whether the prison is a prison"—was answered. "For the first time in years I turn westward without the prison gate sense. That's a good deal to get out of a five weeks' trip. And there too you helped—so subtly that you may be unaware and I should find it hard to formulate. You see you really are a Liberator, even where you least expect." He had found that his life lay in California. "I plan with avidity instead of reluctance. The twenty years sunk in this soil are no longer a means to something else; they are to be capitalized on the spot. It may not wholly last, but just now I'd hate to have a gate open that led elsewhere."[76]

Reflecting on the pieces of their broken relationship, Kroeber requested of Elsie, "Be gentle because you do see. Where I haven't been it was from blindness. After all, whatever my deficiencies of inherent imagination and insight, I was under the added disadvantage of inexperience even greater, I believe, than you fully realize. . . . If one is without experience—which in my case means repressed—for over forty years, one doesn't release the first time without harsh vehemence on the other. . . . I wish it were consolation that you are not the only one that has been hurt, and myself perhaps most of all."[77] Though he did frequently take the blame, Kroeber was able to see Elsie's leverage in their breaking apart. He wrote, "I have felt that you wished to limit rigorously what you took from me, and naturally I resisted or in my turn contradicted." Elsie accused him of self-centered preoccupation. He acquiesced, "Granted that I'd rather talk about myself than listen to anything, I hardly think it's a wholly continuous obsession." He suggested that when he was "raw," she should "bat" him down with his "own weapons" and talk about herself, a subject about which he would "infinitely rather hear . . . than about most other things." He concluded, "There's nothing gained by meeting my childishness with aloof dignity, nor—because after all I am grown up mostly—with firmness." On a trip to New York to attend a meeting of the Social Science Research Council, Kroeber was able to see Elsie. He wrote asking her to sail down the Hackensack on Thursday, April 22. Their time together was not pleasant, and he suggested, "Let's admit we have mismanaged and look into ourselves. We've both been lacking in sympathy. But don't let us allow that to stand and grow into new aloofness. . . . I'll never let you be hostile again."[78]

Kroeber put his energies into his work and settled into his teaching. In the summer of 1925, he began seeing Theodora Brown. And on March 26, 1926, he married her. Kroeber wrote in response to a letter from Elsie, " 'Getting married' runs along very pleasantly. 'What more telling comment on wedding ceremonial—anywhere?' made me smile. We won't argue it nor even tease; but the fervor with which you hate all ritual makes me realize how little I know about you after all. There are so many other things to hate—and tolerate—that there must be a reason for your choice; but I'm as much in the dark as five years ago. Perhaps you too. But I don't mind. Score that to the credit of psychoanalysis, please."[79]

Time passed, and with it went the bitterness. What was left between Elsie and Kroeber was a genial, if somewhat detached, friendship that focused on shared professional concerns. Even so, after all the years, Elsie wrote Kroeber in 1939, asking him, perhaps somewhat nostalgically, "Would you like to return to Zuni with a gang?" As if to excuse her invitation, she admitted to a lack of interest in others who might accompany her, be they Mexican anthropologists or "the Americans," whom as she said, "I would rather see in Chicago."[80]

In sum, there was in this "narrow circle" of Columbia anthropologists not only a feeling of camaraderie—it was, after all, referred to as "our gang"—but also an intensity of emotion. There was an excitement that came of sharing ideas and plans. The social and the intellectual merged in a heady mixture. Behind it all there was the driving force of fieldwork, and, ultimately, the concern with publishing the results of the research and filling in the gaps in the literature. With the constant exchange of ideas, suggestions, fieldnotes, and plans for the future came an intermingling of personalities. For Elsie, the combination was powerful, for it proferred a blend of the personal and the intellectual.

NOTES

1. ECP, Boas to ECP, 28 Mar. 1926.
2. Esther S. Goldfrank, *Notes on an Undirected Life* (New York: Queens College Press, 1978), p. 17.

3. ECP, Kroeber to ECP, 12 June 1918.

4. UCA, Lowie to Kroeber, 29 June 1919.

5. ECP, Boas to ECP, 12 June 1924.

6. ECP, Lowie to ECP, 10 Feb. 1936.

7. ECP, ECP to Lowie, n.d.

8. ECP, ECP to Lowie, penciled note, n.d.

9. Charles Peabody, "Minutes of the Twenty-seventh Annual Meeting of the American Folklore Society," *JAF* 29 (1916): 297.

10. ECP, Boas to Parsons, 24 Nov. 1915.

11. ECP, ECP to HP, 28 May 1919.

12. ECP, Boas to ECP, 3 July 1919.

13. ECP, Boas to ECP, 9 July 1920.

14. ECP, ECP to HP, 29 Sept. 1921.

15. Goldfrank, *Notes*, p. 56.

16. ECP, Boas to ECP, 20 June 1927.

17. ECP, Boas to ECP, 22 Oct. 1924.

18. Rye Historical Society, ECP to HP, Thursday, A.M.

19. ECP, Boas to ECP, 1 Jan. 1929. Boas wrote 1929 by mistake; the correct year was 1930.

20. ECP, ECP to Boas, n.d.; Boas to ECP, n.d. Parsons was referring to the popular writer, James Willard Shultz.

21. ECP, Boas to ECP, 30 Sept. 1936.

22. Boas Papers, ECP to Boas, 8 Sept. 1936.

23. ECP, Boas to ECP, 11 Sept. 1936.

24. ECP, Boas to ECP, 18 Oct. 1938.

25. Parsons, letter to editor, *New Republic* 103 (1940): 554; ECP, Boas to ECP, 22 Oct. 1940.

26. ECP, Boas to ECP, 25 June 1925; 26 Nov. 1925.

27. ECP, Boas to ECP, [1931]. For information on Boas's Northwest fieldwork, see Ronald P. Rohner, *The Ethnography of Franz Boas* (Chicago: University of Chicago Press, 1969), pp. 269, 288–301.

28. ECP, Boas to ECP, 10 Feb. 1931.

29. ECP, Boas to ECP, 14 Oct. 1940.

30. Goldfrank, *Notes*, p. 4.

31. ECP, Boas to ECP, 25 June 1925.

32. Boas Papers, ECP to Boas, 18 Aug. 1926.

33. ECP, Boas to ECP, 12 June 1924.

34. Boas Papers, ECP to Boas, 18 June 1924.

35. Lowie Papers, ECP to Lowie, 6 Jan. 1938.

36. Lowie Papers, ECP to Lowie, 6 Jan. 1938.

37. ALK, Goddard to Kroeber, 28 Dec. 1916.

38. Peter Hare, *A Woman's Quest for Science* (Buffalo, N.Y.: Prometheus Books, 1985), p. 136, quoting ECP, Goddard to ECP, 8 Nov. 1913.

39. ECP, Goddard to ECP, n.d.

40. Hare, *A Woman's Quest for Science*, p. 136, quoting ECP, Goddard to ECP, 2 Feb. 1914.

41. ECP, Goddard to ECP, 25 Jan. 1915, his emphasis.

42. ECP, ECP to HP, 17 May 1915.

43. ALK, Kroeber to Goddard, Jan. 1915; Goddard to ALK, 17 Feb. 1915.

44. American Museum of Natural History, Goddard to Lucas, 7 May 1917; Director to Lowie, 19 June 1917; "Appointment of Robert H. Lowie," *AA* 19 (1917): 323.

45. ALK, ECP to Kroeber, 6 Feb. 1916.

46. ALK, ECP to Kroeber, 3 June 1916.

47. ECP, Kroeber to ECP, 11 June 1916.

48. ECP, ECP to Kroeber, 2 Feb. 1916.

49. Kroeber Papers, ECP to Kroeber, 2 Feb. 1916; 3 June 1916; 11 May 1917.

50. Kroeber Papers, ECP to Kroeber, 11 May 1917; Parsons, *Notes on Zuñi* (Lancaster, Pa.: American Anthropological Association, 1917), p. 281, n. 1.

51. ECP, Kroeber to ECP, 5 Oct. 1916.

52. ECP, Kroeber to ECP, 24 June 1917.

53. ECP, Kroeber to ECP, 23 Dec. 1916.

54. ECP, Kroeber to ECP, 6 Aug. 1918; 8 Aug. 1918.

55. ECP, ECP to HP, 22 May 1918; 22 May 1918; 13 June 1918.

56. ECP, Goddard to ECP, nd.

57. ECP, Kroeber to ECP, 9 June 1918.

58. ECP, Kroeber to ECP, 9 June 1918.

59. ECP, ECP to HP, 13 June 1918.

60. ECP, Kroeber to ECP, 17 June 1918; 22 June 1918.

61. ECP, Kroeber to ECP, 23 July 1918; 2 Aug. 1918.

62. ECP, Kroeber to ECP, Tuesday [Aug. 1918].

63. ECP, Kroeber to ECP, 29 Aug. 1918; Saturday, [30 Aug.] 1918; Saturday, 4 hours later.

64. ECP, Kroeber to ECP, n.d.

65. ECP, Kroeber to ECP, 29 Aug. 1918.

66. ECP, ECP to HP, 5 Sept. 1918.

67. ECP, ECP to HP, 10 Sept. 1918; 13 Sept. 1918; 26 Sept. 1918.

68. ECP, Kroeber to ECP, 9 Oct. 1918.

69. ECP, Kroeber to ECP, 14 Oct. 1918; n.d.

70. ECP, Kroeber to ECP, 18 Dec. 1918.

71. ECP, Kroeber to ECP, 18 Dec. 1918.

72. ECP, Kroeber to ECP, 26 Jan. 1920.

73. ECP, Kroeber to ECP, 19 Jan. 1919.

74. ECP, Kroeber to ECP, 22 Feb. 1919; n.d. [1919?]; 10 Aug. 1919, his emphasis.

75. ECP, Kroeber to ECP, 11 Nov. 1919; 7 Jan. 1920.

76. ECP, Kroeber to ECP, 5 Oct. 1916; 7 Jan. 1920; 26 Jan. 1920.

77. ECP, Kroeber to ECP, 26 Jan. 1920.

78. ECP, Kroeber to ECP, Tuesday; 24 May 1920.

79. ECP, Kroeber to ECP, n.d. For information on his marriage, see Theodora Kroeber, *Alfred Kroeber* (Berkeley: University of California Press, 1970), pp. 119–42.

80. ECP, ECP to Kroeber, 31 Aug. 1939.

9

Of Tales, Riddles, and Proverbs

Elsie had already begun her fieldwork in the Southwest when Franz
Boas encouraged her to pursue still another area, the collection of
folktales from the Caribbean. She wrote him on November 25, 1915,
that she could see him "any time before Dec. 7 about the negro number." She continued, "I shall be at your disposal. I'd like to try it, particularly if it would require doing and directing fieldwork in the West
Indies and getting correspondents there. From visits to Hayti and the
Bahamas . . . I believe there is a rich, unexplored field." She mentioned her "native friends in both groups" and her acquaintance with
the new governor of the Bahamas.[1]

Elsie took up the work on black folklore with relish and zeal. She
began collecting in Rhode Island (Newport and Providence) and Massachusetts (Fall River, New Bedford, and Cape Cod). She worked with
Portuguese blacks who had immigrated from the Cape Verde Islands
for employment as laborers, waiters, cooks, dockhands, and harvest-
ers in the cranberry bogs. In a letter to Boas, she wrote of the plentiful yield, "As a result of four days & nights pretty steady work at N.
Bedford . . . & in cranberry bog cabins on the Cape and of four evenings in Newport I have 26 tales of the European type, told completely and excellently and 27 tales of the African type together with
a number of obvious hybrids."[2] Early on a Sunday morning, she wrote
to her husband of her fieldwork in Providence, Rhode Island: "Sitting
in car in an alley where the windows are full of heads calling out to
one another that she wants someone to tell stories. It being day time,
however, none as yet will. Last night I worked here till 11:30 with
ease. Not as pleasant as a cranberry bog cabin but much nicer than
the slum of Fall River where we spent yesterday afternoon."[3]

Elsie planned to devote two months to collecting the Cape Verde
tales and, during this time, as she said, to acquiring "as much of the
Portuguese dialect as I can." Challenged by the language and con-

cerned about achieving accuracy in recording, she wrote Boas, "In taking down the tales I am careful about getting the creole as they call it for special words & significant phrases, but the translation of two or three sentences at a time is necessarily pretty free." Parsons was working with Gregorio Teixeira da Silva, a resident of Newport, and "a good interpreter, a man 15 years in this country, painstaking & much interested in the job." She also planned to work with "a young woman of the second generation." Still, as she wrote Boas, there was a concern: "But failure to get the tales in the dialect is worrying me. I don't care so much about getting in the dialect the long thoroughly European tale, but I would like to get in dialect the African type (the stories about Lob[o] Wolf and Jubinh[o] Wolf's nephew). Don't you think it would be worthwhile taking considerable trouble about that? It is on this I particularly want your advice."[4] Boas expressed his interest in her work and acknowledged that it would "be important to get the material in the original. However, he cautioned, "I fear that would increase your labor very much." Suggesting that she might have a student of Romance languages record the tales, he concluded, "Anyway, it seems to me that you ought to take what you can get." A few days later, he wrote, "I am glad to hear that you are overcoming the dialect difficulty."[5]

In 1923, the two-part *Folk-Lore from the Cape Verde Islands* was published as Volume XV of the Memoirs of the American Folk-Lore Society. The dedication was to Gregorio Teixeira da Silva, whom Elsie referred to as her interpreter and teacher. He had died in 1919 and thus did not see the yield of their work. Together Elsie and da Silva had visited boardinghouses operated by Cape Verde women who provided lodging for people from their own or their husbands' island: "They constitute colonies within colonies, so to speak, people from the same island to a certain extent keeping together. It was such boarding houses we were apt to visit in search of informants. In the houses of Fogo Islanders our welcome was particularly cordial. Mr. Silva was from Fogo, and frequently he had to overcome a certain shyness in himself and in others when we visited the houses of other Islanders. But in Fogo houses, where Silva was very apt to find an old acquaintance or an acquaintance of an acquaintance, he was always at ease."[6] Elsie recalled the boardinghouses as pleasant places with "clean and orderly" rooms opening to "sunny little" yards. Referring to other Cape Verde residences, she continued, "But even in the bog-cabins where there were no women, or in the rooms of the slum-houses of Providence or Fall River,—and some of these buildings are a vile disgrace to the municipality,—cleanliness and neatness were characteristic. The cleanly personal habits and the tidy housekeeping of the Islanders have been preserved in spite of their American environment."[7]

Save for two exceptions, the Islanders had retained "their gracious Old-World manners." Elsie and da Silva had spent "pleasant and profitable evenings" in several of the bog cabins, but in one they met their "most signal defeat." Elsie recalled, "It was on Nantucket; and we had driven our livery-stable hack through long stretches of sand or swamp, to be challenged with some suspicion when we reached the isolated cabin. The boss had been to the West Indies,—all over the world, in fact, he said,—and he was more intent on demonstrating his sophistication and his control over his men than on giving them and us a good time. He insisted that they knew no stories." Fearing dismissal, the others could not contradict him. The next day, in a boardinghouse yard, Elsie met one of the men from this cranberry bog. He apologized "in the characteristic friendly and charming manner of his people," and then "joined in the story-telling and riddling." In the boardinghouses, Elsie recalled the kind and hospitable reception, though here as in the cranberry bog cabin, she met with one exception: "The only instance of rudeness I personally encountered was from one of these men of the world, who, when the other men were not looking, slapped me on the back as we went into the room where we were to spend the evening a-riddling." Elsie dismissed this as "the outcome of a faulty classification, due to experience, which, though wide, was misleading," for, as she said, "we no sooner fell to riddling than the mistake was rectified."[8]

Elsie was launched on her research in folklore. In her fieldwork and her publications she was unstoppable. She followed the path of folktales from Rhode Island and Massachusetts (1916–17), to North Carolina (Sanford, N. C., 1916), to Virginia (Hampton Institute, 1920), to Pennsylvania (State Reform Farm School, 1916), to Maryland, to South Carolina (the Colored Public School, the Andrew Robertson Institute, and Schofield School in Aiken, 1920; the South Carolina Sea Islands, 1919), to Florida (1916), to the Caribbean (Andros, 1916; Bahamas, 1918; Barbados, Jamaica, Grenada, and Antilles, 1924; Puerto Rico, 1925; Haiti, 1927), Nova Scotia (1924), and to the Sudan and Egypt (1926). While initially she focused on black folktales, she expanded the scope of her research to include riddles, proverbs, folk beliefs, legends, and myths. She also extended her research in folklore to her work with Native Americans, with the Kiowa (1927), the Tewa (1920–21), the Taos and Laguna Indians, the Zuni, the Hopi, the Navajo, and the Zapotecans in Mexico. This research resulted in numerous articles and books, including the following: *Folk-Tales of Andros, Bahamas* (1918), *Folk-Lore from the Cape Verde Islands* (1923), *Folk-Lore of the Sea Islands, South Carolina* (1923), *Folk-Lore of the Antilles, French and English* (Part I, 1933; Part II, 1936; Part III, 1943), *Tewa Tales* (1926), *Kiowa Tales* (1929) and *Taos Tales* (1940).

Parsons extended her work in black folklore to schools in North and South Carolina (1916, 1919, 1920). She gathered folklore from students informally out of class as well as while classes were in session. At Penn School in Beaufort, South Carolina, she was even able to get "a bout of riddles" going in the schoolroom.[9] From the Hampton Institute in Virginia, she wrote Herbert: "A lot of work in very comfortable circumstances. Must have gathered in 200 riddles this morning in the classrooms of Whittier School, the feeding school to the normal dept., & established plans for written stories for prizes. From 3 to 5:30 I keep office hours in the Museum for students to come singly to tell tales."[10] While recognizing that "stories . . . lost the vivacity of narration" when written down, still Parsons found this collecting technique profitable and used it on other occasions.[11] In February, 1916, she wrote Herbert from Sanford, North Carolina, about her trip to the Summerfield Colored School, where she had asked, "Teacher to get her pupils to write out stories for me. I offer 2 or 3 prizes. Nice two room building with 2 teachers, husband and wife. She teaching the younger children and he the older. I told both sets what I wanted, and read the story Beulah had written out for me, Beulah being by good fortune among the older girls."[12]

While at the Hampton Institute in February, 1920, Elsie met with a group of graduate students who provided her with "old ms. material." They offered to add to the collection that she could then edit.[13] In 1922, this appeared in *Journal of American Folklore* as "Folk-Lore from Elizabeth City County, Virginia." Elsie explained, "Two decades or more ago Miss A. M. Bacon conducted a folk-lore society in Hampton Institute. Through the kindness of Miss Herron of the Institute the unpublished material was given to me to edit, and appears in the following collection."[14] The tales were drawn from the Bacon manuscript, Parsons's own fieldwork, and other published texts, while the riddles were divided into her 1920 collection and Bacon's 1894 compilation.

In February, 1919, Parsons conducted fieldwork in the Sea Islands of South Carolina, where the majority of the inhabitants were black. She visited Port Royal, St. Helena, Hilton Head, and Defuskie. The area was sparsely populated—Dataw with approximately twelve

families, Coosa with between twenty-five to thirty families. "The metropolis" of Beaufort had almost three thousand people. Parsons described her arrival: "Just off a train from the North, as I stood on a
street-corner in Beaufort, keeping an eye on the little dock where the
sail-boat put in for passengers to Ladies' Island or to St. Helena, I noticed a ditch-digger make ready to quit his job for the day; and I
heard him call back to a mate, 'Mos kill bud don' make soup!' Later
that moonlit evening on Ladies' Island I swapped riddles with the
woman who had been induced to hitch up a neighbor's horse to her
own buggy and drive me across the Island and inland on St. Helena to
Penn School."[15]

Elsie found that "every Sea-Islander . . . knew, and was seldom too
shy to tell, a few riddles." Collecting tales, she said, was "more a matter of circumstance," which depended in part on ambience and location. She recalled, "Savannah, I was told more than once, is a place to
hear tales; and several of the tales told me were first heard by their
narrators in Savannah or on boats bound for or from Savannah. 'You
could get story on the Savannah boat—dat's whey dey tell 'um.' " Elsie
heeded the advice, "In an oyster-boat sailing to Savannah from Defuskie between midnight and dawn I did, in fact, listen to tales,—the
tales of Henry Ryan as he stood at the wheel of the sloop he had been
sailing for the past eight years for the oyster-factory of Defuskie."[16]

The tales of the black Sea Islanders of South Carolina were a treasure of esoteric knowledge, which set them apart from others. They
served as markers of ethnic pride and identity. As Elsie noted,
"Southern Negroes feel that their stories belong to the part of life,
that major part, which they do not share with their white neighbors."
She continued, "James Murray, in whose cabin on Hilton Head I had
been enjoying a very good and fruitful time, told me that, had I staid
on in the house of the white man where I first suggested story-telling,
he would have told me no tales, 'fo' no money, not fo' a week.' And he
added on the subject of racial relations: 'We pay dem fo' what we git,
an' dey pay us. We don' boder wid dem, an' dey don' boder wid us. We
wouldn' tell riddle befo' dem, not even if we was a servan' in deir
house.' "[17] However, Elsie, as a white woman from the North who was
genuinely interested in the people and their traditions, was able to
"hear tale upon tale." It was only the rain that kept people, as her host
said, from "flockin' in to my house" to tell her tales.

When collecting folklore, Parsons was tenacious. On one occasion,
she missed her train rather than forego the transcription of a folktale.
As she wrote Herbert from the railroad station in Sanford, "We were
in the middle of a story, Uncle George Marshall and I, when it was

time to leave for the morning train and so—I didn't."[18] Elsie followed the trail of folklore wherever it lead her. Arthur Huff Fauset, who worked with Parsons in Nova Scotia, recalled: "I was impressed by her fearlessness. I remember one character, a mixed black-white youth, sailor and bohemian, obviously one who was alert to the main chance, whom Dr. Parsons had singled out and cultivated to give her entree to the community of rough folk from whom she wished to extract folk material. One night she said to me, 'Basil is taking us far into the woods to meet an old man . . . who has some ghost stories I want to hear.' 'Aren't you afraid to go far into the backwoods alone, with unknown characters, during the night?' I asked. She smiled simply. Her only answer was, 'This is Canada, not the United States. With British law in control, one doesn't have to fear a thing.'[19]

Elsie was ever aware of the possibilities of collecting folklore, even when she was not specifically engaged in fieldwork. In March, 1919, she and her friend and companion, Grant La Farge, were making breakfast in their "canoe-camp" on the Lumbee River in North Carolina when a young boy, ostensibly out hunting rabbits, appeared. Elsie recalled, "After a greeting, he sat down on his haunches by the cook-fire and watched. He asked no questions, but he answered them unconstrainedly. He was Claymiller Lockley, named, as his mother told us later, for a son of Jesse James, the 'dressparader;' and he had a brother Coleyounger, named for the other son of the desperado. Seeing the camp-smoke, Claymiller had told his mother he was going to take his gun and make out he was hunting rabbits, and find out about the camp."[20] Elsie followed him to his family's tenant farm, where the boy's mother, Mrs. Lockley, called her husband in from the field because she wanted Elsie to see "a real Indian." To Elsie's query, " 'What Indian tribe are you?' " Mrs. Lockley replied, " 'Cherokee.' " To Elsie's question about the size of their tribe, she responded, " 'Thousands 'pon top of thousands. Dere's only us up dis way; but you'll see more down to Maxton, an' mo' an' mo' in Pembroke an' Lumberton.' "[21] Elsie met other local inhabitants, too, for her encampment was close to a road that lead to Maxton. She recalled time with a family where she passed "hour on hour, watching the quilting that was in progress, riddling and story-telling, and learning odds and ends from the three generations of the household and from their visiting friends." The quilting frame had been lowered from the ceiling where it was stored. Elsie helped with preparing the cotton batting. "Handfuls of raw cotton grown on the farm were . . . thrown by Mother on the cloth, where it was 'beaten' with light 'sticks' to separate it and get out the 'trash.' The girls joined in the switching, which was repeated three times; and the grandmother and little boys and I would collect the wisps of cotton as they flew about the room."[22]

Elsie was careful to find local people who could assist her in her work. In a 1916 letter headed, "On Way to Jacksonville," she wrote Herbert, "Yesterday at Miami I collected 15 stories, getting the cooperation of my hackman and working the negro quarter." From Aiken, South Carolina, in March, 1920, she reported, "I began folklore collecting with Freddie, aged 12, who sits all day long in the buggy waiting on anyone who wants to go out." From Martinique in March, 1924, she wrote: "The folklore is rich, and I am hard at work, with a one leg man who lost his leg from snake bite, in the morning teaching me idioms, and discussing customs and beliefs and in the afternoon or evening working the phonograph or recording stories from visitors of all kinds. When the old people fail, there is always a child at the door to speak *tim tim,* i.e. riddles. I better stick to it for another two weeks or so, before moving north, reaching N.Y. towards the close of April." One year later, she was working on St. Croix, an island she found "far prettier than St. Thomas" with "people less spoiled." As she wrote Herbert, she was "working hard, another one leg man my chief informant, with a band of boys, a toothless old man called Boss Make and a young woman who works by day in the cane field as auxiliaries."[23]

Elsie engaged some of the people whom she met during her fieldwork as correspondents. They would collect stories, proverbs, riddles, and folk beliefs and mail these to her in exchange for various forms of payment. A young woman from Mangrove Cay on Andros Island wrote Elsie in December, 1916, "Rafuleta Rolle she is in Florida but she leave me her sister Zilpha Rolle to recive [*sic*] what you send I recive the ribbons and I send you more stories." A man from Nicoll's Town of Andros wrote thanking her for the watch and continued: "You didn't send me word whether you wanted any more storys. But I have ventured to send you this one and I hope that you will like it."[24]

Parsons was intent on recruiting others to work in the field of folklore. In a 1918 talk to Boas's anthropology class, she spoke of her work as being "too big for one person." She invited "partners" and offered to help launch several expeditions.[25] In a 1920 lecture at the Hampton Institute, she focused on both the importance of folktales and the urgency of collecting black folklore. She noted that work had been undertaken in Jamaica, the Bahamas, Louisiana, Georgia, and South Carolina but that "Brazil, other parts of South America, Barbados, Lesser Antilles, Hayti, San Domingo, and many places . . . in [the] South" remained untouched. This, she said to the students of the Hampton Institute, was "your part."[26]

When she did succeed in finding someone who was interested in collecting folklore, Elsie offered encouragement but also stipulated certain rigorous standards of recording. She had met a man from Port au Prince, Mr. Gold Refined Wilson, who she hoped would be able to gather folktales in Haiti. She wrote to him that the American Folklore Society would be interested in such a collection and that she would be glad personally to offer him an honorarium. However, she stressed, she needed some assurance about the quality of the material. "You recorded no tales, I recall, in the folk lore study you made a year or so ago. Recording tales in the French Negro dialect is of course difficult."[27] She requested him to send a sample of his work, to include "one tale of the European fairy tale type (you must be careful that these are not book learned, as I have found them at times in Martinique & Guadaloupe) and one of the Lapin or Boukie type or whatever the personage of the animal tale may be called in Haiti." Parenthetically, she cautioned him: "(Dont overlook the riddles, by the way, which are probably as interesting as in the other French Islands.)" Following the directions she had given him, Wilson went to Haiti, learned to speak the dialect, and made acquaintances especially among the Jamican-born inhabitants, in whom Parsons was particularly interested. He assured her that he was ready to undertake a collection of folktales and that he would accept the salary that she suggested.[28]

Parsons also funded people who were already working in anthropology and folklore. She supported Aurelio Espinosa's collection of Spanish folktales in Spain and New Mexico, Harold Courlander's folksong research in Haiti and Santo Domingo, and Zora Neale Hurston's collection of black folklore in Florida and Alabama.[29] Most successful among her recruits for collaborative research was Arthur Huff Fauset. When Parsons decided to follow the folktale trail into Nova Scotia, she contacted Frank Speck at the University of Pennsylvania to help locate a black student who might be able to assist her. Fauset recalled: "Early in my student career at the University of Pennsylvania, I took an evening course in Anthropology with Dr. Frank G. Speck, then head of the department of Anthropology. One evening he announced to the students, 'I am expecting in a week or two a visit by an eminent folk-lorist who is a friend of mine. She is a very wealthy lady who has a distinguished career in Negro folk-lore research.' . . . As the class was disbanding, Dr. Speck said to me, 'Arthur, I'd like to talk with you a moment.' He then informed me that Dr. Parsons had asked him if he had a black student whom she could use during the summer as an investigator of Black folklore in Nova Scotia. All expenses would be paid, and there would be an honorarium." When Parsons arrived, he was introduced to her in Dr. Speck's office. He recalled her puffing "interminably on a cigarette" and asking questions in a quiet, direct manner. To her query as to whether or not he was interested in such a study, he replied positively. Fauset continued: "But to her question whether or not I had ever collected folk material, I had to reply in the negative. She then turned to Dr. Speck and said, 'I would want him to collect samples here in the Philadelphia area, then send them to me. If I am satisfied that he appears to be a person who could do what is required, I will use him.' "[30]

Fauset, who taught seventh grade at Edwin M. Stanton Public School in Philadelphia, began collecting riddles from his students.[31] He collected tales from people in "barber shops, cafeterias, at churches." Parsons was pleased. Together they left for Yarmouth, Nova Scotia, in July, 1923. Once there, Parsons took up residence in a hotel, while Fauset stayed with a black family to make acquaintances. He recalled: "During the next two or three days, Mrs. Parsons took me in tow, showing me how she proceeded to obtain folk material. She was, of course, very simple in her manner, quiet, direct, and although readily observable as not being one of 'the people' nevertheless one who faded almost into anonymity among them. There was a *savoir faire* about her that taught me much about how one maintains one's identity, uniqueness, individuality, yet merges with the surroundings, inconspicuously, in order to achieve desired ends."[32]

Fauset learned certain "mechanical things" of fieldwork from Parsons, "such as having paper and pencil handy on all occasions." She encouraged him to develop a form of shorthand to record with accuracy and speed "the essential utterances . . . and then to find some way to put down the more extensive notes as rapidly as possible, while the memory was fresh." Fauset had been anxious about being able to listen to the story and record it at the same time. Additionally, he was certain that the process of transcription would distract the informant. "But," he said, "from Dr. Parsons I learned to lose my personal identity in the aura and intent of the informant, with the result that even essential interruptions, in order to make sure the transcription had been accurately made, did not prove fatal distractions."[33]

Fauset stayed on in Nova Scotia after Elsie left in mid-July. He worked in New Glasgow, where he fruitlessly attempted to locate a "colored person who [spoke] Gaelic." He traveled to Annapolis Royal, where he "had a very successful time with the Indians . . . spending several days working with them." As he told Elsie, "Your name was the touchstone." Lucy Picton made him "a little charm," and John Picton gave him a basket. He continued, "The mention of your name had as much to do with the success as anything, I guess. They all wanted to help the friend of 'the lady.' Mrs. Picton in particular desired to be remembered to you." He was, however, disappointed in not being able to collect any riddles from the Indians. He wrote Elsie, "I tried, tried, tried. John Picton, my Indian guide tried to get the Indians to tell under the urge of a handsome reward if he was successful, but with no success. The one Indian in Bear River who might have given us some was off on a guiding trip." Fauset was told that the Indians called riddles "unspirited stories . . . which signified that they were undesirable." As he said, "All the Indians I approached on the subject of riddles said, 'I dont know none of this kind of stuff.' "[34]

In St. John, New Brunswick, Fauset took a rest before the "final plunge in Digby and Weymouth." As he wrote Elsie, he had been "chasing thru the hills of Lejuille and Granville, to say nothing of Bear River, often without taking dinner because it was inconvenient to get back to the hotel." At the library in St. John, he had consulted William Roy MacKenzie's *The Quest of the Ballad*. Wistfully, he noted that the work would have been helpful to him before he had begun his work, for it assisted him in collecting ballads, "of which I obtained variants from a girl in Liverpool, one of them called 'Polly,' I believe, quite important. . . . I got some ballads, English and Negro from an old colored man in Annapolis Royal, and a few approaching the ballad type, tho inferior in character, in Shelburne county and Dartmouth, some rollicking songs from a colored fellow in Annapolis Royal, and a few sailor songs here and there. In one of the stories I got from an old lady in New Glasgow is a suspicious trace of some old English ballad."[35]

On his return home to Philadelphia, Fauset thanked Elsie for the "wonderful experience." As he wrote her, "You literally made it possible for me to pursue my work under conditions so new to me that I could hardly believe myself at times." He lauded her "splendid spirit of democratic fellowship and cooperation" and credited her "absolute confidence" in him with making the "experiment" a success. He asked her permission to dedicate the volume to her, which, he said, "would be a sublime pleasure."[36] Fauset's *Folklore from Nova Scotia* bore a dual dedication: "I am at a loss to express in words my indebtedness to Dr. Elsie Clews Parsons who not only sponsored this investigation, but whose kindly interest and advice, and co-operation on and off the field, have been of invaluable assistance. I owe a similar debt of gratitude to Dr. Frank G. Speck, Professor of Anthropology in the University of Pennsylvania. He has been more than an inspiring teacher to me. Counselor, teacher, above all a friend, his words of advice and

encouragement are priceless treasures for which there can be no fitting tribute. To dedicate this volume to these friends crowns my task
with genuine happiness."[37]

Elsie and Fauset joined forces in another endeavor, the collection
of material for *Folk-Lore of the Antilles, French and English.* Elsie made
three trips to the Caribbean from 1924 to 1927, while Fauset traveled
to the northern British Isles of the Lesser Antilles in 1927. Of her
first trip, Elsie recalled, "I visited the most southern islands of the
great crescent, reaching them by steamer or by mail boat schooner,
Trinidad, the Grenadines, St. Vincent and St. Lucia, and then for several weeks I kept house in Martinique, at Morne Rouge, on the slope
of Pélée."[38] While on St. Lucia, she had written Herbert, "From
Grenada I went by sail boat to Carnacou, and there again by schooner
to St. Vincent, and to this island. . . . St. George's Grenada was a
charming town, the prettiest I've seen. . . . The material is pretty
good. . . . I can write the patois now pretty well, after practice of several hours a day! It is much harder in these tropical islands to stick to
the job than in New Mexico; one can sleep, sleep, sleep."[39] In 1925,
she visited Guadaloupe, where, as she recalled, she "lived in a mountain inn kept by a Syrian merchant who occasionally sold me sweets
and told tales." In 1927, she chartered a schooner and sailed to islands
"otherwise accessible only by dint of patient waits for very uncertain
vessels—Marie Galante, Les Saints, Saba." She also revisited the south
coast of Haiti and Dominica.

In Trinidad, Elsie began her study of French Creole "under the tu-
telage of [a man] whom I met on a dock in Port of Spain."[40] The results were fruitful, for as she wrote to Herbert, "Now I can write the
dialect pretty well when it is dictated slowly. And my note books are
full up."[41] Her tutor she remembered also as "a devoted interpreter,
runner in of story tellers, sponsor, and guide." On later trips to other
islands, his role would be filled "by other lads." Of these, she wrote,
"To the water boys of the islands, dock rats in our ugly speech, these
collections are much indebted."[42]

During the course of her work, Elsie became increasingly interested in, as she said, the "study of the patois with some systematic instruction about puzzling syntax." She was able to work with Felix
Mordock of Morne Rouge, Martinique, who recorded the majority of
the Martinique materials. Elsie recalled: "Mordock could write both
French and patois and he had all the time in the world for me, for he
was a one legged man, having been stung while cutting wood, by one
of the dreaded snakes of the island and having resorted first to the
[curer] and then to the hospital doctor . . . to neither, as each said,

soon enough. Mordock was a very intelligent person and we learned much each from the other, so that after I left the island for several years he continued to record folklore." Mordock's cousin also recorded tales for Elsie. With pleasure, Elsie remembered time spent in the yard of her house where she "listened of moonlight nights to the stories told and sung naturally."[43] In the morning light, they would record the tales on the phonograph.

Elsie spent her afternoons in Morne Rouge calling on the neighbors, collecting riddles from them, and listening for good storytellers. Recording tales on such visits, Elsie noted, was "almost out of the question so eager and clamorous was the mob that instantly grew up to push into the two roomed cabin, and outrage the sense of propriety of an ever courteous hostess." She would return home, as she recalled, and retreat "behind my bamboo fence, jasmin and rose bushes." There she would find "Louise to snatch bits of lore from when she was not too busy cooking or cleaning or gossiping or bickering with the *marchande* who brought us fish from the coast or milk or vegetables, those long striding, long necked girls who give their greatest charm to the island highways. . . . Louise was not much of a story teller, but she sang over her pots and authenticated traditions."[44]

In 1926, Elsie went to Egypt and the Sudan in search of folktales. She had originally planned to travel from Khartoum to Abyssinia, but the British Sudanese Government Office looked with displeasure on such a journey. So she compromised with a study of Egypt and the Sudan. From the Savoy Hotel in Luxor (Upper Egypt), she wrote her son, "In Cairo I got an Arab dragman & a motor boat & spent 12 days coming here putting in at villages & towns to see tombs or temples or listen to stories in villages unfrequented by tourists where the children are mannerly & the *sheikh* gives you coffee and urges a dinner upon you & lets you smoke his water pipe & shows you—if the village is Arab—his horse. Also, if you ask, his ladies who kiss your hand, you in return kissing theirs. Later the story tellers gather around the light you set up on the river bank and you hear the origin stories of those you once heard in the Bahamas or the Sea Islands & wondered where they came from, knowing they were not European."[45]

In Khartoum, she stayed at the Grand Hotel, where her veranda overlooked "the date palms of the zoo where the lion roars throughout the night." She told her son, John, "At first he sounded like the plumbing gone wrong at Harrison."[46] To Mabel Dodge Luhan, she wrote, "Folk tales here & in Egypt, antiquities in stone, heat & cold alternating, and sand storm have been my lot. After such a sand gale as is this moment on, one will never complain of N.Y. March winds. Even the lion's roar in the zoo next door can not be heard. Only the English sparrows are indomitable. The British have achieved more than sparrows here or a caged lion,—a great feat of order and efficiency in their own likeness. I benefit, but I am glad too that folk tale recording takes me into other than colonial society."[47]

Elsie relished the variety in her surroundings. She remarked on the "medley . . . of peoples" in Khartoum, where all save a few Britishers spoke Arabic. Her search for interpreters yielded an American who was born in Luxor and taught in a Greek Catholic school, a Syrian, and a Sudanese employee of the Governor's Office. She wrote John: "My life is varied. Last night I slept very well in the sitting room of a Greek Catholic mission, after listening all evening to Syrian tales in the house of a merchant where our large audience was served with coffee & sponge cake. . . . This morning a school boy told tales of Egyptian Copt source. This afternoon I spent in the American Protestant mission house, with an Arab for a story teller, and another Syrian to translate. Tomorrow afternoon will be spent in the Sudanese Negro quarter, with a Sudanese civil servant as interpreter."[48] The yield of tales was bountiful. She filled her notebooks with Egyptian folktales and with Sudanese material collected in Khartoum. Her Sudanese interpreter wrote tales in Arabic, while a student provided an English translation.

On all her travels and for all her collections, Elsie had a certain approach toward the study of folklore. Above all she was interested in thoroughness, in gathering as much material as possible. The text, then, was paramount, and as such had to be respected. Editing, whether for a publisher's concern with length or an editor's concern with propriety, was not permissible. As she wrote to one collector of Taos tales, "Your rendering is almost too good. I am not charging you with the felony of 'dressing up,' only with the misdemeanor of rendering the narratives' inadequate English too indulgently."[49] Her attitude toward the collection of folklore was in keeping with her approach toward research in anthropology. "She was," as Gladys Reichard said, "above all things a respecter of evidence." And the evidence for Parsons was in the material—in the folklore collections themselves. Indeed, her folklore material was presented almost entirely as collections of texts. She would begin an article or a book with a passage on the fieldwork situation, a list of the informants, a bibliography of related works but the body of the work would always be the texts. These folklore texts were part of the mosaic of her work, from which, as she had told Reichard, "she hated to omit any detail."

As Elsie reasoned, a seemingly irrelevant piece of information might one day provide the missing clue for another researcher.[50]

To the dismay of her publishers, the detail in the texts extended to the inclusion of variants. Of this she wrote, "If folk-tales have indeed the cultural significance imputed to them, their growth and decay are of moment, and such processes can best be studied by an accumulation of variants. Indeed, the time may come when the collector will feel called upon to publish as well as record *all* the variants he hears." Elsie suggested that a study of variants might prove useful for those interested in the development of folklore—a successful variant might give rise to new tales. She viewed the analysis of tales as important for acculturation studies. Stories, she said, were "great travellers." In this "passing from people to people changes [were] made" in the tales that might cast light on the "differences in life between the two peoples." Elsie stressed in a talk on "The Value of Folk Tales," delivered at the Hampton Institute, that there was no better opportunity "for studying this very important subject [of acculturation] . . . than in contacts between Indians and Whites and Negroes and Whites."[51]

In following the folktale trail, Elsie was on a quest for origin. She quite literally hoped to follow the tales to their source. In this she was not alone, since Boas and his students were tracing the diffusion of culture traits, and the European and American folklorists were launched on historic-geographic studies of tales to determine the *Ur* type—the original form of a narrative. In his early letters to her regarding the Cape Verde fieldwork, Boas wrote, "I feel quite certain that Portuguese & Spanish influence account for a great deal of our Negro folklore. They must have acquired a great deal in Africa before coming here."[52] Parsons herself became convinced that the origin of the black folktales was largely European and Asiatic. Of this she wrote in *Folk-Lore of the Sea Islands:* "The Cape Verde Islander on Cape Cod, Jack Brown in Carolina, were but repeating an old process,—the transmission of Asiatic or European tales to the Americas by way of Africa. Unsurpassed as hardy voyagers and explorers, the men of the Iberian Peninsula, together with their descendants, black and white, are also unsurpassed as carriers of folk-tales."[53]

In remarks to Boas's class in anthropology, Parsons spoke of the complex problem of origin, which she presented as the puzzle to be solved. "You have doubtless heard from Prof. Boas," she said, "that many negro folk-tales are of European origin, learned in Africa from some of the most remarkable tale carriers of the world." It was "the Portuguese and Spanish Negro slaves" who carried the tales to North and South America. However, they also "brought African stories &

stories that probably reached Africa directly from Asia." The challenge, as Parsons presented it, was "to work out what is Asiatic in this
folklore, what African, what European." The path of the folktale,
however, was not firmly etched. While origin of the tales, as she pos-
ited, might ultimately be from the Iberian peninsula, the actual trail
of diffusion was a mystery. For the Sea Islands of South Carolina, the
tales might have come from the Spanish settlements of St. Helena or
Port Royal, or from contact with Spanish sailors, or from the original
contact in Africa with "Hispanic tales brought to the African West
Coast." Additionally, the corpus of tales was not all of one piece. Of
the Cape Verde Island repertoire, she wrote, "The greater number
are European, and told probably much as they are told in Portugal;
others are European in substance, but given an Island or African setting; others, again, may be entirely African." She noted "a general appreciation . . . that the animal stories were less to be identified with
their Portuguese culture than the stories that began, let us say, with
three brothers in search of adventure." The tales with animal characters, including those about Wolf (Lob') and Wolf's Nephew (Jubinh'),
were felt to have "no place at all in American culture," so much so
that the Cape Verde immigrants ceased telling these tales when they
came to the United States.[54] From her work with the Andros Islanders, Parsons was most emphatic about the location where the tales
were originally acquired. She wrote, "Whatever may have been the
provenience of the tales in Africa, Portuguese or other, I have no
doubt that by far the greater number of the Bahama tales were
learned there,—learned, not in America, but in Africa."[55] Her trip to
Egypt and the Sudan in 1926 was to be the ultimate search for origins: she intended to follow "Arabic folk tales on their way into Africa." Her pleasure was in finding just such connections. As she wrote
her son, "My first folktale was told by a boy of twelve whose Copt
grandparents came from Egypt. It is an excellent place to study Arabic influence in Negro folk tales which is what I am after in
particular."[56]

Parsons was keenly concerned with doing justice to the oral rendi-
tion. She found this particularly challenging in her collection of black
folktales. She wrote: "The heaviest handicap that the white recorder
is under, in taking down Negro tales, is the pressure which he exerts,
willy nilly, upon the use of language. In the effort to use school English, dialect tends to pass into bad grammar. Dialect is not uncommonly more vigorous and expressive . . . ; but the narrator, naturally enough, fails to realize this, and attempts to eschew dialect. To
one who opines of his people, like Frank Murray of Defuskie, that

'dere is not'in' de matter wid us but bad grammar,' the temptation to try to use school-taught language in telling tales to a white is strong."[57] For one familiar with the Negro dialect, a substitution could be made, Parsons remarked, "but there are risks to fidelity of transmission involved by this method, and I for one have not enough self-confidence to use it." She noted an even greater challenge in recording "characteristic emphasis of Negro tales, the drawl, and the tricks of speeding up." While the use of italics and exclamation points were but "feeble indicators," one certainly could not express "by printers' signs the significance of what is *not* said . . . —a significance conveyed by manner or by quietness of intonation, of which a good story-teller is past master."[58]

As an aid for achieving fidelity in transcription, Elsie recorded tales on a phonograph. She began this in February, 1916, during fieldwork in North Carolina. She wrote Herbert, "I got a lot more stories towards the end, and considerable experience with the phonograph."[59] She used this method extensively for the songs that she collected from the Andros Islanders. Never relying entirely on the recording device, she also transcribed the lyrics by hand. In the process, she discovered the disparity between the two versions. She noted, "As usual in records of Negro songs the phonograph record and the text as dictated do not altogether correspond."[60]

It was precisely because she recognized the limitations of recording that Parsons was exacting in the transcription of texts. She attempted to convey on paper the way the folklore was rendered verbally—this included concern with orthography. She was known for her insistence "on precise transcription, with no doctoring for effect, and no editing; she wanted the raw utterance."[61] She was wary of literary influence on oral tradition. After one tale recorded in her Khartoum notebook, she wrote, "Heard from grandmother who does not read. NO Arabian Nights in house."[62]

Parsons's work with the Cape Verde Islanders showed the difficulties she encountered when trying to achieve both a true and a precise transcription. Her translator, Gregorio Teixeira da Silva, could record with ease in the Fogo dialect, but was unable to take down stories in the dialect of the other islands. Parsons explained the process: "The stories had to be told slowly in order to be translated and recorded. In the stories in both Portuguese dialect and translation the translation made on the spot served as notes for Mr. Silva to write the story in dialect at a later date. The English translations as printed are of his stories. This method of collecting and translating is laborious, nor is it quite free from the danger of literary elaboration; but the method seemed necessary, as neither of us could take down the stories in the dialect; at least, in the first summer of our work, when the bulk of the stories were collected." With this method of recording, Parsons recognized that the "dialectical differences between the Islands—and they are considerable—are for the most part overlooked." However, she viewed it as a necessary compromise. In all cases, she was insistent that the stories be told in dialect, even when the narrator could speak English better than the translator, for, as she said, "I had learned from experience that when the foreign-born narrator told his story in English, it suffered greatly from paraphrases or short cuts."[63]

While Parsons wanted the tales "pure" of literary influence, she did not necessarily want them clean. The mosaic of folklore included obscene tales. However, if Parsons would not edit the material, her informants would. Said one Sea Island resident, " 'Some is so evil, I don' like to go t'rough wid 'em'.' " Of her attempt to record one of the most common of Bahamian tales, which she titled "Man under the Bed," she wrote: "One day I happened to ask Mr. Jack if he knew it. 'Oh, you want dem kin' o' tales too! I could tell you a heap o' dem tales, but I blush fo' you,' he said. 'You must not,' I rejoined, 'for it is my business to take down all kinds of tales, no matter what they are about, and just as they are.' " Elsie finally convinced him to tell her "out of the 'heap o' dem tales" precisely the one she had asked about, as well a variant entitled "The Three Sweethearts." While he acquiesced to the request, the informant gave the barest sketch of the tales, thus rendering them totally innocuous. Still another informant was more emphatic in censoring what he would tell Elsie. "James Murray said that he knew twenty-five or thirty 'man's tales;' 'but,' added he, and too firmly for challenge, 'I wouldn' go t'rough wid 'em.' Artistic storyteller as he was, he would forego part of the point of a story rather than commit the moral impropriety of telling it. 'I leave it dere,' he would say."[64] In Bermuda, Elsie met a thirty-year-old cab driver who assured her he

> knew "boyish tales" which he said he was "not in suitable circumstances to tell," since "the stories men tell are not the way women tell stories." Among his "boyish tales" I surmised he included one which at last after prompting he did give, very sketchily, as,

TWO POPPERS

> Woman had a visitor. Her husband comes back. Little boy says, "Two poppers." —"What you say, Jack?"—"Two daddies, one under de bed, one eating supper."[65]

Elsie applied the same standards to those who worked with her in folklore research. As with the informants, so with the collectors, this proved uncomfortable. Fauset wrote Parsons, "A good many of the tales which remain are men's tales of the 'meanest' kind. I shall go thru with them solely out of respect for my obligation to the American Folk-Lore Society, and to you, for frankly I am loath to include them."[66] Following Parsons's standards and not his own, Fauset included the obscene material only to find himself criticized by an offended reader. Ruth Benedict, editor of the *Journal of American Folklore*, wrote Parsons, "I am enclosing the letter I have received from Professor Krauss about the publication of the so-called smutty stories and riddles from the Fauset mss."[67]

Sensitive to people's own view of their material, Parsons paid heed to what they themselves called their folklore. In her work with the Cape Verde Islanders, she noted, "The Portuguese term *proverbio* is not in use by the Islanders; in general, the term is not even understood." While she was not able to ascertain a single designation, *piada* or *rafolh'* seemed "to approximate the sense of 'proverb.' " The meaning of *piada* in Portuguese as deceit or dissimulation, Parsons indicated, did not pertain to the meaning of the word in the dialect. Rather, for the Cape Verde Islanders, *piada* denoted an indirect reference, and *rafolh'*, an indirect reference more personal or pointed. The meaning of these native terms was a clear statement about the way in which this genre of folklore was used—that is, for indirect reference. Parsons remarked: "Of *rafolh'* and *piada* the Islanders are undoubtedly very fond. I have been told that quite a lengthy conversation may thus be indirectly conducted, particularly in the presence of those to whom the speakers wish to keep their meaning obscure. Besides, if only you do not refer to a person by name, you may talk 'at him,' as we say, as much as you like, and, theoretically at least, he may not take offence."[68]

Among the Sea Islanders of South Carolina, a folktale was referred to as a story or a riddle or sometimes a fable or little joke. Parsons tried to have "Mr. Jack . . . explain the difference," which he did in a straightforward manner: "How you spli de diffunce between riddle an' story? Dere is singin' in story."[69] For the Andros Islanders, "sings," or musical passages, were frequently inserted in the tales. Parsons recalled, "Pa Black of Jamaica and Andros sometimes took steps as he sung; so did old Jack Armbrister, one of the so-called 'Congo' in New Providence." She continued, "Old Armbrister had taught the words and dance-steps to his grandson, John Richardson. He was impatient when the bashful boy refused to perform with him. Like a true artist, he explained that he could not do justice to song and dance without, as he said, a 'partner.' "[70]

The Andros Islanders had a set phrase to refer to a folktale. Parsons explained, "You *talk* ol' storee. The emphasis is on 'ol.' " If pronounced properly, "talk ol' storee" is a formula understood by every one." As she candidly related, ignorance of this phrase had posed initial difficulties in her fieldwork: "Not knowing it during my first hour in Nassau, when I asked for old-time story-tellers, I was directed to fortune-tellers." However, once she learned "the formula," she was able to "get a group of women and children around me eager to talk "ol' storee" for a penny or two." This method of collecting, while "particularly useful . . . to ascertain the circulation of a story already heard," Parsons said, was not ideal. "The best way to hear the stories," she opined, "is in the evening, the time they are wont to be told, and, if possible, in the house of a mutual friend."[71]

To "talk ol' storee," a narrator needed to incorporate elements from the present situation as well as to adhere to a traditional format. As Parsons explained: "The tales allow for individualistic variation, deliberate variation, only in their conclusion. The narrator is expected to connect the tale with the occasion of its telling,—an opportunity for personal garnish or wit. This feature of talking 'ol' storee,' whenever the tale is properly told, is very marked." Tradition, however, held check on individual variation by stipulating the characters and the format of the narrative. Parsons observed, "The personages of the tales are . . . formulaic, possessed of fixed attributes or names." She continued, "Rabbit is always temperate and crafty, Boukee always greedy and sluggish. In the tales of a 'boy' hero, Jack or Jock is almost invariably his name. Greenleaf is the name of the heroine."[72] The narrative itself was set off by traditional markers, a formularized beginning and ending. Parsons noted, "To be properly 'talked,' every 'ol' storee' should have one of these openings and closings." Here also, as with the extemporized conclusion to the tale, there was allowance for individual variation, for there was a long list of formulae from which to choose.

Among the Cape Verde Islanders, Parsons also noted the importance of formula openings. In order to begin a storytelling session, someone might say, "There was an old man with an old woman with an old basket. The old man was putting his foot in and out. The old woman was putting her foot in and out. From here on what it is, he knows?" Openings could also be quite simple, such as " 'Was a man married to a woman,' [or] 'Was a boy.' " Tales ended with what Parsons referred to as "comparatively detachable formula-closings." She continued, "Indeed, the *offerice*, the offering or *l'envoi*, should attach to every well-told story. The *offerice* . . . is supposed to refer, however slightly, to the plot of the tale, and this reference taxes the skill of the narrator." In "The Poor Friend and the Rich," a tale of problems that money could not solve, Parsons gave an example of such a closing: "Even yesterday I went there, I saw them as contented as ever. I went there to pay him a debt I owed him. He said, 'Money! money! if you mention money in my house, I will kill you.' " Tales could also be ended with "closings . . . which are entirely irrelevant to the tale." The narrator might also succinctly state, " 'It is finished.' "[73]

Parsons referred to the formularized openings and closings for Cape Verde riddles. One might say, " '¿Cusa é uma cousa? [What is a thing?]'. . . . '¿Cusa é cousa?' . . . , or merely '¿Cusa?' " She noted the element of individual choice, for "some riddlers use the formula before every riddle, others drop it." To begin a riddling session, one used the "quasi-opening formula" "Mi' 'li, mi' lá" ["I am here, I am there"]. In the Windward Islands (San Anton, San Vicente, or San Nicolao), one might say, " 'Dibinhâ dibinha' or 'Divinha.' " In place of a spoken opening, in San Anton one could pick up a pebble and rub it in the palms of the hands. If a pebble could not be found, the person might throw up "the hands . . . to show that there is no pebble" and then rub the palms together. In Fogo, to spur on a reluctant riddling group, one could say, " '¿Cusa é uma cousa: Francês na mar, Orlandês na terr' [What is this: French at sea, Irish on land]?' There is no answer. In San Anton, 'Vamos deitar divínhas [Come, let us lay down riddles]!' some one may propose." A riddle session could be held between two men with "first one asking, and then the other; the aim being not only to give . . . hard riddles, but to exhaust the supply of your opponent." For the Cape Verde Islanders, this type of competition was called *desfio*, which also meant horse race. Parsons recalled, "I was told one night that the preceding night, after I had left the circle, two men . . . asked riddles in competition until one o'clock."[74]

Parsons was keenly aware of the importance of context. The time, the place, the season, the audience, all these contributed to, indeed in many cases, determined the type of folklore she was able to collect. Of her fieldwork in Robeson County, North Carolina, she wrote, "Telling riddles fitted in nicely . . . with the quilting and with the grandmother's pipe." She continued, "Mother did not smoke, but chewed. She was remarkably skillful in spitting into the fire from wherever she sat at the quilting frame. She spat through the index and middle fingers of her right hand held to her lips." After the quilting frame was raised to the ceiling and supper had been served, the family and a few visitors gathered around the fire. The comfortable, cozy setting was ideal for telling tales, but not for recording them. As Parsons related, "Circumstances precluded taking the tales down at the time (the only light was the fire, around which, on the floor, lay the children, and the talk was freer without a note-book)."[75]

In "Spirituals and Other Folklore from the Bahamas," Parsons explained how the destruction from a natural disaster had determined where and what type of material she could collect. In 1926 a series of three violent hurricanes had struck the islands, "destroying fishing and sponging fleets, snapping off the tops of cocoanut trees or uprooting them, tearing off the roofs, tipping or leveling the walls of the houses of the settlements." Parsons described her arrival: "One day the following January, I went ashore on the beach at Devil's Point, Cat Island, and with a group of welcoming islanders walked up the dunes to look at the devastated settlement. 'Mah sister house; she have no man to build it up again.' This was a pile of coral rubble. Other houses had been more or less restored, if only with palm leaf thatch, but the usual warm invitations to visit failed, so I turned into the Zion chapel, part stone, part palm leaf, to sit down and lead away from the tale of hurricane to ol' time tale and riddle." However, she found that the stories and riddles were not forthcoming, because "a chapel is not a proper place for riddling." The people, knowing what was appropriate for the context, asked her, " 'Wouldn' mistress cyare to hear anthum?' And then and there I learned that spirituals were as common in the Bahamas as . . . in the Carolinas." She described the performance: "The middle-aged woman who asserted herself as hostess became the leader, carrying the tune and the new lines, the others coming in with the refrain. The leader remained seated, but she so swung the upper part of her body, gesticulating with her arms and tossing her head, as to produce virtually a dance accompaniment to the song. The other girls and women shared in some of these motions, but were far less vehement than the leader, particularly the younger ones."[76]

In Haiti, Parsons found that church was *not* the proper context for singing spirituals or "anthums." She had conducted fieldwork in what was called the American Colony of Samana Bay, among the descendants of American blacks who had immigrated there in the early nineteenth century. These people referred to themselves as Americans and retained English as their language. While other Haitians called them "Combeltieu (Converti), the Converts," they remained, "in part at least, Protestants, Wesleyan Methodists." Parsons had been interested in finding what had remained of American folklore. She found that only spirituals or anthums remained and that they were "sung at the night time weddings and on moonlit nights at parties for 'pealing' (shuking) corn (*sheshé*), and not in chapel." As Parsons recounted, the minister had never heard an anthum: "When at my request his missionary congregation at Clara sang us some 'anthums,' he was a much surprised man. The unusual self-consciousness of the congregation as they sang their 'anthums' complemented the surprise of their minister and bore witness to the statement that anthums were never sung in chapel. I for one enjoyed the morning's innovation. Outside the open windows the pigs were rooting and the cocoanut palms crackling in the smart breeze off the blue bay as the somewhat shamefaced girls and their more complacent elders sang to their American visitor and to the minister who had finished preaching in an accent foreign to us all."[77]

In "The Value of Folk Tales," a talk delivered at Hampton Institute, Parsons rhetorically posed the question as to why it was important to collect tales. Why did one need to travel to "Canada, the West Indies, Mexico," or the southern part of the United States? She answered her question: "Because knowledge of old stories contributes to knowledge of civilization and to the history of the human mind. Unwritten stories [had come] before written stories, [and] traditional tales before literature." Tales, she said, revealed the life of the people, "the homely ways of living." They told about "ways of thinking and feeling." Using information gleaned from tales, one might "bit by bit" piece together life as it was once lived. Tales, she said, also provided "a record of language and of those variations in language . . . call[ed] dialects." Storytelling, she asserted, was an art. Addressing her black audience, she said,

[I] don't have to tell you that Colored people are remarkably good story tellers. It would be a great pity to sacrifice this gift to the notion that story telling is un-American, foolishness, a waste of time. It is all this in pretty much the same way that gracious manners, a love of music, and a love of color, are to many Americans a waste of energy. But there are quite a number of different kinds of people in this country. Some of them White and Black, hope that the particular Negro gifts of gracious manners of expressiveness in color and in music and in the spoken word, including the art of story telling, will be, not withdrawn from American culture, or crushed out of it, but contributed to its enrichment.

For Parsons, collecting folktales provided a "sense of romance." She found excitement in the connections she could make between "an Apache tale from the Southwest or an Indian tale from Penobscot Bay [and] a tale you have heard the day before from a Cape Verde Islander on Cape Cod." Pursuing folktales, Parsons was led "to islands and other places more or less romantic," and she encountered people whom she otherwise would not have met. She remarked,

> Recently, on a visit to the Sea Islands, had I not been sitting by the fire one night in the house of old Mr. Jack . . . , it is likely that one aspect of the charming little town . . . [would have] escaped me. We were in the middle of a tale about the Devil Bridegroom when a goodlooking young woman came in from the street and, looking over the screen between the hearth and the open door, said, "Mr. Jack, didsh yer hear dat cyar jus' now in dis street? Ef I could fin' out who dat chauffeur, I git after him. . . . Six, sewen sojers pile out an' ax me ef I wan' mek some money. I say, "Not day way." . . . We had heard a motor, but Mr. Jack was not to be interrupted. "I hear' nothin,' " he answered. "I des tellin' riddles to dish yere ladee."

Clearly a practical joke intended to insult, the white sailors delivered to the doorstep were a way of reminding Elsie and Mr. Jack of racial segregation. For this reason, because of inequalities in status, southern whites knew nothing of the tales of the blacks. Parsons continued, "Arrogance or condescension stand in the way of story telling. It would be strange indeed if Southern Negroes told stories to Southern Whites. It takes something of an artist to listen to a folk-tale as well as to tell it, and between artists theories of social inequality do not obtrude."[78] Though Parsons had set aside her political work for her scientific research, these lines echo her statements on social equality expressed in the earlier works, *Social Rule* and *Social Freedom*. Implicitly, her work in folklore had a political counterpoint, for she was recording the voices of those who had for so long gone unheeded. In so doing, she accorded to the tellers of the tales, the riddles, and the proverbs the respect due to a creator of something beautiful.

NOTES

1. Boas Papers, ECP to Boas, 25 Nov. 1915.
2. ECP, ECP to Boas, July 1916.
3. ECP, ECP to HP, 31 July 1916.
4. ECP, ECP to Boas, 22 July 1916.
5. ECP, Boas to ECP, 29 July 1916; 5 Aug. 1916.

6. Parsons, *Folk-Lore from the Cape Verde Islands* (New York: G. E. Stechert & Co., 1923), Part I, p. xi.

7. Ibid., p. xii.

8. Ibid., pp. xii-xiii.

9. Parsons, *Folk-Lore of the Sea Islands, South Carolina* (New York: G. E. Stechert & Co., 1923), p. xiii.

10. ECP, ECP to HP, 10 Feb. 1920.

11. Parsons, *Folk-Lore of the Sea Islands*, p. xiii.

12. ECP, ECP to HP, 24 Feb. 1916.

13. ECP, ECP to HP, 10 Feb. 1920.

14. A. M. Bacon and E. C. Parsons, "Folk-Lore from Elizabeth City County, Virginia," *JAF* 35 (1922): 250–327.

15. Parsons, *Folk-Lore of the Sea Islands*, p. xiii.

16. Ibid., p. xv.

17. Ibid., p. xiv; see also Parsons, "Joel Chandler Harris and Negro Folklore," *The Dial* 66 (1919): 493.

18. ECP, ECP to HP, 24 Feb. 1916.

19. ECP, Fauset to Hare, Aug. 1970.

20. Parsons, "Folk-Lore of the Cherokee of Robeson County, North Carolina," *JAF* 32 (1919): 384.

21. Ibid., p. 385.

22. Ibid., pp. 386–87.

23. ECP, ECP to HP, 27 Feb. 1916; 26 Mar. 1920; 25 Mar. 1924; 5 Mar. 1925.

24. ECP, anonymous letters to ECP dated 13 Dec. 1916, 21 May 1917.

25. ECP, "Remarks to Prof. Boas's Class in Anthropology," 25 Mar. 1918.

26. ECP, "The Value of Folk Tales."

27. ECP, ECP to Gold Refined Wilson, n.d.

28. ECP, Gold Refined Wilson to ECP, 1 Oct. 1925.

29. Parsons provided Aurelio M. Espinosa, and his son, J. Manuel Espinosa, with support for fieldtrips to Spain and to the Southwest. For Parsons's funding of Espinosa, see Aurelio M. Espinosa, *The Folklore of Spain in the American Southwest* (Norman: University of Oklahoma Press, 1985), p. 40; Rosemary Lévy Zumwalt, *American Folklore Scholarship* (Bloomington: Indiana University Press, 1988), p. 89, and Boas Papers, ECP to Boas, 4 Nov. 1919; Boas to Parsons, 9 Apr. 1923; ECP, ECP to Espinosa, 22 Feb. 1925; 12 July 1927; Espinosa to ECP, 18 June 1931. For Parsons's support of Courlander, see ECP, Courlander to ECP, 4 Mar. 1938, and ECP to Courlander, 16 Mar. 1938. For her support of Hurston, see Robert E. Hemenway, *Zora Neale Hurston* (Urbana: University of Illinois Press, 1980), pp. 88–89; ECP, Boas to ECP, 7 Dec. 1926. Amy Horowitz has, with great sensitivity, examined the relationship between Boas and Hurston in "Franz Boas and Zora Neal Hurston: Resetting the Margins" (American Folklore Society Meeting, 1989).

30. ECP, Arthur Huff Fauset's recollections of ECP, circa 1923, Aug. 1970.

31. Fauset's collection was published as "Tales and Riddles Collected in Philadelphia," *JAF* 41 (1928): 529–57.

32. ECP, Fauset's recollections, Aug. 1970.

33. ECP, Fauset's recollections, Aug. 1970.

34. ECP, Fauset to ECP, 2 Aug. 1923; 15 Aug. 1923; 17 Aug. 1923.

35. ECP, Fauset to ECP, 17 Aug. 1923.

36. ECP, Fauset to ECP, 29 Aug. 1923.

37. Arthur Huff Fauset, *Folklore from Nova Scotia* (New York: G. E. Stechert & Co., 1931), p. vi.

38. ECP, preface to work on West Indies. A marginal note in ECP's hand reads "not used."

39. ECP, ECP to HP, 13 Mar. 1924.

40. ECP, preface to work on West Indies.

41. ECP, ECP to HP, 1 Mar. 1924.

42. ECP, preface to work on West Indies.

43. ECP, preface to work on West Indies.

44. ECP, preface to work on West Indies.

45. ECP, ECP to JP, 2 Mar. 1926.

46. ECP, ECP to JP, 13 Mar. 1926.

47. ECP, ECP to Mabel Dodge Luhan, 14 Mar. 1926.

48. ECP, ECP to JP, 13 Mar. 1926; 17 Mar. 1926.

49. ECP, draft of letter in ECP's hand, no addressee, n.d.

50. Gladys Reichard, "Elsie Clews Parsons," *JAF* 56 (1943): 47.

51. Parsons, *Folk-Lore of the Sea Islands*, pp. xiv, xiii-xiv; ECP, "The Value of Folk Tales."

52. ECP, Boas to ECP, 5 Aug. 1916.

53. Parsons, *Folk-Lore of the Sea Islands*, p. xvi.

54. Parsons, *Folk-Lore from the Cape Verde Islands*, p. xiv.

55. Parsons, *Folk-Tales of Andros Island, Bahamas* (New York: G. E. Stechert & Co., 1918), p. xii.

56. ECP, ECP to John Parsons, 2 Mar. 1926; 13 Mar. 1926.

57. Parsons, *Folk-Lore of the Sea Islands*, p. xx.

58. Ibid., pp. xx-xxi.

59. ECP, ECP to HP, 24 Feb. 1916.

60. Parsons, "Lord Bateman," *JAF* 41 (1928): 585. For *Folk-Tales of Andros Island*, Parsons made phonograph records of the songs, which were transcribed by H. W. Loomis.

61. ECP, Fauset's recollections, Aug. 1970.

62. ECP, Khartoum notebook.

63. Parsons, *Folk-Lore from the Cape Verde Islands*, p. xiii.

64. Parsons, *Folk-Lore of the Sea Islands*, pp. xx. For "The Three Sweethearts" and "Man Under the Bed," see ibid., pp. 89–90.

65. Parsons, "Bermuda Folklore," *JAF* 38 (1925): 241.

66. ECP, Fauset to ECP, 21 Sept. 1923.

67. ECP, Benedict to ECP, 12 Aug. 1930.

68. Parsons, *Folk-Lore from the Cape Verde Islands*, p. 194.

69. Parsons, *Folk-Lore of the Sea Islands*, pp. xiii, xix.

70. Parsons, *Folk-Tales of Andros Island*, pp. xii-xiii; xiii, n. 1.

71. Ibid., p. x, n. 2.

72. Ibid., pp. x, xii.

73. Parsons, *Folk-Lore from the Cape Verde Islands*, pp. 66, xv, 234.

74. Ibid., p. 215. *Desfio* is not a word in Portuguese, though most probably it was in the Portuguese dialect that Parsons was studying. *Desafiu* means a competitive challenge or provocation carried out until one wins; *desafiar* means to challenge or to dare; and *desfilar*, to walk or to show a horse before a race. I am grateful to my friend and colleague, Professor Celso DeOliveira, for this clarification.

75. Parsons, "Folk-Lore of the Cherokee," pp. 388, 390–91.

76. Parsons, "Spirituals and Other Folk-Lore from the Bahamas," *JAF* 41 (1928): 455.

77. Parsons, "Spirituals from the 'American' Colony of Samana Bay, Santo Domingo," *JAF* 41 (1928): 525–26.

78. Parsons, "Joel Chandler Harris," p. 493.

10

The Filigree of Cultures

In a letter to her son John, written from Athens, Greece, in 1938, Elsie spoke of her "passion for cultural overlays" that was "gratified . . . in stone, in ritual, and otherwise" by the street scenes about her: "the spiral stair to what was once a Turkish minaret in the corner of the Parthenon; a Christian angel painted on one of its stones; the Roman market not far from the ancient Greek one." Part of Elsie's approach to anthropology lay in the analysis of such cultural filigree. Alfred Kroeber had remarked on this predilection when he wrote her, "You . . . are enough of an individualist to be at bottom a bit anti-cultural, and when two civilizations get tangled and fuse their patterns perceptibly, it gives you a bit of satisfaction at the break-up of the patterns, as I feel shock."[1]

At base, Parsons was historical in her orientation. On the completion of *Pueblo Indian Religion,* she referred to herself as "severely historic."[2] Of this bent, Gladys Reichard wrote, "Her research and field experience have convinced her that motives, attitudes, and forms of behavior may be largely explained by history and she believes that any attempt at social control should proceed from an awareness of all available historical data."[3] This approach was apparent in one of Parsons's first letters to Franz Boas in which she spoke about the arbitrary division between anthropology and history. She remarked that " 'primitive' cultures are taken as the subject matter of ethnology, and the 'civilized' or 'semi-civilized' as that of History, a purely artificial separation and a remarkable, if unremarked, instance of folk lore." She pointed out a need for "studies, historical and contemporaneous of the civilized peoples," as vital for the study of ethnology. She continued: "In particular does the student in the Southwest wish for studies in Spanish History as an aid in his inquiries into what happened when Indian culture came into contact with Spanish culture. Inquiry into the problems of acculturation throughout the world are handicapped by ignorance of the culture of the civilized members in the contacts." She pointed out that in "a study of Pueblo Indian witchcraft, or Haytian voudoo, we are more handicapped by our ignorance about medieval Spanish or French belief than by ignorance of Indian or Negro."[4]

For Elsie, history entailed an understanding of past contact and a concern with the impact of one culture upon another. Using a combination of documentary sources and comparative ethnographic study, Parsons attempted to trace the origin of cultural practices and thereby reconstruct culture history. In a note to Leslie White, written in 1937, Parsons stressed just this combination of the documentary and ethnographic approach. Referring to an article in the *New Mexico Historical Review* about a campaign against the Hopis carried out by the Spanish in 1716, she wrote, "It is immensely valuable to me, at least more than any historical document. It proves that the Tewa of Hano are Southern Tewa or Tano, about which I had been speculating. It reveals that a large group of Jemez lived twenty years in Hopiland. I *knew* from the parallels that there had been some contact, & here it is like finding your planet after observing its influence!"[5]

Present also in her work was the culture area concept that grouped American Indians according to shared traits. Coupled with this was an emphasis on diffusion of culture traits from one area to another. She found the pueblo cultures, as she said, "an unusually interesting field for a study of the distribution of traits within the same general culture area." Such an approach necessitated comparative research, which proceeded from "town to town, not merely from tribe to tribe."[6]

Parsons stressed the need for the integration of information. For her, atomistic studies on one subject were anathema. In her Hopi fieldnotes, she wrote, "Asked what handicap the ethnology of the Southwest labors under, every anthropologist would answer, I presume, 'lack of integration.' Interested in potshards or the type of kiva the archaeologist pays little attention to current variations in pottery—in a certain ceremonial at Zuñi where food bowls are conspicuous I once counted at least fifty elaborations of one design—or to such problems as contemporary Isleta presents with its two square, undetached kivas and its one 'round house.' Analogously in concentration upon clan migration tales the student of social organization overlooks actual clan organization or study of migrations within the last half century." As an example of this lack of integration, she referred to the accounts of Frank Hamilton Cushing and Matilda Coxe Stevenson on Zuni ceremonialism. She saw these as "notorious illustration" of the absence of a uniform approach within even a single pueblo. As she said, "The same data are seldom recorded in the same terms." Extending beyond Zuni, the anthropologists had grossly failed "to equate Zuñi with let us say Zia or Hopi data."[7]

Most striking for Parsons was the absence of the comparative view-point. She remarked, "There is today, despite all the energy and de-votion that has been lavished upon the ethnology of the Southwest, no comparative study of the ceremonial life, of the material culture, or even of the popular subject of kinship systems."[8] She was impatient with what she called " 'Walpi, the world' non-comparative attitude." As she wrote Robert Lowie, "I have no special kick against the so-called psychological interest any more than against travel books but when it affects the education of the student I find it objectionable." She was impatient with students who developed theories "about Pueblo character from observing that little attention is paid to infants (i.e. that visitors are expected not to notice them)," while being igno-rant of the belief in the evil eye of the neighboring Mexicans.[9]

Parsons's focus on culture change preceded her work in anthropol-ogy. In 1903, she had translated Gabriel Tarde's *The Laws of Imitation* from French to English. As she remarked in her 1919 presidential ad-dress to the American Folklore Society, Tarde's was "the first theory in science to make an effectual demand . . . on my imagination." Still, while drawn to his explanation of change, she found that "there is lit-tle or no attempt to analyze why a model is imitated or why it fails of imitation."[10] In her own work, Parsons hoped to arrive at such an un-derstanding. She was interested in the ways in which a culture changed when it was influenced by another, whether this be through culture contact, a borrowing of culture traits, imitation, disintegra-tion, or acculturation. Her work in the Southwest, in Mexico, and in Ecuador all fed into this fascination with the blending of traditions. Her journey through Spain in 1923 was a search for the ceremonial trappings of what she referred to as Spanish Indian culture. Much of Elsie's pleasure in tracing the paths of influence lay in uncovering connections of which all others were ignorant or that they preferred to discount. And much of the delight came from the often incongru-ous blending of customs, the humorous juxtaposition of the old and the new, and the creative twist of mind employed to explain what might otherwise seem inexplicable.

In the preface to *Mitla, Town of the Souls*, Elsie spoke of the Spanish influence on Indian culture, which formed a basis for many tradi-tions—traditions that were presented as Indian. The newcomer to Mexico City, she said, would find very little that seemed Indian, but people make "references of all kinds to the Indian," and the visitor would be taken "from suburb to suburb or from town to town in the valley on the assurance that here they speak *idioma*, Indian idiom," and that their customs are very ancient, "*muy índio*, very Indian." Elsie was perplexed at first by this insistence on the Indian basis for much of Mexican culture. She wrote:

> It was not until after a visit to Huizquilucan, a hill town in the state of Mexico, an Otomi town, *"muy índio,"* . . . that I began to realize the source of the confusion. Delfino had taken his American visitors to the parish, or barrio, of San Martín, the saint who gave his hat and cape to the mendicant. In the barrio chapel the image of the charitable saint is regaled annually with a new hat and cape, and as we were being shown the discarded ones, a veritable museum collection of century-old Spanish fashions, Delfino told us that in the annual carnival the barrio of San Martín was pitted against the barrio of San Juan; stones were thrown across a barrier and insults shouted; the Virgen de la Candelaria was even reproached with slipping away from the barrio of San Juan to pass the night with San Martín: burlesque and *combate* of the early Spanish type of carnival. But by Delfino combat and burlesque as well as the offerings to San Martín were all described as *índio, muy índio,* and I foresaw that at least one of the visitors would sometime write in English about the Indian customs of Huizquilucan, and perhaps he would refer to the saint of Tours and the scandalous Virgin as Indian gods or idols in disguise.

Elsie pointed to the root of the problem. Both the American visitor and the mestizo host lacked knowledge of early Spanish or European customs, "and so each could speak unrestrictedly of such customs in Huizquilucan as *muy índio*—not being of modern Mexico must they not be from the Indians?"[11] In a letter to Kroeber, Elsie pursued the same thought with perhaps more candor. In her study of "the religious folk dancing and other medieval forms" retained so well in Mexico, she had noted that "the Mexicans and their American journalist friends have a funny way of calling medieval ritual, Indian, partly as anti-Catholic propaganda, partly from ignorance of the medieval in Europe."[12]

Parsons's interest in the interplay between Spanish and Indian cultures had been an enduring concern in her work. As she explained, it was long before her visit to Huizquilucan that she had become "interested in the analysis of Spanish-Indian relationships."[13] In her fieldnotes recorded in 1920, while she was staying at Sichumovi on the First Mesa of Hopi, she had written, "It is impossible to understand the ceremonial life of the Southwest, I venture to say, without knowledge of Spanish influences, and yet these influences are rarely if ever noted."[14] In *Mitla, Town of the Souls*, she remarked, "As a student of the Pueblo or town-dwelling Indians of New Mexico and Arizona I was for years face to face with the query of what these sometime Spanish Indians had borrowed from their Spanish or Mexican neighbors, captains and colonists and friars, more especially the friars."[15] She pondered "the indigenous Pueblo rites of fasting, continence, flagellation, aspersing, making vows in sickness, hairwashing, and naming or baptism." To what extent were they of Indian origin? To what extent Catholic? She puzzled about the derivation of witchcraft beliefs, ceremonial organization, and systems of communal labor. And she wondered, "Were some of their masks suggested by the Franciscans, who remembered the masked impersonations of the saints in Spain, particularly Catalonian Spain, where to this day San Juan dances on his feast day in a mask, between two girls who carry eagle heads of painted cardboard?" These questions were, she said, "alluring," but they were also "baffling when studied only within a few tribes." She felt the need to widen her scope, to search for "comparative clues." And so she turned to Mexico, which was a perfect source because "in tribe upon tribe the process of cultural assimilation has also been going on for centuries and in such varying degrees that sometimes the Indian is foremost, sometimes the Spanish." Here she was sure she would find "touchstones" that would direct her toward the answers as to what was Spanish and what was Indian.[16]

Interested in the effect of one Indian culture on another, Parsons was eager to examine the influence on the southwestern Indians by the Indians of the Plains, the Southeast, California, and Mexico. Parsons's work with the Caddo, who had originally come from the area of Louisiana before settling in the Plains, tied in with her pursuit of parallels between the southeastern and southwestern native cultures.[17] Just so, in her work with the Kiowa, she hoped to connect aspects of the Plains and southwestern Indians. In 1927, she wrote Lowie, "I am jumping off for Oklahoma to have a look at the Kaiowa, on my way to the Hopi winter solstice ceremony. Between Pueblo and Pawnee there ought to be some links somewhere." She queried, "Have you ever had any theory about the Pueblo-Pawnee similarities?" and added, "the provenience of the war traits of the Pueblos, including those suggested in their clown societies, intrigues me."[18] On still another occasion, she had puzzled over the relationship between the Zuni *newekwe* or ceremonial clowns, known in other pueblos as *koshare*, with the ceremonial warriors of the Plains Indians who were required to do everything in the reverse. She wrote: "The *newekwe* use backward speech . . . , they carry a baton (bow-spear?), they smear face and body with grey clay. Their 'foolhardiness' takes the form of filth eating and of breaking all rules of behaviour; . . . in one of Cushing's accounts he describes a *newekwe* as saying, 'We must now go and kill a Navaho'—a dog is caught, torn apart and eaten to symbolize the Navaho."[19] Elsie concluded, "It is quite exciting. What do you think?" Lowie agreed that there should be "a systematic attempt to trace connections between the Pueblo and Plains Indian ceremonialism." This was hampered, he noted, through a lack of knowledge about the southern Plains Indians, precisely the ones with whom the southwestern Indians were most likely to come into contact. He observed: "The feature of backward speech and anti-natural conduct is widespread in the Plains. The Dakota *heyoka* cover themselves when it is hot, walk about naked in the cold, plunge their arms into scalding water, etc. Logically the *newekwe* practice certainly belongs to the same category,—eating the negation of food, so to speak."[20] Lowie concluded that this "parallel" was "a clue" that should be pursued, specifically with a study of clowning behavior among the Witchita.

Years later, when reading *Mitla*, Lowie offered further encouragement. He wrote, "I intend to jot down various items of comparative interest as I proceed. . . . We must all collaborate in an attempt to discover what features are pan-American in range."[21] Elsie responded with enthusiasm, both about collaborating and about extending the scope to include all of the Americas. She saw this as especially crucial for the study of ritual distribution, which had been neglected "even in North America."[22]

In her southwestern work, Parsons was relentless in singling out similarities and differences in the daily and ceremonial life of the pueblos. From visits to Acoma and Laguna in 1917, she became "convinced that comparative study of all the pueblos" was necessary. She wrote Kroeber, "I would like next to try out Cochiti or better still Sant Anna."[23] In this manner, by working from one pueblo to the next, Parsons intended to build up a reliable body of comparative material. When there was insufficient information on a particular pueblo, she would either undertake fieldwork herself or encourage others to do so. At times, she felt compelled to publish material from her fieldwork, even though she knew it was incomplete or questioned its accuracy. This she did to stimulate further research and to provide the mortar for filling in the gaps.

Over the years, from her beginning work at Zuni, Acoma, and Laguna, to the publication of her four-volume *Pueblo Indian Religion* (1939), Parsons's goal was the comparative study of southwestern Indian cultures, with particular attention to ceremonial life. She did not limit her study to parallels between the pueblos, but also delved into the connections between pueblo and nonpueblo cultures, especially in terms of ritual practices. In 1935, she and Gladys Reichard organized a symposium for the American Folklore Society meeting "to make a start on the much neglected subject of Navajo-Pueblo relation in ceremonialism."[24] In 1937, she began collecting what she referred to as a "hunt list," literally a compilation of rituals associated with hunting. Gifford had sent her some information on San Ildefonso, which she found to be "dubious" ("They are a lying lot at San Ildefonso"). She was planning to get similar lists for the Apache from Morris Opler and Grenville Goodwin.[25]

An ambitious, though ultimately fruitless, comparative undertaking planned by Parsons was the concordance for southwestern mythology, which was to have been a compilation in abstract form of all southwestern myths and folktales. For this project, Elsie engaged Erna Gunther, who had previously worked with Leo Frobenius in excerpting tales for the Atlas Africanus. The relationship between Parsons and Gunther was not an easy one. In 1932, Elsie wrote Boas, "No word from Gunther about the concordance." Since Erna would not answer her letters, Parsons remarked, "Perhaps you will have to order her to send on the ms. as it is." Again in 1935, Parsons appealed to Boas, "Wont you please write Erna Gunther to send you at once a carbon copy of what she had done. Since I paid for it, to put it crudely, I think I am entitled to it." That same year, Ruth Benedict, editor of the American Folklore Society, was preparing the concordance for publication. Benedict was pleased to receive the final section of the concordance, though, as she said, "There is considerable editorial work to do . . . , and I do not dare risk the delay of sending it back to Erna." One year later, Parsons wrote Boas, "The Concordance ms. is an outrageous mess. Unless it is checked and completely revised for errors of statement, omission and classification the A[merican] F[olk] L[ore] S[ociety] can not afford to publish it." After a decade of work and an investment by Parsons of over two thousand dollars, the concordance of southwestern mythology was dropped.[26]

Parsons's comparative orientation, her interest in the impact of one culture on another, was inextricably linked to another concern, that of social change. In the preface to *Pueblo Indian Religion*, she wrote:

Contacts with Mexico, with both White and Indian Mexico, produced changes in Pueblo society, in historic or prehistoric periods. The nomadic tribes of the Southwest also affected the town-dwellers with whom they fought, traded, and now and again mated. In the eighteenth century there was a great deal of circulation not only between Pueblos and Southern Plains tribes, Athapascan Apache and Navaho, Shoshonean Ute and Paiute, but among Pueblo tribes themselves, rendering a discussion of borrowed traits rather difficult. During the last hundred years and particularly during the recent decades further changes have taken place as a result of contact with Americans. . . . To all of us, whether we are with or without faith in that development toward our own values which we call progress, social change is of the greatest interest.[27]

Elsie recognized that the southwestern pueblos had been exposed to differing degrees of foreign contact in the historic period and that the extent of subsequent change had been uneven. There were, therefore, variations among the pueblos as a result of this contact that augmented differences present in the prehistoric period in kinship systems, ceremonial groupings, language, and handicrafts. All of this, she maintained, needed to be carefully documented and examined.

Parsons argued repeatedly against assuming a uniformity to Pueblo culture that did not exist. To Fred Eggan's proposal for a study of social change of the east and the west pueblos to be based on a similar format, Parsons wrote, "But you are assuming there was once a homogeneous culture—in face of 4 different stock languages & no end of other cultural differences."[28] In *The Social Organization of the Tewa of New Mexico,* Parsons reiterated her position on variation among the pueblos. Discussing each town separately or, as she said, in a "particularized" arrangement, she conceded that "this may seem overmeticulous" and that "further work among the Tewa will undoubtedly show that in many cases a general statement would have sufficed for what will prove to be a widespread or general practice." However, she cautioned, "social organization . . . will never be found to be quite the same in any two pueblos of any of the Pueblo tribes."[29]

While Elsie stressed the variety among the pueblos, the inhabitants themselves were unaware of all but the most apparent distinctions. They were especially "blind to the religious differences." Elsie recalled, "When Crow-Wing and I set out from First Mesa to visit the other Hopi pueblos, he told me that I would find just the same ceremonies and the same clans in all the pueblos. 'They *have* to be the same,' [he] said, . . . and it was not until he interpreted for me on Second Mesa that he admitted they were not the same." In similar fashion, an Acoma Indian was forced into a recognition of differences among the pueblos. As Elsie commented, "Certain variations he had known, but the concept of variability was utterly strange."[30]

This lack of awareness about the distinctiveness of pueblo life was significant for the study of culture change. As Elsie observed, "People do not borrow that which they are unaware of." While esoteric kiva ritual was not accessible to outsiders, the kachina dances were. The relative openness of kachina performances sparked the spread of what Parsons referred to as the kachina cult and fostered "comparative uniformity." At the same time, the underlying organizational aspects were not shared with others.[31] When nothing in one culture resembled a certain trait, or when a new trait clashed with existing traits or was incomprehensible to the new culture, then there was resistance to its incorporation.[32] As an example of this process, Parsons referred to the reactions in Taos to the peyote cult. The traditionalists who were said to face "towards the south and the Katchina cult" opposed the "Peyote boys" who were said to face toward Oklahoma. The cause of dissension arose over a clash of values. The peyote religion, with its emphasis on individual experience, was perceived as contrary to the traditional religious system and to the spirit of Pueblo culture where the group was paramount.[33] Parsons suggested that the degree of resistance might be lessened if only a few traits, rather than a whole complex, were adopted. She added, "A few traits can be fitted into existing schemes." In just this way, Lucinda of Isleta learned a new style of pottery from her Laguna neighbor, "and they went together to get clay and the neighbor taught Lucinda how to ask the Clay Mother for her substance. One more Mother, that was not hard for corn-mothered Lucinda!"[34]

Innovation and invention were also vital components of social change. While, as Elsie noted, "in an unlettered people it is . . . hard to 'catch' the birth of an innovation through an individual," still she was able to provide a few examples. She referred to a Hano woman, Nampeyo, whose husband had helped with the excavation of Sikyatki. She was able to study the shards "and in the course of years produced designs inspired by the old pottery and yet distinctive, and this famous potter has been copied by all her neighbors."[35] Elsie recalled Margaret Lewis's husband as gifted in composing songs: "In particular I recall a song that I heard in a Comanche dance. The sweeping feathered headdress was Comanche, the staffs were made in imitation of Spanish halberds, but the song had unusual melody and the melody was certainly reminiscent of Marching Through Georgia. 'Yes, we heard that tune one day on a hand organ in Gallup,' said Margaret

Lewis."[36] So Lewis had set the tune to a Zuni rhythm, composed the song, and introduced it as dance music.

Disintegration, as Elsie explained, was a negative component of social change, which at times resulted in "a kind of abortion." Borrowed customs poorly "integrated into the ceremonial life" would simply no longer be observed, and other more imbedded aspects of social life would either wither in the face of ridicule by outsiders or strangle in the grip of economic change. While the clown societies had been affected by the elimination of war, the most powerful factor in their disintegration was the utter scorn accorded to the burlesque sexual play by the Anglos. Woman's participation in ceremonial life declined in direct relationship to her loss of economic power. She became more subject to the whim of her husband, who resented the restrictions placed on her for sexual continence during ritual. As Parsons remarked, "This is an inroad on the Zuni or Pueblo principle of identifying personal with community welfare." Other factors that contributed to the disintegration of Pueblo culture were the introduction of western commodities, the adoption of the Julian calendar, the requirement of school attendance, and the impact of wage earnings.[37] Parsons remarked on "the substitution of foreign materials for native materials. . . . Parrot feathers, important for fetish or mask or dancer's array, have become very scarce, possibly because it is easier or cheaper to use dyed chicken feathers than to trade for parrot feathers or to keep live birds. When cotton or other local yields of nature are substituted for by commercial supplies, the ritual of gathering lapses, and animistic theory is undermined. Cotton Woman, for example, will cease to be named in prayer." Similarly, when modern technology was substituted for traditional methods, there was a threat to the old way of life. An irrigation system that could operate apart from rainfall would undermine the power of the kachina. " 'Why dance kachina when you have only to open a sluice gate?' young men of the most conservative pueblo of the East are beginning to ask . . . , just as years ago Hopi asked, 'Why practice running, when you have a horse?' "[38]

Disintegration could be countered by substitution whereby one person might fill a vacant office or an existing group might assume the functions of an extinct organization. Elsie discussed substitution in ritual: "At the last and final Scalp ceremony of Acoma, who should perform the adoptive head-washing (aspersing) ritual for the Scalps but the church sacristan! The sacristan baptizes the living, so why not the dead? Indeed, he may asperse the dead townsman, so why not the dead enemy? Substitution works on the basis of resemblance, more or less logically."[39]

Parsons discussed the importance of a strong, intricate cultural framework, which she referred to as "involution," for absorbing and balancing change. Change and involution—or "mobility within steadfast design"—were characteristic of pueblo life. She spoke of a "mobile habit, a habit of mind or spirit" that manifested itself in ceremonial life, "for Pueblo Indian ceremonialism thrives on foreign accretions, whether of myth or song or dance or design of mask or costume."[40] Yet this attraction to the foreign had to be balanced against the accepted. Elsie observed: "Pueblo ritual or ceremonial has developed very largely . . . through the spread or flowering of the same pattern. This involuting process seems to be related to a sense of order or gratification derived from familiar, orderly design. Change will proceed along orderly, involutional lines and whatever is disorderly, immoderate, or unamenable will be disregarded."[41] In this way, a certain style would emerge in the arts, and there would be a sense of harmony to life. She opined, "As long as people are working at or playing with their cultural patterns, their way of life appears integrated, sincere, and vital." Without this creative urge, the culture would lose its life breath, and decadence would seep through it.[42]

Acculturation, according to Parsons, was the result of a borrowed element, either a single item or an organizational complex, being incorporated fully into a new culture. Elsie related the story of a Laguna man, the first Pueblo Indian to read, who had been educated for seven years by the priests in Durango, Mexico. When he came back to the pueblo, he brought with him a book that was said to contain songs. She continued, "The book was kept under the *samahiye* ('idol') of his altar. After his death someone once wrapped the book up in a blanket of a deceased relative. It was discovered before the burial . . . and removed. Subsequently it disappeared." Elsie added, "It is a striking little instance of acculturation."[43] As is apparent in this account, the sense that Parsons attached to the concept of acculturation differed markedly with the interpretation accorded it in other works, including her own. Here, Elsie simply meant that a borrowed item became a part of the culture. The emphasis was on the *item*, or the *form of behavior* that became incorporated into the new society—the book, for example, became fully incorporated into Laguna ritual pattern—and not on the process whereby an individual or a group adapted to new cultural patterns.

Parsons's approach was not always so particular in focus. For *Mitla, Town of the Souls,* she was lauded for her study of acculturation. Sol Tax called it "a milestone . . . in such studies in Middle America because it is the first work definitely committed to a statement of what parts of a local culture are Spanish in origin and what parts are Indian *and why*."[44] Laying bare "the heart" of her inquiry in the last chapter of *Mitla*, Parsons puzzled about why some traits had survived from the original Zapotec culture, why others had died, and what accounted for the adoption of certain Spanish customs and the rejection of others. Her answers paralleled in large measure those given to similar questions in *Pueblo Indian Religion*. A lack of knowledge by one culture of the other fostered a retention of traits. As Parsons said, "Ignorance . . . is a great protection of custom." She spoke, for example, of the Zapotecan and Mestiza woman, neither of whom had knowledge of the domestic ways of the other. She identified intermarriage as the most significant factor "in cultural breakdown or cultural assimilation, whichever way you look at it." This was especially the case if the woman belonged to the dominant culture, because then the traditions of the home would change almost immediately and the children were not likely to gain fluency in the Indian language. As Parsons said, "Almost at once at intermarriage *idioma* is lost, and with language a great many mental attitudes controlled by language."[45] Just as a woman from outside the culture might stimulate change, so a woman within the culture would retain tradition. As Parsons observed, "It is notable that the aspects of culture more closely associated with women—'remedies,' weaving, cookery, and feasting—have outlasted the cultural activities of men—hunting, war, the ritual arts, and ceremonial and political organization, all of which have either disappeared or been largely hispanicized."[46]

At times, an old custom might survive simply because it seemed fitting and right to the new culture. For example, the Indian practice of separating men from women outside the home was compatible with practices of the Catholic Church.[47] The reverse, of course, frequently happened: a traditional custom gained the disfavor of the new and more powerful society and was successfully excised. For the ancestors of the Mitleños, the suppression of their calendrical cycle by disapproving Spaniards had had devastating results, since it was not merely an item that was removed, but an entire organizational complex, including rituals, the priesthood, and the arts.[48] Recognizing the alienation that occurred through such suppression, the Catholic Church attempted to gain favor by incorporating aspects of the native belief system. The early priests had the churches and monasteries constructed on top of old temple mounds, and they astutely incorporated aspects of the native calendrical cycle in Christian rituals.

Parsons referred to the "prime principle of assimilation" in which a new trait was similar to elements in the traditional culture. The new, then, provided a link with the old, a way of making otherwise foreign practices compatible. The use of candles, Parsons said, was a Spanish introduction, but "it was probably assimilated with the use of copal or of ritual torches or braziers such as were used by the Aztecs." Indifference occurred when there was no such link between the old and the new. For example, the Catholic concept of sin and holiness was utterly alien to Zapotecan ideology, where the emphasis was not on individual relationship with the gods, but rather on adherence to the rules and taboos of the group. And in the cosmological system, the Christian concept of going up to heaven did not fit with the downward path of the Zapotecan dead. Nor would the Indians pray *for* the souls of the dead who were said to be in purgatory; rather they would pray *to* them.[49]

While indifference might be possible with respect to church doctrine, Parsons did not see this choice available for the impending source of social change, capitalism. The notion of accumulating wealth, Parsons stressed, would provide "a very easy path" for the social transformation of Mitla, "and in two or three generations will be accomplished what the Church failed or did not seek to accomplish during centuries. Celebration of *mayordomías* and of weddings in their festival form will go; the system of communal service will break down; class distinction based on wealth will be made; and personal distinction will be sought. The *comisario* system which is destroying local self-government in other parts of the Republic will be imposed, and the town government will go by the board. Within fifty years, perhaps much sooner, Mitla will be a modern town, for good and bad, a backward modern town."[50]

While in her own society, Elsie challenged the customary and the conventional, in traditional cultures she viewed change as a threat to the integrity of the social order. "A large measure of meticulous conservatism," she said, "is essential to the life of ceremonialism."[51] Parsons recognized this contradiction in herself. She wrote, "Being one of those wholly irrational persons who is not interested in religion for himself, but very much interested in religion for others, during this recent visit to Zuñi, I was beginning to worry perhaps more than any Zuñi elder about the town's irreligious tendencies."[52] She spoke of the "germs of cultural disintegration" that had been planted in pueblo culture from exposure to non-Indian cultures,[53] and she rued the effect on ceremonial life. In writing of a saint's dance at Santa Ana, Elsie observed that "legs, arms and hands and upper body are painted a violet blue (a commercial dye, alack, which is being used, I am told, for the first time) . . . " and that "the hair of some of the younger men and boys is short (another unhappy Americanism)."[54] In *Notes on Zuñi*, Parsons remarked on the threat to ritual life through "Americanized," or non-Indian, influence. Of the *newekwe* (ritual clown) society, Parsons said, "The changes seem to be in the direction of making the cult less exacting. This feature is in itself significant of decadence." She referred to the use of "commercial articles" in ritual. Dance leaders would carry sacred meal in a glass bowl or a cup rather than in the traditional pottery bowl. The kachina masks were being decorated with "store-bought ribbons and artificial flowers." Parsons observed, "If this use increases, the same tawdriness in ceremonial make-up and complete lack of style characteristic of other pueblos may be expected in Zuñi ceremonials." Parsons viewed the commercialization of ritual as a spiraling threat. She spoke of "the increase of the practice of largess at the dances," which she saw as "a secular practice" that ultimately would lead "from a devout to a more secular point of view." With the expectation for a lavish exchange of gifts, people felt reluctant to host rituals.[55]

Still, in her observations on ritual life in Zuni, Elsie felt reason for some optimism. On one occasion, she was pleased to admit error. " 'Presumedly there will never again be an initiation ceremony or scalp dance at Zuñi,' I happened to write in August, 1921. Among Pueblo Indians prediction of any ceremonial extinction is rash." The following month, the initiation ceremony was held.[56] In June, 1933, Elsie had visited Zuni to study the ritualized kick-stick race and was struck by the changes in all aspects of life. An article on her experiences began, "We motored in from Gallup over the new road, in two hours. Twenty years ago I once made the trip in a wagon in eight hours, by the old road, which is five or six miles shorter." After describing the changes, Elsie concluded, "There is still much to learn about the Zuñi kick-stick race, but incomplete as was my ethnographic information when I left the Pueblo, I left with lessened despondency. As long as men bet gaily, risk stone bruise or cactus wound whether for pleasure or for profit, and dread black magic, the spirit of old Zuñi will live on, despite schools, wage system and foreign spouses."[57]

For Parsons, the understanding of a culture included a recognition of its complexities. It was precisely this—the intricacies of pattern upon pattern—that attracted her to issues of social change. "But society in Mexico or anywhere else," she wrote, "is not a tapestry to pick threads from and expect to find a new design in one's hand; and assimilation is one of the most subtle and elusive of social processes, which does not reveal itself by plucked threads, by isolated facts."

Thus, in order "to tie up the threads," one needed knowledge of context and appreciation of detail. For this reason, Parsons elected in her southwestern work to focus on specific pueblos—to study first one, then another, in order to compile an ever-increasing record of the complexities of pueblo life. Similarly, in Mexico, she chose to study Mitla, as she expressed it, "until I learned something coherent about its people and culture."[58]

Kroeber had remarked on this orientation in her work. As he said, she "sensed at once the necessity of context, and empiricism." These, he noted, "appealed to something fundamental in her nature." In her work, Kroeber continued, "accuracy came first, overwhelming confirmation by mass of evidence next."[59] Reichard had spoken of Parsons's careful compilation of fact and detail as a mosaic that she was constructing. Of *Mitla, Town of the Souls*, Reichard wrote, "If we may use an artistic simile, she indulges in no great color splurges or in bold brush work, but builds a mosaic bit by bit. Each minute stone is cut and fitted so nicely that gradually out of the welter of details comes the finished picture, and the little town and its poised citizens fairly glitter, so sharply are they done."[60]

Parsons's tapestry was woven from her detailed observations, her careful fieldwork, and her diligent reading of the literature. She drew these together, never losing hold of the complexity that she so valued. Even at the risk of being "overmeticulous," she avoided simplifying accounts, for as Kroeber said, she disdained "the rash of brilliance and the premature conclusion."[61] Her accounts were rich with lived experience, for, in her writing, she included colorful illustrations from her research, related from her own narrative perspective. For her reader, there was no doubt that Elsie was part of the observational process, that she was right there having her head ritually washed at Sichumovi and receiving her Hopi name, that she was with the family at Zuni when the masked god, *A'doshle*, entered their home to discipline the little three-year-old boy, that she was present at Mitla when the curandera sucked the intrusive object out of her neck to relieve her of headaches. The people and Elsie's interactions with them gave vibrancy to her works.

Elsie's filigree of cultures was also a description of cultures. She was gifted with the ability to bring life to the printed page. As Kroeber remarked both admiringly and enviously, "I wish we could write our anthropology as well as you do."[62] The richness of life in the Southwest and at Mitla was conveyed through the skill of Parsons's prose. Through her description, one can hear the Zuni men bringing in the horses at night, whistling to keep away the witches; one can smell the bread baking in the Eckerman's oven as she collected folktales in their New Laguna home; and one can see the destruction of the earth-quake at Mitla as she explored by flashlight the darkened inn with her hosts. Elsie was careful in her selection of stylistic devices to convey mood. For an article on change at Zuni published in the *Scientific Monthly*, she adopted an "impressionistic" tone[63] that allowed her to discuss the effects of modernization from her own perspective. In *Mitla, Town of the Souls*, Elsie shifted verb tense from the past to the present in order to draw the reader into the scene. From the vantage point of her room at the inn, she wrote, "I have not visited San Mar-cos, but its pottery vendors come frequently to Mitla. Some are sitting today in front of La Sorpresa, under the ash tree."[64] The reader feels the presence of the visitors from San Marcos, for they "are sitting *today* . . . under the ash tree." With an emphasis on the unfolding of events, Elsie described her trip from Mitla with Eligio to mountain villages.

> Descending into the pueblo we make our way to its one adobe house, and Eligio asks the old man in the yard where we may spend the night. "Right here . . . ," and he shows me into the large adobe chamber where we unpack and are to spend two nights. The fire in the cook shed and water are at our disposal. Food we have with us. *Zacate* for the animals we buy from our host. During our brief stay several other travelers, traders, ar-rive, and all are given the same facilities. Some stop merely for their meal; others stay overnight. None of us pays anything for shelter.
>
> The night is cold and I am glad of a *posada* indoors, in spite of fleas and practice by the town band inside our chamber. There are about twenty instruments and as the players are learning a new piece each instrument is played independently of the oth-ers. I withdraw to my mat in a corner and Eligio rests in the hammock and proceeds to touch up his sketch of the serpents.[65]

The reader feels the warmth of the adobe room, the aggravation of the fleas, and the discordance of the various instruments. Elsie suc-ceeded in drawing the reader to her, to sit beside her on the mat in the corner, to hear, see, and feel all of this. Undoubtedly, as Elsie had sug-gested, Mitla and the surrounding towns have changed drastically from her account penned in the 1930s. But from her sensitive de-scription, life in Mitla, as recorded by Elsie, endures.

For Parsons, the filigree of cultures depended on the maintenance of "definite cultural patterns in mobile combination." Characteristic of the Pueblo Indians of the Southwest, this blending of stability and change yielded "from an aesthetic point of view . . . style, and from the standpoint of general culture, . . . vitality and durability."[66] To this, she was drawn—to tradition and change and to a layering of cultures, which she found most hardily expressed in the Southwest.

NOTES

1. ECP, ECP to John Parsons, 17 June 1938; Kroeber to ECP, 18 Oct. 1923.

2. ECP, Robert Redfield to ECP, 10 July 1939; Clark Wissler to ECP, 12 June 1939.

3. Gladys Reichard, review of *Mitla, Survey Graphics*, Jan. 1937, p. 44.

4. ECP, ECP to Boas, n.d.

5. ECP, ECP to White, 17 Sept. 1937.

6. Parsons, *The Social Organization of the Tewa of New Mexico* (Menasha, Wis.: George Banta Publishing Company, 1929), p. 8.

7. ECP, "Hopi Notes."

8. Ibid., p. 2.

9. Lowie Papers, ECP to Lowie, 8 Jan. 1937.

10. Parsons, "The Study of Variants," *JAF* 33 (1920): 87–90.

11. Parsons, *Mitla, Town of the Souls* (Chicago: University of Chicago Press, 1936), p. ix.

12. UCA, ECP to Kroeber, 26 Mar. 1929.

13. Parsons, *Mitla*, p. x.

14. ECP, "Hopi Notes."

15. Parsons, *Mitla*, p. x.

16. Ibid., p. xi. See also Parsons, *Pueblo Indian Religion* (Chicago: University of Chicago Press, 1939), p. viii, for a discussion of the Pueblos as "Spanish Indians" and the need for a comparison with other Hispanized Indians.

17. ECP, Erminie Voegelin to ECP, 14 Feb. 1940.

18. UCA, ECP to Lowie, 11 Nov. 1927.

19. ECP, note to Lowie, n.d.

20. ECP, Lowie to ECP, 24 July.

21. ECP, Lowie to ECP, 17 Oct. 1936.

22. ECP, ECP to Lowie, 24 Oct. 1936.

23. Kroeber Papers, ECP to Kroeber, 11 May 1917.

24. UM, ECP to White, 14 Dec. 1935.

25. UCA, ECP to Gifford, 1 Mar. 1937.

26. On Gunther's work with Frobenius, see Boas Papers, Boas to Reichard, 4 Nov. 1926; Parsons to Boas, Aug. [1932]; 19 Jan 1935; ECP, Benedict to Parsons, 4 Oct. 1935; Boas Papers, Parsons to Boas, 13 July 1936. For a discussion of the attempt to compile a catch-word concordance, see Rosemary Lévy Zumwalt, *American Folklore Scholarship* (Bloomington: Indiana University Press, 1988), pp. 118–19.

27. Parsons, *Pueblo Indian Religion,* p. viii.

28. ECP, marginal note on Eggan to ECP.

29. Parsons, *Social Organization of the Tewa,* p. 8.

30. Parsons, *Pueblo Indian Religion,* p. 941.

31. Ibid., p. 944.

32. Ibid., p. 1085.

33. Ibid., p. 1094.

34. Ibid., p. 1097.

35. Ibid., p. 1118. J. Walter Fewkes assigned the name Sikyatki to the first major archeological excavation in the Hopi area, dug in the 1890s on the eastern terraces of First Mesa. The pottery associated with this excavation was black-on-yellow with the addition of red, a style called Sikyatki polychrome. In the 1890s, the trader Thomas Keam was distributing art pottery made by Nampeyo that was modeled after this style. See J. O. Brew, "Hopi Prehistory and History to 1850," 9: 516–17, and J. J. Brody, "Pueblo Fine Arts," 9: 604–5, *Handbook of North American Indians, Southwest,* ed. Alfonso Ortiz (Washington: Smithsonian, 1979).

36. ECP, "The Governor of Zuñi," p. 3, in the unpublished manuscript, "In the Southwest"; and Parsons, *Pueblo Indian Religion,* p. 1119.

37. Parsons, *Pueblo Indian Religion,* pp. 1127–42.

38. Ibid., pp. 1142–43.

39. Ibid., p. 1145.

40. Parsons, "Waiyautitsa of Zuñi, New Mexico," *Scientific Monthly* 9 (Nov. 1919): 457.

41. Parsons, *Pueblo Indian Religion,* p. 1155.

42. Ibid., p. 1150.

43. Parsons, "Notes on Acoma and Laguna," *AA* 20 (1918): 180, n. 1.

44. Sol Tax, Review of *Mitla, American Sociological Review* 2 (1937): 135–36.

45. Parsons, *Mitla,* p. 515.

46. Ibid.

47. Ibid.

48. Ibid., p. 519.

49. Ibid., pp. 528, 530.

50. Ibid., pp. 535–36.

51. Parsons, *Notes on Zuñi* (Lancaster, Pa.: American Anthropological Association, 1917), p. 248.

52. Parsons, "Spring Days in Zuni, New Mexico," *Scientific Monthly* 36 (Jan. 1933): 50.

53. Ibid., p. 51.

54. Parsons, "Fiesta at Sant'Ana, New Mexico," *Scientific Monthly* 16 (1923): 182.

55. Parsons, *Notes on Zuñi,* p. 248.

56. Parsons, *The Scalp Ceremonial of Zuñi* (Menasha, Wis,: American Anthropological Association, 1924), p. 7.

57. Parsons, "Spring Days," pp. 49, 54.

58. Parsons, *Mitla,* p. xi.

59. Kroeber, "Elsie Clews Parsons," *AA* 45 (1943): 254.

60. Gladys Reichard, review of *Mitla, Town of the Souls, Barnard College Alumnae,* Feb. 1937, p. 15.

61. Kroeber, "Elsie Clews Parsons," p. 254.

62. ECP, Kroeber to ECP, 13 Jan. 1916.

63. UCA, ECP to Kroeber, 7 Oct. 1932.

64. Parsons, *Mitla,* p. 367.

65. Ibid., p. 372.

66. Parsons, "The Pueblo Indian Clan in Folk-Lore," *JAF* 34 (1921): 209.

11

In the Southwest

> If anyone ever gets around to writing the inside history of
> the development of Southwestern ethnology, your contri-
> butions, both personal and vicarious, will bulk very large.
> Many individuals and institutions are very deeply indebted
> to you, and I trust you realize how much your assistance is
> appreciated on all sides.[1]

So wrote Alfred Kidder to Elsie in March, 1929, after hearing that she
had been providing financial support for Morris Opler's work among
the Apaches. What had begun as the lure of the Southwest and a
horseback ride to the Apache dances in 1912 had expanded for Elsie
to an intense and consuming ethnographic concern. From Zuni, she
went to Hopi, Acoma, Laguna, Cochiti, Isleta, Jemez, Santa Clara,
San Juan, San Ildefonso, Taos, Santo Domingo, Nambé, and Tesuque
to the Pima and the Navajo. Her goal became the documentation of
southwestern cultures, first in order to understand each society, then
to compare one with the other, to determine historical precedence, to
single out unique innovations, syncretistic elements, and areas of culture change. She became interested in broadening the comparative
perspective to encompass the influence of the Plains and of the southeastern Indians on the cultures of the Southwest. For this reason she
undertook a study of the Kiowa and the Caddo. In her desire to flesh
out the record completely, Elsie provided financial support for others
in their research and often collaborated closely with them, offering
copies of her fieldwork notes, suggesting directions of inquiry, and fa-
cilitating entry into communities. In the Southwest, Elsie would become the grande dame of anthropology.

The majority of Elsie's southwestern fieldwork was conducted
from 1915 (her initial research at Zuni) through the 1920s (her later
research among the eastern pueblos).[2] Her published works on the
Southwest include four edited volumes, more than seventy articles,
and sixteen books, among which are: *Notes on Zuñi* (1917), *Notes on*

Ceremonialism at Laguna (1920), *Winter and Summer Dance Series in Zuñi in 1918* (1922), *Laguna Genealogies* (1923), *The Scalp Ceremonial of Zuñi* (1924), *The Pueblo of Jemez* (1925), *The Social Organization of the Tewa in New Mexico* (1929), *Isleta, New Mexico* (1932), *Hopi and Zuñi Ceremonialism* (1933), *Taos Pueblo* (1936), *Pueblo Indian Religion* (1939), and *Isleta Paintings* (1962).

In notes captioned "Getting Information from Pueblo Indians," Elsie sketched her manner of, as she phrased it, getting down to work. The "most formal [and] systematic" approach involved interviewing, text dictation, and a category that she referred to as "revelation of texts." There was "observation of ceremonies or processes," which as she cryptically noted lasted "many hours: from one day to ten or sixteen. Inside, outside. Exact time uncertain. No note-taking on spot." She stressed the necessity to observe everything and to be particularly attuned to the informative nature of gossip. She concluded with a list of "principles of conduct: 1. Avoid whites. Know nothing, less than nothing. . . . 2. Avoid moralistic interest. Newspaper reporters can't afford to be moralists, still less ethnographers. . . . 3. Patience."[3]

Once Elsie established a relationship with an informant, she was careful to maintain it. When she returned home, she corresponded frequently with many Pueblo Indians. In turn, they wrote to her about their families, about school and work, about their problems, and they answered questions she had asked. One young Hopi agreed to keep a daily journal for Parsons and wrote thanking her for the check and the stove. He told her that he was making something to send to her children that would not be for pay, but for friendship.[4] A young Pueblo girl who attended boarding school in Kansas corresponded frequently with Elsie, told her about her life at school, her serious concerns about her family at home, and answered questions about ritual practices. Her letters were replete with sketches of the kachinas as well as accompanying tales.

Elsie's most important correspondents, Margaret Lewis and Mabel Dodge Luhan, used their husbands and other contacts in order to answer Elsie's questions. Margaret Lewis, the Cherokee who had married a Zuni, answered in detail Elsie's questions about activities in the pueblo. In 1919, she kept a calendar of the ritualized kick-stick races, information that greatly enhanced Parsons's research. And in 1932, she responded to Elsie's typed list of questions with information for the article "Spring Days in Zuñi, New Mexico."[5] To Mabel Dodge Luhan, Elsie sent "Discreet Questions," which included queries such as the following, "About when were turkeys last kept in town? Are wild turkeys ever eaten? Are there any tame ducks? Are wild turkeys shot or snared? Are dogs given names?" Mabel felt quite free to ask such innocuous questions of her husband, Tony Luhan, a Taos Indian. She wrote to Elsie, "I can't see *what* you get out of these tips but I can get you *any* amount of information of *this* kind you want." Elsie responded to Mabel, "Why do I want the kind of information asked for in Discreet Questions? Because I am interested in the *whole* life, economic as well as ceremonial, and only concrete data make the study worth while."[6]

Though much of her research focused on ritual, Elsie was interested in all aspects of Indian life. Just such an inclusive approach was apparent from her beginning work at Zuni in 1915. In one fieldwork notebook, Elsie sketched the "lines of inquiry," which included the following:

> *The Household and the Family:* to show how there is a continuous regrouping according to household requirements. Take a list of cases.
> *The Brittle monogamy of Zuñi:* case method.
> *Witchcraft:* What idiosyncracies, failures to conform, subject a person to suspicion of witchcraft? What coincidence or accident?

In a fieldnote entry pertaining to witchcraft, Elsie wrote, "Last night we slept on roof. Margaret L. and I. We heard the young men singing in the fields." Margaret Lewis explained that they were " 'Taking out the horses. They sing to keep the witches off. There surely are witches. Not long ago they dug up a girl in the cemetery, took away all the beads & bracelets & money. All the village was talking about it. Men & women witches, old or young. They used to hang them.' " In another notebook, she jotted entries on "assimilation, owl, sun lore, beliefs, practices, lightening," and "Questions for the Time Keeping Calendar." She recorded information on pregnancy and birth, and childrearing practices, including the supernatural enforcer of norms, *A'doshle*, who was called on to punish recalcitrant children.[7]

Parsons's fieldtrips to the Southwest were frequent, but not of long duration. She would plan a stay of two, sometimes three months, usually one in mid-winter and one in late summer or early fall. Often she traveled to more than one pueblo, sometimes dashing off to observe a specific ceremony in one and then returning to the other for more intensive work. Just such a situation arose in her fieldwork at Jemez in September, 1921. She was hard at work, secretly collecting ritual information from one informant, when she heard of an important ceremony at Zuni. She caught a train to Gallup and rode in a wagon to Zuni, arriving just in time for the last day of the ceremony.[8] She wrote

Herbert, "It was the close of the scalp dance at Zuñi, what we had supposed was an extinct ceremonial, but they had got some hair, Nick said from the barbers, and found an old man, Crazy Joe, willing to become a war priest, and so they initiated him, dancing eight nights, all night, around the scalp pole, making war god images & on the last day which I saw setting out the war altar in the plaza, with much dancing."[9] When the scalp dance was over, she returned to Jemez, hoping to see a masked dance, which as it happened, she had seen before. This dance, however, provided her with new information, for as she observed, "They are so naive that there under one's eyes they burlesque the very type of ceremony not for anything would they let you into."[10]

Elsie encountered varying degrees of difficulty, from ease to impossibility, in conducting her fieldwork among the pueblos. By good fortune, she had selected the Zunis for her first trip. In her field entry dated August 14, 1915, she had written, "Leave Gallup for Zuñi 5:20 A.M. with rig from Quinn. . . . Turned off road in direction of Black Rock & east 9 1/2 hrs . . . to Z[uñi]." She found her way to the "Governor's house," where Margaret Lewis and her husband had served as "Kroeber's comforters" in his fieldwork and would be so for her as well. Her entry into Hopi was not quite so felicitous. On March 8, 1918, Elsie left Zuni with a young man who had been serving as her interpreter for a week's visit to Hopi. From Gallup, New Mexico, she wrote Herbert that the road was "impassable, . . . so at a large price I got the best motor in town to take me out to the Hopis." The trip was difficult. She had spent the night "in the wilderness on the back seat of the motor & at 6:30 A. M. having walked in 8 miles & wagoned in on a springless Navaho wagon, 8 miles. On top of 12 hours of motoring two successive days the tires had completely given out, likewise the pump." On their arrival at the Hopi Indian agency they were told that "there was smallpox in the mesas. They were in quarantine & if I went in my stay would have to be at least 3 weeks, perhaps 6, perhaps 9 etc." Elsie found the agent to be a "most objectionable petty overbearing official . . . with a prejudice against scientists & a determination to make it all just as hard for me as possible." Since there was no telegraph office, she could not "very easily get the whip hand over him." She added that she "felt rather responsible for my Zuñi boy" and that she was "awfully tired, so I just turned back." In frustration she realized that people in Gallup had known that "the mesas were quarantined & yet they let me take that fruitless & expensive journey!" And she vowed that her next attempt to reach Hopi would be successful.[11]

Elsie did try again to reach the Hopi mesas. Her Zuni friend, Flora, had given her a photograph of a Hopi man, who was Flora's friend, and letters to her acquaintances. These proved to be "a charm," as Elsie described: "Thirty-six miles from Zuñi to Gallup, a hundred odd miles to the first mesa, and at the post-office and store at the foot of the mesa I asked a woman coming out if she happened to know John Kochisi and where he lived. I showed the photograph. 'I am his aunt,' said she. . . . 'He lives on top of this mesa at Sichumovi.' "[12] Elsie invited her to ride up the mesa with them. They found John Kochisi "sitting at his door." Relatives were gathered "at the end of the room . . . in a circle about the loaves and piles of wafer bread and the bowls of mutton stew," which had been their compensation for their work in the family's fields. With the photograph and the letters as introduction, Elsie was taken in and given a room. Of her accommodations, she commented: "It was the same room that Douglas Fairbanks had lived in when he was there a few weeks past, making a film, and I was shown the photographs from the envelop the aunt had just brought from the post-office—photographs of the slim actor dancing with a portly Hopi matron and winking an eye at the motley crowd of Indian and white lookers-on."

Her hosts decided that it would be well for Elsie to have her head ceremonially washed, so that the Hopi family would not be unduly criticized for having a stranger stay with them—rumors had already circulated that Elsie "had books about the ceremonies." As Elsie wrote to Kroeber, "At the end of 4 days I acquired a father & had my head washed in my father's sister's house—a very interesting rite, carried out exactly as if I were non-White."[13] Her ceremonial father, Sixtaime, was the head man of the winter solstice ceremony. As Elsie described the ritual, early in the morning, "Sixtaime came into my room to fetch me and lead the way across the plaza to his sister's house, a Water clan house. Sleeping pallets had been rolled up and put away, and the household of three generations, mother, daughter, and daughter's husband and children, and two clanswomen from outside were sitting against the wall on box stools and chairs. In the middle of the room was a chair for me, and on the floor nearby the large pottery bowl in which my head was to be washed. There was some water in it, and the yucca roots lay at hand." Elsie sat down and removed "the one hair-pin that held up" her hair. Her "father's" sister, Chii, brought forth the ear of corn, which was crucially important for the ritual, and kneeled on a sheepskin beside a bowl. She stirred the yucca roots briskly in the water. "The suds mounted, a pretty sight. Chii beckoned me to take her place on the sheepskin. I knelt, facing east, and with the bestalked corn-ear as a dipper Chii put some suds on the top of my head, dabbing twice with the corn-dipper. She did this four times, praying the while." Then the washing was repeated by Chii's daughter, the grandson, the baby, and the two clanswomen. After the ritual washing, Elsie's "aunt" vigorously washed her head and face, and then rubbed her face and chest with cornmeal, which stuck to the wet skin. Her right hand was filled with cornmeal, and the ear of corn was placed on top of the meal. Then each one who had washed her head gave her a new name. They stepped up, knelt beside her, took the ear of corn "and with a circular motion waving it four times" toward Elsie, the individual would pronounce the new name. One clanswoman named her Talasveñsi (Corn Pollen); the little boy, Suñawaimana (Pretty Girl); Chii and her daughter, Kümayaunöma and Kümawaisi (Corn-Meal); and the other clanswoman, Yuyuhöññoma (Cloud-Covered Rain-Streaks). "Yuyuhöññoma appeared to appeal to them most; that was the name they thought would 'stick.' I, too, liked it best." In the ceremonial washing, Elsie's "family" had "washed away my 'old name and life.' " The cornmeal rubbed on her body and cradled in her right hand signified that she "was being given new life." Elsie wanted to thank her ceremonial father. She took his right hand in hers, and "Zuñi fashion," raised it toward her mouth and breathed in. "Without unclasping my hand, my 'father' drew it in turn toward his mouth and breathed in."[14]

To Herbert, Elsie wrote about the ritual headwashing, her new name and her "father & . . . large number of aunts." She signed her letter (with yet a different spelling), "Yuyuhuöma or cloud-covered-falling-rain."[15] Her Hopi father had explained the significance of her name by drawing "the cumulus cloud and falling rain 'glyph' familiar to all Pueblos,"[16] which represented "a heavy rain-cloud fringing along its lower edge into slanting streaks of rain."[17] In another letter, she told Herbert, "My own family here are particularly pleasant folks. 'My sister' has just washed my hair for me in yucca suds. After the ungraciousness of the Laguna & San Felipe people, it is a treat to be appreciated." However, her status as daughter did not entitle her to unlimited ritual access, for as she recounted, "Doing well in every way, altho' 'my father' wouldnt take me into see his ceremony, the private part of it, because, said he, I was a woman. But George, my host & interpreter, thinks he was merely putting me off, as a white. However, the public part was very interesting, and there was a Buffalo dance thrown in."[18]

Of her fieldwork at Sichumovi, Elsie said, "It was a success beyond all anticipation." She worked with her host and his wife as well as with a girl in Hano. She found the Hopi ceremonial system and the customs of daily life much more similar to those of Zuni than had been pointed out in the literature. Her friend, Grant La Farge, who had accompanied her, "photographed endlessly & started ethnobotany— 38 plants collected & identified with a certain amount of data."[19]

Elsie left Hopi on June 16, 1920, pleased with the results of her fieldwork and with her acceptance by the Hopis. She wrote Kroeber, "Came out yesterday from the First Mesa—driving from 5:50 a.m. to 1:30 p.m. but I questioned my host most of the way, & there was . . . a new kind of country to be seen. Motoring in to Zuñi this afternoon."[20] When she arrived in Zuni and told of her adventures, including the ritual initiation, the Zuni quickly informed her that they "could not make *kihi* with white or Navaho." She was told this, as she said, "because they felt as if having had my head washed at Hopi, I might think it was up to them to wash my head."[21]

Elsie began her research on Laguna not in the pueblo itself, but rather three miles to the west, in the town of New Laguna. There lived the Eckerman family, whom she first met in February, 1918. Mr. Eckerman, who had worked first as a brakeman on the Santa Fe railroad and then as a miller at Laguna, was married to a Laguna woman whose mother, Gawiretsa, belonged to the Sun Clan. Mrs. Eckerman's mother and another Laguna friend, Tsiwema, who was knowledgeable about the sacred traditions, came to talk with Elsie. On the day of the visit, as Elsie recalled, there was an "opaque and devastating sandstorm without, but cheer and gaiety in our kitchen, where Mrs. Eckerman was baking bread and interpreting at the same time." Gawiretsa and Tsiwema spoke of the old Laguna feud, which had resulted in a rending of the pueblo between those who sided with the Protestants and those who supported the Indian traditions. This sort of casual gossip, Elsie remarked, was much more informative than direct interviews. As the day passed, "when the bread needed particular attention or the baby lapsed from her extraordinary goodness, one of the little girls would take a turn interpreting." In the late afternoon the next-to-the-youngest child "interpreted a long folk-tale from beginning to end. The children loved and respected their grandmother and they were proud to be able to interpret her stories and pleased to find in me too an appreciative auditor. The story of the Rabbit Huntress I had heard before and I have heard it since, but never as pleasantly as on that gale-swept day."[22]

While the Eckermans, their relatives, and friends would help Elsie, this was only up to a point *and* from a distance. Neither Gawiretsa nor Tsiwema, both conservative, traditional members of the community, would introduce her to others. As Elsie explained, "Gossiping with me three miles out of town or even making ceremonial objects for the Museum were one thing, to champion me in public was quite another. Nobody would take that risk, much less [Tsiwema,] the foremost sacerdotalist of town." Elsie decided that she needed to meet more people, to become a familiar "object . . . about town." She concluded, "On my next visit I would have to live in the pueblo."[23]

Indeed, on her return, it was even more imperative for Elsie to take up an abode in town, for she was accompanied by Franz Boas, who in his study of the Keresan language needed constant exposure to native speakers. They began their work at Laguna on June 1, 1919. The first two nights they stayed with the Eckermans in New Laguna; and then they, as she said, "broke loose and established ourselves in town in an Indian house." She wrote Herbert that they found it "comfortable enough except that meals are a little uncertain. Today, e.g. our hostess Tsaidyiwi, otherwise Mrs. Joe Johnson went off to the fields to feed her husband getting in his alfalfa, & Boas has been trying to make a fire for me to cook coffee & eggs."[24]

As part of her study of kinship, Elsie was mapping the town. In the early mornings, Boas would accompany her for his exercise, which consisted of "pacing off the houses, house by house," and then he would return to his work on the language that, as Elsie reported to Herbert, he found "hard and so to him interesting, & we have enough informants."[25] Elsie was compiling genealogies that, as she said, "necessitated visiting about." She went around town on her own, since her hostess "would take no responsibility for her lodgers." Elsie was able to make several friends, though the reception was not always warm. She recalled one occasion when her hostess's little girl took her "to the house of a kinswoman where some women were holding a corn grinding party and singing their clan songs. In the grinding room there were eight sets of grinding stones in two rows, four women to the row. They faced one another and were chatting merrily or singing until I appeared in the doorway and asked permission to enter. 'If you give each of us one dollar,' said the spokeswoman. I smiled and left."[26]

Boas and Parsons were able to overcome the minor difficulties and discomforts. What they most wanted was permission to attend the summer solstice ceremony. Together they presented a formal request to a gathering of men in the assembly house. Of this experience she wrote:

> When we walked up to the platform on which [the men] were sitting and asked for the governor, Governor Frank Pisano came

forward. With proper deliberation I set forth the reasons why we were in Laguna, how we had come to study their language and to find out a way of writing it down so that in the future they would be able to write letters and keep records in their own tongue, that the Professor was a student of many Indian languages from the country in the far North to Mexico in the South and that it would interest people to compare all these different Indian languages, nor should Laguna language be omitted, that I myself travelled about from one pueblo to another, making friends and learning the rules people lived by. These rules were changing, the old rules were passing away, they should be written down so that people would know how their grandfathers had lived. . . . The time might come when their young people would no longer care to hold the *shiwannatyia* . . . ; but their children's children would like to know about it. I concluded by saying that we came from New York, from the big school there and the museum, we did not come from Washington, we had nothing to do with Washington. "*Tsa* Washington," *not* Washington, the governor repeated to a man who was sitting at a desk, with paper and pencil. "*Tsa* Washington," repeated the man at the desk picking up the pencil. And *tsa* Washington, I believe, was all of the speech that got recorded. "I will tell my war captains," said Governor Pisano. "They look after it tonight, they have to say." We bowed and left.[27]

Apparently Elsie had decided that some official verification of their status was necessary and that this should come from Washington. She wired Herbert, asking him to "get some official in Washington . . . to telegraph" Frank Pisano "that Boas and Parsons are respectable persons worthy of consideration."[28] Herbert telegraphed Senator William Calder who, in turn, contacted Pisano as Elsie had requested.

Finally the issue was resolved. The war captain came to their house, and quietly, with sternness and gravity, told them that they could not go. Elsie responded, "*Tauwa e*, it is good. . . . We are sorry, and . . . some day other people, too, may be sorry." While the whole pueblo participated in the ceremony, Elsie and Boas were confined to their house with the owner posted as guard against their leaving. She recollected: "It was a warm night, the windows of the house across the way were left open and from our terrace we could hear the singing of the *cheani* [medicine men]. . . . For an hour or so we sat listening to the singing and looking at the dark figures that now and then passed under the terrace, then the Professor betook himself to his . . . baffling verbs and I in no agreeable state of mind went to bed."[29]

Eventually their petulant hostess tired of their presence. One afternoon, after Elsie had left for Acoma, she began whitewashing Boas's room. Elsie returned to find "everything from the walls heaped on his bed, and the Professor absent. 'Where has he gone?' I asked. . . . 'To the minister's house.' "[30] Thus, as Elsie reported to Herbert, they were "turned out of our 3 weeks Indian home." The Presbyterian missionary gave them shelter. Of him, Elsie said, he had not "a convert in the town," but he was "a good carpenter," and his wife was "a good housekeeper." She opined, "Window frames & canned food will win out, of course, but the Franciscan father in his white satin & golden vestment or in his brown monk gown with his simple ethics and his mystical prayer, still holds his own." The chief medicine man of Laguna was the sexton who served the pueblo well by cutting prayer-sticks on saints' days. As Elsie observed, "No early Christian town in Europe could have presented a more interesting commingling of belief and ritual from different sources."[31]

Parsons returned to Laguna in June, 1920, accompanied by Grant La Farge, who served as photographer and sometimes chef. Together, they joined up with Boas and Esther Schiff Goldfrank, who had volunteered as his assistant. As Goldfrank recalled, the accommodations at the "Eckerman's Hotel" were comfortable, but Margaret Eckerman was an "atrocious cook." She continued: "After joining us, Mr. Lafarge, who was quite a gourmet and fancied himself as a chef, took over whenever he could. Once, as the *pièce de la resistance* he served up a cheese omelet with jelly. Dr. Boas strongly disliked melted cheese. He looked at me across the table, took one mouthful and quit. Nothing was said, but Mr. Lafarge was obviously dismayed. I cheered him by eating with gusto. Mrs. Parsons just ate. Food meant little to her—good or bad—and she was quite content to eat an apple at midday and call it lunch."[32] All four moved on from Laguna to San Felipe, where La Farge was run out of town for photographing the church. Parsons was able to recruit only one informant to work with Boas. Goldfrank recalled, "A frightened soul, despite his daring decision, he was brought to Dr. Boas, who was trying to establish dialectical deviations between Laguna and other Keresan pueblos." Esther stood guard outside the door and as soon as a stranger appeared, she was "to rush indoors to see to it that Dr. Boas and his San Felipan were concealed behind closed doors." The three left Boas with his informant, and they drove on to Santa Ana where Parsons had located a family to work with her. From there, they went to Albuquerque, where they interviewed an Isleta woman and her aunt. Goldfrank, who was suffering from appendicitis, lay in bed, surrounded by notebooks and plants. Parsons was at the bedside with two Isleta women who were to identify the plants.[33]

In September, 1921, Elsie traveled to Jemez, New Mexico, where she called on the same family she had spent three nights with in 1913. She wrote Herbert: "They remembered me, the old lady from Santa Clara and her husband & said that for their part I could spend the winter with them. So they have given me a mattress in their back room, and the never failing coffee which isnt coffee at all, fortunately, one has to drink so much of it, and sour bread & they cook my eggs."[34] With the family, Elsie conversed in Spanish, though, as she said, she would not "feel really at rest" until she had obtained an interpreter. She continued, "But that is a very delicate matter indeed, with everybody so potentially suspicious."

Her days at Jemez were, as she said, "informing and full of the romantic," though she added, "I *would* like a little more food. Today, before setting out, I am promised, however, a real meal here." She wrote Herbert of the beauty of the countryside and of a rabbit hunt: "Whole families out to hunt, here two little boys on the same horse, their father giving them the clubs they throw at the rabbit, there a woman with a baby on her back, girls in their best clothes to run up to the man who kills the rabbit, the girl who gets there first getting the rabbit & the next day taking the man a basket of bread." Elsie had been able to observe her first woman's harvest dance. She described it to Herbert as "hours of, at times, hot & tedious watching," but it had been productive. While her family slept, she seized the opportunity to write up her notes and "to make diagrams unobserved."[35]

Elsie began work at Taos in 1922. She returned frequently over the years to stay with her friends, Mabel Dodge Luhan and Tony Luhan. Mabel, Elsie said, was "generally known throughout the country as the woman who married an Indian."[36] While marriage for Mabel in April, 1923, brought notoriety, for Tony it brought ostracism. He was forced to give up his ceremonial position, and he was not fully reinstated in his pueblo until 1934.[37] Elsie was one of many who were welcomed into the Luhan home. Indeed, Mabel took a delight in "collecting" people—intellectuals, artists, writers, politicians, photographers. She wrote Elsie in August, 1922, "At present I am distracted by too many disparate human beings about me—St. Geronimo Day is the 30th & I have young Alice Henderson—& my son John—Dr. Light & her companion . . . , John Collier on indian business, another friend of distant youth—and Tony—and the Lawrences. These last, particularly he, I find difficult to incorporate!" D. H. Lawrence, Mabel said, was "the typical lower middle class, puritanical conventional englishman; a mass of taboos & prohibitions, inferiority & mother complexes, not to mention the Jehovah complex." Still, she said, "the genius is there, buried under the small meannesses, & the unhappiness & the conflicts."[38] Of her time with Mabel, Elsie wrote, "I lunch or sup very agreeably with her and the odd collection of Easterners and Britishers and Indians of Taos."[39]

Elsie recalled her introduction to the pueblo: "When first I visited Taos a June day in 1922, and saw the tall terraced houses with their small, high placed windows without frame or glass and then heard called from the top of the highest house the gubernatorial order of the day, I wondered if this most northern of the pueblos was going to reveal other early pictures of Pueblo culture."[40] She remarked that "Zuñi's small windows" had begun to disappear after 1870, and in no other eastern pueblo had she seen "a house of more than two stories." Tradition there was in Taos, and distrust of outsiders as well. Elsie attempted to assemble accounts on ceremonials. She would frame her questions based on knowledge of other pueblo groups, a problematic approach since much of what she referred to did not have relevance for Taos. The answers to her questions were not reliable. As she remarked, "To distinguish between what was being withheld by my astute informants, past masters in the art of evasion and subterfuge, and what was merely different was no easy job. Sometimes I thought I was easy to baffle just because of my knowledge of Pueblo culture elsewhere. I asked so many questions about things which did not exist or occur."[41]

A Taos resident explained to Elsie the need for secrecy: " 'People want to find out about this pueblo; but they can't. *Our ways would lose their power if they were known,* just as Zuñi ways and the ways of other places have lost their power.' "[42] The Taos people recalled the warning they had received from Sia in 1881. It was said that government people had been making inquiries at Sia, and when they left many people died. This ill fortune was connected in the people's minds to the investigations. They sent a warning to other pueblos, including Taos, about white people "who came to find out about their customs and beliefs." The mistrust of anthropologists was etched in indelible memory, so that when Matilda Coxe Stevenson arrived to conduct fieldwork, she was forced to stay outside of town in what she named "Camp Defiance." Any Taos resident suspected of working with an anthropologist risked ostracism by the community. Maria, a woman whose husband's father had died suddenly after a visit by Stevenson, explained to Elsie, " 'They will be mean to us and to our children .' " Of this pervasive fear, Elsie remarked, "It is no exaggeration to say that during my acquaintance with María and Pablo I was presented daily with a vision of death from giving information." Elsie found that "the obsession of danger from giving information" was attached to "almost any occurrence or situation." One woman informant told Elsie that "she was very much worried because she had forgotten to bring . . . her contraceptive root and she was ten days past her menstrual period." She feared conceiving during the time she was working with Elsie, because after having given such "information she would have a specially hard pregnancy."[43]

A large portion of Elsie's research was concerned with the most sacred aspects of pueblo life. So it was that the desire of the people, to keep their secrets, and the desire of Elsie as fieldworker, to gain access to *all* their secrets, was in conflict. As her research progressed, she came to view the Pueblo concern for privacy as a "characteristic and deep-rooted Indian attitude" connected with the belief that "religious knowledge and ritual, when divulged to the noninitiated, lose their potency." Just as a prayer or a cure would lose efficacy if imparted, "so the life of the Pueblo will be impaired if outsiders know about it." To safeguard their culture, as Parsons noted, "Pueblo Indians are trained from earliest childhood to keep the major part of their life hidden from their White neighbors and visitors."[44] Leslie White referred to this as "cultural quarantine," and spoke of the consequences of nonobservance: "It is virtually certain that anyone among the eastern Keresan pueblos (with the possible exception of Cochiti) who was convicted of aiding an ethnologist would be severely punished, if not executed. According to Curtis, a man at San Ildefonso was executed for assisting Matilda Coxe Stevenson; two Santo Domingo men were executed for dancing tribal dances while on a trip to Washington. . . . The present writer's Santo Domingo informants not infrequently expressed fear of punishment for aiding an ethnographer. Every effort, then, from instruction and exhortation to drastic punishment—even execution—is made by many of the eastern pueblos to guard their 'secrets,' to preserve the old ways."[45]

The challenge was there for Elsie. She *would* gain access to the information. The endeavor, as she saw it, was for science, and her driving concern was for thoroughness and accuracy. To succeed, she could be silent and patient, observing and asking seemingly innocuous questions, the compounded answers to which eventually filled in areas of the puzzle. She could be devious and secretive, meeting with informants far away from their pueblos and working with them for days at a time in order to extract as much information as possible. In her 1918 fieldwork at Zuni, her attempt to arrange secret meetings with key political and religious figures failed. She wrote Herbert that she "was in a nest of suspicion & fear so that the greatest patience was necessary & results were sometimes exasperatingly meagre. For example after careful planning to have two informants come separate evenings, one a high priest . . . , the other a fraternity officer, the two would come to supper the same evening, & so fearful of one another would they be that no information at all would be forth coming except the observation of mutual fear."[46]

Of her brief visit to Acoma and Laguna in January, 1917, Elsie remarked on the difficulty of gathering information due to the "extreme distrust of Whites." Her introduction was "of the best," since she was traveling with Zuni friends who had relatives at Acoma. While she was "most hospitably entertained" by a family in Acoma who provided her with a place to stay, still, as she said, "I was unable to overcome the distrust altogether and much of my time was squandered in merely trying to differentiate myself from the picture-taking tourist or from the Washington representative from whom every ceremonial or intimate detail of life is to be hidden." (Elsie had yet to learn about the eastern Pueblos what Leslie White later observed, that "United States government representatives and missionaries are bad enough, from the Indian's point of view, but they are more tolerable than journalists and, above all, ethnographers!"[47]) Of her attempt to conduct research in Acoma, she said, one of the two people who would desultorily answer her questions was the storekeeper. This he did because he wanted her business, but he would also be evasive, answering obliquely or incorrectly or, as Elsie explained, staying in the store, "for he knew I would not question with customers about or people passing by." She recalled, "Only once had he to warn me, my back was to the door. 'Hide your paper,' he said, 'I see the governor come.' " Elsie had met the governor earlier at the house where she was staying. Spurred on by the rumors in town, he had come to ascertain whether or not her traveling case contained a camera. Finding that it did not—"indubitable proof," as Elsie said, that she was not a tourist—he agreed to take her to visit his uncle, the cacique, from whom Elsie hoped to collect folktales. Of this, she wrote: "The Cacique lived in a house in the rear of the kiva towards the north of Middle Row. We went up an unusually broad ladder with ornate tips and crossed the roof of the kiva to reach the second story room and in it to descend by a narrow and steep little ladder into the room where the old man, a woman and little girl were preparing for their night sleep." The cacique, an old and feeble man, greeted Elsie with a welcome speech and thanked her for her gift of tobacco. He agreed to tell her a folktale about "how the pigeons loaned their feathers to Coyote, one of the many Spanish folktales the Indians heard long enough ago to have forgotten their origin and claim as their own. In the middle of the story where the birds take back their feathers and Coyote begins to cry, the old man broke off, and . . . explained that before going on he wanted my assurance that I would not report the story to Washington."[48]

Elsie found it more productive to work with a single informant away from the constraining influence of the pueblo. She observed, "As I had expected, he was more communicative away from Acoma than he had been in Acoma. Besides, he learned that the next day I was leaving the country. Even so, he balked about telling me even the group names of the *cheani* or medicine-men."[49] She realized that the people of Acoma would have rearranged a scheduled kachina dance rather than have her see it. The date for the dance had been set for the day after her departure. When she mentioned to her hosts that she might stay longer, they told her the dance had been cancelled.[50] Years later, reflecting on her fieldwork in Acoma, Elsie concluded, "If I were trying it again I would go to Grants on the [railroad] & try to get an informant to come there away from observation." She added, "There are certain Pueblos where it is impossible to work *in* the town."[51]

In Jemez (1921), Elsie found a haven in the monastery where she was able to work in private. Father Barnabas, whom she had found to be "one of the most helpful people ever I met,"[52] had introduced her to the sacristan of the church. In her words, this was "the only man we can trust to inform." She wrote Herbert, "I am writing as usual in the monastery, waiting for my informant to get away from ringing the church bells, or perhaps to finish drawing some masks for me in his house."[53]

For her work among the Tewa of New Mexico, Elsie followed "the secretiveness observed in all the Rio Grande pueblos." She took up residence at the San Gabriel ranch in Alcalde, a "Mexican town two or three miles north of San Juan." Elsie described her accommodations to Herbert, "A dude ranch indeed. . . . The living is one more novel experience in this inexhaustible country. In a Mexican town, an adobe house, built around a patio [with] flowers, chili pendants [tied] to the columns of the porches, above, the seven mountains & blue sky. . . . Delicious food, a warm room, quiet at night, a few too many other guests."[54] With the help of her hosts, she located informants from the Tewa pueblos of San Juan, Santa Clara, and San Ildefonso. As she explained in *The Social Organization of the Tewa of New Mexico*, "My informants worked singly or in couples, niece and uncle, sister and brother, mother and daughter, one interpreting for the other."[55] More candidly, she wrote to Herbert, "This week I have cleaned out one woman and last night started with her as interpreter for her uncle, one of the ceremonialists of this town. He told two beautiful tales, one my pet White Buffalo or Escape up the Tree. These from San Juan. Today I hope to get somebody from Santa Clara. It is a good technique, I think, to work like this away from the towns."[56]

In all, Elsie made three trips to Alcalde where she pursued work on the Tewa. In 1924, she wrote Herbert, "Taos man not here yet, it is aggravating. The Tesuque man I got up was only moderately good enough for two days work. Meanwhile I ride in the afternoon and take Spanish lessons from the school teacher who is a native and knows the Mexican folktales which he is dictating in Spanish. This time I will know some Spanish. And I am very glad to have the tales as some of them I get from the Indians. Comparison will be of interest." The man from Taos arrived along with his wife. Elsie found him to be "a good storyteller," but he knew "too much English for the best work." The main difficulty was, however, that he would not "give up on some of the ceremonial [information], claiming that his career at Carlyle precluded early ceremonial education."[57]

During her visit to Alcalde in 1925, Parsons wrote Esther Gold-frank, "I stopped off at Albuquerque & motored to Isleta and within the minutes had kidnapped [Juan] . . . *without* his daughter who had to stay to care for the grandfather." After working with him for two weeks at the San Gabriel ranch, she took him to Taos, ostensibly so he could visit with his relatives for a week, but also, Elsie hoped, for "detective work." Juan had, Elsie remarked, "a very striking imaginative turn of mind." He was both "shrewd [and] . . . exceedingly credulous."[58] Ritual magic was to him not a symbolic slight of hand, but a potent reality: "Had he not seen a living deer walk through the door of the hunt chief's house, and a medicine man fly away as an eagle to a great distance, to return within an hour to the ceremonial chamber?"[59]

Elsie attempted to corroborate the information that she had collected from the Isleta informant. She worked with an Isletan woman, Lucinda, who scrupulously avoided all ceremonial topics. "She was," Parsons wrote, "absolutely close-mouthed." Lucinda regarded herself as of " 'one heart.' " Parsons continued, "It undoubtedly pained her to hear me allude in any way to the secrets of religion. When I referred to the war spirits as living in the mountain under whose feet we were one day passing—Sandia Mountain—Lucinda began to weep."

After telling Elsie a folktale, she added, " 'I hope I won't die soon.' " The consequences for revealing Pueblo secrets were clear to her: " 'If I tell about our religion, some time when I am out in the hills a bear or some other wild animal might get me and hurt me.' " She related to Parsons "what had happened to the Hopi Indian who lay the altars in the Harvey House at Albuquerque. 'In two days he began to swell up. His tongue was swollen and hanging from his mouth.' "[60]

In 1926, and again the following year, Elsie established herself at "a ranch between Santa Clara and San Ildefonso, too near either pueblo for adventure by the townspeople, always apprehensive of spies." It was here that she was able to obtain "invaluable information from San Juan and Nambé, with sidelights on Tesuque, the most conservative and tight-bound of all the Tewa pueblos." As a white, Elsie was never allowed to spend the night in any of the Tewa pueblos, thus in her work she was unable to give a "general picture of town life." Her brief visits to the pueblos were sufficient "merely to check up in a general way on maps of houses and kivas and to give me impressions I could compare with the life in other pueblos in which I have lived."[61]

Elsie came to regard the sequestering of informants as crucial for successful fieldwork among the pueblos. In her support of Leslie White's research, she counseled him on the importance of absolute secrecy. She advised, "I suppose you are aware that for the sake of fellow workers one must never show Pueblo Indians any publications." While he was conducting fieldwork at Acoma, she sent him copies of her *Laguna Ceremonialism, Laguna Genealogies,* and the monograph on Jemez, along with Kroeber's *Zuni Kin and Clan.* She reiterated, "Do not fail to keep these publications under lock & key. It is most important to our work that no Pueblo Indian see them, and they will take a book with pictures of masks when they wont take anything else from your belongings." In a marginal note, she warned, "Do not lend them to Father Shuster or any other White." When he offered to conduct research on prayer sticks at Acoma, Elsie cautioned, "Collecting prayer sticks is a risky & most secretive business and I would not advise it unless you have some special opportunities, & at the close of your trip." After White's years of research among the eastern pueblos, Elsie encouraged him to begin work at Taos. She wrote, "You and I are the only two people in this world, I believe, who can work Taos with any success, in view of our comparative knowledge and more particularly of our knowledge of the secretive technique."[62]

When possible, Parsons would take advantage of divisions between people to gather information that otherwise might not be readily given. She was aware of the schism in the Tewa pueblo of Santa

Clara between "progressive pro-Americans and conservative anti-Americans." This followed the moiety division between Summer people and Winter people. The feud had progressed to the point that the Winter people had been electing their own governor. However, in spite of the divisive intensity, no one would speak of it publicly. As Parsons commented, "They are not washing their dirty linen in public, a decency I exceedingly regret, since it leaves the history of the quarrel unrecorded." Elsie had singled out a "short-haired, English-speaking young man" who she had hoped would serve as "historian." She commented that he turned out to be "one of the most tongue-tied Pueblos it has been my misfortune to meet." Members of his family had died recently, because, it was believed, they had "told some white person something."[63]

From some informants, secrets could be had for a price. As one person queried, "How much will you pay for my fear?" Passing on information, Parsons explained, was regarded as so dangerous that there should be a very high payment as compensation. For example, when Elsie read the names of the Taos kivas to a woman, the latter responded, " '*I* would not tell you *that* for one dollar!' " When the fee offered by Parsons was too low, the informant might refuse to cooperate or attempt to raise the amount. The same woman who exhibited dismay over Elsie's knowledge of the Taos kivas demanded more money for two short Spanish folktales she had related. To Parsons's playful rebuke, " 'Don't be greedy,' " the woman responded, " '[I'm] not greedy, but if I get sick & die, [I] want more money to enjoy, [I] want a silk dress!' "[64]

In 1936, Parsons was able to negotiate a long-term secret negotiation. An Isletan Indian who had read her book, *Isleta, New Mexico*, had found the written account correct, but the illustrations inadequate. Surreptitiously he wrote to George Dorsey at the Bureau of American Ethnology in Washington where the book had been published. Eventually this letter and a sample of his drawings were forwarded to Parsons. The artist explained that the pictures were secret and that only those who believed could see them. No one else would paint such pictures because they feared death. He emphasized that he wanted no one to know so long as he lived that he had drawn the pictures. He had done this only because he had no other way of making money. Though he had worked for the Atchison Topeka and Santa Fe Railway Company for approximately eight years in Clovis, Gallup, and Albuquerque, he had been forced to leave work due to poor health. He asked for help in securing employment so that he could once again support himself. There was in his letter an expression of both desperation and shame. Reduced to poverty, he had been forced to betray his own people.[65]

Parsons immediately responded, "Your letter and two enclosures were forwarded to me as the proper person to attend to them. I enclose two five dollar bills. I will be glad to pay at the same rate for others equally good."[66] The letters that accompanied Felipe's paintings showed his continuing concern with earning money and his fear of exposure. Acknowledging receipt of payment, he told about the picture of the Town Chief. He said that the drawing had been emotionally difficult for him to do, but that he needed the money. Felipe gathered additional information from specialists in order to portray accurately the details of ritual. He attended a ceremonial held in Gallup so he could learn the secret of the feather dance from the medicine men, and he traveled to Zuni to attend the secret fire dance, which he planned to draw for Parsons.[67] The artist continued his work for a period of five years, completing over one hundred watercolors. Parsons stipulated that the artist's real name never be revealed. On the title page of the manuscript, she wrote, "I refer to my informant as Felipe. His true name is never to be used. Very important."

In this exchange with the Isletan artist, Parsons was an enthusiastic participant. There was no hesitation on her part, only on his. There was for her no ethical issue. The result of the engagement would advance science: secrets would be recorded in detail unmatched by verbal description.[68] In an ethical twist, she stood in judgment of him and acknowledged, "Of moral scruples in our terms there are a few expressions." She continued: "After referring to offerings to the dead made on the ash piles, Felipe writes: 'I don't know if I am doing right to tell all this or not. Sometimes I feel funny.' Again, 'If I had not seen the History [the Bureau publication] I would not give you or anybody any drawings.' This appears to be the familiar rationalization for telling a secret—'You know it anyway.' It is also an illustration of the general attitude of the Pueblo Indian who tells you something only when in his opinion you know enough to understand."[69]

Parsons had attempted to limit access to her works on the pueblos. In 1936, she had decided to publish *Taos Pueblo* in Yale University's General Series in Anthropology because she thought "the circulation . . . so limited that it [would] be almost impossible for a copy to reach the town."[70] In her agreement with the press, she stipulated that the work not be made available to people in New Mexico.[71] It was agreed that a note would be slipped into each copy that would read, "We would greatly appreciate an effort on your part to keep this paper from getting into the hands of people in and around Taos. It may cause conflict in the pueblo and create difficulties for future ethnographic investigations there." Parsons expressed the same desire when she sent a copy of the monograph to Grenville Goodwin, who was conducting fieldwork among the western Apache. He acknowledged receipt and assured her that he would be cautious about allowing others to see it.[72] Once "the Taos affair" erupted, and the people were in an uproar over her work, Elsie still insisted on selective distribution of the monograph.

Leslie Spier, as editor of the General Series in Anthropology, assured Elsie that he would follow her requests and not sell any copies of *Taos Pueblo* to residents of New Mexico. He told her that he had, indeed, refused sales to the Southwest, save for requests from individuals whom he judged trustworthy. For the latter, he wrote asking them to be discreet with the book, and not to show it to any Indians or to any whites in the Taos area.[73] Apparently Spier's request was taken seriously, for Ruth Underhill was unable to gain access to a copy in the Albuquerque public library. She wrote Elsie, "Have you a spare copy of your Taos? The library here keeps it where I can't get it."[74] Elsie was still following this policy in 1939 when *Pueblo Indian Religion* was published. Robert Redfield, as representative of the University of Chicago Press, wrote her that he had sent some complimentary copies to people not on her list. He assured her that for those living in the Southwest, he had included a request that the book not be made available to Indians.[75]

This informal policy of limited access failed, and some of Parsons's books inevitably reached the people about whom they were written. In fact, some of the most avid readers were the people themselves. The revelations on the printed page caused reverberations throughout their communities. In both Jemez and Taos, there was outrage that Parsons had succeeded in finding out secrets that had been protected with such care for so many centuries. The anger was partially directed toward the author, but most intensely it was internalized. Someone within the pueblos had betrayed the people, and the immediate concern was to single out the guilty one. Precisely what Parsons had worried about had come to pass. She was powerless, try as she might, to undo the forces that the discovery of her works had set in motion.

An inhabitant of Jemez wrote Elsie demanding to know who her informants were for *The Pueblo of Jemez*. She responded: "I got my information from a great many persons, practically everybody told me something in one way or another, not knowing they were telling me anything. As for giving you names, I could not possibly do so, as I know very well that no Pueblo Indian wants to have his name mentioned in such a way." She assured the man that she relied heavily on information derived from other pueblos that she had visited prior to Jemez. The book, Elsie explained, was not intended for the general public, nor was it in general circulation. She emphasized, "Tourists and disagreeable white people do not read it. They can not understand it and they do not care about it. When I meet such people, I am as careful in talking to them as any Indian would be." The book, she said, had been "written for a very few white people, all of whom are friends of the Indians." In addition, she intended the book for the man's great-grandchildren. Elsie continued, "You know quite well that the customs are changing, and that many will be forgotten, and unless the history is written your descendants will not know about the ways of their old people." She asked the correspondent, "Why don't you try to explain this both to your old men and your young?" The consequences of his not doing this, Elsie asserted, were apparent: "Because you don't try to explain, the persecution situation is entirely your own fault." She asked the man from Jemez to explain to his people that "everything about all the Pueblos is known to a few wise white people who keep the books merely as a record, not because they are going to make use of the customs themselves and not because they want to have the customs interfered with." Indeed, she assured him, these are the very people who want the customs preserved. Elsie acknowledged that "it is hard work explaining this," but suggested that if he kept at it "instead of trying to get information that will harm people," he would eventually succeed, "particularly with the younger men." She continued, "For one thing you must explain that nobody makes any money from a book of history. It costs them money. I think I paid about $1000 towards the printing of this book. In my opinion it was a present I made to the people of Jemez, as their friend." Elsie signed the letter, "Your friend and friend of Jemez."[76]

The Jemez Indians had convened several times to discuss Parsons's letter and, as a result, had reached a unanimous decision. They assured her that they had read her letter very carefully and had thought about what she had said. They agreed that she deserved credit for traveling to Jemez, for depriving herself of customary comforts, and for expending the effort to write the book. They were in accord with her viewpoint, that their descendants would now have a record of their way of life. She had compiled, they said, a very good work, one of which the Indians could one day be proud. After this initial praise, they elaborated on their grievances. She was, they insisted, mistaken about the number of books in circulation. There were several copies in the pueblo, over fifty in the state, and others in libraries throughout the United States. The real point of dispute was the source of her information. The people of Jemez were certain that she could not have gathered the material by simply talking with people at random. They insisted that she had worked with knowledgeable individuals who were also skilled at drawing and that she must have done this over a period of time. Her book, they insisted, contained information that even old men of the Pueblo did not know. At this point, the writer of the letter shifted from a discussion of the group response to his own reaction. He and his family had been singled out as the guilty ones. He had been summoned before the governor and the council on numerous occasions. He had been denied his irrigation rights for two years and was unable to raise a sufficient crop. In addition, there was the shame; he and his family were publicly humiliated. To vindicate his honor, he asked for the names of the people who had given her the information. He assured her that since the book had been in circulation for several years the responsible parties would suffer no harm if their names were revealed. He saw it as the only just and honest thing for her to do, considering how he and his family had suffered. It would be easier if she would give the information voluntarily, but he and the people of Jemez were prepared to force such revelations. This, he assured her, would prove embarrassing for her and a poor advertisement for Columbia University.[77]

By September, 1937, there was trouble brewing at Taos as well. A copy of Parsons's monograph had reached the pueblo. Elsie suspected that John Collier, the commissioner of Indian affairs, had given the Taos Indians the book, though she later found that it had been a soil conservationist. She explained to Mabel Dodge Luhan, "I have written Collier asking him to deny or admit sending the Taos monograph to Taos. Sparks may fly." Elsie continued, "The editor and author have been taking great pains that no copy should reach Taos or any non-anthropologists." She said that she had "held back from publishing [for] several years until I found a way, as I thought, to restrict the thing to the profession that was in need of it." Elsie had been most concerned about Mabel and Tony, since she was their friend and had stayed with them at their home in Taos. She continued, "The dedication is true, of course, but I put it in as an alibi for you and Tony in case of necessity."[78] Clearly intended for Tony Luhan, the dedication read, "To my best friend in Taos, the most scrupulous Pueblo Indian of my acquaintance, who told me nothing about the pueblo and who never will tell any white person anything his people would not have him tell, which is nothing."[79] She assured Mabel, "On your account I had a great many qualms over publishing at all, but it had to be made available for students not merely of the Pueblos but of all the Southwest." Elsie assured Mabel that the book was compiled so "that no one faction can use it against another faction, I think, or one individual against another." She added, "But you never can tell." She expressed her fondness for all of her Taos acquaintances and her regret at upsetting any of them. Elsie concluded, "Of course what they most value, prayers, songs, and rituals I did not learn and there is little or nothing that other Pueblos would object to having known about themselves, nothing esoteric from the Pueblo point of view." She felt saddened to know that Tony would not understand her motivation for publishing the book, but she was sure that he would understand that "there is nothing *precious* or *valuable* in the book at all."[80]

Mabel wrote Elsie, "I have to tell you the Taos Indians are raising Cain over your book and have been doing so for months." Mabel continued, "While I was away . . . they had a government employee sent from San Juan and he read it out loud to the assembled council for nine days and nights, and they had two interpreters . . . translating. Now they are simply wild." Two individuals who felt especially impugned by the book were "about to engage a lawyer outside the Indian Bureau to sue you for libel." One had announced to the council three times "that if he killed someone over this he would be justified." The problems were not limited to misunderstandings and confusion. As Mabel said, "There seem many angles and horrors to them over it. For instance members of different clans were present and heard each others' 'secrets,' things they had never known, so you can imagine how they take it!" The Taos Indians had launched an investigation to determine who had provided Parsons with her information. Mabel explained, "They are using very ingenious means to discover who the three people are who sold out to you." They had located someone who worked at a place where Elsie had stayed, and that person recalled that a particular Taos Indian had visited with her there. Next they consulted "old pueblo secretary books" for financial information on this same individual. Mabel assured her, "They are bent on tracking the traitors down if it takes forever—the penalty will be unguessable—maybe death—you can see what storm is raging." Mabel had spoken with the son of the man who was planning to sue Elsie for libel. Of this she said, "I asked Luis . . . why wouldn't it be a good thing for Dr. Elsie Parsons to come and visit the Indians and have some talks and try and clear it up and he replied gently: 'I am afraid we will have to scalp her.' " Rather weakly, Mabel asked Elsie, "Have you any suggestions? Do you think a visit from you would help?"[81]

The Taos Indian who had suffered the most as the result of Parsons's book dictated a letter to Mabel, who then sent it to Elsie. As he said, those who were opposed to the old ways delighted in the opportunity to castigate him. He had lost his power, his prestige, and his honor. No one would listen to him now. In fact, he was derided by people who accused him to his face of "coming out from under his blanket," of telling the secrets of the people. He asked Elsie what she could do to help him now that his life had been thoroughly disrupted. Could she come talk to the council? Could she give the names of the people who had given her the malicious information? If she could not do these things, who then would protect him?[82]

Elsie did not travel to Taos, but she did send Mabel a list of suggestions. First, it might be pointed out to the individual who felt most maligned that there had been mistakes made in the translation when the book was read aloud. Second, he should know that part of the book was concerned with town gossip and was not intended to be taken as accusations. As she wrote, "I am merely repeating the general gossip of the town, and I state it is gossip. In both references I say very carefully 'it is said' or 'it is supposed in town.' " And, third, it must be made clear to him that Parsons had actually praised him and his family for protecting pueblo secrets. The family of the aggrieved individual had originally come under suspicion in 1897, when they provided lodgings for a young student from Chicago. She clearly stated that this family had kept all esoteric matters from Merton Miller. As she said, "This is the first complete vindication for the . . . family, and should remove from them the long standing suspicion." Elsie concluded, "At any rate you might explain all these points to Tony and then he can use them or not as he sees fit. My own view is that you and Tony had better keep out of the picture as much as possible."[83]

Elsie also wrote a letter to the governor and the council of Taos. She began, "My Friends, I hear you are troubled about a book written about Taos. I am very sorry indeed about it, but perhaps the trouble is not as bad as you think it is." She assured them that there was "little if any secret information in the book; no songs, or prayers, or medicine." Some information that might appear to be secret was actually "known about in all the other pueblos and has been for many years." This had been told to her "many years ago by persons who are dead as far as I know." She explained that the book was "nowhere on public sale; very few people want to read it." Whites, she said, were not interested in reading such a book. However, if the Taos people drew attention to the book, or if they "make a row about it and go on talking about it people may try to get the book and publish pieces from it in the newspapers." She advised, "Better for secrecy at Taos not to pay any attention to it. Then very few people will read it." One family, she had heard, had been particularly offended by her book. She continued: "Let me say to you that I have never had any secret information from any members of that family and what I say about any of them is only what I have heard from people in Taos. You know people talk about that family a good deal and I wrote down some of the talk only to show what people talk about and not because I thought it was true." Indeed, she said, the two men of this family "are among those most careful to guard the secrets of the pueblo." She assured them that anyone reading the book "would see that I like and admire Taos people and do not wish to hurt their feelings or disturb them in any way." She wrote the book out of a regard for the traditions of Taos, and not from a desire to "change its ways of life." Parsons closed the letter with the assurance that the few white people who would read the book "are like myself people who do not want to see the old ways changed."[84]

Parsons's efforts did nothing to ease the suffering of the individual who had been singled out as guilty. Mabel wrote Elsie that she had seen him in the plaza and that "he looked very badly as though he is going to have an illness." She continued:

> I told him all you said but it always came back to the same refrain: "I started our granary. I got the indians to buy indian grain & store it so we can sell it to good advantage in the spring. I wanted to go on & start our own butcher shop so we could stop selling our stock to the butchers in town & then buy it back by the pound. I meant to go on & persuade the old men to save out a small per cent of the grain in the granary & the money we get when we see it & make a fund to take care of the old people. But now that's all finished. No one will listen to me any more. Every man on the council believes because my name comes in that book so much I have been making money here & there in every little way." I felt so sorry for him. I told him you would answer his letter soon. That maybe you would come out & meet the council & explain to them how mistaken they are.

Mabel asked Elsie, "Can you fix it up somehow?" and added, "We should help him repair his power & restore his influence."[85]

Parsons was furious that a government employee should have read her monograph to the Taos Indians. It was, she said, a "very stupid and outrageous" thing to do.[86] To convey her displeasure, she wrote to Sophie Aberle, the general superintendent of the United Pueblos Agency with the Office of Indian Affairs. Parsons explained, "An unexpected situation has developed at Taos in connection with the monograph I published in one of the anthropological series." These publications, prepared in unappealing offsets, were ordinarily consulted by a few anthropologists. It had not been distributed to the public, and the editor was careful never to sell "a copy to anybody in Taos, either in the White or the Indian town." In spite of the intended audience, and the restricted sales, Elsie continued, "A copy reached the Indians over a year ago through a land conservation man. Why he happened to use the book I can not guess for there is practically nothing about land in it. Of course he was ignorant of the trouble he was starting. So with the approval of Mr. Collier I wrote to him and described quite fully the disaster caused by any anthropological report in any pueblo town, how it stirred up suspicion, malice, and persecution, as it is always used as tool or evidence to feed old-time feuds." Parsons referred to the public reading of the book in Taos during which an Anglo, assisted by two Indian interpreters, had spent several nights reading the entire book aloud. She continued, "The book was very difficult to translate and in certain places it was certainly mistranslated." Even if the translation had been entirely accurate, still "it would have disturbed some of the old men who believe that not a word of the language and nothing at all about the customs should be communicated to White people." Though there was little to object to in the monograph itself, there was controversy following "the feud pattern of Taos." This had resulted in "unjust charges of all kinds" directed toward certain individuals. Parsons expressed her concern that similar incidents might be repeated at other pueblos "where any anthropological report of the last fifty years or so might be read and work the same sort of havoc. . . . I am sure you want even more than I do to preclude such rows among *your* people and you will know how to instruct Government employees."[87]

In her response to Parsons's letter, Aberle indicated her regret for the problems that had arisen due to the Indians' reactions to Parsons's monograph. However, since the book had been read to the Indians and explained to them, much of the misunderstanding had dissipated. She said that the governor, the officers, and the principal men of Taos had had the monograph in their possession for several months. Since they could not read English very well, the interpretation of what was written had generated numerous rumors. Both the governor and the council had requested that Aberle's office appoint someone "entirely impartial who would carefully and slowly read the book to them and they, in their turn, wanted to appoint well qualified interpreters." She had sent someone from her office to read the book. The result, she assured Parsons, had eased the situation. Much of what they thought was in the book was not there and other information was treated in an unobjectionable manner. Aberle concluded: "Although I was not in the Government Service at the time of the controversy at Jemez when the Indians learned of the contents of your book about that pueblo, that incident resulted in more bitterness than I believe you will find at Taos today, and I feel as if the Taos incident has been minimized by the fact that the Taos Indians know exactly what the pamphlet contains."[88]

Parsons was not calmed by Aberle's reassurances. She had penned a series of exclamation points all down the margin of the letter. Elsie responded, "I wish I too could feel cheerful about the Taos situation. I wrote the Governor and Council allaying certain suspicions aroused by the reading of the book, but I fear there is a man hunt on there, and as Taos is a comparatively violent pueblo who knows the end?"[89]

Parsons was preparing herself for a libel case. She had retyped all of the letters pertaining to "the Taos affair," and she kept complete documentation on all matters. Anticipating that the suit might include her publisher, she forwarded copies of the Taos correspondence to Spier. Acknowledging receipt, Spier commended her on handling a difficult situation astutely. He expressed his concern for her in the event that there might be a lawsuit and assured her of his support. Spier was of the opinion that ultimately the secrecy issue would diminish, and that this would be a direct result of Parsons's book. It would be an acknowledged fact that the "secrets" were known, and efforts to protect that which was already published would cease. This he thought was beneficial for science. Without such a loosening of restrictions, further publications on the pueblos could be a difficult matter. University presses might respond to pressure from the pueblo communities and from their allies in the white community not to publish material that was regarded as secret.[90]

The dissonance at Taos over Elsie's book seemed to grow quieter with time. Underhill wrote that a lawyer from Albuquerque, much trusted by the Taos people, had attempted "to put the quietus on the whole thing" in 1938. The threats and accusations that surfaced in 1939, he regarded as "a belated echo" of earlier resentments.[91] These reverberations grew more distant. In May, 1940, a friend wrote Elsie,

"The Taos Indians didn't trek down here again after they had me write to you a year or so ago about something or other in some book you had done. I suppose they made up and forgot whatever grouch they had been enjoying."[92] And in November, 1941, Mabel Dodge Luhan wrote, "I persuaded the indians your book was not to buy & be seen by trying to send for one & not getting it & they seem to feel alright."[93] Still, while the public outcry had stilled, the internal investigation did not cease until the people of Taos felt they had identified Parsons's informant, a man who had died two years before the monograph had been published. The sins of the father were visited on his innocent and uninvolved son, who was divested of his share of the communal lands.[94]

Parsons's tenacity in gathering the esoteric secrets of the Pueblo Indians and her insistence on publishing sensitive material were linked to her idea of science. For her, only a complete account would provide the substance for future study. Her work was directed toward thorough documentation, including the actual names of individuals, so that other anthropologists might locate them, or their descendants, for future research. Genealogies linked families with house sites, naming patterns, and ceremonial organizations. Even the gossip about people was recorded, replete with the names of those involved. When she changed or omitted names, it was to protect the identity of informants who had given her, usually for a price, bits of precious traditions. Parsons fitted these pieces together to form the life pattern of the Pueblo Indians. This intricate picture that emerged after years of work was grounded in her fundamental respect for science. For Parsons, the precise documentation of the life of a people was justified, no matter what the repercussions. Ultimately it was anthropology as a science that mattered, and this above all else. The cares and worries of individuals, herself among these, were subsumed within the greater sphere of science. Unfortunately, many people were hurt, and hurt badly, by the publication of her pueblo research. For some, it meant a loss of family honor and of pueblo affiliation, including land and irrigation rights. For all, it meant disruption of life in the pueblo, and a wariness toward anthropologists that has never dissipated. To be fair, Parsons was not the only anthropologist who engaged in such secretive tactics, but she was certainly one whose presence was among the most pervasive in all of the pueblos.

Parsons was adamant that the true record would yield good results. Sincerely as she regretted the pain and unhappiness she had caused the Indians of Jemez and Taos in the controversy over her books, still she was sure that in future years they would be grateful for the record of their lives. Thus, in her view, not only would the science of anthropology benefit from her work, but also the Indians themselves. She attempted to explain this in a letter she wrote to Tony Luhan in April, 1932. "I *am* a friend to the Indians. I have always tried to help them, together and singly. Because I like them; in many ways I like them better than white people. You and I think the same about what is good for them. But on one point we do not think the same. I think that a true, written record should be made of their life, of their *costumbres*. Fifty years from now the *costumbres* will be different in many ways. . . . For the sake of the Indians and of all the world I think a true record should be made of the *costumbres* before people change them and forget them."[95]

Parsons had turned to the Southwest as an escape from the disappointments of political action and movements for social change. She soon found that here also she could not avoid the consequences of political events. Along with so many others, she was swept up in the organized opposition to the Bursum bill, which posed a vital threat to Pueblo life. In September, 1922, Senator Holm O. Bursum of New Mexico introduced Senate bill 3855, which came to be known as the Bursum bill. This piece of legislation was the product of a close-knit group from New Mexico. At the behest of Secretary of the Interior Albert B. Fall, who had been a former Senator from New Mexico, two attorneys from Santa Fe, A. B. Renehan and Ralph Twitchell, drafted the bill. There was clearly a conflict of interest, since Renehan was a lawyer for Mexican and Anglo clients with disputed claims to Pueblo lands, and Twitchell had been appointed special U.S. attorney to defend the rights of Indians by Secretary Fall. The Bursum bill was presented to the Senate with the support of the Bureau of Indian Affairs, the secretary of the interior, and, it was incorrectly asserted, with the approval of the Pueblo Indians. No public hearings were held on the bill.

While the bill passed the Senate without dispute, news of it, as John Collier said, brought "a public wrath of nation-wide proportions." The bill ostensibly gave jurisdiction of Pueblo Indian land claims to the U.S. courts. Its critics said that the result of the bill would be quite different. In an impassioned article, entitled "Politicians Pillage the Pueblos," Collier charged that if made law, the bill would facilitate settlement of claims made by trespassers on Pueblo lands, that there would be no provision for adequate compensation for land sales, and that jurisdiction in matters of land and of water would be given "to the inimical New Mexico state courts."[96] Collier served as the director of research for the Indian Welfare Committee of the General Federation of Women's Clubs, one of the most vocal groups opposing the Bursum bill. In an article in *The World*, entitled "Robbing the Pueblo Indians," he wrote, "The nature of the present crisis can be stated in few words. The Pueblo life rests on the land. The whole social system—even the religious system—of the Pueblos . . . rests on the foundation of agriculture."[97] The loss of their land, Collier asserted, meant extinction for the Pueblo Indians.

In an unpublished manuscript, "Indians Ku-Klux-Klanned," Parsons addressed this same issue. If the Bursum bill became law, the Indians would lose a total of 60,000 acres, which would be divided as follows: "to Taos, 4000 acres; to San Juan, 1700 acres; to Tesuque, 1164 acres; to Pojoaque, 5785 acres; to Nambé, 1000 acres; to Cochiti, 10000 acres; to Sandia, 1500 acres; to San Felipe, 2100 acres; to Isleta, from 2500 to 3000 acres, to Acoma, 1000 acres, to Santo Domingo, 25000 acres."[98] The disputed land was taken, Parsons said, "by the methods of adverse possession or squatting, of taking evidence without color of title." Collier compiled further statistics, "Taos has lost over 3,000 acres of its best land. Tesuque has been robbed of all its water. Santa Clara retains the use of about 200 acres of arable land. Picuris retains only about forty acres."[99] In San Juan, outsiders "occupy all but 588 of about 4,000 irrigable acres and 432 Indians subsist on what is left." The result of this, Collier reported, was near starvation in some of the pueblos. Crops had failed because the Pueblo Indians had been unable to irrigate. Their water had been diverted "by non-Indians within and outside of their boundaries." They had, he said, "been deprived of the means of self-support and [were] being rapidly crowded to the wall by stronger neighbors."[100]

The Bursum bill stipulated that boundaries would be established by reference to the Joy survey, which had been conducted in 1914–16. Parsons referred to this as "the burlesque touch," since it entailed using as "evidence of the validity of claims" a map that was compiled from claims made by non-Indians against Indians. In a *New Republic* article, entitled "The Death of the Pueblos," Alice Corbin Henderson characterized the Joy survey as a preliminary mapping of the area, showing "every small cabin, ranch or field within the Indian boundaries, giving to each claim such dimensions as the claimant chose verbally to define." Written on each of the hundreds of blueprints comprising the survey was a statement to the effect that "this was merely 'a depicting of present conditions' and that it was never to be used in any way as proof of title."[101]

The opposition organized. On November 5, 1922, a little over one month after the Senate had passed the Bursum bill, Santo Domingo

and Cochiti called a meeting of the twenty Pueblos. As it was reported
to the *New York Times,* "United in action for the first time since they
drove out the Spaniards in 1680, nearly one hundred delegates, including eight Governors, traveling on foot and horseback, representing 8,000 Pueblo Indians in 19 pueblos in New Mexico assembled at
the Pueblo of Santo Domingo on Sunday, adopted a memorial to the
American people 'for fair play and justice and the preservation of our
Pueblo life.' "[102] Charlie Kie of Laguna, who worked as a car inspec-
tor for the Santa Fe Railroad, served as chairman. As the *Santa Fe New
Mexican* reported, the proceedings unfolded slowly "with long inter-
vals of silence," but the issues were addressed in a "methodical" manner that clearly "showed the experience gained in village councils."
Each pueblo attempted to reach accord with the others, so that any
action taken would be thoroughly representative. "The committee
whose personnel was unanimously approved by all the Indians, retired to another house late Sunday afternoon and deliberated for two
or three hours before reporting its findings to the council." While the
deliberations were carried out exclusively by the Pueblo Indians
themselves, the council did request that Father Shuster, a Franciscan
priest from Laguna who was trained in shorthand, take notes and
that Collier type all the documents. The delegates signed according to
pueblo affiliation.[103] Mabel Dodge Luhan wrote to Elsie of the meeting, "I will send you soon a copy of the petition the indians framed up
down at San Domingo & signed with their thumbprints—most of
them. There were over a hundred delegates there & it was very impressive. They had five interpreters—english, spanish, & three indian
languages."[104]

The statement the council issued was an appeal "for fair play and
justice and the preservation of our pueblo life." The representatives
of the twenty New Mexico pueblos addressed the issue of land and
water needs: "Today, many of our pueblos have the use of less than an
acre per person of irrigated land, whereas in New Mexico 10 acres of
irrigated land are considered necessary for a white man to live on. We
have reached a point where we must either live or die." The Bursum
bill, they said, would complete their destruction. They continued,
"Now we discover . . . that congress and the American people have
been told that we, the Indians, have asked for this legislation. This, we
say, is not true. We have never asked for this legislation. We were
never given the chance of having anything to say or do about this bill."
The Pueblo representatives had attempted, they asserted, on numerous occasions to have officials of the Indian office and the attorneys of
the government explain the bill to them. The result was that they had
"always been put off and even insulted, and on one occasion when a

Pueblo Indian talked with the government attorney who drew this Bursum bill, about the bill, he was told that he was 'ungrateful' and 'no good.' " Aware that the bill was being framed, a delegation from Laguna, the largest of the New Mexico pueblos, "waited 11 hours for a chance to discuss it with the Commissioner of Indian Affairs at Albuquerque. At the end of this time, the commissioner granted 10 minutes, in which he answered no question that the Pueblos had come to ask." They said that they could not understand "why the Indian office and the lawyers who are paid by the government to defend our interests, and the secretary of the interior, have deserted us and failed to protect us this time." They took their plea to the American people, saying that "the bill will destroy our common life and will rob us of everything which we hold dear—our lands, our customs, our traditions." They asked, "Are the American people willing to see this happen?"[105]

Elsie was charged to action. She wrote Mabel, "What an outrage! I am writing to the Speaker of the House, Gillett, an old friend, & to Ogden Mills, a competent & energetic Congressman from N. Y., also a friend. Also I'll get Herbert to make me a list of others worth writing to." She would attempt to get the American Museum of Natural History and the American Ethnological Society to pass resolutions. She continued, "And through Wiley of the Times I'll work for some publicity on that paper, even to being interviewed which is the last proof of devotion." In two weeks, Parsons had succeeded in rallying some professional groups to the cause. She wrote Mabel, "The Peabody Museum people have come across handsomely with resolutions & letters. Tonight the American Ethnological Society is to pass a resolution. I have invited reporters, & wrote to Lippmann [of the *New Republic*] to send one." The next day Elsie wrote Mabel that she had received from her in time for the meeting the pamphlets and copies of "An Appeal by the Pueblo Indians of New Mexico to the People of the United States," which she distributed to the reporters. Elsie forwarded Mabel a copy of the resolution passed by the American Ethnological Society and suggested, "It might be a good idea to get it printed in a Santa Fe paper."[106] *The World* reported on the meeting: "Mrs. Elsie Clews Parsons, who sponsored the resolutions, said the bill validates the right of squatters encroaching on Indian reservations, thereby reducing more than 8,000 Indians to a per capita acreage too small to support life and forcing them to become shifting groups of day laborers. The Pueblo colonies, she said, are examples of the highest Indian cultures."[107] Elsie was not impressed with the coverage, and wrote to Mabel that *The World* "will have to do better than that."[108] News of her work reached the *Literary Review*, where it was reported,

"To mention again the fight for the Pueblo Indians, it seems that now *Elsie Clews Parsons,* herself a member of the Hopi tribe of the Pueblo Indians, has instigated the American Ethnological Society to protest against the Bursum Bill."[109]

In response to the threat posed by the Bursum bill, an organization of non-Indians, called the Eastern Association of Indian Affairs, was formed. Among the members of the committee were Elsie Clews Parsons, Pliny Earle Goddard, and Stewart Culin. The stated purpose of the group was "the defeat of the iniquitous U. S. Senate Bill 3855." In addition to this association, the Indian Welfare Committee of the General Federation of Women's Clubs had been actively opposing the bill from its very inception, and the American Indian Defense Society joined the efforts. These groups launched an organized effort to defeat the Bursum bill, and together they distributed the poignant statements made by the Pueblo Indians themselves—"An Appeal by the Pueblo Indians of New Mexico to the People of the United States," "An Appeal by Pablo Johnson of Laguna," and "The Appeal of the Acomas," as well as "The Protest of Artists and Writers Against the Bursum Indian Bill," signed, among others, by Zane Grey, D. H. Lawrence, Carl Sandburg, William Allen White, Vachel Lindsay, Maxfield Parrish, Grant La Farge, and Elsie Clews Parsons.

The publicity and the protest worked. As the *Santa Fe New Mexican* reported,

> Seldom has a proposed piece of national legislation or a public man had to bear the brunt of such a universal press fusillade as that now being directed throughout the country against the . . . Bursum Indian Bill and against Secretary of the Interior Fall. . . . Newspapers and magazines from San Francisco to New York, organizations ranging from the National Federation of Women's Clubs to the Girl Scouts, and art, archaeological and ethnological associations have united in the barrage, and it is doubtful if any measure so "purely local," as Senator Bursum says, in its effect has ever before aroused in this country such an upheaval of popular indignation.[110]

William Allen White was inspired to draw a political cartoon for the *New York Tribune* showing "a diminutive David with brush and palette, who, with a small sling and a pebble labeled 'publicity,' has laid low an astonished Goliath bearing the legend, 'Bursum Bill.' "[111]

The Bursum bill was recalled from the House of Representatives and returned to its place of origin, the Senate Public Lands Committee.[112] However, the threat had not passed, for Representative

Homer P. Snyder, chairman of the Indian Affairs Committee in the
House, had introduced what Collier called a "denatured version of
the Bursum Bill." The Pueblo Indians themselves, aided by the Wom-
en's Federation, the Franciscan Fathers of New Mexico, and the New
Mexico Association on Indian Affairs, were drafting their own legislation, referred to as the Jones-Leatherwood bill. The groups that
had lobbied against the Bursum bill rallied to the support of this measure. Elsie wrote Mabel of the action taken by the American Association for the Advancement of Science at its annual meeting: "Its
executive committee was most insistent for a resolution from the
American Anthropological Asso. against the Bursum bill. The AAA
appointed a committee on Indian policy, & Spinden, Morehead & I
drafted resolutions in favor of the Jones bill & of general changes in
Indian administration. I'll get copies to send you, for local use."[113]
The Jones-Leatherwood bill received the endorsement of the American Anthropological Association and the Eastern Association of Indian Affairs.[114] This substitute bill, Mabel wrote Elsie, would provide
for a commission to visit the pueblos to settle the land disputes "in a
manner *as fair* to the indian as to the white settlers & squatters." Collier was at work compiling information on the economic conditions of
the pueblos. Mabel wrote Elsie, "Crops & livings of some of these people . . . will shock you as well as others when it is made public."[115] Collier had found that San Juan, the most prosperous of the pueblos, had
a per capita annual income of approximately thirty-two dollars. The
pueblo of Tesuque, where nearly all of the irrigation had been ap-
propriated by non-Indians, had a per capita annual income of just
over sixteen dollars, and San Ildefonso had a per capita income of
thirteen dollars.[116]

The Pueblo Indians had voted in the All-Pueblo Council Meeting,
as the *Santa Fe New Mexican* reported, "to send their appeal against
the Bursum bill by Indian delegates to Washington to be given to the
president and congress."[117] As Mabel reported to Elsie, plans were
made to send "a group of 12 to 15 from the different pueblos to Washington possibly around the 1st of December & they will then carry the
original petition to the president." They might travel, she said, to
New York to meet with groups of people at the Natural History Museum and at Columbia University. She was hoping that the novelist
Mary Austin would arrange for them to appear at the National Arts
Club, and she asked Elsie if she could arrange for the Indians to
spend an afternoon or an evening at the Colony Club. She continued,
"They will be a fine number of the best older men & will be very interesting to people who have never seen them & maybe more so to

those who have. John Collier will introduce them with a talk about
their situation & he is a splendid speaker. Maybe they will sing—
if pressed!" Mabel noted that, in addition to publicity, they would
need "to raise money by contributions both for their expenses for
the journey, & also to help them through this winter which is going
to be a terror to pueblo indians for they have raised practically no
crops."[118]

Elsie organized gatherings, as Mabel had requested, with influential people for the delegation of Pueblo Indians. When she found that
the clubs would not allow meetings connected with legislation, she
made other plans: "The Cosmopolitan audience has been arranged
for by Mrs. Tonette in her studio, a meeting next Sunday. And when
I called on Mrs. Charles Platt on the subject she offered her large
room." Elsie was distributing a pamphlet on the Jones bill and asked
Mabel for "a dozen or more copies." In turn, she sent Mabel a copy of
a letter that Herbert had drafted to "Snyder, extracts of which you
might like to use in Mr. Renehan's own state." The meetings were a
success. On January 24, 1923, Elsie wrote Mabel, "The Indian meetings are in full swing. One today at the Town Hall, tomorrow at Dorothy Straight's house. Friday, a party at the American Museum." Elsie
also arranged for the delegation to visit her son's school. She wrote
Mabel, "Mac told me two days ago after a visit by the Indians to his
Lincoln School that he had a surprise for me. . . . This morning he
confides that they are poems. 'We were so inspired by the visit of
the Pueblo Indians that we made up a song, the class made one, I'd
made my own already.' " The children were collecting money to contribute to the Indians' travel fund.[119]

The press gave enthusiastic coverage to the delegation of Pueblo
Indians. An article in *The World,* entitled "Pueblo Indians Appeal
Against Bursum Bill Disinheriting Them," included a photograph of
Santiago Narango of Santa Clara Pueblo. In full regalia, complete
with feathered head-dress, Narango held his cane of office. The caption read, "SANTIAGO NARANGO, BY WORLD STAFF PHOTOG-
RAPHER YESTERDAY." The article opened: "While other speakers
denounced the Bursum bill as an attempted theft by 'land-grabbing
politicians,' representatives of the Pueblo Indians who, according to
expert opinion, face extinction if the bill is passed, limited themselves
to a quiet, confident appeal for justice at a reception in the Explorers'
Club yesterday afternoon. Dressed in regalia their ancestors have
worn for centuries, they told of the squatters who have stolen their
lands. . . . 'We are not afraid to speak before you,' they said, 'because
we know we are right.'[120]

A front-page article in the *Santa Fe New Mexican* reported that the members of the Pueblo delegation had made appearances before large gatherings in New York and Washington and that they would stop in Chicago on their journey home. The delegation was present at the Senate hearings on the Bursum bill. The article declared, "The hearings have created a sensation throughout Washington official circles and undoubtedly mark the beginning of a general movement toward rectification of Indian policy." Under cross-examination, one of the framers of the Bursum bill, R. E. Twitchell, had "acknowledged the validity of nearly all the criticism of the bill. . . . The Indian Bureau finally agreed to the cancellation of nearly every paragraph of the Bursum bill."[121]

The problem was not simply that the framers of the Bursum Bill had self-interest and not Indian interest in mind. It went much deeper. Stella M. Atwood, head of the Indian Welfare Committee of the General Federation of Women's Clubs, testified in the Senate hearings that the governmental policy toward American Indians was " 'inhumane, expensive to the tax-payer and largely fruitless of good to the Indians.' " She was especially critical of Indian Commissioner Charles H. Burke and the special government attorney for the Pueblos in New Mexico, R. E. Twitchell. Burke bristled and informed Mrs. Atwood that the Indian Bureau would not tolerate further investigations by her organization among American Indians. As it was reported in the *Santa Fe New Mexican*, "Mrs. Atwood pleasantly but caustically reminded the Commission that he was the servant, not the master of the American people, and that the Indians did not belong to him as his private property."[122]

Burke was not chastened by the public criticism. Just four months after the Senate hearings on the Bursum bill, he issued an order in person at Taos Pueblo. Elsie received a letter, dated "Easter Sunday," which described this event, "The pueblo is very sad and all upset. Yesterday, the Commissioner of Indian Affairs, Burke, came thru here on a tour of inspection and told the Indians that they must put a stop to their ceremonies. What a stupidly cruel thing to do."[123] Commissioner Burke, accompanied by Interior Secretary Hubert Work, had "invaded the Taos Pueblo's Council," and accused the Indians of being " 'half animals' by virtue of their 'pagan worship.' "[124] The writer of the letter continued that for his part he considered this as "another case of American bullying, of the hundred percent variety." Since the Bureau of Indian Affairs was ignorant "in all that is Indian," the writer would not "do them the honor of believing them capable of understanding that to take away his religious ceremonies from the Indian is to take away his heart, and leave him a corpse, ready for quick disintegration. It is just plain, stupid, brutal, arrogant Nordic superiority." Commissioner Burke was determined that the Indians would not dance in summer ceremonies but would spend their time working. As explained in a *New York Times* article, "The objections of the Commissioner, which are held also, he says, by the superintendents and the missionaries among the Indians, are that the dances take up too much time, that they interfere with work, and that they are evil and foolish." Burke had issued his " 'message' to 'All Indians' " following a conference with missionaries in the Sioux country.[125]

As soon as she received news of this, Elsie began work to contravene the Burke order. She contacted Burton E. Livingston, the secretary of the American Association for the Advancement of Science. Livingston wrote in response, "Thank you for calling my attention to the Burke order about Indian dances. I will bear this in mind and do anything possible. It looks as though we might get definite action at the Executive Committee in April, and then proceed to publish resolutions."[126] She also contacted Geoffrey Parsons of the *New York Tribune:* "I read that Commissioner Burke has issued an order that the Pueblo Indians are not to 'dance' in summer. Do write an editorial about it. It seems incredible, either as ignorance or malice. It hits Indians, pro-Indian whites, *and* the Catholic church almost as much as a land grab bill. It even hits the 'Mexicans' who are fond of going to the Saint's day dances in the pueblo, for amusement & for trade." Elsie noted that the Zuni and the Hopi Indians would suffer even more than the eastern pueblos from such an order. The Catholic Church was not established among the western pueblos, and the people depended on their native ceremonial calendar for the pacing of their life. The Burke order, she continued, would destroy "the Hopi snake ceremony, the Flute ceremony and the Farewell Kachina ceremony. In Zuñi too it will destroy the summer solstice ceremony and a series of rain dances." These ceremonies, Elsie emphasized, did not really draw from the work force of the pueblos. At most, they required the energy "of but a few old men." As she noted, "They interfere far less than would compulsory Sunday observance with the work time of the younger men." The problem, she said, was that the Bureau agents were displeased "to see people working on Sunday & dancing, perhaps, on Saturday, even every other Saturday, or every third or fourth Saturday." Of the consequences, she remarked: "To the Indians this order will seem like the most overbearing of religious persecution, & it is. It will cause untold fear and distress. That the Indian Bureau may not appreciate what the order means is hardly to its credit. It is not merely a silly order, as the World calls it, . . . it is a criminal order."

Burke was acting in petulant revenge. As Elsie expressed it, it was as if he "were saying to the Indian delegation who dared to come to criticize his Bureau as well as to his White critics, 'I'll show you! I can hit back, & I have the power.' It's really an amazing gesture for a public servant." Elsie suggested that Geoffrey Parsons might use any portion of her letter for an editorial; she offered to send him a shortened version of her article on Ku-Klux-Klanning Pueblo Indians. She concluded: "This last piece of Ku Klux Klanning somehow gets my goat even more than the land bills. The land grab bills were simple enough to explain. Before the devilishness of this executive order the Indians are much more helpless. And coming at this particular time it looks like such preposterous malice."[127]

The writer of the letter about Burke's Easter visit to Taos had said that the Indians wanted him, because he was an anthropologist, to inform the scientists, to "get Boas and Elsie and Wissler, Kroeber, Lowie, Goddard et. al. to do something." He had hoped for "perhaps a sort of manifesto, protesting against the interference with the religious freedom of the Indians, and endorsed by all the anthropologists of note." Yet, he despaired of this, because he did not think "the anthropologists want to be bothered."[128] He was proven wrong. The anthropologists had successfully organized in opposition to both the Bursum bill and the Burke order. The Bursum bill was defeated. On a not entirely unrelated matter, the instigator of the bill, Secretary of Interior Albert B. Fall, had resigned his post in April, 1923. Four years later, he was found guilty of having accepted a bribe in 1922 in exchange for lease to a private company of federal oil reserves in Elk Hills, California, and Teapot Dome, Wyoming. Fined one hundred thousand dollars and sentenced to one year in prison, Fall was the first former Cabinet member to be convicted of a felony.[129] In 1929, five years after the public outcry against the Bursum bill and the Burke order, Burke himself was forced to resign. Responding to the pressure of the Senate Indian Investigating Committee, with its thirty-seven volumes documenting the poverty and repression of the Indians, Burke accused Senator William Bliss Pine, of Oklahoma, a member of the committee, and John Collier "of subverting the Indians, and of organizing them against the government."[130] Called before the Senate committee to substantiate his charges, Burke resigned from office. Collier gained a reputation as a champion of Indian rights and was appointed commissioner of Indian affairs under Franklin Delano Roosevelt. In this instance, Parsons and the other anthropologists who worked to defeat the Bursum bill and the Burke order must have felt vindicated.

Elsie's interest in the Southwest had always extended beyond her own fieldwork and writing. She envisioned a research plan for the entire Southwest that would necessitate coordinated work by many anthropologists. As she wrote Clark Wissler on January 3, 1918, "Research in the Southwest is being done in a desultory, individualistic fashion." What was needed, she said, was a "plan of cooperative work and a general research program." She suggested the possibility of compiling an encyclopedia of southwestern culture. Scholars could agree upon "a tentative list of encyclopedia articles." Then each researcher responsible for a certain area would "prepare a memorandum of the comparative data lacking in his particular topics."[131] Should the Museum of Natural History, of which Wissler was curator of anthropology, be interested in sponsoring such an undertaking, then the memoranda would be kept on file there, along with all the available literature on the Southwest.

Such an energetic plan did not materialize, though Elsie continued to press for institutional coordination of southwestern research. In January, 1938, she wrote to H. Scudder Mekeel of the Laboratory of Anthropology in Santa Fe, New Mexico: "I have always thought that one important function of the Laboratory should consist of being a clearing house of information, so that students should not overlap and should be well informed as to what has already been done, and I think that reports in manuscript should be circulated as much as possible." Elsie added that she carried "on a little of this sort of cooperation" on her own and would be glad to furnish the laboratory with any information that might be helpful. Pueblo culture, she noted, was alive and changing, and afforded "a rare chance for a dynamic study." For this reason, she hoped that the laboratory might keep annual records on all the pueblos. Such a chronicle for a ten-year period would provide invaluable information about culture change. She added, "Very important changes have occurred during the last five years, but do you know of any ethnological records?"[132]

While Parsons was unable to gain the institutional support necessary for the coordination of southwestern research, in her own life she came to fill this role. She became the "clearing house" for information on fieldwork and publications, and she served as the facilitator, making contacts and financial support available. The interconnectedness of southwestern work was also reflected in letters to her from the field. Anthropologists, whose work was often supported by funds from her, would write to Parsons about the progress of their own work and the contributions of others. In short, she promoted, organized, and sponsored research in the Southwest.

In her correspondence, Elsie customarily summarized current projects and publications, as it were, spreading the information through the network of southwestern scholars. For example, in a 1929 letter to Alfred Kroeber, she wrote: "I have been putting through with Stirling an annual report consisting of material on the Southwest, which pleases me very much—one volume on the Keres, White's Acoma, some Acoma material that Stirling got himself from an informant in Washington, some Boas and Benedict material from Cochiti; and one volume on Isleta (social organization, by myself) and two papers on Zuñi by Bunzel, Zuñi ritual poetry and Zuñi kachina cult."[133] In a letter to Mekeel, Elsie wrote about Morris Opler's collection of folktales from the Lipan Apache, which would appear as a Memoirs of the American Folk-Lore Society, and about Grenville Goodwin's general ethnography of the five groups of western Apache. She added, "His Folktales of the White Mountain Apache is in press (A.F.L.S.). . . . Parsons, Taos Folk Tales will soon be in press; Frager is planning to publish his study of Tanoan and Whorf, his Hopi grammar."[134] With a similar summation in a note to Matthew W. Stirling, she said, "Dr. Boas and Dr. Benedict are writing the introductions to their Cochiti papers and Dr. Bunzel is working on her katchina paper."[135]

As part of her stress on collaboration in research, Elsie freely shared her fieldwork notes and carbon copies of articles and books that she was preparing for publication. To Robert Lowie she wrote, "I've been rereading your 'Exogamy and the Classificatory Systems of Relationship,' and it occurs to me you might like to see my notes, scant as they are, on Zuñi kinship terms. Besides, any questions they might suggest to you would be a help to me on my next trip."[136] J. O. Brew returned her manuscript copy of a paper on Hopi-Keresan connections with the notation, "I have made notes of your description of altar set-ups and am hoping one of these days to find chamahias actually in position."[137]

Parsons worked toward the location and publication of manuscripts on the Southwest. If the author was deceased, she would take on the responsibility of editing the work; if the author was living, she would offer encouragement and assistance in preparing the manuscript for press. In 1918, she wrote to James Walter Fewkes, head of the Bureau of Ethnology, "I have become interested in getting published as soon as can be whatever unpublished mss. there are on the SW."[138] In 1937, she wrote Lowie, "No end to new mss. and publications on the Southwest. Be sure to point out if I am overlooking any important one—new or old."[139] Through her alertness to their value, she found lost treasures. From Stewart Culin, she learned of a manuscript at the Brooklyn Museum on Cochiti ceremonial life. It had been written by Father Noel Dumarest while he served the pueblos of Cochiti, Santo Domingo, and San Felipe from 1893 to 1900. With painstaking care, Elsie translated the "difficult ms., in a poor hand, in French,"[140] inserting editorial comments for a comparative perspective with other pueblos. *Notes on Cochiti* was published as part of the Memoirs of the American Anthropological Association (1919).

In 1922, Elsie began work on "a veritable treasure house,"[141] the copious and rich fieldnotes of Alexander M. Stephen, which at the author's death had been purchased by Culin for the Brooklyn Institute Museum. The majority of Stephen's entries were from 1892 to 1893 and focused on the ceremonial and daily life of the people on First Mesa (the Hopi pueblo of Walpi and the Tewa town of Hano), with information on Second and Third Mesas as well. Parsons provided funds to Benjamin Whorf to work on the Hopi glossary, which he found to "a very considerable job," because of errors in the translations.[142] Parsons organized the journal according to ceremony, gathering together the descriptions for the various years, and introducing the ritual with a prefatory note. She included comparative notes, appendices on calendrical cycles, kinship, place names and ritual terminology, and material culture (the organization of which she referred to as "my particular hell"[143]), and an extensive glossary of Hopi terms. The *Hopi Journal of Alexander M. Stephen* was published by Columbia University Press, with Parsons paying two thousand dollars of the expenses and donating future royalties to the Council for Research in the Social Sciences.[144] On receipt of a copy of *Hopi Journal*, Morris Titiev wrote Elsie from Oraibi, "I am carried away by the deep significance of your edition of Stephen's Journal. No present or future student of the Hopi can hope to make an interpretation of this material without consulting that work."[145]

When Elsie heard that Frances Densmore had been collecting Pueblo songs, she wrote, "It occurs to me that in preparing notes on ceremonialism in connection with the songs I might be of service." She added, "Pueblo ceremonialism is so intricate and information so hard to come by that I have always thought that between those working in the field there should be as much informal cooperation as possible."[146] Responding to Elsie's suggestion with appreciation, Densmore indicated that she would be unable to work on the songs for a long time and would be receptive to any cooperative form of publication that Parsons might suggest. Elsie immediately wrote to Stirling, who was head of the Bureau of American Ethnology, which sponsored Densmore's research, volunteering her assistance: "Of course I do not wish my name to appear in the publication, and I may not be able to contribute much information, but it seems probable that some information I *could* contribute which would add a little value to the publication."[147]

In 1929, Elsie corresponded with Stirling about his Acoma manuscript, which he had compiled with the informant, Henry Hunt. She said, "The great value of old Hunt's narrative is the picture it reveals of the man's mind towards the whole ceremonial life." Elsie suggested that Stirling's manuscript should be published along with Leslie White's work on the Acoma. She wrote, "I think Dr. Boas would be glad to do a little standardizing of the phonetics if you wished. . . . And I would be glad to supply some comparative notes." She emphasized the importance of collaboration on research: "My plan, involving you, White, Boas and myself, represents a kind of cooperation which appeals to me very much. If there had been more of it in the past, we would know more of the ethnology of the Southwest today." In 1937, Elsie was still trying to get Stirling to finalize his manuscript on Acoma mythology, again offering Boas's assistance on Keresan words, and her own on paraphrases that Hunt might have used. Finally in August, 1937, Elsie received Stirling's Acoma manuscript, which she found "exceedingly interesting. . . . novel [in] detail and interpretation." The help that Elsie had offered as a labor of love was a challenge to deliver. In May, 1941, eleven years after she had first inquired about the manuscript, she wrote, "At long last I am returning . . . the Acoma material."[148]

In 1918, as a means both to encourage fieldwork and to channel her financial support, Elsie created the Southwest Society. She had mentioned its formation in a letter to Fewkes, "A few of us—Kroeber, Goddard, Laufer, etc.—have talked over organizing a Southwest Society to bring together those interested in the Southwest and to dispose of a few hundred dollars each year in cooperating with institutions in fieldwork."[149] The official minutes conveyed a more formal organization: "The Southwest Society was organized on November 25th [1918] at a lunch club made up of members of the American Museum of Natural History, the Museum of the American Indian, and Columbia University. Dr. Goddard was chosen temporary chairman, and Dr. Parsons temporary Secretary-Treasurer. Dr. Boas, Dr. Hodge and Dr. Parsons were appointed a committee to draw up a

Constitution."[150] The stated purpose of the society was "to promote inquiries into the culture of the peoples of the Southwest through field-work undertaken independently or, whenever possible, in coöperation with other institutions; and to arrange for the publication of the material collected."[151]

Pleased with the results, Elsie wrote Herbert, "My enterprise, the Southwest Society, got new members, & was permanently organized. . . . I have high hopes it will mean cooperation in Southwest research, fresh research where most needed &, incidentally, somewhat of a syndicalist experiment in the research workers running their own machinery & controlling their own funds."[152] Membership dues were one dollar a year, which raised a modest sum as indicated by the total amount of forty-four dollars in 1918 and thirty-three dollars in 1919. The coffers were filled by donations from Parsons that matched the funds allotted for fieldwork. For example, in December, 1918, four hundred dollars were credited to the Southwest account, and that precise amount was awarded to James Alden Mason for his work with the Papago. In 1919, Parsons donated four hundred dollars to support Leslie Spier's work among the Yuman, and three hundred and fifty dollars as the "Boas payment."[153]

Parsons was not simply "pecuniarily responsible" for projects; she was also intellectually involved. She identified research topics that she thought crucial, located capable students, guided their investigations, and required that their written reports be completed within the year of funding.[154] In her search for potential fieldworkers, Elsie worked closely with others, especially with Lowie, Boas, and Kroeber. Just such a situation arose in November, 1927, when Elsie found that the initiation ceremonies on the Hopi First Mesa were to be "in their long form, for the first time in several years." She wrote Lowie, "I am wondering whether you or Kroeber has any promising Southwest student whom you would like to send to the Hopi to observe, say the *powamu*, in February." She added, "The Southwest Society would be glad to defray expenses."[155] Lowie responded suggesting Julian Steward.[156]

One of Parsons's most important collaborative relationships grew out of just such sponsored research. With Edward Sapir's assistance, Elsie had located a young student to carry out fieldwork in the eastern Pueblos. She wrote Sapir, "Mr. White sounds promising and the Southwest Society will be glad to finance a field trip for him."[157] Parsons had intended for Leslie White to begin work after June in Laguna; White decided to begin in May at Acoma. Displeased with his initiative, she wrote, "May I recall to you that I wrote Dr. Sapir . . .

and Dr. Boas wrote also advising against going to N[ew] M[exico] until June, also that we had concluded that Acoma would be too difficult.
Perhaps you are learning that now." She scolded him for not knowing
the literature on Zuni and Laguna, which was necessary for good
work at Acoma. She advised that " 'making contacts' is not a help but
a hindrance among the Pueblos. Most of us have got our material for
any town from a single informant, & away from his town. They watch
and terrorize one another." And then she added, sternly, again, "This
was the sort of thing I wanted to tell you about at the appointment in
Chicago." White was chastened, and Parsons responded, "I am sorry
I stirred you into feeling badly, and yet not altogether sorry for I still
think you went off rather half-cocked."[158]

In spite of her initial displeasure, Elsie was pleased with White's
work. She wrote him in August, 1926, "If your trip is coming to an
end merely for lack of money, I would be glad to send you some if you
let me know how much you need. It is trying to leave a field before
you feel that you have exhausted it." When he despaired of his
progress, she offered encouragement, "I am sorry you feel discouraged about the summer's work. I knew you would not get the 'heart
of Taos' unless you had some lucky break, as Goldfrank and I had at
Isleta, but no doubt the data you did get will add up to the good with
what we already have. And your personal experience was certainly
widened, wasn't it, by acquaintance with those Taos conservatives?"
She cautioned him, "They have their eyes on you now and you won't
be able to work at Taos at all, and will have to be, of course you know,
most circumspect about getting anybody to come away from Taos to
the ranch." She praised him for his success. In 1931, from her fieldwork in Mitla, she wrote, "By the way your role of anthropologist was
undiscovered, I infer, at Taos. Tony Luhan and his white wife turned
up in Mexico City and I gathered they had not heard of you at Taos."
Parsons also conveyed the excitement she felt about his work. She
wrote, "Your letters make me feel very restless. I would like to be up
with you in the front line. However, the next best thing is to hear
about it in the full way in which you write."[159]

Parsons encouraged collaboration between George Herzog, whose
research she was also supporting, and White. She wrote, "You may
hear soon . . . from George Herzog who is recording music for Dr.
Boas. After Santa Fé & the Tewa he will be on his way to Zuñi and I
have advised him to try & tie up with you." She hoped that the two of
them might be able to obtain recordings of Acoma kachina songs. She
added, "This is his first trip & I doubt if he was helped much in Santa
Fé. I cautioned him to be secretive."[160]

Taking on the role of mentor to White, Parsons guided and organized his research. In October, 1927, she wrote him, "You will be getting your notes into shape, I suppose. Another field-trip next summer to the Keres? Perhaps a summary on Acoma or a comparative Keres paper for the Anthropological Asso. meeting this winter?" She suggested that, after he finished his survey of Acoma, he might want to prepare a monograph on that pueblo for publication as a Memoirs of the American Anthropological Association. She counseled that it was "important . . . for the sake of one's own work and that of others to get out monographs on the separate towns in advance of comparative work." She continued, "This has no bearing on your proposed paper for the *Anthropologist* on Keresan medicine societies. I think that would be a good thing to do. For the same issue I might do a review among the other pueblos—Zuñi, Isleta, Hopi, Tewa."[161]

Of her numerous articles, monographs, and books, Parsons's *Pueblo Indian Religion* marked the culmination of her years of research. In 1943, Reichard commented that it contained "all that is known of the ethnology of the Pueblo Indians, for she searched the historical records, and combed archaeological reports for clues to the interpretation of modern rituals and beliefs." And in 1972, Alfonso Ortiz called this two-volume work "monumental": it "marked the first time any scholar had ever attempted to summarize and synthesize what was known of all the cultures of the 'Pueblo crescent.'" Of this work, Parsons herself commented that she had tried to combine "subjective interpretation, as well as objective description," and added, "It's damn hard."[162]

Elsie had been drawn to the Southwest by the beauty of the land and a fascination with the Pueblo Indians. Challenged to discover what the Indians would not willingly reveal to her, she focused her work on the ceremonial. She was aware of the contradiction in herself: that she could accept among the Pueblo Indians what she could not accept in her own society. Elsie dismissed it simply as her own irrationality. With her vision, dedication, and energy, Elsie Clews Parsons had vitalized research in the Southwest. Not only in her own work, but also in her encouragement of others, she had made this area crucial for American anthropology. So identified was she with the Southwest that Alfred Louis Kroeber commented, "I think you have all the anthropologists thinking you committed [yourself] to it forever." He added, "I used to wonder, finally gave it up, and perhaps unconsciously pigeon-holed you too."[163] Always rebellious against classification, Elsie would not be confined, even to the spaciousness of the Southwest. She went south from the pueblos to Mexico.

NOTES

1. ECP, Alfred Kidder to ECP, 14 Mar. 1929.

2. The dates for Parsons's southwestern fieldwork as ascertained from her correspondence, fieldwork notebooks, and publications are the following: Acoma (Jan., 1917, Jan., 1927); Caddo (1921–22 [interviewed Caddo graduate of Carlyle in New York], Nov.-Dec., 1927, Oklahoma], notebook dated 1922–40); Cochiti, Hopi (Nov.-Dec., 1920, June, 1920, Dec., 1924), Isleta (July, 1920), Jemez (Sept.-Oct, 1921, July, 1922, Nov., 1925); Kiowa (Dec., 1927); Laguna (Jan., 1917, Oct., 1918, 1919, June, 1920); Nambé (1926); the Navajo (Oct., 1918); the Pima (Dec., 1926); Santa Clara (Nov.-Dec., 1923); Santo Domingo (July, 1920); San Ildefonso (Nov.-Dec., 1923); San Juan (Nov.-Dec., 1923, 1926); Taos (Nov.-Dec., 1923); Tesuque (Nov., 1923, 1925); and Zuni (Dec., 1915, Feb., 1918, June, 1920, Sept., 1921, Dec., 1923, Apr., 1932).

3. ECP, "Getting Information from Pueblo Indians."

4. ECP, George to ECP, 15 Feb. 1921.

5. ECP, ECP to Margaret Lewis, 27 Apr. 1932; Parsons, "Spring Days in Zuñi, New Mexico," *Scientific Monthly* 36 (Jan. 1933): 49–54.

6. ECP, Mabel Dodge Luhan to ECP, n.d.; Beinecke, ECP to Mabel Dodge Luhan, 6 Feb. 1923.

7. ECP, Zuñi Notebooks, 1915.

8. Parsons, The *Scalp Ceremonial of Zuñi* (Menasha, Wis.: American Anthropological Association, 1924), p.7.

9. ECP, ECP to HP, 29 Sept. 1921. In *The Scalp Ceremonial of Zuñi*, Parsons gave another version as to how the scalp was acquired: the initiate had found a dead Navajo girl lying in the bush (p. 7).

10. ECP, ECP to HP, 29 Sept. 1921.

11. ECP, ECP to HP, 9 Mar. 1918.

12. Parsons, "A Hopi Ceremonial," *Century Magazine* 101, n.s. 79 (Nov. 1920): 177.

13. ECP, ECP to Kroeber, 17 June 1920.

14. Parsons, "A Hopi Ceremonial," pp. 177–80.

15. ECP, ECP to HP, 17 June 1920.

16. Parsons, *Pueblo Indian Religion* (Chicago: University of Chicago Press, 1939), p. 1023.

17. Parsons, "A Hopi Ceremonial," p. 180.

18. ECP, ECP to HP, 27 Nov. 1920.

19. ECP, ECP to Kroeber, 17 June 1920.

20. ECP, ECP to Kroeber, 17 June 1920.

21. ECP, Zuñi fieldnotes, June 17–19, 1920.

22. ECP, "Laguna Lodging Houses," in "In the Southwest," unpublished manuscript, p. 6.

23. ECP, "Laguna Lodging Houses," p. 7.

24. ECP, ECP to HP, 3 June 1919.

25. ECP, ECP to HP, 3 June 1919.

26. ECP, "Laguna Lodging Houses," p. 8.

27. Ibid., pp. 10–11.

28. ECP, Herbert Parsons, 1919, copy of telegram.

29. ECP, "Laguna Lodging Houses," pp. 10–11.

30. Ibid., p. 14.

31. ECP, ECP to HP, 25 June 1919.

32. Esther S. Goldfrank, *Notes on an Undirected Life* (Flushing, N.Y.: Queens College Press, 1978), p. 44.

33. Ibid., pp. 54, 55.

34. ECP, ECP to HP, 17 Sept. 1921.

35. ECP, ECP to HP, 9 Oct. 1921; 17 Sept. 1921.

36. ECP, ECP to JP, 23 Nov. 1925.

37. Lois Palken Rudnick, "The Unexpurgated Self: A Critical Biography of Mabel Dodge Luhan," Ph.D. dissertation in American Civilization, Brown University, 1977, p. 272; and *Mabel Dodge Luhan* (Albuquerque: University of New Mexico Press, 1984), p. 155.

38. ECP, Mabel to ECP, 28 Sept. 1922.

39. ECP, ECP to JP, 13 Dec. 1931.

40. Parsons, *Taos Pueblo* (Menasha, Wis.: George Banta Publishing Co., 1936), p. 5.

41. Ibid., p. 5.

42. Ibid., p. 14, emphasis in the original.

43. Ibid., p. 15.

44. Parsons, *Isleta Paintings,* ed. by Esther S. Goldfrank (Washington, D. C.: Smithsonian Institution, 1962), p. 2.

45. Leslie A. White, *The Pueblo of Santa Ana, New Mexico* (Menasha, Wis.: American Anthropological Association, 1942), pp. 9–10.

46. ECP, ECP to HP, 9 Mar. 1918.

47. White, *Pueblo of Santa Ana,* p. 10.

48. ECP, "In the Room Below," from the unpublished manuscript, "In the Southwest," p. 7.

49. Parsons, "Notes on Isleta, Santa Ana, and Acoma," *AA* 22 (1920): 56.

50. Parsons, "Notes on Acoma and Laguna," *AA* 20 (1918): 162.

51. ECP, ECP to Leslie White, 17 May 1926.

52. ECP, ECP to HP, 9 Oct. 1921.

53. ECP, ECP to HP, 29 Sept. 1921; 9 Oct. 1921.

54. ECP, ECP to HP, 17 Nov. 1923.

55. Parsons, *The Social Organization of the Tewa of New Mexico* (Menasha, Wis.: George Banta Publishing Company, 1929), p. 7.

56. ECP, ECP to HP, 17 Nov. 1923

57. ECP, ECP to HP, 26 Nov. 1924; 4 Dec. 1924.

58. ECP, ECP to Esther Goldfrank, 24 Nov. 1925. Parsons was introduced to this informant through Esther Goldfrank.

59. Parsons, *Isleta, New Mexico* (Washington, D.C.: U.S. Government Printing Office, 1932), p. 201.

60. Ibid., p. 202, n. 1.

61. Parsons, *The Tewa,* pp. 8–9.

62. ECP, ECP to White, 17 May, 1926; Leslie White Papers, UM, ECP to White, 3 June 1926; 17 July 1926; ECP, 14 Mar. 1934.

63. Parsons, *The Tewa,* p. 9.

64. Parsons, *Taos Pueblo,* p. 15, and ECP, Taos fieldnotes, Nov. 1926.

65. In *The Artist of "Isleta Paintings" in Pueblo Society* (Washington, D.C.: Smithsonian Institution, 1967), Esther S. Goldfrank revealed the artist's name for the first time and reproduced the letters that he wrote to Parsons. To be consistent with Parsons's work, I use the pseudonym that she had adopted. ECP, Felipe to Dorsey, 1 May 1936. For comments on Parsons's and Goldfrank's work, see Alfonso Ortiz's review of *The Artist of "Isleta Paintings",* *AA* 70 (1968): 838–39.

66. ECP, ECP to Felipe, 17 May 1936.

67. ECP, Felipe to ECP, n.d.; 27 Nov. 1936.

68. Parsons, *Isleta Paintings,* p. 3.

69. Ibid., p. 2.

70. Leslie White Papers, ECP to Leslie White, 9 June 1935.

71. ECP, Spier to ECP, 22 July 1935.

72. ECP, Grenville Goodwin to ECP, 3 May 1937.

73. ECP, Spier to ECP, 15 Jan. 1939. See also Spier to New Mexico Book Store, 28 Jan. 1939, for Spier's query about an individual ordering a copy of *Taos Pueblo.*

74. ECP, Ruth Underhill to ECP, n.d.

75. ECP, Redfield to ECP, 2 June 1939.

76. ECP, ECP to Gwinn, 3 June 1932.

77. ECP, Juan G. to ECP, 5 July 1932.

78. Beinecke, ECP to Mabel Dodge Luhan, 15 Sept. 1937.

79. Parsons, *Taos Pueblo.*

80. Beinecke, ECP to Mabel Dodge Luhan, 15 Sept. 1937.

81. ECP, Mabel to ECP on 30 Dec. [1938].

82. ECP, Tony M. to ECP, 3 Jan. 1939.

83. ECP, ECP to Mabel Dodge Luhan, 4 Jan. 1939.

84. Beinecke, ECP to Governor and Council of Taos, 7 Jan. 1939.

85. ECP, Mabel Dodge Luhan to ECP, n.d.

86. ECP, ECP to Mabel, 4 Jan. 1939.

87. ECP, ECP to Sophie Aberle, 9 Jan. 1939.

88. ECP, Sophie D. Aberle to ECP, 18 Jan. 1939.

89. ECP, ECP to Sophie D. Aberle, 23 Jan. 1939.

90. ECP, Leslie Spier to ECP, 5 Apr. 1939.

91. ECP, Ruth Underhill to ECP, 1 Feb. 1939. On U.S. Department of the Interior letterhead.

92. ECP, anonymous to ECP, 24 May 1940.

93. ECP, Mabel Dodge Luhan to ECP, 7 Nov. 1941.

94. Claire Morrill, *A Taos Mosaic* (Albuquerque: University of New Mexico Press, 1973), p. 58.

95. Beinecke, ECP to Antonio Luhan, 11 Apr. 1932.

96. John Collier, "Politicians Pillage the Pueblos," *The Searchlight*, 31 Jan. 1923, p. 16.

97. John Collier, "The Crisis in the Affairs of the Ancient Pueblo Indians That Has Brought the Country's Federated Women to Their Aid," *The World*, 21 Jan. 1923, sec. cc, p. 1, col. 1–3.

98. ECP, "Indians Ku-Klux-Klanned," p. 2.

99. Collier, "The Crisis in the Affairs of the Ancient Pueblo Indians," p. 1, col. 1–3.

100. Collier, "Robbing the Pueblo Indians," editorial, *The World*, 27 Nov. 1922, p. 12, col. 1.

101. Alice Corbin Henderson, "The Death of the Pueblos," *New Republic*, 29 Nov. 1922, p. 11.

102. "Pueblos Unite in Petition," *New York Times*, 7 Nov. 1922, sec. 1, p. 6, col. 2.

103. "Indian Bill Will Destroy Pueblo Life, Say Indians in Memorial to Country," *Santa Fe New Mexican*, 6 Nov. 1922, p. 1, col. 1–2. For a view of Mabel Dodge Luhan's part in the opposition to the Bursum bill, see Rudnick, *Mabel Dodge Luhan*, pp. 175–82.

104. ECP, Mabel Dodge Luhan to ECP, 11 Nov. [1922].

105. ECP, "An Appeal by the Pueblo Indians of New Mexico to the People of the United States."

106. Beinecke, ECP to Mabel, 13 Nov. 1922; 27 Nov. 1922; 28 Nov. 1922.

107. "Denounce Indian Land Bill," *The World*, 28 Nov. 1922, news clipping in ECP's files.

108. Beinecke, ECP to Mabel, 28 Nov. 1922.

109. Kenelm Digby, "The Literary Lobby," *Literary Review*, 9 Dec. 1922, p. 310, emphasis in original.

110. "Terrific Barrage Aimed at Pueblo Indian Bill All Over United States," *Santa Fe New Mexican*, 6 Dec. 1922, p. 5, col. 1–2.

111. "More about the Indian Bill," editorial, *Santa Fe New Mexican*, 28 Dec. 1922, p. 4, col. 1.

112. "Protests Halt Pueblo Indian Bill in Senate," *Tribune*, 3 Dec. 1922, p. 1.

113. Beinecke, ECP to Mabel, 3 Jan. 1923.

114. Collier, "Politicians Pillage the Pueblos," pp. 16, 17.

115. ECP, Mabel to ECP, 28 Nov. [1922].

116. ECP, John Collier, unpublished information under the heading "Provisional Data on the Economic Condition of Five of the Northern Pueblos."

117. "Indians Will Take Appeal to Washington," *Santa Fe New Mexican*, 7 Nov. 1922, p. 6, col. 4. See also "Pueblo Delegation Going to Washington First of its Kind Since the days of Lincoln," *Santa Fe New Mexican*, 9 Jan. 1923, p. 5, col. 1–2.

118. ECP, Mabel to ECP, 11 Nov. 1922.

119. Beinecke, ECP to Mabel, 16 Jan. 1923; 24 Jan. 1923; 27 Jan. 1923.

120. "Pueblo Indians Appeal against Bursum Bill Disinheriting Them," *The World*, 15 Jan. 1923, p. 4, col. 2–3.

121. "Lenroot Roasts Twitchell, Backs up on Indian Bill," *Santa Fe New Mexican*, 22 Jan. 1923, p. 1, col. 1–2, p. 3, col. 7.

122. "Mrs. Atwood Brands All Indian Policy as Inhumane and Expensive," *Santa Fe New Mexican*, 22 Jan. 1923, p. 1, col. 2, p. 3, col. 7.

123. ECP, anonymous, Taos, Easter Sunday [1 Apr. 1923].

124. John Collier, *From Every Zenith* (Denver: Sage Books, 1963), p. 136. Hubert Work had just replaced Albert Fall as interior secretary. This invasion of the Taos Pueblo council on April 1, 1923, was his first action in office.

125. Alida Sims Malkus, "Those Doomed Indian Dances," *New York Times*, 18 Apr. 1923, pp. 1–2; Editorial, "Preserving Indian Dances," *New York Times*, 8 May 1923, sec. 1, p. 16, col. 4–5.

126. ECP, Livingston to ECP, 15 Mar. 1923.

127. ECP, ECP to Geoffrey Parsons, n.d.

128. ECP, anonymous, Taos, Easter Sunday [1 Apr. 1923].

129. For information on Albert B. Fall, see "Ex-Secretary Fall Dies in El Paso, 83," *New York Times*, 1 Dec. 1944, sec. 1, p. 23, col. 1; and Lawrence C. Kelly, *The Assault on Assimilation* (Albuquerque: University of New Mexico Press, 1983.)

130. Collier, *From Every Zenith*, p. 145.

131. ECP, Parsons to Wissler, 3 Jan. 1918.

132. ECP, ECP to Mekeel, 25 Jan. 1938.

133. UCA, ECP to Kroeber, 18 May 1929.

134. ECP, ECP to H. Scudder Mekeel, 22 Mar. 1938.

135. NAA, ECP to Stirling, 19 Oct. 1929.

136. Lowie Papers, ECP to Lowie, n.d.

137. ECP, J. O. Brew to ECP, 13 Feb. 1936.

138. NAA, Parsons to Fewkes, 31 Oct. 1918.

139. Lowie Papers, ECP to Lowie, 23 July 1937.

140. NAA, ECP to Fewkes, 24 Apr. 1922.

141. Leslie A. White, review of *Hopi Journal*, *AA* 40 (1938): 307.

142. ECP, Whorf to ECP, 4 May 1934. Cautioning her against the plan of illustrating the use of keywords in phrases, Whorf suggested that she "heave the lot of Stephen's phrases overboard and [not] waste any regrets on them." Parsons decided instead to insert a cautionary note to the reader, that there were "undoubtedly many errors in these linguistic notes due both to the recorder and to the editor," but that they might nonetheless prove useful, especially in a study of ritual terminology (Alexander M. Stephen, *Hopi Journal* [New York: Columbia University Press, 1936], p. xxi).

143. Leslie White Papers, ECP to White, 26 Oct. 1933.

144. ECP, contract for *Hopi Journal* with Columbia University Press, 9 Dec. 1936; Philip M. Hayden to ECP, 8 Nov. 1933; 7 Apr. 1934.

145. ECP, Morris Titiev to ECP, 14 Aug. 1933.

146. NAA, ECP to Densmore, 24 June 1933.

147. NAA, ECP to Stirling, 5 July 1933.

148. NAA, ECP to Stirling, 28 May 1941.

149. NAA, ECP to Fewkes, 15 Nov. 1918.

150. UCA, Report of the Secretary-Treasurer of the Southwest Society, 28 Dec. 1918.

151. *Constitution and By-Laws of the Southwest Society* (New York: Gilbert T. Washburn & Co., 1919), p. 3.

152. ECP, ECP to HP, 28 Dec. 1918.

153. ECP, Ledger of the Southwest Society. Treasurer's accounts begin on Nov. 25, 1918, and end on Jan. 22, 1923, though the Southwest Society continued funding projects through the 1930s. For the funding of J. Alden Mason's research, see UCA, Mason to ECP, 19 Nov. 1918; and Report of the Secretary-Treasurer of the Southwest Society, 28 Dec. 1918. A partial list of those supported by the Southwest Society include the following: Esther Goldfrank (Laguna, 1920, 1921, Isleta, 1924); Ann Gayton Spier [$275] (Supai); Pliny Earle Goddard and Gladys Reichard (Navajo, [$700] 1923); Julian Steward (Hopi [$228.35], 1928); Father Berard Haile (Navajo [$500], 1929; [$500], 1931); C. Daryll Forde (Pueblo agriculture [$250], 1929); Paul Radin (Zapotec, 1930); Helen Roberts (Songs of Acoma, Cochiti, Pecos, Santa Clara, San Ildefonso, Taos, Tesuque [$500], 1930); Leslie White (Acoma [$800] 1926, 1928; Taos, 1930; Santo Domingo memoir [$1437], 1934); Eduard Kennard (Hopi [$350], 1937, [$175], 1938); Morris Opler (Apaches [$400], 1931, [$250], 1935, [$172.78] 1938); Frances Toor (Sonora and Nayarit [$200], 1931); John Adair (Zuni silver work, Zuni and Navajo, motion pictures, 1938); Ralph Beals, (Mayo-Yaqui, Cora, and Huichol, 1932 [$2,200]); E. Adamson Hoebel (Publication of Comanche Lawways, 1939); Dorothy L. Keur (Archeological excavation of Navajo site, Gobernador, New Mexico [$798.36], 1940); George Herzog (Eastern Pueblo music, 1927, [$833], 1940).

154. ECP, Leslie White to ECP, 29 July 1935; ECP, Ann Gayton Spier to ECP, 29 June 1920.

155. UCA, ECP to Lowie, 12 Nov. 1927.

156. UCA, Lowie to ECP, 5 Dec. 1927.

157. ECP, ECP to Sapir, 26 Dec. 1925.

158. Leslie White Papers, ECP to White, 27 May, 1926; 18 June 1926.

159. ECP, ECP to White, 8 Aug. 1926; 9 Oct. 1930; 14 July 1930; 7 Feb. 1931; 14 July 1930.

160. Leslie White Papers, ECP to White, 13 July 1927.

161. Leslie White Papers, ECP to White, 5 Oct. 1927; 13 Nov. 1927.

162. Reichard, "Elsie Clews Parsons," *JAF* 56 (1943): 46; Ortiz, "Introduction," *New Perspectives on the Pueblos* (Albuquerque: University of New Mexico Press, 1972), p. xv; Lowie Papers, ECP to Lowie, 19 Oct. 1922. Parsons provided $4,297.75 for the publication of *Pueblo Indian Religion* (ECP, Robert Redfield to ECP, 29 Mar. 1938).

163. ECP, Kroeber to ECP, 7 July 1921.

12

Mayo-Yaqui, Cora, Huichol, and Mitleño

In 1930, Elsie wrote to Matthew W. Stirling, the director of the Bureau of American Ethnology, "I had an interesting time last winter in the state of Oaxaca where I made Mitla my headquarters and took riding trips into the mountains for some Zapoteca ethnology. Any Mexican programs in the Bureau?"[1] Finding no organized research through the bureau, she planned her own. From 1929 to 1933, she worked among the Zapotecan Indians; and in 1936, *Mitla, Town of the Souls*, appeared. Along with Ralph Beals, she conducted fieldwork in the state of Sonora among the Mayo and Yaqui (1932), and with him co-authored "The Sacred Clowns of the Pueblo and Mayo-Yaqui Indians" (1934). In 1932, again with Beals, she worked among the Cora and Huichol in the state of Nayarit.

Elsie had first visited Mexico in 1913, when she stayed in Mérida and explored the Maya ruins of Chichén Itzá with the archaeologist Sylvanus Griswold Morley and the eccentric and impassioned Ernesto Balch. Her return to Mexico was initially for her "winter season," during which time she would find a quiet location to work on her material from the Southwest. Her visit in 1929 did not yield such peace. She was caught in an uprising that ultimately led to the formation of the National Revolutionary party. Elsie left Mitla, where she had begun research among the Zapotec Indians, for refuge in Mexico City. Here perforce she passed her time in social engagements. As recorded in her diary, she had "tea at Mrs. [Zelia] Nuttall's [with] Czecko-Slovakian minister & wife, French minister, deaf, [and] Cockney wife of blond Mexican" on one day, and on another, "invited [Gordon] Wiley to lunch, but Am[erican] Embassy invited me instead." George Vaillant took her to view his excavation at Guadalupe Hidalgo, and she met Diego Rivera, who proclaimed that there were "only 2 communists" in existence, but that this was all that was needed "to populate the world." She managed to catch a train for Vera Cruz, where a boat named the *Morazon*, which belonged to the American

Fruit and Transportation Company, was bound for New Orleans. At midnight, after the cargo of bananas was stowed aboard, they set sail. In spite of the seizure of the *Morazon* for three hours by twenty-eight rebels who demanded to be taken to Tampico, the crew, the bananas, and Elsie arrived in New Orleans four days later. She disembarked, visited briefly with Oliver La Farge at Tulane University, and caught the train for New York.[2] In a letter to her son John, she condensed the adventure into a simple explanation, "I came out of Mexico by the back door of Vera Cruz and New Orleans, a diversified and much pleasanter trip than by the north, just now safer too, although trains had begun to run."[3]

Subsequent trips to Mexico were more tranquil. In Mazatlán, she worked while relishing the beauty of her "Mexican Riviera." From the Hotel Belmar, she wrote Franz Boas, "Here I have been finishing my Taos material, incorporating it into the rest of the Taos record of the last ten years. . . . Mazatlán is comfortable and an ideal place to write." Elsie tried to shield herself from distractions, but there were enticements. As she told Boas, "I hoped I was not to hear of a dance, but I did yesterday, from a driver, *muy indio*. . . . His account sounded quite a little like Tarahumara, Mayo and Yaqui, so I may be tempted away. Luckily my chambermaid has no memory for tales." On the shores of Lake Chapala, she worked on *Pueblo Indian Religion,* departing only briefly to escape "the congestion of Semana Santa." She wrote John, from Chapala, "It is so pleasant being an anthropologist in a warm climate, with no trusteeship for anything but science." To Alfred Kroeber, she emphasized her isolation from her usual concerns, "There are no Indians at Chapala and no editing."[4]

Of course, Elsie was not successful in remaining so detached. She found the Indians, and in them, a connection to the Southwest. She told Boas of her trip to Tepic, Nayarit. "At last, *real* Indians, in psychology and culture! And they link up with the Pueblos in most interesting ways. The political organization is just the same, including a lifelong war chief and assistant and lifelong *principales*. . . . The tree cotton sticks . . . are undoubtedly related to the war god netted shield sticks of Zuñi. And I am guessing that the ceremonial jars of Zuñi . . . which are encrusted with turquoise are related to the wax and bead ritual bowl . . . about which our informants had so much to say." To Kroeber, she also mentioned the similarities with the Pueblos: "The Coras have a snake hunt and dance (around the altar!), . . . and . . . their masks they consider impersonations of the rain spirits, the dead." Her enthusiasm for tracing lines of influence was infectious. Beals, in his fieldwork with Elsie, was caught up in the excitement.

"The Cora," he wrote his wife, "are a Pueblo people in all probability, but with closer affiliations with Mexico [and the] Aztec."[5]

Elsie was in pursuit of still another enduring interest, the connection between the Spanish and the Indian. In January, 1930, she moved on from Mexico City to the state of Oaxaca in order, as she said, "to follow up the *fiestas* elsewhere and see how Spanish patterns of culture combined with Indian."[6] She selected Mitla as a research site, she confessed, from a "somewhat blind . . . theoretical point of view," but with assurance that "both Indian and Spanish cultures were represented." She hoped to find the connections between the Indian and Spanish "in government, in religion, in manners, and other personal ways."[7] Certainly, she would enjoy the hunt, for the surroundings were to her liking. On her second trip to Mitla (the first having been abruptly shortened by a "revolution"), she wrote to John, "I am working now in a Zapotecan family. The climate is perfect. . . . A full moon last evening over hills and a trickling river that reminded very much of Rio Grande country. The great ruins I haven't yet visited."[8] She was drawn to the Mitleños. As she wrote in the opening passage of *Mitla, Town of the Souls:* "I noted the low, self-contained voices, Indian voices, the unhurried gait of the barefoot women with bowl or basket on their head, their small hands and feet, the quiet children playing adult, the composure of all the townspeople, their order and style, and sentimentally I felt at home; the people reminded me of my Pueblo friends."[9] Mitla, itself, was for Elsie "closer to a New Mexican pueblo than any place in Mexico I have seen."[10]

Her residence in Mitla was in La Sorpresa, home of the Queros, a mestizo family of solid reputation and great importance in the community. Don Félix Quero, who had been known as a cacique in the surrounding mountain towns, had converted the family home into an inn, with the front portion as a store. Built in 1840 in the style of the time, La Sorpresa was constructed from large stones that had been plastered over and tinted. The rooms had high ceilings, supported by beams, and the large windows were covered on the outside with iron grills. Each room had a heavy wooden door, which opened onto a corridor lined with pillars. The central patio was ablaze with flowers, and a large cypress tree offered its shade to the birds that nested there.[11]

At first, Elsie stayed in the inn simply for its charm and comfort; it served as a good base for her fieldwork. Rather abruptly, during her third season, she became more than a guest at La Sorpresa, and more than an observer in the town. Along with the Mitleños, she lived on life's uncertain edge during *el grandote*, the big earthquake of January 14, 1931. As she remarked on her return to New York, "Yes, last season in Mitla was good. I lived *with* the people, particularly after the earthquake brought us together."[12] And in the midst of the days of the earth's trembling, she wrote John, "I have slipped into all sorts of little personal relationships in this very agreable town."[13] In *Mitla, Town of the Souls*, she recalled:

> It hit us, according to my watch, at 7:45 P.M., and lasted with uniform violence from two to three minutes. It had been a bleak and windy afternoon and . . . I was writing my notes very comfortably in the cot in the corner of my high-ceiled room. I jumped from the cot and the two candles were thrown off the stand, at the same moment. My nearer and safer exit was the wooden window-door. . . . It was bolted, but I drew the two upper wooden bolts and one of the lower iron bolts, the fourth bolt stuck. In that moment of panic, as I leaned out the open part, I heard cries from . . . across the road. The dogs were barking and the cocks, crowing. Behind me I heard things falling. I stooped again, succeeded in drawing the bolt, and stepped into the open. "Señora! Señora!" calls Angélica. As I pass back through my room the air is thick with the dust of plaster.

Elsie made her way to the Queros in the front of the house, where Josefa, the elderly spinster, was "crying quietly and calling on all her Virgins;" Lidia, who tended the store, was calmly cleaning up broken glass and preparing to serve customers; Don Rafaél was taking a drink to steady his nerves; and Angélica, ever-composed, was surveying the damage. "With flashlights," Elsie recounted, "Rafaél and Angélica and I make a turn of inspection." Her room was covered with plaster and concrete; and her cot was buried in adobe bricks and debris from the ceiling. In another room, a beam had fallen; and in others, there were holes in the ceilings. Two columns had fallen in the corridor, and the rear wall of the store was severely damaged. " 'My house is wrecked!' says poor Angélica. 'Do me the favor to allow me to aid you in repairing it.'—'God will reward you!' The next day Josefa with tears in her eyes will tell me I am 'an angel from God.' "[14] Amused and touched by the comparison, Elsie wrote Mabel Dodge Luhan, "I myself was called *ángel de Dios* [angel of God] on making a regalo [gift] of adobes and other building materials to reconstruct our shaken mansion."[15]

The family and Elsie sat down to supper in a room littered with broken china and shattered glass. Already miraculous stories were being told, of the picture of the Virgin of Guadalupe, which had remained unscathed amid all the destruction in the corridor, of the

Cristo safe amid the fallen plaster and concrete in one of the bedrooms. The family was going to spend the night in a wooden house across the road, but Elsie decided to stay in her room. "The ceiling beams look sound enough and I will sleep in the center of the room, with the window-door open. 'Do not undress!' urges Josefa. Angélica provides a night-light. They leave the dog behind, but he keeps up such a howling that Rafaél comes back for him. After midnight there is a slight tremor and twenty minutes later another which makes the dogs bark but no plaster falls and I get to sleep until I am waked up at seven by another small quake. As I stand by the window-door I hear the band and through the cactus hedge I see the procession pass by, the candle and marigold procession of the *mayordomía*. The worse the quake, the greater the need of paying one's obligation!"[16] Tremors and quakes continued for several weeks. A series of Catholic masses were offered, the first three at the request of the bishop and the fourth by the pueblo. Elsie commented, "Whether by God's mercy or otherwise the quakes are letting up—not more than one in the 24 hours, and some days without any, and they are little ones."[17]

Those who lived in houses constructed of stone built thatched dwellings out in the yard. Elsie, however, continued sleeping in her room, and, as she wrote Mabel Dodge Luhan, "acquired a nice sensitiveness to the degree of quake which was worth jumping into the neighbor's patio."[18] The sight of Elsie leaping out the door for the safety of the Delfino's yard was remembered with humor by those who saw her. Years later, when Mabel visited Mitla, Angélica pointed out the door through which Elsie made her hasty escape.[19] Finally, Elsie saw the wisdom of the Mitleños: "The earthquake technique, practical and psychological, is really quite interesting. You sleep soundly in a wattle and thatched house in the patio. In the daytime in your room of masonry you keep your bolts free, and then you dont give a damn. It is the way to live one's life anyhow, earthquake or no earthquake." She left her high-ceiling room for the "sweet smelling and warm" thatched hut in which she slept quite soundly.[20]

From the closeness she had established with the people, largely through the shared experience of the earthquake, Elsie opined, "My book ought to be good."[21] So it was through the lived experiences that she was able to bring immediacy and vibrancy to the pages of *Mitla, Town of the Souls.* The customs and traditions were more than just described; their significance was conveyed by the actions and the words of the people. In one passage, Parsons explained that Mitla was a town focused on trade. Everyone was vitally interested in economic matters, particularly in the price of items. Often, she said, this was expressed in an exceedingly direct manner. She recalled, "We are talking of the earthquake—'May God pardon us!' murmurs Felícitas, and in the same breath, 'How much did you pay for your sandals?' " At a wedding, she had joined the crowd of women at the groom's house who were congregated in the cook shed. "One woman is beating the chocolate to a froth, using a green glaze pitcher of Azompa pottery, and the chocolate beater of the country. The groom's mother presides passing out the replenished dishes to the young men who serve the table. We all sit on mats, and there is much talk and gaiety. Someone fetches me a leafy necklace and a bouquet. My amber beads are admired: 'From China.'—'How much did they cost in that pueblo?' "[22]

Through personalized accounts, Elsie captured the sense and tenor of her fieldwork. She told of assisting at a difficult birth in Zaachila. The mother could not expel the placenta, and scrapings from a deer horn were administered, as well as a drug obtained from a pharmacy. Elsie suggested that the woman's abdomen be massaged, and it was to this that the new father attributed the success: "I was showered with confetti—it was carnival in town—the infant was held up for me to bless, and I was invited to become his godmother."[23] Elsie recounted her visit to the *curandera*, Agustina, who treated her for *aire*, which was causing her headaches. Agustina asked her, " 'Why do you think so much. . . . You think and then . . . the air catches you, you hear a drum in your head.' " In San Baltazar, she consulted a *curandera* who divined the answer to her questions by casting kernels of corn. Elsie had queried, "Are my children well? Shall I remarry? Is my married daughter to get a divorce? For each question she rearranges the grains and blows, and she asks a few questions herself. How many children have I? How long widowed? Has my daughter children? The corn tells her that two sons are sad, thinking of me; the third is selfish and disobedient. They are going to abandon something important; I should go back to look after my affairs. I have a lover the children do not like. I had better not marry him, life with my family would be unhappy. I get angry quickly. . . . I shall live long."[24] She told of the little girl who was nicknamed *la Tehuana*, "because of her bold manners and brown *huipil*. In the street, she would call after me, 'Elissa! Elissa!' as no other child would think of doing." This same child, whose given name was Encarnación, sat next to Elsie at a domestic ritual. Elsie recalled: "With us was a youth who was too drunk to keep from falling down when he danced, and much too drunk to know what he was saying. I was telling Encarnación about my earthquake experience, how I leaped from my bed—here the youth interrupted. 'He wants to

know when you will take him into your bed,' said the little girl. As I did not answer, she looked at me in her usual eager way, but a little anxiously. 'You are not angry?'—'No, it is only a joke, a poor joke.' "
On another occasion the little girl sat as close to her as possible, and, as Elsie recalled, "gently strokes my arm and side, a most unconventional girl!"[25]

In *Mitla, Town of the Souls*, this personalized narration culminated in the next-to-the-last chapter, "Town Gossip." Here immediacy was conveyed as if all were happening in the present. The Mitleños who had been introduced by name and photograph throughout the book were shown again in vignettes, which featured the individual and brought life to the cultural setting. Parsons was very conscious of her purpose. She wrote: "In any systematic town survey much detail is necessarily omitted and the life appears more standardized than it really is; there is no place for contradictions or exception or minor variations; the classifications more or less preclude pictures of people living and functioning together. In my last visit to Mitla I spent a good deal of time visiting and gossiping, and I would recall these scenes, as well as a few from earlier years, in order to convey personal aspects of the townspeople and some of the variability in their lives."[26] She hoped to convey through these impressions a true sense of the Mitleños, including what they found amusing, what pleased them or offended them, how they felt about their customs and about the passing of certain traditions. She was also aware that in dealing with the personal she was treading on the potentially volatile. She wrote to John, "I am . . . pegging away at my Mitla book. My chapter on town gossip is getting quite novel like, full of murder and intrigue and couldnt be published if there were a Mexican libel law or pueblo folk read books."[27]

On her last fieldtrip to Mitla in 1933, Elsie succeeded in reviving a fiesta tradition, that of *el palo en sebado,* or the greased pole. Two years earlier at the Fiesta of San Pablo, she had attempted to sponsor this event, but the president of Mitla had insisted it was too dangerous and that *la cucaña,* or the walking pole, be substituted. (As Elsie reported, the president had arranged for a cinema production and did not want such strong competition.) Both involved men competing for prizes that were hung at the most inaccessible location. The week-long fiesta drew pilgrims to venerate the statue of San Pablo. Two brass bands and a drum and fife band provided the music; and there was the traditional riding of the bulls, and "the latest thing, a basket-ball match." For the greased pole, Elsie provided, as she told her son, "the prizes on top—overalls, hat, sandals, belt, sweets to throw down, and of course colored paper. The pole was about 50 ft. high and climbed by 3 loops around the pole, one fastened to the belt, the other two serving as stirrups, the climber standing in one while he shifted the other—no shimmying at all."[28] The victor made it to the top, accompanied by the music of "Dian," and, as Elsie described, he "throws down the prizes, scatters the fruit, sets off the wheel, and slides down. . . . The *síndico* has gathered up the goods and the president distributes them, giving a kerchief to one competitor, the sandal materials to another, and the rest to the successful climber." As a fitting end to the fiesta, and to her last fieldtrip, which was drawing to an end, the gallant young victor, with the bundle of prizes in his arms, "to the surprise and laughter of everybody, turns to me and says, "*Señorita, vamos a bailar!* Come and dance!" and away he goes gaily, with the little boys tagging behind."[29]

In his restudy of Mitla, the anthropologist Charles Leslie was able to locate the people with whom Parsons had worked. "Townspeople," he wrote, "enjoyed looking at Parsons' book, identifying familiar names and the pictures of themselves or their friends." While he criticized her book on the basis of the historical and sociological approach, Leslie praised Parsons for her energy, her interest in people, and her "lack of intellectual pretension." The archaeologist John Paddock commented that "those who have occasion to corroborate her work frequently testify that her accuracy was extraordinary."[30]

In January, 1932, just before sailing from San Francisco to Mazatlán aboard a mail steamer, Elsie stopped for a visit with Alfred Kroeber in Berkeley. At a gathering in his home, she met Ralph Beals, who was a postdoctoral National Research Council Fellow about to depart for his second research trip to Mexico. Elsie indicated her interest in joining him for a few days at his field site in Navajoa, Sonora. Kroeber acted as a liaison, advising his student, "Mrs. Parsons sailed this morning for Mazatlan. . . . I think she certainly means to visit you later on if you are still both in the field. I suggest your keeping her informed of your movements and asking her to do the same."[31] Elsie did travel to Navajoa, and in March, Beals wrote his wife, "How much work I will get done in the next few days will depend. Elsie Clews Parsons is arriving on the noon train and will probably take some of my time and may want to be taken up to the Yaqui country." In his next letter to his wife, Beals wrote, "Elsie Clews Parsons has been here three days now to the infinite curiosity of the entire population."[32] To ease suspicions, Beals conveniently became Elsie's nephew.

Clearly, Elsie found the field situation to her liking, for, as Beals remarked, "Considering that she came intending to stay a few days and is planning to stay three weeks, I feel a personal triumph, although the Indians deserve all the credit." He found her "quite a help" with his research, and added, "Now that the edges are wearing off, a quite good companion."[33] Of her time in Navajoa, Elsie wrote John, "About two weeks ago I came here to be motored about to see some dances by Ralph Beals, one of Kroeber's students, who is studying Mayo and Yaqui. The Indians were so interesting in relation to the Pueblos and Beals such pleasant company that I decided to stay on through the Easter week ceremonies. These we shall see a little farther north, in a Yaqui town."[34]

Beals marveled at Elsie's ability to extract information from informants and he confessed to his wife, "worse [yet] out of my own informants, that I would never have gotten." He saw her success, in part, as "proof of Leslie's theory that one should know everything possible about the surrounding peoples, because much of the significant data she is getting is due to her ability to ask leading questions from her wide southwestern experience." Beals, of course, had no way of knowing that Leslie White had learned this lesson the hard way, through a feeble start at Acoma, and Elsie's pointed advice, that one must know the literature before beginning fieldwork. Of course, Beals also realized that Elsie had a head start at Navajoa. He had provided her with his best informant, an old Mayo woman whom it had taken five months to locate. As Beals explained to his wife, he and Elsie set up a comfortable pace for their research: "I get started late in the morning . . . and Elsie . . . and I eat rather leisurely, comparing notes and planning work."[35] Elsie described her schedule to John, "Most of the time I spend working with an old woman in my room, or at an all-night fiesta."[36] Beals took Elsie to the places where he had done research: to the Indian settlement of Navajoa Viejo, to San Ignacio, and to the weaving and sheepherding communities.

Parsons and Beals worked well together and jointly were able to obtain more information than either one could have alone. Beals reported to his wife: "The ceremony last night was quite interesting and by compromising Mrs. Parsons to the extent of saying she had taken a promise to attend the ceremony and getting acquainted with the host beforehand, we were treated, as she remarked, more like royalty than ever before in our lives. And had a better view of things than ever before."[37] They attended several rituals that marked the start of the Easter cycle. Some of these lasted all night in the plaza of Navajoa Viejo, where crowds of people jostled one another to see the groups of dancers perform, and festival foods were prepared and served. At the same time, inside the church special rites were being conducted. They were also present for the Lenten ceremony where the community of believers visited the Stations of the Cross, marking each with special prayers and rituals. Parsons and Beals followed the masked clowns from house to house and attended the night-long rituals conducted in people's homes. Under these circumstances, taking notes at the time of the rituals was almost impossible. So together they worked out a method for verifying the accuracy of information that they often could not record until the following day. Individually each would write an account, and subsequently they would compare their versions. When there was a discrepancy, they would ask an informant for clarification.

Two weeks after the beginning of the Lenten season, Parsons and Beals made preparations to go north to a Yaqui village of Vicam Station. Because there were still Yaqui living in the mountains who did not accept the peace terms that ended the uprising of 1928, this area had been subject to martial law. The year before, Beals, as a foreigner, had been ejected from Yaqui country by the military. So it was with difficulty that in 1932 he had received permission to return. While exhausting the official channels for approval, which went from the university to the state department to the Mexican ministry of foreign affairs, Beals, through the assistance of friends, managed to meet the commanding general who sternly questioned him about the purposes of his trip and then granted him permission. When Beals returned to request that he be allowed to take his "aunt" with him, the general reluctantly agreed. They were directed, however, to remain in the hotel at Vicam Station unless accompanied by the army lieutenant who had been assigned to them.

Initially, the requirement for a military escort was strictly enforced. Parsons and Beals would walk about the town with their lieutenant conspicuously at their side. The uniformed officer was a distinct disadvantage in their attempts to meet and talk with inhabitants of the town. However, when they did find a person who would talk to them, the officer, who spoke fluent Yaqui, acted as an interpreter. In fact, Parsons and Beals found that he was a good source of information, with quite a bit of knowledge about Yaqui customs. So they walked about the town, talking to their officer and observing what they could. The focus of their fieldwork was to have been the Lenten ceremonies and processions. With their army escort, they could hardly carry on as they had with the Mayo, following the dancers and the ritual clowns on their nightly circuit, which included the ranchos in outlying area.

This close supervision ended abruptly one day, when Elsie, who bridled against the constraints, quietly rebelled. Beals, Elsie, and the lieutenant had climbed into their Model A Ford for a Friday morning drive to Pitahaya, a village that reputedly adhered to the old ways. They arrived at about 10 A.M. and drove to the enormous, dusty plaza where they planned to observe the ritual of the Stations of the Cross. The lieutenant insisted on parking at the edge of the plaza. On the other side, a good distance away, they could make out the clowns cavorting in front of the church. The three of them sat in the front seat, with Elsie between Beals and the lieutenant. After a long while, Elsie remarked that it was impossible to see what was happening and that she was going to walk over to the church. The lieutenant objected, reasoning that the Indians were unpredictable and dangerous. As Beals recalled, "Elsie . . . patted him on his rather plump knee and said, 'What is the matter, are you afraid? I am not, so please let me out of the car.' " The officer, embarrassed and angered by her challenge to his bravery, walked with them to the church. Beals continued: "Yaqui ceremonies in the main have few if any observers as virtually everyone is a participant, if only to kneel at proper times, cross oneself very elaborately and take part in the chants and responses. . . . After a short time, the clowns motioned to us to join the group, after which we were ignored, the clowns especially acting as if we were nonexistent as they carried on their task of policing the event."

When they returned to their village, the officer convinced his superiors that Parsons and Beals were able to take care of themselves; and from that time forth they were allowed to go about unescorted. At Vicam Station and Vicam Viejo, they were accepted in all ceremonial celebrations. During the evening stops on the clown pilgrimages, chairs were provided for them so they could watch the proceedings in comfort, and, perhaps more importantly, so Elsie would be positioned far enough away from the clowns for whom all female contact was forbidden during Lent. Beals's presence became a foil for the clown's play. At Vicam Viejo, the pascola dancers gave him native tobacco and corn husks and then laughed at his efforts to roll a cigarette. On another occasion, the presence of Parsons and Beals sparked a monologue in Yaqui. Playfully one of the clowns insisted that he could speak English: "You doubted? But of course he spoke English. After carrying this on to the limit of its possibilities, he said, 'Well, I'll show you,' and shouted very loudly in English, 'All right, all right, all right, god damn.' "[38]

Toward the end of her stay at Navajoa, Elsie told Beals that she had been "maturing a plan" for him in the event that he found no employment for the next year. With a fellowship from the Southwest Society, Beals would come to Mexico to join up with her. They would spend two or three weeks with the Cora and Huichol in Nayarit, then travel to Mexico City where Parsons would "instruct" Beals on "what should be seen there." Next, they would journey to Oaxaca where Parsons, who had already begun research there, could introduce Beals to "a working knowledge of the Zapotecs." Finally Beals would go up "in the mountains a couple days ride on horseback" to begin research on the Mixes, who were, as he said, "one of the least known and entirely unworked groups in Mexico." Elsie had contacted the appropriate people and had "ascertained that the living conditions would be fairly good." Customarily, the Southwest Society would only pay a stipend for field expenses, but Parsons assured Beals that in his case she was sure that the society would provide support for his family. Beals told his wife, "This promise seems fairly reasonable as I discover by questioning that the Southwest Society is Elsie Clews Parsons to all intents and purposes and is the form in which she has 'organized' so to speak to help needy anthropologists and get work done in which she is most interested." All this, he added, was "on the hush-hush," because Elsie had not made him a firm offer, but had simply inquired about his reaction to her plans. After Elsie had left, Beals wrote his wife that he thought "Elsie would come through with the money for the trip," though she might well decide not to accompany him on all of it. He added, "Apparently money is no object with her and she became quite fond of me—her ambitions to have fifteen sons having been thwarted by a mere three and a . . . daughter so she is apparently prone to collect sons vicariously." The timing of Elsie's offer was crucial for Beals, for, as Kroeber wrote him, there were no jobs and he should grab "a life raft." Beals told his wife, "The most obvious one is Elsie's proposal providing she doesn't have a saner moment on her return back home."[39]

Beals wrote Elsie to inquire circumspectly about the trip: "Have you thought any more about your plan for next year? . . . if you still are seriously considering it as a possibility, I should rather like to know." He had begun the letter, "Dear Elsie: Or should I make it more dignified by saying Aunt Elsie?," to which she responded, "Dear Raoul (in or out of Mexico, but I am only *tia*, by God, in Mexico. Even legitimate nephews are not allowed 'Aunt Elsie.'" After setting him straight on the form of address, she wrote, "I had not thought any more about the plan for next year, but I think just the same." She suggested that Beals would precede her by about a month, going first to the Yaqui: "After you have put your manuscript into shape, you are sure to find points that you would like to look up. You might even try to get into the mountain Yaqui country direct from the border, without going through the military rigamarole." Aware of his concern about the effect of the *"piquante,"* or spicy foods, of the Yaqui on his delicate stomach, she counseled, "You could take some food supplies with you and I really think you would be just as well off from a dietary point of view in the mountains as on the railroad." She would meet him at Tepic toward the end of November; and when they had completed their work, they would move on to Mexico City. From there, they would go to Oaxaca, to see Mitla, and Beals would go to the Mixes. She assured him of "Expenses and whatever stipend you consider proper."[40]

Elsie was excited by Beals's research among the Yaqui. After she had left him in Vicam Station—a departure that he said was "timely," since the temperatures soared to 110—he had gathered information on the governmental system. As he wrote her, he thought that he had "exploded the myth of Yaqui democracy." What had been described in the literature as an election was simply an installation ceremony. The governor from one year chose his successor, with the approval of the *principales*. This pattern was followed for all positions, save for the one of "real power," the oldest *maestro*, who would choose both his own successor and the first governor. Beals suggested that he might be a substitute for the *padre*. He told her of the ceremonial division of the upper and lower towns and the arrangements for policing the Yaqui territory. "And as a final shock," Beals added, " . . . the war captains are called bow chiefs, wíkori yáut." Elsie responded, "I am very much interested in the explosion of the Yaqui democracy idea. It is about the same as Pueblo democracy. The *maestro* who knows the prayers would correspond to the Pueblo priests or societies, possibly more than to the *padre*. Calling the war captains bow chiefs is very interesting. There is a Keresan term *wíkoli* (never etymologized) for the supernatural patron of their clown group, which I am going to look into." Intrigued by the connections between the Pueblos and the Yaqui, Parsons suggested to Beals that they might collaborate on an article for the *American Anthropologist* on the Yaqui-Pueblo parallels. In the postscript, she added, "But perhaps we dont know enough yet about the Yaqui."[41]

Elsie finalized the arrangements for Beals's stipend. She wrote Kroeber, "I propose that your department direct the research and handle the funds which I will contribute in my own name." The salary for the year was set at $1500, which Beals, with great embarrassment, had requested; field expenses totaled $700, with supplemental funds available. The research, as Elsie described it, would entail an ethnographic study of the Mixes, as well as an account of their relations with their Zapoctecan neighbors. She concluded, "Probably

Dr. Beals will be in the field six or seven months and I should like to stipulate that his report be completed by September 1, 1933." The publication of the material was to be the responsibility of the Kroeber's department.[42]

In October, 1932, Beals arrived in Tepic, Nayarit. He rented a large room on the top floor of the Hotel Boro del Oro and reserved an adjoining room for his "Aunt" Elsie. The balcony, shaded by palms and decorated with lush ferns, spanned the length of the building and provided a view of the plaza, with the cathedral off to one side. Elsie was to have arrived a few days after Beals, but it was two weeks before she would appear. With no word from her, Beals dutifully met every northbound train. He wrote his wife, "Elsie should arrive tonight and perhaps life will be more active and less of a bore." In a postscript, he added, "Elsie failed to show up, drat her. Another train tonight at the ungodly hour of midnight which I suppose I must meet." While awaiting her arrival, Beals nursed a cold and made plans for their research. He wrote his wife, "The future of the Cora trip is still uncertain. Everyone holds up their hands in horror at the thought of a woman making the trip. Five to six days riding 8 or 9 hours a day, sleeping in *rancherias*, eating where one can, over very rough trails, doesn't sound too good for Elsie."[43] The other possibility, he said, was to travel to the coastal villages where the Cora go for employment.

Elsie arrived with a cold, and so there was a change of plans. Beals wrote his wife, "There are to be no mountain trips on Elsie's part—or any horseback riding beyond an hour or two. So probably we will stay in Tepic's beautiful winter climate." Elsie began immediately locating Indian informants. She enlisted the aid of the hotel personnel who brought Cora and Huichol right in off the streets. Beals wrote his wife, "Today we corralled three Huicholes but did not get much from them. It is evident, however, both from them and what we hear that we are dealing with real Indians—afraid of us, suspicious, and close mouthed. 'Would you like to stay here and work awhile?' 'No, I want to go home.' 'I'll pay you well. . . . ' 'I want to go home.' 'We are hungry. We have to go eat.' Which, beyond two pages of vocabulary was all the satisfaction we got."[44] Years later, Beals assessed this method of gathering informants as "a complete failure; the victims were terrified and sure they were being taken to jail. We got nowhere."[45] Elsie's curiosity was piqued, for, as Beals recalled, these were to her "the most Indian Indians by far of any she has seen in four years of hunting through Mexico, except possibly the Mixe."[46] Furthermore, from what little information they were able to gather, Parsons and Beals were both convinced that previous work on the Cora and Huichol had been entirely inadequate.

To occupy their time when not conducting interviews, they explored the town. One night, they attended a rehearsal for the dance of *La Conquista*, which was held on the outskirts of town in "a simple house . . . [with] one coal oil flare, a circle of blanketed watchers, and the dancers." Another afternoon, they walked out to the Chapel of the Miraculous Cross to see the miracle of the grass, never watered, which grew in the shape of a cross. Even when the bandit, the Tiger of the Sierras, had ripped it up, it had grown back again in its blessed spot, precisely at the opposite side of the earth from the location of Christ's crucifixion.[47] On one particular excursion, they happened on to a tannery that produced the highest quality leather. Elsie with persistent questioning forced the embarrassed proprietor into admitting that the fine and supple leather was "cured with dog faeces brought to him by a corps of small boys he had scouring the city." As Beals observed, "Elsie was annoyed as well as amused by his reticence. She did not see why the facts should not be discussed."[48]

Parsons was pleased. She wrote Mabel Dodge Luhan, "You said I would enjoy it and I have been doing so for ten days. Perfect weather, sun and clean air. And this time I have the best room, the corner on the balcony."[49] To John, she described the town as "the prettiest in the Republic. Hill vistas at the end of every street of low pink and blue houses; a river with a three arched bridge; and a very graceful cathedral overlooking the befountained plaza." She wished for cooler nights so "that the town might go to sleep earlier than 4 A. M." She was kept awake by "a loud speaker, strolling ballad singers, automobiles under repair, raucous church bells, and . . . a drunken German [who] sent for the brass band to serenade him at 3:30 A. M."[50]

Charmed by Tepic, Elsie had just one wish: "If only there were more Indians!"[51] The Cora and Huichol came to town in groups of six to twelve men. They had walked six or more days for the market, which was held on Saturdays and Sundays; and they would leave immediately after it closed. During the week, the town was deserted by Indians. Parsons and Beals managed one good day of collecting from a group of Cora, but even this was limited to simple vocabulary. When a group of Huichols who had just arrived refused an invitation to come up to the hotel, Parsons and Beals went to their lodgings, which were known as *mesones*, somewhat akin to old-fashioned inns with a large courtyard for their animals and a communal kitchen. There they found a Huichol who was a willing informant for half a day. Beals recalled, "He gave information quite freely about some very important things—prayer sticks, burial beliefs, shamans,—which even in bare outline show Pueblo and also Oaxaca connections." They tried to convince him to stay in town, but he had to return to his village for a fiesta.[52]

Parsons and Beals took to visiting with the Indians in the evening after business in the market was completed. On occasion, they would single out one member of a trading party who agreed to work with them during the day for a substantial payment.[53] However, for the most part, as Elsie told Kroeber, no sooner had they obtained a qualified informant than they lost him; and she added, "Such are the habits of traveling men."[54] Still, following the flow of the market, they managed to work with a number of informants. Once they settled on visiting the Indians in their own surroundings, rather than attempting to bring them into their hotel, they were able to establish a good relationship, as Beals remarked, "perhaps much better than we might have had in their home towns where neighbors might criticize them for talking freely on some subjects." He attributed this, in part, to "Elsie's experience and her confident approach." They would begin by trying to put "the Indians at ease by asking for simple vocabulary. What is the word for this and that every day object—the plants and animals, and parts of the body, etc." Next, with Elsie initially wary from her Pueblo experience, they would ask questions about kinship terminology. With ease, they moved on to questions about ritual and belief, and they were even able to gather information on the often taboo subject of witchcraft. Beals recalled, "That this was a special relationship was illustrated one evening when a young man [who] had been giving us some very esoteric religious material . . . suddenly began giving me list of words for basic vocabulary. The word for maize is—for lion is—, etc. Following a well-known anthropological principle, I kept on writing down everything he said, although I was puzzled by the shift." Then Beals realized that the innkeeper's daughter had come up behind him and was listening to the interview. Soon bored with the listing of vocabulary, she left. "The young man, without any prompting, took up his account of religious activities and beliefs." To Beals, this illustrated that he and Elsie had been able to communicate their sincere interest to the Indians; they "would not make fun of their 'superstitions' as a mestizo would have done."[55]

Beals recalled Elsie's method of working. When she wanted information on a particular topic, she would give an example of how something was done in her "pueblo," often the examples were drawn from several pueblos in which she had worked. This led, Beals said, to an animated discussion, often with the Indians wanting to hear more about Elsie's village. "They also told her what they did in their own village. And for good measure they might add in what they had seen or heard was a variant way of doing things in some other village." Beals identified what he called "Elsie's basic field work approach; to try to imagine every life situation and ask how it was dealt with, not only the obvious life crises of birth, marriage, sickness and death but all the other problems of life. How do you know when to plant; how do you do it; do you say prayers." Particularly interested in ritual and the supernatural, Elsie was able to collect a great deal of material in a short time, though, as Beals remarked, "it was not always possible in the time available to be absolutely confident that the accounts we were getting were of actual practices or referred to some mythical or folkloric past."[56]

Above all, Beals said, Parsons "did get enthusiasm." The evening sessions frequently turned into group affairs, "almost a seminar with everyone crowding around and adding to the conversation." So involved was one group that they delayed their departure for half a day in order to finish a session that had started the night before. Elsie would pass around a rare book on the rituals of the Cora, written by Konrad Theodor Preuss and published in the nineteenth century. Both Cora and Huichol were fascinated by the illustrations of ritual objects, altars, and shrines. They would draw close "to look at the pictures, identifying objects, explaining how they were made, by whom, and for what they were used."[57]

In late November, Parsons and Beals left Tepic for Guadalajara, where they passed a few days in a luxury hotel. Save for occasional groups of Huichol Indians making their way down the main street in single file, there was little of interest for their research. They journeyed in a chartered car to Chapala, where they took lodgings in an inn perched over the lake. During their ten-day visit, they explored this town and the villages on the east end of Lake Chapala, paying particular attention to the ceremonial dance groups responsible for the performance on the day of Guadalupe. On December 15, they spent the day in Ajiji, an isolated and traditional village, where they followed the processions and observed the rituals honoring the patron saint of Mexico. From Chapala, they took passage on a mail launch across the lake where they were able to catch the train for Mexico City. Here Beals was hospitalized as a result of a swollen lymph gland. Elsie, who had taken a room in the San Angel Inn, a converted monastery, came every day to visit him and to bring him gifts and reading material. To occupy him during his period of recovery, she encouraged him to work on the article they were co-authoring, "The Sacred Clowns of the Pueblo and Mayo-Yaqui Indians," and to organize the Cora and Huichol field notes. After his release, Beals convalesced at the San Angel Inn. Then they were off by train for Oaxaca, where they stayed for a short time before chartering a car for Mitla. Here Elsie would stay for several months of fieldwork, while Beals, after ten days, would move on to work with the Mixe.

Elsie took Beals around Mitla, introducing him to friends she had made on previous visits, instructing him in Zapotecan culture, and soliciting his help in her research. Elsie would spend the mornings writing, while Beals explored the surrounding countryside, often on horseback to strengthen him for his trip to the Mixe. In the afternoons, they would go about visiting her old friends or making new acquaintances. As Beals recalled, "Not only was this in part to educate me as rapidly as possible about Mitla culture, but to help build up Elsie's data on material culture, a subject which bored her but in which I had some practical knowledge." On one trip about town, they were invited into a home to join the wedding party for a Zapoteca bride and a Mixe groom. Beals recounted, "All went well until we had finished the ritual meal at which Elsie and I had been featured at the head table. Finally, well into the evening a lull came. The musicians played but nothing happened. . . . The host came to me and asked if I would not start the fandango with his daughter, the bride. I explained my health, and my ignorance of how people danced in Mitla. He left, and again nothing happened. Then he returned and we repeated the performance. Again nothing happened. Then the enormous Mixe groom appeared beside my chair and in a most truculent manner asked what was the matter with his bride that I refused to dance with her. So I danced." Elsie enjoyed the incident immensely, until it was her turn to dance with the groom. Beals with the bride and Elsie with the groom graced the otherwise empty dance floor for, as Beals recalled, "a painfully long interlude." At the end of the evening, they unwittingly committed another *faux pas*. Ignorant of the Oaxacan custom at ritual meals in which the guests were expected to carry away large quantities of food, Parsons and Beals simply thanked their hosts, congratulated the newlyweds, and left. "The hosts," Beals said, "were understanding of the ignorant foreigners and sent the food by messengers to the inn."[58]

Their trip together ended here in Mitla. Beals left on horseback for Ayutla, where Elsie had made arrangements for his research through the political boss of the area whom she had met in Mexico City. To Kroeber, Elsie wrote, "Beals and I are a good team,"[59] and so they had been.

NOTES

1. NAA, ECP to Stirling, 30 June 1930.

2. ECP, Mexican Notes. The anthropologist Grant La Farge was the son of Elsie's friend, Oliver La Farge.

3. ECP, ECP to John Parsons, 24 Mar. 1929.

4. ECP, ECP to HP, 20 Jan. 1932; Boas Papers, ECP to Boas, 23 Jan. 1932; ECP, ECP to John Parsons, 27 Mar. 1935; UCA, ECP to Kroeber, 12 May 1934.

5. ECP, ECP to Boas, 21 Dec. 1932; UCA, ECP to Kroeber, 16 Dec. 1932; AA, Beals to Dorothy Beals, 9 Dec. 1932, his emphasis.

6. ECP, ECP to John Parsons, 14 Jan. 1930.

7. Parsons, *Mitla, Town of the Souls* (Chicago: University of Chicago Press, 1936), p. xi.

8. ECP, ECP to John Parsons, 14 Jan. 1930.

9. Parsons, *Mitla*, p. xi.

10. Beinecke, ECP to Mabel Dodge Luhan, 1 Feb. 1931.

11. Parsons, *Mitla*, p. 15, n. 31; ECP, Mabel Dodge Luhan to ECP, 19 Mar. [n.d.].

12. UCA, ECP to Lowie, 17 Sept. 1931.

13. ECP, ECP to John Parsons, 4 Feb. 1931.

14. Parsons, *Mitla*, pp. 462–64.

15. Beinecke, ECP to Mabel Dodge Luhan, 18 Feb. 1931.

16. Parsons, *Mitla*, p. 464.

17. ECP, ECP to John Parsons, 4 Feb. 1931.

18. Beinecke, ECP to Mabel Dodge Luhan, 1 Feb. 1931.

19. ECP, Mabel Dodge Luhan to ECP, 19 Mar. [n.d.].

20. ECP, ECP to John Parsons, 4 Feb. 1931; Parsons, *Mitla*, p. 23; Beinecke, ECP to Mabel Dodge Luhan, 1 Feb. 1931.

21. ECP, ECP to John Parsons, 4 Feb. 1931.

22. Parsons, *Mitla*, pp. 12, 106.

23. Ibid., p. 76.

24. Parsons, "Curanderos in Oaxaca, Mexico," *Scientific Monthly* 32 (Jan. 1931): 60, 66, ellipses in the original.

25. Parsons, *Mitla*, pp. 405, 406.

26. Ibid., p. 386.

27. ECP, ECP to John Parsons, 10 Mar. 1933.

28. ECP, ECP to John Parsons, 2 Feb. 1933.

29. Parsons, *Mitla*, p. 249.

30. Charles Leslie, *Now We Are Civilized* (Detroit: Wayne State University Press, 1960): xi; ECP, Charles Leslie to Peter Hare, 29 June 1970; John Paddock, *Ancient Oaxaca* (Stanford: Stanford University Press, 1966), p. 372.

31. NAA, Kroeber to Beals, 12 Jan. 1932. See also ECP, Beals to ECP, 17 Jan. 1932, and 13 Feb. 1932, in which Beals made arrangements for Parsons's visit.

32. NAA, Beals to Dorothy Beals, 3 Mar. 1932; 5 Mar. 1932.

33. NAA, Beals to Dorothy Beals, 9 Mar. 1932.

34. ECP, ECP to John Parsons, 20 Mar. 1932.

35. NAA, Beals to Dorothy Beals, 5 Mar. 1932; 9 Mar. 1932; 12 Mar. 1932.

36. ECP, ECP to John Parsons, 20 Mar. 1932.

37. NAA, Beals to Dorothy Beals, 9 Mar. 1932.

38. ECP, Beals to Peter Hare, 31 July 1978.

39. NAA, Beals to Dorothy Beals, 15 Mar. 1932; 30 Mar. 1932; 7 Apr. 1932.

40. ECP, Beals to ECP, 26 Apr. 1932; ECP to Beals, 1 May 1932.

41. ECP, Beals to ECP, 26 Apr. 1932; ECP to Beals, 1 May 1932.

42. ECP, ECP to Kroeber, 7 Aug. 1932; Beals to ECP, 8 June 1932; 11 July 1932; 13 July 1932; Kroeber to ECP, 12 Aug. 1932.

43. NAA, Beals to Dorothy Beals, 20 Nov. 1932; 18 Nov. 1932.

44. NAA, Beals to Dorothy Beals, 23 Nov. 1932.

45. NAA, Beals to Hare, 31 July 1978.

46. NAA, Beals to Dorothy Beals, 23 Nov. 1932.

47. NAA, Beals to Dorothy Beals, 23 Nov. 1932.

48. NAA, Beals to Hare, 31 July 1978.

49. Beinecke, ECP to Mabel Dodge Luhan, 1 Dec. 1932.

50. ECP, ECP to John Parsons, 2 Dec. 1932.

51. Beinecke, ECP to Mabel Dodge Luhan, 1 Dec. 1932.

52. NAA, Beals to Dorothy Beals, 27 Nov. 1932.

53. ECP, Beals to Peter Hare, 31 July 1978.

54. UCA, ECP to Kroeber, 16 Dec. 1932.

55. ECP, Beals to Peter Hare, 31 July 1978.

56. ECP, Beals to Peter Hare, 31 July 1978.

57. ECP, Beals to Peter Hare, 31 July 1978. Preuss's book on the Cora was *Die magische Denkweise der Cora Indianer,* in Proceedings of the International Congress of Americanists 18th Session, Jalisco, Mexico.

58. ECP, Beals to Peter Hare, 31 July 1978.

59. UCA, ECP to Kroeber, 16 Dec. 1932.

13

Peguche

Mother is an anthropologist by profession. You may have
met her through your reading—Dr. Elsie Clews Parsons.
She is also among other things a lover of scenic beauty. I
have told her that although she has travelled widely, I am
sure she has yet to see anything comparable to the magnificence of your Andes.[1]

So wrote Lissa to an acquaintance whom she had met in 1926 while
traveling in Peru. Elsie had decided in 1940 to visit Bolivia, Ecuador,
and perhaps Peru. She apparently had considered, for the first time
in many years, traveling as a tourist. However, as Gladys Reichard recalled, "When, after a two-months absence she returned, we asked
her such questions as a tourist might answer and she replied, 'As soon
as I got to Quito I learned of a village I could study very easily. I went
there at once and stayed until it was time to come home!' "[2] In actual
fact, she had prepared for this study. Prior to her departure, she conveyed to Julian Steward her support of the prospective *Handbook of
South American Indians,* and added, "I plan to fly to Peru late this winter and would be glad to have any chore wished on me." Steward suggested that she study acculturation in Otavalo, Ecuador.[3]

Elsie left for Ecuador with a list of "Notes on Letters for Mrs. Parsons," written by F. L. Stagg.[4] She carried a letter of introduction
from him to Sr. Don Victor Eastman Cox, the former minister pleni-
potentiary from Chile, who was married to Doña María Lasso de la
Vega y Chiriboga, a member of one of the leading noble families of
Ecuador, descendants of the conquistador Don Diego de Sandoval.
She also carried a letter to Sr. Don Francisco A. Uribe, a statesman
and diplomat and a successful rancher and industrialist in Quito; and
to Sr. Don Juan Marcos, a descendant of conquistadors and, with his
father, owner of a major bank in Ecuador. However, it was the letter to
the British minister to Ecuador, Guy Bullock, and his wife, which
yielded results. The latter introduced Elsie to Juan Gorrell who, as

she described him, was "a talented and understanding American . . . engaged in business for several years in Quito," as well as in farming in the Cayambe Valley. As Elsie related, "Mrs. Guy Bullock . . . introduced Mr. Gorrell, who in turn introduced Rosita Lema of Peguche, who in turn introduced me to Peguche neighbors."[5]

Elsie was launched on her fieldwork. She stayed in the city of Otavalo and spent her days in Peguche. As she said, "The time spent in Otavalo was not a loss, for it enabled me to observe contacts between the Whites and the Indians and the particular forms of Hispanic culture from which the Indians have borrowed."[6] On her return from the first trip, Elsie wrote Robert Lowie: "Back from Ecuador. . . . I spent two months in Imbabura province in the north, working in a hamlet of about 1000 Quechua-speaking Indians only three miles out from a very attractive White town. Quite early I began to think that the Indians of this valley might be descendants of Inca colonists and now I am piling up Peruvian parallels." She was interested in the relations between the Indians and, as she said, "the Whites or near Whites." Elsie continued, "Ecuadorians think that their mestizos or Cholos are Indians without a pigtail, as they say. There is racial mixture throughout Ecuador, of course, but as far as the Cholo culture can be defined it is early Spanish peasant. The borrowing between Indian and Cholo is not all one way, e.g. the Chola (woman) of Peguche (my hamlet) and nearby places weaves belts on the Indian man's loom (no Indian women weave). . . . I will have more to tell you later."[7]

Her contact with Rosita Lema was crucial for Parsons's work. In notes for the preface of her book, Elsie reminded herself to "tell about the family." She continued: "When I made the acquaintance of Rosita Lema, she was advanced in pregnancy and within a few days the baby was born, about two weeks ahead of time according to Rosita's reckoning. As my visits were still welcome it was a special opportunity to learn the details of birth, confinement, and of the care of a young infant."[8] Rosita became Elsie's "teacher," instructing her in the Quechua language and telling her about life in Peguche. Elsie recalled Rosita, her younger brother and sisters, and her daughter, all sitting on the bed, teaching her to count in Quechua.[9] On most occasions, as Elsie remarked, "Rosita was inclined to put her Spanish foot foremost, partly because it had in her own eyes more prestige and partly because she thought, at first at least, that it would have more prestige in my eyes." Elsie wrote, "When I asked her about luck, *buena (mala) suerte,* the closest approach in Indian Spanish to omen she first gave me a Spanish aphorism: 'Quando [*sic*] no se tiene buenas espaldas no se tiene buena suerte,' ('When you have not good shoulders you have not good luck'), and only after a little probing did she tell me that to meet a weasel was bad luck."[10]

Rosita also taught Elsie about proper etiquette, specifically with regard to consumption of alcohol. "Any acceptable stranger," Elsie remarked, ". . . will be offered a drink." At a dance, she would accept the proffered drink, however, "in the casual roadside drinking of which I knew Rosita did not approve I did not join, giving the only possible excuse, . . . 'I do not know how to drink.' But only girls are supposed not to know how, so that excuse was not wholly acceptable. . . . 'Yes, she knows, she doesn't want to,' was the ready retort." Elsie encountered just such a situation one afternoon when she and Rosita's husband, José, were returning from a walk. Their path would take them right past a *chicheria*, a place where *chicha*, a drink made from sprouted maize, was sold. José decided to leave the road and take a circuitous route across a cornfield in order to avoid the inevitable offer of a drink. Elsie recalled, "Besides, he knew that I, too, because I was along with him, would be offered a drink and would probably decline it, and that would add to the awkward situation." On their return home, Rosita told Elsie that she might just have tasted the *chicha* to see what it was like. "She got out a gourdful and for me a glass. I was given some, with white sugar in it stirred with a spoon, then José got a drink, then the servants, and then, to my surprise, little Alberto. Only Lucila was omitted. Girls are supposed not to drink. But Lucila was far from being acquiescent, this was merely a tasting party in the family. So Lucila finally got her taste, too. . . . Everybody got a drink excepting Rosita; her confinement was not yet concluded." Elsie decided that perhaps it would have been better "just to take a sip," as she had been advised at Mitla. She added, "Ethnologists cannot afford to be reformers."[11]

Wanting to visit a curer, Elsie relied on Rosita and José to take her. The two were wary, for curers were regarded as witches. As she recalled, they "kept putting me off, being very loath to introduce me to [Misías] Terán; but at last Rosita went with me to his house. It was in the middle of the morning, and Misías had not yet slept off the effects of two treatments given the night before—treatments are supposed to be given at night, and at each treatment a bottle of rum is drunk. Practitioners are reputed to be hard drinkers and generally incapacitated by day."[12]

Terán rose from his bed and agreed to treat Elsie. He spread a mat on the bedroom floor and asked Elsie for money to buy a candle and a bottle of rum. Terán had Rosita sit next to him, and Elsie, opposite, facing the light of the open door. In her field notes, Elsie wrote: "Places candle in black clay candlestick between us, forcible expulsion of breath 3 times. . . . Asks my name, now and again cant remember it. Looks fixedly at candle, from his small basket takes a paper with powder in it & sprinkles on candle which sparks a little. This is the divination—tells me that after husband died—I had said I was a widow—un amorado wanted to marry me, but I would not, so he sent *gusanos* [worms] into eyes and head from the neck up. Told me to re-move glasses. Looked fixedly at my eyes. From time to time holds my hand. Looks at my tongue, 'Pobre!' "[13] With the diagnosis completed, Terán told them to return the next day. He left the room and fell asleep in the corridor. On their return, he arranged the ritual ob-jects—the bottle of rum, a piece of cinnamon, a sprig of the herb, *ti-grecillo*, a piece of white paper with the ashes of a cigarette, and a special powder—and knelt opposite Elsie. He blew smoke on her an-kles, chest, head, and both sides of her neck, and asked her to repeat after him three times, " 'Yo creo en Dios (I believe in God),' and . . . 'Yo creo en la Virgen Santissima [*sic*] (I believe in the Holy Virgin).' "[14] In her notes, she wrote, "Bids me take off: stockings, ker-chief, glasses. Straighten out my legs, manipulates my toes, fingers, neck, head. . . . Takes mouthful of aguadiente & standing sprays vio-lently from mouth feet & legs, another into face and head, asks me to put out tongue. I decline, suggest neck instead. Asks me to pull down sweater a little & sprays neck. Goes to door, asks if I want him to take out the *gusanos*. Yes. Standing over me he growls & snorts, pounces on me & sucks side of neck (not *very* hard) & takes out from mouth a dark brown object . . . (like a chewed quid of tobacco) puts it in pa-per near candle."[15] He continued the procedure for the other side of her neck, and for the back of her neck, each time taking the "animal-ito" to the door for disposal. Elsie was to return for a total of twelve treatments, as she said, "to be rid of all the destructive 'animals' inside my head. Three I am rid of, but the others are still there, for I did not return."[16]

Elsie was content with the result of the cure. While she admitted to discomfort—"One finger ached a little, my dress was stained, and I was reeking of rum"—still she was pleased to have experienced "one of the oldest of American Indian rituals." Rosita and José had a dif-ferent reaction. "Rosita, who had never been cured for witchcraft or attended a cure before, said that at first she felt like laughing but that then she began to be frightened. It was, of course, funny to her to see me take off my stockings, and afterward with a laugh she wondered what Señor Andrade would think when he drove me back to town and smelt the rum." José found the whole episode ridiculous. " 'Yuga brujo [Lying witch],' " he responded. When Elsie asked him why he thought it was lies, he answered, " 'Because it is not true.' "[17] This, Elsie concluded, was the attitude of most of the Indian inhabitants of Peguche toward the sorcerers—a mingling of José's skepticism with Rosita's amusement and fear.

When Elsie left Ecuador after her first trip in 1940, she arranged for Gorrell to conduct research for her. In May, he wrote, "I have not forgot [sic] my promise to gather data for you, and have been at it as much as time has allowed since you left." Elsie had sent him a copy of *Mitla, Town of the Souls*, which he was reading to get an idea about what type of information she needed. He was also studying, as he told Elsie, " 'Notes and Queries on Anthropology,' that has been very helpful in making me look at things with a slightly more 'professional' eye."[18]

Gorrell had begun research immediately. As Elsie had requested, he had inquired about funeral practices in the town of Amaguaña. He interviewed the mayordomo's wife, who "proved not too accurate or reliable," save for one piece of information that she told him, as he said, "in front of some Indian women peons, to whom she referred occasionally for details." Gorrell was certain that Elsie would be interested in the custom, since she had recorded a similar practice for Mitla. "When a person died in a house," he wrote Elsie, "the funeral party, after the person is buried, goes back to the house of the dead man, and sweeps the floor as clean as possible. They then sift ashes all over the floor, and shut the house up tight . . . , and the whole party . . . bathes . . . with all clothes on." After they return home, "el que sabe," the one who knows, examines the floor for footprints of "the soul of the dead man, that has returned." When the footprint is found, the ashes are swept up, and all sit down to a feast consisting of all the things the deceased had liked to eat and drink.[19]

In addition to conducting interviews with the mayordomo's wife in Amaguaña, Gorrell had rented a car and had driven to the Corpus Christi feast at the hacienda of San Rafael. His detailed notes on the Corpus Christi celebration covered over five single-spaced typed pages. Not only was he excited about the research, and willing to devote time and energy and endure discomfort in pursuit of information, he had another valuable asset: he recognized his own limitations. Remarking on the dances at the Corpus Christi celebration, he noted that the "guía" called the turns, and added, "Unfortunately, as the shouting of the guía was all in Quechua, I couldn't tell when he said what, nor with what effect." Unwilling simply to abandon this, he obtained from one of the leaders the following summary of the calls: "Year after year we come like this, passing the village, passing Amagüaña. . . . Afraid, with sadness we are coming. . . . From other farms they came hitting, they made a minga, they said a mass, but they couldn't hit us. . . . The feast, feast, only for the feast we have come down from the grassy wastes to the village. . . . Lion, tiger, bear wanted to eat us, we escaped, came for the day of Corpus. . . . The priest has called us, for that reason we have come to make a feast."[20]

Gorrell had employed a photographer, Bodo Wuth, to take pictures of the Corpus Christi celebration in Sangolquí. As Gorrell had become interested in the research, so also did Wuth. Gorrell wrote Elsie: "The other day Bodo Wuth was in the office when Rosita and her family were in, and asked me if I thought Rosita would mind his taking her picture. Of course Rosita just loves it, so he took quite a few pictures of her and her family. He also took one of her hands, showing her ornaments, as he thought you might want it or be able to use it. . . . I think the enclosed picture of Rosita and Matildita is marvelous, and no doubt you can use it."[21] Elsie appreciated the pictures. She wrote Gorrell, "Ever so much thanks to you and to Mr. Wuth. Tell him he is an excellent *ethnographic* photographer, nor are his aesthetic values lost on me."[22] The stunning portrait of Rosita and her baby, Matilda, is the frontispiece of *Peguche,* and the picture of Rosita's bejeweled hands appears with the caption, "The bracelets or red beads and innumerable rings worn by women."[23]

Before she left Ecuador, Elsie had mentioned her interest in working with Indian schoolchildren from whom she might collect information on aspects of daily life, customs, and traditions, and from whom she might record folktales. Gorrell located two young Indian boys who attended the Normal School in Uyumbichu. They were brothers of a man who worked in his office, and so Gorrell had occasion to visit with them. He wrote Elsie, "They talked very intelligently on various points that I know are just what you want, so, . . . I made a proposition to them. I told them that if they would gather and write down certain information, I was sure that you would pay them for their work." Gorrell emphasized that Parsons wanted "simply facts and no interpretation" and that "they are to draw not at all on their imaginations, . . . as exaggerations and inventions always come out in the wash, and we would not be interested in any more collaboration from them if they are not reliable." He continued: "I have told both boys to write me a detailed description of the San Pedro festivities in Cayambe, taking their own section apart, and then adding what they know of the other sections. I have asked them to describe the costumes, dances, mimicries, actions, and songs and cries. They are going to Cayambe on vacation in a couple of weeks, and have promised to do all this." On their vacation, Gorrell asked them to record beliefs "about spirits, rainbow, herbs, illness, birth, death." He also requested that they record folktales "of which their mother knows a great number." Gorrell said they were "very earnest boys," and assessed them as "A rare find for us."[24]

Gorrell kept the Maldonado brothers busy recording information under the following headings: "The age of puberty, matrimony and its customs, choosing the marriage day, . . . sexual anormality, homosexuality, . . . the belief that the monkey is the transformation of a lazy man, the belief that single men or single women who die are condemned, the beliefs about lizards, the way of curing a cow that gives little milk, . . . how to discover a thief, how to find something lost." When the boys answered his queries, Gorrell's work began. He wrote Elsie, "On these and other topics there are thirty pages, closely written by hand, so you can imagine that the transcription and translation will be quite a job."[25]

Anxious to extend the network of schoolchildren, Gorrell asked the Maldonado brothers to put him in touch with boys from other parts of the country.[26] The boys succeeded only in recruiting their cousin, Francisco Andrango, whom Gorrell had set to work on "customs and beliefs about pregnancy, . . . the cause of accidents, . . . [and] old stories and beliefs." Gorrell found Francisco's accounts "better than I ever expected." But he also found that the young boy on occasion inserted "moral texts," and he assured Elsie that "when I send him the money I shall tell him to stick closer to what we ask for."[27]

The headmaster of the Normal School of Uyumbicho, which the Maldonado and the Andrango boys attended, paid a visit to Gorrell. Thinking he had a good source for funding, he tried to raise money for his school by selling Parsons a manuscript magazine in Quechua with themes describing life in Ecuador. In marginal notes on Gorrell's letter, Elsie wrote "can't use; try him out on the marriage customs."[28]

Elsie was pleased with the information that Gorrell had compiled from the schoolboys. The material gathered from José Antonio Maldonado, Segundo Felix Maldonado, and Francisco Andrango, and translated from Quechua by Juan Gorrell, appeared as the appendix to *Peguche*. In the preface to her book, Elsie said that she used this information from Cayambe as a check for Otavalo, but that she kept it separate because the informants were more sophisticated than those in Peguche, and the two locales, twenty miles apart, were divided by the Otavalo Valley drainage.

Parsons's research in Ecuador was closely related to her work in the Southwest and in Mexico. She was interested in the interplay between Spanish and Indian culture; and she was drawn to the ever-present puzzle, what was the origin of the present-day practices? In an opening passage of *Peguche,* she stated her approach: "Among our problems are to what degree Indian ways may have penetrated Spanish culture and to what degree Spanish ways have penetrated Indian culture."[29] In notes for the book, Parsons wrote, "Interest in Hispanicized Indian—in our Southwest, in Southern Mexico, between Spanish and Indian cultures. But here as elsewhere until the ethnography is clear accult[uration] must await. So this book is first of all an ethnographic picture."[30] Thus, the first step in an acculturation study for Parsons was ethnography.

There was, as Parsons noted, an absence of a baseline study of Ecuadorian Indians at the time of the Spanish conquest. As she recorded in her notes, "Meager picture of Ecuador at and after the Spanish conquest. No Garcil[asso]. No Landa. No Sahagun." She continued, "So it has to be reconstructed through documentary researches from archaeological data."[31] In this way, her interest in acculturation studies led her to archeological accounts, and from these she was drawn to historical works. Of this, she wrote to Lowie, "I have been working on a book about the Andean Indian group I visited last spring and plan to visit again, perhaps this autumn, and digesting the Peruvian chroniclers who have been read more by archeologists than by ethnologists. For an acculturation study Garcilasso is rich." With a certain satisfaction, she added, "When I asked Dr. Boas who had first described pitch accent among American Indians he did not know it was Garcilasso."[32] She also wrote to Gorrell of this: "The Peruvian data from Garcilasso de la Vega's Royal Commentaries of the Incas—a most fascinating book . . . —throws light on no end of Ecuadorian ways. I believe Peguche was actually one of the famous Peruvian colonies." She spoke of customs that were "straight from Inca, Peru," and remarked, "The parallel traits with Peruvian pile up."[33] In her own notes for *Peguche,* she cryptically summarized this approach: "Thorough analyses of the contemporary life knowledge of Peruvian life before and since the Spanish conquest of value, since the Inca conquered Ecuador and introduced Peruvian culture & colonists. So the analysis of accult[uration] must root back."[34]

In *Peguche,* Parsons was primarily concerned with Indian and mestizo cultures. Specifically, she focused on issues that now are linked to the concept of ethnicity, a concept that had not been developed at the time Parsons was writing. As she emphasized in a letter to Gorrell, she was "referring to *culture not to race*."[35] In the first chapter, Parsons

stressed just this point: "Between race and culture there is considerable confusion of thought in Ecuador, as elsewhere. A mestizo or
Cholo is thought of both as a half-breed and as a person of low economic status and cultural inferiority derived from Indian contacts."
She noted the historical derivation of the term "Cholo": "According
to Garcilasso . . . , the term came from the Caribbean Islands and
meant dog. It was a term of contempt, as it is more or less today in
Ecuador; one would not use the term in speaking to a mestizo."[36] For
her work, she decided to refer to Cholo or mestizo culture (which she
regarded as primarily derived from Spanish peasant or village culture) as white; and Indian culture, quite simply, as Indian.

With this complex blending of cultures, with conflicting values and
measures for being human, Parsons was curious as to how people
reached a sense of self. On this subject of establishing cultural identity, she was aided by Gorrell's perceptive observations. Of the Maldonado brothers, he wrote: "But Elisa, I must warn you on one or
two points: the boys have thought of themselves as mestizos much
more so recently than before. It is they who have made their mother
use a stove, eliminate guinea pigs from the kitchen for hygenic [*sic*]
reasons, put in flooring and beds in the house . . . from what they
learned away at school. So the fact that they live in the mestizo culture
is not so much because of their mestizo descent [from their father]
as because of their schooling." Gorrell said that all of these changes
and more had occurred during the seven-year period of school attendance, and he wagered "that if you go back . . . in another year
you will find the Maldonados living . . . even nearer white than Mestizo." He added that the mestizo aspects present in their family life
before the boys had entered school were not due to their mestizo father, but rather "to the pride and ambition of the fully Indian
[mother] Clara."[37]

Parsons herself concluded that the Indians alone had a secure
identity, with no ambivalence. In notes for her book, she wrote, "The
only people I met in Ecuador who are not confused were the Indians
because in their way of thinking if you are living like an Indian you
are an Indian, if you are living like a Blanco, you are a Blanco, and
they distinguish between the two ways of life without hesitation or
uncertainty."[38]

However, if the Indians were secure in their cultural identity, they
were impoverished economically in a system controlled by the elite of
the hacienda. Through Peguche and neighboring Quinchuquí flowed
the Rio Grande, known in Quechua as Jatunyacu, or Big Water. The
river was channeled into numerous conduits, to which, as Parsons

noted, "the Indians own only partial water rights. . . . They may wash in them or use the water for drinking or cooking; they may not divert water to irrigate their fields. In time of drought, with water streaming past their failing crops, the best they can do is to pay a Mass in Otavalo for rainfall—unless covertly they irrigate a little by hand." In addition to water, the owner of the hacienda controlled pasture land and firewood. Parsons remarked, "Between White town or settlement and hacienda lands in some places it tends to be a tight squeeze for the Indians."[39]

Parsons examined the relations between the whites and the Indians, which she typified as "mutual economic convenience." She continued: "Rarely do Indians cross the charming flowery plaza or sit on its benches, and in the churches they keep to one side, except at their own very early hours or at special services. Relations with the priest do not extend, except in connection with baptism, to even the most casual relations with the congregation." The Indians had not the slightest trace of subservience toward the whites. Rather, she said, they were "indifferent and impersonal" in their relations with whites. They kept to themselves "as a guaranty of independence." She remarked that "the nearest comparable relationship I know of is, curiously enough, that between masters and European-born servants in large households of the northeastern Atlantic seaboard."[40]

The indifference of the Indians toward the whites was not returned in kind. Whites, Parsons said, were extremely curious about the ways of the Indians. As she observed, "Indian withdrawal excites the curiosity of White neighbors, who seem glad of a pretext to visit an Indian house and look around. Their staring and their questions are naturally objectionable. They get little information, and that little, if possible, is misleading." Elsie encountered this on a daily basis during the course of her fieldwork. The hotel in Otavalo where she was staying would send a car to pick her up, and as she recalled, "The pretext of telling me the car was waiting was used by all the girls in the hotel who, uninvited, would walk into Rosita's bedroom." Finding Rosita in bed, one woman named María asked, " 'Are you sick?'. . . . Receiving no answer, she added, 'Probably you are sick with the influenza.' " Parsons added, "The baby was five days old and was tucked away with Rosita in bed, but Rosita did not show off the baby or mention her birth."[41]

However, when Rosita desired, she could successfully bridge the gap between Indian and white culture. She possessed an awareness and knowledge of white culture that gave her the flexibility to adapt to it when this was useful. As Parsons observed, "Because of her comparatively close relations to the Church, of her trading relations abroad [in textiles], and of her fluent knowledge of Spanish, Rosita is becoming more and more aware of White culture and more and more critical of several aspects of her Indian culture, for example, of the validity of dreams or of witchcraft." Rosita provided an example "of the opportunities for acculturation through unusual personality." In fact, Parsons said, she was "one of the most outstanding instances I have ever observed."[42]

In addition to relations between Indians and whites, Parsons was interested in the attitudes of the inhabitants of Peguche toward the people of other lands. She quickly found out that they had little knowledge of anything outside their own world: "They have heard of the Oriente and of cannibalistic Jibaros; Colombia and Venezuela are known by name, but Mexico and North America are wholly unknown, and, curiously enough, Peru." They would make reference to an "Inca *rey,* to the obsidian or potsherds they turn up in plowing as Inca money (*plata de Inca*) or Inca jars (*olla de Inca*), but no world before the advent of the Spaniards is conceived of, nor any part of the world today as unoccupied by Spaniards." They had trouble understanding, as Elsie recalled, "That there were few if any Spaniards in parts of my 'land.' Once I was asked if the sun rose and set in my 'land.' " On another occasion, the following exchange took place between Rosita and Elsie on the subject of Chinese and Japanese people:

> "Blancos, White people?" asked Rosita.
> "No."
> "Are they baptized?"
> "No."
> "Then they are Masons?"
> "No, they have another religion." This amazed her.
> "How is that possible?"
> "They have other gods."
> "How is that possible! Are they married in the church?"
> "Married, but not in the church."

The exchange ended at this point, and Rosita returned "to the always fascinating subject of the high buildings of Nueva York, an equally extraordinary but more intelligible matter. 'Fifteen to twenty stories! Three thousand more than everybody in Peguche in one house!' "[43]

The results of Elsie's fieldwork in Peguche was received with enthusiasm. Alfred Kroeber wrote Lissa saying that he considered it to be one of her mother's best works. In his review for the *Hispanic American Historical Review,* Paul Radin opined, "Her study can, in fact, be said to be perfect . . . and it will remain, for many years to come, a model of what can be done by the new method of approach to the study of acculturation, of which she was one of the founders."[44]

NOTES

1. ECP, Lissa to Colley, 1 Mar. 1940.
2. Gladys Reichard, "Elsie Clews Parsons," *JAF* 56 (1943): 47.
3. ECP, ECP to Steward, 26 Nov. 1939; Steward to ECP, 27 Nov. 1939; 26 Feb. 1940.
4. ECP, F. L. Stagg to Don Victor Eastman Cox & Sra, 13 Feb. 1940.
5. Elsie Clews Parsons, *Peguche* (Chicago: University of Chicago Press, 1945), p. v.
6. Ibid., p. iv.
7. Lowie Papers, ECP to Lowie, 21 May 1940.
8. ECP, Notes "For Preface."
9. Parsons, *Peguche*, p. 154.
10. ECP, Notes "For Preface."
11. Parsons, *Peguche*, pp. 123, 153.
12. Ibid., p. 69.
13. ECP, Peguche fieldnotes.
14. Parsons, *Peguche*, p. 71.
15. ECP, Peguche fieldnotes.
16. Parsons, *Peguche*, p. 72.
17. Ibid., pp. 72–73.
18. ECP, Gorrell to ECP, 27 May 1940.
19. ECP, Gorrell to ECP, 27 May 1940.
20. ECP, Gorrell to ECP, 27 May 1940.
21. ECP, Gorrell to ECP, 4 Oct. 1940.
22. ECP, ECP to Gorrell, 2 Aug. 1940, her emphasis.
23. Parsons, *Peguche*, Plates I, XVIII.
24. ECP, Gorrell to ECP, 15 Aug. 1940.
25. ECP, Gorrell to ECP, 10 Feb. 1941.
26. ECP, Gorrell to ECP, 29 Oct. 1940.
27. ECP, Gorrell to ECP, 10 Feb. 1941.
28. ECP, Gorrell to ECP, 5 May 1941.
29. Parsons, *Peguche*, p. 1.
30. ECP, Notes for *Peguche*.
31. Ibid.
32. Lowie Papers, ECP to Lowie, 10 Feb. 1941.
33. ECP, ECP to Gorrell, 2 Aug. 1940, n.d.
34. ECP, Notes for *Peguche*.
35. ECP, ECP to Gorrell, n.d., her emphasis.
36. Parsons, *Peguche*, p. 1.
37. ECP, Gorrell to ECP, 13 Oct. 1940.

38. ECP, Notes for *Peguche.*

39. Parsons, *Peguche,* pp. 8, 9.

40. Ibid., p. 10.

41. Ibid., p. 11.

42. Ibid., p. 151.

43. Ibid., pp. 13, 151.

44. Paul Radin, review of *Peguche, Hispanic Historical Review* 26 (1946): 246–47.

14

A Position of Power

In 1941, Elsie Clews Parsons was at the apogee of her career as an anthropologist. She was president of the American Anthropological Association, the first woman to occupy the office. She was the associate editor of the *Journal of American Folklore,* and, in a de facto position, acted as the stabilizing force for the American Folklore Society. And through her benefactions—the funding of individuals and of publications—she had helped shape the discipline of anthropology. In sum, she was a woman of power in her profession. A letter to Parsons from Ann Gayton, who was book review editor for the *American Anthropologist,* serves as a marker of this: "I couldn't find any body better to review Lowie's book because there isn't anybody better. There are few people who have your knowledge, experience, and perspective with regard to anthropology and social theory."[1]

Parsons's position as a leading American anthropologist was linked to her work in professional organizations. In 1915, she had become affiliated with the American Anthropological Association and the American Folklore Society. In 1918, she was treasurer of the American Ethnological Society and, from 1919 to 1920, president of the American Folklore Society. From 1923 to 1925, she served as president of the American Ethnological Society; from 1930 to 1931, as second vice-president; and from 1934 to 1935, and again in 1937, as first vice-president.[2] For the American Anthropological Association, she was appointed to the Committee on Policy in 1920 and to the Committee on Indian Policy in 1922; and she served on the council from 1919 until her death. In 1925, and again in 1938 and 1939, she served on the executive committee of the American Anthropological Association. In 1940, she was vice-president and, in 1941, president, of the American Anthropological Association.

From her first involvement in the discipline, Parsons began to use her influence, in consort with Franz Boas, to help direct the affairs of anthropology. In 1917, she worked out with him a plan to finance the publication by the American Folklore Society of her *Folk-Tales of Andros Islands, Bahamas.* Responding to his explanation of the way the

Memoirs were usually subsidized, she suggested, "It might be simpler if I paid the full $500 or whatever the cost of printing. If that would release funds in the treasury for the publication of other memoirs, I would be glad to do it."[3] When, at the 1918 meeting of the American Anthropological Association, a rift arose between Boas and C. Hart Merriam, Elsie played the role of mediator. Merriam had convened, by invitation, a meeting of anthropologists to discuss the position of anthropology in the National Research Council. Boas had not been invited, quite obviously because he would have opposed Merriam. As Boas viewed it, "The essential point at issue is that [Merriam seemed] to wish to make a section in the general Research Council on anthropology and psychology, or in some other way in which anthropology will be subordinated to other science." There was further discussion in public forum, at Section H of the American Association for the Advancement of Science and in the American Anthropological Association. However, it was Elsie who provided the means for mending the rift. "In the evening," Boas recalled, "Mrs. Elsie Clews Parsons had invited Merriam, Goddard and myself to dinner, and we had the matter out then in a very friendly matter." Boas acknowledged that Merriam had "behaved very decently," that he had indicated his sympathies were with Boas's group, but that he had felt constrained to follow the dictates of the National Research Council. Boas continued, "The up-shot of the discussion at dinner was that I suggested to him that we would make a report to the Research Council summarizing . . . what types of affiliations might be needed from time to time and to show that such affiliations must always be temporary and that anthropology would have to be an independent development."[4]

Of her first American Folklore Society meeting, held at the National Museum in Washington, D.C., in December, 1915, Elsie had written Herbert, "My turn comes this morning. The papers werent very interesting with a few exceptions—Boas, Kroeber, Goddard. But more interesting was lunching with Kroeber and looking at the Zuñi exhibit with him in the Museum. I had Mr. & Mrs. Boas, Kroeber, Lowie & Goddard to dine with me here [at the New Willard Hotel]."[5] At this meeting, Parsons was appointed to the editorial board to work on the publication of material on Negro folklore.[6] By the next annual meeting in December, 1916, Boas reported that "the material for the first Negro Number has been collected by Mrs. Parsons, who is in charge of this subject, and it is hoped that the first Negro Number may appear early in the coming year."[7] The following year, Elsie served as a member of the council of the American Folklore Society.

In December, 1918, three years after Elsie had become a member of the American Folklore Society, she was elected president. She wrote Herbert, "Our annual Amer[ican] Anthropological Ass[ocia-tion] & Amer[ican] Folk-Lore Society meetings have just come off in Philadelphia. They were unusually interesting & full of side shows. The men now take me as one of themselves, & to my surprise I was elected president of the Folk-Lore Soc[iety]." Cognizant of the source of her appointment, she added, "I feel flattered that Boas thinks I am fit."[8] Boas in a letter to Alfred Tozzer had commented on the selec-tion of Parsons, "In the Folk-Lore Society we have elected Mrs. Par-sons president, in the hope particularly that she may be able to devise some means of increasing our membership. She is very energetic and resourceful, and I shall try to work with her towards that end."[9]

Parsons soon became part of the inner circle of anthropologists who directed, often from behind the scenes, the affairs of the Amer-ican Folklore Society. In December, 1923, Tozzer, as treasurer of the society, wrote her that he would not be attending the meetings to be held in New York, and for this reason he was sending her the reports of the treasurer and secretary. He wrote, "I shall also present my res-ignation. I have served for ten years and I insist that someone else be found. I think that the Society could be more easily run from New York. I suggest that you be the Secretary and that someone near you be Treasurer."[10] New York people were selected: Pliny Earle God-dard, as treasurer, and Gladys Reichard, as secretary.

Just as Tozzer had done, so also did Boas ask Parsons to attend to matters in his absence. In preparation for the American Folklore So-ciety meetings to be held in Washington in December, 1924, he wrote her, "I shall not be able to stay in Washington after 3 P.M. Friday. For this reason I am sending you the enclosed letters and the Editors re-port." Boas asked Elsie to help set both the location of the meeting and the election of the new president. He noted, "There will presum-ably be an invitation from the University of Chicago to meet with the Modern Language Association next year." Boas was aware that the joint-membership agreement, which enabled a person to join both or-ganizations by a single payment to one, had resulted in an imbalance. He wrote, "Considering that we have received more than sixty new members from the Modern Language Association while they have re-ceived hardly any from us, I think it would be a good plan to elect one of the Modern Language people, perhaps Miss Pound of Nebraska, president, and to meet with the Modern Language people and try at the same time to arrange the time so that members may also attend the Anthropological Association meeting."[11] Elsie attended to busi-ness. Louise Pound was elected president of the American Folklore Society in 1925 and reelected in 1926. Since Pound did not attend the meeting in Washington, she was informed by letter of her new position, and of the location of the next annual meeting, a "double meeting," one to be held in Chicago with the Modern Language Association, and the other in New Haven with the American Anthropological Association.[12]

In 1925, and in 1927, the society formally recognized the assistance that Parsons had rendered. Recorded in the minutes of the thirty-seventh annual meeting of the American Folklore Society was the following: "The Secretary was instructed to send a resolution of thanks to Dr. Elsie Clews Parsons for the cooperation and help she has given the Society."[13] In her capacity as secretary, Gladys Reichard wrote:

> My dear Dr. Parsons:
>   At the meeting of the American Folk-Lore Society on Dec. 29, 1927, The Council requested the secretary to send you a letter expressing the deepest thanks of the Society to you for the large amount of help and interest which you have rendered us particularly during the last year. It was decided that a letter to this effect be sent you and that a copy be laid upon the minutes.[14]

The source of such gratitude was Parsons's financial support of both the *Journal of American Folklore* and the Memoirs of the American Folklore Society. As Keith Chambers observed in "The Indefatigable Elsie Clews Parsons—Folklorist," from 1916 to 1941, Parsons had contributed in excess of $30,000 to the society.[15] Susan Dwyer-Shick appraised Parsons's support of the society and the *Journal:* "An examination of the Treasurer's Report published for the years 1919 through 1940 . . . shows that Parsons contributed *at least* $12,113.54 to the *Memoirs* series. Moreover, Parsons assumed support for five volumes in this series for which figures are *not* available, since in each case she had sent the necessary funds directly to the publisher." Dwyer-Shick noted that Parsons had paid for sixteen of the twenty-six Memoirs of the American Folklore Society published between 1918 and 1943. "And of these sixteen, seven were written by Parsons herself, including two Memoirs published as multiple volumes—the two-volume *Folk-Lore from the Cape Verde Islands, South Carolina* (XV) and the even larger three-volume *Folk-Lore of the Antilles, French and English* (XXVI)."[16]

Parsons felt the economic necessity to reduce the amount of her support for anthropological work in 1932 and 1933. She had written Boas, by way of apology for cutting her annual contribution to his secretarial fund to $1500: "My income has been considerably cut; the reduction overtook me before I realized and for the time being I feel rather squeezed. I have to make retrenchments all along the line to readjust to the new scale. The family retrenchments I mind least, but they . . . bring pressure to bear on scientific reductions which I mind most."[17] For this reason, Parsons lessened her contributions to the *Journal of American Folklore*. Reichard wrote, "Many thanks for the cheque. We understand perfectly about the Journal. We are most grateful you have slung us a lifeline as long as you have. As the affairs of the Society now stand we can perhaps manage to keep going." Reichard added that the year before, "in a moment of optimism," the society had agreed to publish Thelma Adamson's memoirs, "and when your letter came it gave us a bit of a turn. But the next day we got word that the Council of Learned Societies would give us $500, so that makes us all right again."[18] Ruth Benedict also wrote Parsons of the award, adding, "You have carried it so long when the issues couldn't possibly have been financed without your help that I'm glad that you can be relieved now without feeling that the Journal will go completely on the rocks financially."[19]

While cutting back on her contributions to the *Journal,* Parsons was at the same time contributing a large amount for the publication of various works. In October, 1933, Boas mentioned his concern over the amount to which she had obligated herself. After his talk with the publisher, Heinrich W. Augustin, he was able to tell Elsie of the estimated expenses, which included the Antilles manuscript at $1,512.00 and the Hopi $5,500. In addition, Parsons had ordered Melville Herskovits's Suriname manuscript printed, which would cost $3,850.00. In the margin of Boas's letter, Elsie penned an exclamation point, but she nonetheless paid all the expenses.[20]

Both in official and unofficial capacity, Elsie occupied a central position in the organizational structure of the society. This was exemplified by two communications relating to the reorganization of the American Folklore Society. On February 24, 1940, as the secretary-treasurer, George Herzog, reported, the council of the American Folklore Society called a meeting "to discuss current affairs of the society connected with the change of editorship and the publication of the Journal."[21] In his report of the meeting published in the *Journal of American Folklore,* he mentioned the formation of three new committees: the Membership Committee, a Publication Policy Committee, and the Committee on Policy. Parsons had been appointed to all three of these crucial committees. In the matter of the selection of the editor, Herzog noted that "since Ann Gayton did not wish to serve as Editor, Gladys A. Reichard was elected Editor for 1940."[22] What was not apparent from Herzog's report was revealed in a letter from

Gayton to Elsie, i.e., that even in the selection of the editor, Elsie played an informal role by suggesting her for the position and attempting to persuade her to accept. When Gayton was approached again for the following year, she wrote Elsie, "I think it is high time I put an end to all hopes, doubts, or fears that I might be the next editor of the journal. . . . I know you make plans for the journal and I wanted you to know where I stand in these matters."[23] Thus, both de jure and ex officio, Elsie was at the nexus of events affecting the American Folklore Society.

The efforts to reorganize the American Folklore Society in 1940 essentially concerned achieving a balance between the anthropological folklorists and the literary folklorists. Melville J. Herskovits, as chair of the Committee on Policy, had solicited the views of the committee members on what they regarded as the most pressing concerns of the American Folklore Society.[24] From the responses of the committee members, he concluded that "the major difficulty facing the Society is an absence of definite policy regarding our most difficult problem— the reconciliation of the divergent interests of those whose concern with folklore stems from what may be termed the humanities and 'folk-say,' on the one hand, and, on the other, those who are interested in the folklore of primitive folk."[25] Herskovits drew together the various points raised by the members of the Policy Committee, and in turn submitted twenty-two proposals for their consideration.

Elsie's position on the reorganization of the society was one of inclusion of the literary folklorists, save for two specific concerns, the editorship of the *Journal* and the location of the annual meeting. To Herskovits's query about the "most urgent needs of the Folklore Society," Elsie had responded, "Suggestions: For administration, representatives as far as possible from all centres interested in folk lore; but the editorship of the Journal to remain in the hands of a folklorist who is also an experienced anthropologist." She was also opposed to the rotation of annual meetings between the American Anthropological Association and the Modern Language Association, "unless," as she said, "the Modern Language Association is holding its meetings in the same locality as the AAA." Otherwise, Elsie concurred with most of the proposals that Herskovits had formulated from the committee responses. She agreed that "the American Folklore Society adopt as a definite policy the aim of bringing together and integrating the interests of all folklorists." She was also in accord with the suggestion "that in any given year the President and Second Vice-president be either anthropologists or those concerned with the folklore of non-primitive folk; the First and Third Vice-presidents to be in that category not represented by those two other officers." Elsie suggested that the Committee on Membership should consist "largely [of] 'folk-say' and literary folklorists."[26]

Parsons supported certain policy changes for the publication of the *Journal* and was cautious about others. She concurred with the suggestion that single topic issues be discontinued and that the emphasis should be on shorter articles, as well as theoretical papers that would provide a balance to "the collection of raw data." However, she did not support change in the status of associate editor and disagreed with the opinion expressed by others that "the position is largely honorific."[27] She stressed that the associate editor should continue to be "appointed by the editor, as any working cabinet should be appointed by its head." She did concur with the proposal that the review editor should be nominated by committee and voted on by the council. Elsie was lukewarm to suggestions that topics of interest for the amateur folklorist be included in the *Journal*. To the suggestion that a "News and Notes" section be added, with attention paid to the nonacademic amateur collectors, Parsons responded, "Yes, but without attention to the work of amateur collectors like the WPA. Amateur collecting can be stimulated and directed only by someone who knows subject and field. It can not be done wholesale or directed by a correspondence course in a pedagogical journal." In response to the proposal, "Should it be recommended that the *Journal* include methodological discussions and questionnaires concerning suggested techniques of collecting tales and other folklore materials, these to be particularly directed toward amateurs in the field?" Parsons succinctly responded, "No." To the last proposal, "Should the Memoirs be lithographed or offprinted so as to conserve resources in caring for this portion of the Society's publications?" Elsie must have smiled somewhat sardonically. She responded, "Memoirs are printed only through special contributions. There is no memoir fund to be conserved."[28]

The final report of the Committee on Policy, which had been approved by the council of the society, was presented at the fifty-second annual meeting of the American Folklore Society in December, 1940. Gayton had written Elsie, "I do wish I were going to be at the Christmas meeting just to hear the chatter; so many people suddenly struck with fervor to do something to improve the dear old folklore society. I only hope that whatever remedies are adopted, the cure will be permanent."[29] Elsie's key concerns—that the editor of the *Journal* be an anthropologist and that the meetings of the society be held in conjunction with the American Anthropological Association—were, rather subtly, finessed. It was simply proposed that "the Editor be nominated and elected annually, and that no person serve as Editor for more than five consecutive years." No mention was made as to the disciplinary affiliation of the editor. In fact, however, Archer Taylor, professor of German literature at the University of California, Berkeley, was to be the editor of the *Journal of American Folklore* for 1941. This marked a significant break with the past, for he was the first editor who had a literary orientation to the study of folklore, and the first editor who was not a student or close colleague of Boas. For the selection of the location of the annual meeting, it was proposed that "due consideration be given to the convenience of all members, to the end that meetings shall be held jointly with the Modern Language Association in something of the same degree that they are held with the American Anthropological Association." It was also suggested that "a rigid policy of alternation" should be avoided, but so should the past "tradition of meeting exclusively with the American Anthropological Association" be avoided.[30] On this point, Gayton, also a member of the Committee on Policy, had remarked to Elsie, "I'm not sure . . . that I like the business of meeting with the Modern Language Association. That however will probably be gotten around."[31] As worded, the proposal would have provided for just such maneuvering room, but, in fact, the spirit of the proposal was honored in subsequent years.[32] Parsons had opposed the election of associate editors, and she lost on that point, too, since it was recommended that they be elected on an annual basis. She also had opposed a recommendation, supported by the majority, that the *Journal* include materials for the benefit of amateur collectors.

Parsons and Gayton, the two most ardent supporters on the Committee on Policy of the anthropological approach to the study of folklore, were in essence defeated in most of their positions. Still, they joined with the other committee members—Archer Taylor, Stith Thompson, Leslie White, and Melville Herskovits—in unanimous approval of the report of the Committee on Policy. In good spirit, Gayton wrote to Elsie, "*My* hat *is* off to Herskovits, who, I think, had a very difficult job—receiving the extensive and disorganized complaints of numbers of people and converting them into practical policies."[33]

Until the late 1930s, Parsons did not wield the same degree of power in the American Anthropological Association as she did in the American Folklore Society. Much of her influence was effected behind the scene, through her contacts with those in positions of authority. Her financial contributions to the American Anthropological Association, while generous and substantial, were also not in equal measure to those of the American Folklore Society. Still, she did have her impact. On one occasion, Parsons had attempted to influence Pliny Earle Goddard in favor of continuing the American Anthropological Society Memoirs series. Through his position as editor of the *American Anthropologist,* Goddard had convinced the executive committee to discontinue publication of the Memoirs.[34] Parsons wrote him, questioning the wisdom of such a move, and suggesting that Robert Lowie, for instance, had material in hand that could have been published in the series. Goddard responded that he did not want to publish any Memoirs until the *American Anthropologist* was on schedule. As he said, "It seems to me the first duty of the Association is to get out a live and adequate journal of discussion and method." He continued, "The suggestion of a supplement was to provide for your paper without reopening a series of Memoirs. I must say such supplements do not appeal to me particularly. . . . I don't know what to say about an outlet for your activity. I had hoped there would be an opportunity for you to publish all you wanted in our department series here at the Museum. I hear there is now a congestion of manuscripts and a lack of funds."[35]

A draft of her answer to Goddard read, "Thanks for your note of Oct 21. Zuñi Notes, Pt III will have to go by the board, I think." She concluded, "My ms. on 'Laguna Genealogies' is now about ready to go to the printer. Am I to conclude from your letter that your department will not undertake publication during 1920–1921?"[36] *Laguna Genealogies* was published by the American Museum of Natural History in 1923, and the Memoirs series of the American Anthropological Association was reinstituted in the same year. Clearly, Parsons's financial support was critical for both. She had offered "Gratis, for full measure" for *Laguna Genealogies,* and she had paid publication costs for Memoirs 29 ($448.03), Ruth Benedict's *The Concept of the Guardian Spirit in North America.*[37]

Elsie's financial contributions to the American Anthropological Association were not always a matter of public record. In April, 1934, she wrote to Leslie Spier, the editor of the *American Anthropologist,* "I think you ought to have more than $40 a month for secretarial expense," and she suggested that at the next meeting he lobby for it. She offered, in the meantime, "to be personally resposible for another $40 a month, or at least for an emergency fund of $320, if that is agreable to you." Elsie explained, "I would like it to be anonymous and particularly a secret from Sapir, because I turned him down on something he proposed. But this matter is more important, I think; besides my personal account is looking up a little."[38] Spier responded:

"You're a peach to offer to hire more assistance for the Anthropologist. You cannot know just how much of a relief it will be to have some of the load lifted: the mere thought of it lets me breathe more freely. At the same time it doesn't seem fair to let one person pay for what the Association should be financing, but my selfishness—the necessity for getting some of my own work done—gets the best of my scruples."[39]

In December, 1940, the secretary, Frank M. Setzler, wrote to Parsons, "It is my pleasure to inform you that at the annual meeting of the American Anthropological Association . . . you were elected President for the year of 1941."[40] Her position of power was secured, and a sense of this is conveyed in her correspondence. Deference can be read in letters to Parsons, and authority in her responses. One poor soul wrote after a traumatic encounter with her at the 1940 American Anthropological Association meeting, "You gave me a case of jitters at Philadelphia the other day when you began lambasting me so enthusiastically because of my belief in the authority of Father Velasco."[41] Her position of authority is also conveyed in correspondence with the secretary of the American Anthropological Association, Fred Eggan. She wrote to him, "As soon as I get . . . from you . . . a list of the committee appointments made in recent years I will write you on pending committee appointments." And she sent him directives on organizational affairs: "Before I left Philadelphia I had a talk with Dr. Mason who is, I presume, the Chairman of the Executive Committee, and we agreed that the best way to take up the matter of our representative on the Social Science Research Council was to ask you to send Dr. Mason the names of the three AAA Members. . . . Kindly send me also the same information."[42]

Elsie had taken charge. With characteristic direction and style, she charted her course for her year as presdient of the American Anthropological Association. She had reached the apogee of her professional life, and she enjoyed the vantage point. In notes written for her presidential address to the American Anthropological Association, she had jotted down prospective titles, scratched them out, and circled one, "An Anthropological Excursion." She wrote, "In recent years a precedent seems to be growing up for the retiring President of the A[merican] A[nthropological] A[ssociation] to take an after dinner trans-continental walk, it may be in the northern parts of North America or in the marginal areas of South America."[43] Elsie Clews Parsons's year as president of the American Anthropological Association was, indeed, the culmination of her "Anthropological Excursion."

NOTES

1. ECP, Ann Gayton to ECP, 24 Feb. 1938.

2. To commemorate her contributions, the American Ethnological Society awarded an Elsie Clews Parsons Prize to the most outstanding graduate student paper during the 1960s and 1970s. As Louise Lamphere remarked in her distinguished lecture to the American Ethnological Society in 1989, "When the prize was discontinued, the last medal was given to the president and handed down from president to president as a symbol of office." See Lamphere, "Feminist Anthropology: The Legacy of Elsie Clews Parsons," *American Ethnologist* 16 (1989): 518.

3. Boas Papers, ECP to Boas, 8 May 1917, in response to ECP, Boas to ECP, 4 May 1917.

4. Boas Papers, Boas to Tozzer, 30 Dec. 1918.

5. ECP, ECP to HP, 29 Dec. 1915.

6. Charles Peabody, "Report on the Twenty-Seventh Annual Meeting of the American Folklore Society," *JAF* 29 (1916): 297. In 1916, Parsons was reappointed as assistant editor; and in 1917, this title was changed to associate editor, a position she retained to her death.

7. Boas, "Editor's Report," *JAF* 30 (1917): 270.

8. ECP, ECP to HP, 28 Dec. 1918.

9. Boas Papers, Boas to Tozzer, 30 Dec. 1918.

10. ECP, Tozzer to ECP, 19 Dec. 1923.

11. Boas Papers, Boas to ECP, 29 Dec. 1924. For more on the joint membership agreement between the AFS and MLA, see Susan Dwyer-Shick, "The American Folklore Society and Folklore Research in American, 1888–1940," Ph.D. dissertation in Folklore and Folklife, University of Pennsylvania, 1979, p. 51; and Rosemary Lévy Zumwalt, *American Folklore Scholarship* (Bloomington: University of Indiana Press, 1988), p. 37.

12. UPFFA, Boas to Pound, 12 Jan. 1925.

13. "Thirty-Seventh Annual Meeting of the American Folklore Society," *JAF* 39 (1926): 210.

14. UPFFA, Reichards to ECP, 18 Feb. 1928.

15. *Western Folklore* 32 (1973): 197.

16. Dwyer-Shick, "The American Folklore Society," p. 285. The annual reports of the American Folklore Society meetings provide a record of her generosity. In 1919, included in Tozzer's treasurer report under Publication Fund was "Dr. Parsons' contribution" of $702.67, which covered the expenses for her *Folk-Tales of Andros Island, Bahamas* (Memoirs XIII). In 1920, her contribution was listed as $1,000.00. In 1921, Tozzer reported that she had donated $1,000.00, for Dean S. Fansler's *Filipino Popular Tales* (Memoirs XII). In 1922, he noted, "Dr. Parsons, [Memoirs] ... XII, balance, $899.94; Dr. Parsons, for Sea Island Memoir, $600.00." In 1923, Tozzer listed under the General Fund, "Dr. E. C. Parsons, April-June, 1921, Journal, $500.00; ... July-Sept., 1922, Journal, $412.50"; and under the Publication fund, "Dr. E. C. Parsons, balance on Memoir ... XVI, $1179.10." Appended to his

report, Tozzer added, "The finances of the Folk-Lore Society are in a better state than at this time last year, when we owed over $1000.00. The present condition of our treasury is entirely due to the generous donations of Dr. Parsons who has paid for two numbers of the Journal and an entire memoir." [See *JAF:* Alfred M. Tozzer, "Treasurer's Report," Thirty-First Annual Meeting of the American Folklore Society, 33 (1920): 167; Thirty-Second Annual Meeting of the AFS, 34 (1921): 218; Thirty-Third Annual Meeting of AFS, 35 (1922): 206; Thirty-Fourth Annual Meeting of AFS, 36 (1923): 197; Thirty-Fifth Annual Meeting of the AFS, 37 (1924): 243–44.]

And so it continued on an annual basis: from 1919 until her death in 1941, Elsie Clews Parsons made substantial contributions to the American Folklore Society. In 1926, Ruth Benedict, as editor, reported that Parsons had paid for the publication of Clement M. Doke's *Lamda Folk-Tales* (Memoirs XX), though no dollar amount was given. In 1927, Benedict noted in her report, "We wish to take this opportunity of expressing our thanks to Dr. Parsons, who has also paid for the Negro number of the *Journal* published during the current year." In 1931, Parsons paid for the Southwest number of the *Journal* (No. 167, $443.76), and the Negro number (No. 169, $392.18), as well as for her *Kiowa Tales* (Memoirs XXII). In 1932, Elsie paid for Manuel J. Andrade's *Folk-Lore from the Dominican Republic* (Memoirs XXIII, $1258), and Arthur Huff Fauset's *Nova Scotia Folk-Lore* (Memoirs XXIV, $717). In 1933, she supported the publication of two issues of the *Journal* (Nos. 174 and 177) for $725.83. In addition, under the guise of "Friends of Professor Boas for Bella Bella Memoir," she gave $747.10. Parsons financed the preparation of the Southwest concordance ($2,030.00) and was to finance the publication as well, though the project was never completed. She paid for her *Folk-Lore of the Antilles* (Memoirs XXVI, Volume I, $1,882.00; Volume II, $1900). In 1937, she financed José Manuel Espinosa's *Spanish Folk-Tales from New Mexico* (Memoirs XXX, $911.49), and in 1939, Grenville Goodwin's *Myths and Tales of the White Mountain Apache* (Memoirs XXXIII, Parsons's Southwest Society, $477.40). Parsons paid for her *Taos Tales* (Memoirs XXXIV, $1,441.25), for H. T. Wheeler's *Tales from Jalisco Mexico* (Memoirs XXXV), and Morris Opler's *Myths and Legends of the Lipan Apache* (Memoirs XXXVI; for the latter two, a total of $3,170.55). In 1941, she paid for the printing and distribution of the journals ($563.80). [See *JAF:* Ruth Benedict, Editor Reports, Thirty-Eighth Annual Meeting of AFS, 40 (1927): 210, and Thirty-Ninth Annual Meeting of AFS, 41 (1928): 287; Gladys Reichard, "Treasurer Report," Fortieth Annual Meeting of AFS, 42 (1929): 199; Leslie White, "Treasurer Report," and Benedict, "Editor Report," Forty-Third Annual Meeting of AFS, 45 (1932): 263–64; Benedict, "Editor Report," and Ruth Underhill, "Treasurer Report," Forty-Fourth Annual Meeting of AFS, 46 (1933): 190; Underhill, "Treasurer Report," Forty-Fifth Annual Meeting of AFS, 47 (1934): 259, 261, Forty-Sixth Annual Meeting of AFS, 48 (1935), p. 187; Benedict, "Editor Report", Forty-Seventh Annual Meeting of AFS, 49 (1936): 170; Forty-Ninth Annual Meeting of AFS, 51 (1938): 105; and Benedict, "Editor Report," Gene Weltfish, "Treasurer Report," Fiftieth Annual Meeting of the AFS, 52 (1939): 211,

Fifty-First Annual Meeting of AFS, 53 (1940): 191, 193; ECP, list of checks sent to Treasurer of AFS.]

17. Boas Papers, ECP to Boas, 13 Sept. 1932.

18. ECP, Reichard to ECP, 7 Mar. 1933.

19. ECP, Benedict to ECP, 10 Mar. 1933.

20. ECP, Boas to ECP, 30 Oct. 1933. In a letter dated Apr. 3, 1934, Boas informed Elsie that the first volume of the Antilles manuscript would cost $1,882; the second volume, $1,900; the Hopi manuscript, $3,710 (Columbia University Press was contributing $1200); and Herskovits's Suriname manuscript, $4,250 (ECP, Boas to ECP), all of which she paid.

21. UPFFA, Herzog, Feb. 1940.

22. George Herzog, "Special Council Meeting," *JAF* 53 (1940): 194. For information on the change in editorship, see Elizabeth F. Null, W. K. McNeil, and Lynn Pifer, "The *Journal's* Editors," in *The Centennial Index, JAF* 101 (1988): 26–30.

23. ECP, Gayton to ECP, 5 July 1940. For additional correspondence on Gayton and the editorship of *JAF,* see ECP, Gayton to ECP, 31 Jan. 1940, and ECP to Gayton, 25 Feb. 1940.

24. ECP, Herskovits to Ralph Boggs, Ann Gayton, Archer Taylor, Stith Thompson, Leslie White, and Elsie Clews Parsons, 15 Nov. 1940.

25. ECP, Herskovits to Policy Committee, 2 Dec. 1940.

26. ECP, ECP to Herskovits, 17 Nov. 1940.

27. ECP, Herskovits to Members of the American Folklore Society Policy Committee, 2 Dec. 1940.

28. ECP, Parsons to Herskovits, 4 Dec. 1940.

29. ECP, Ann Gayton to ECP, 23 Nov. 1940.

30. "Fifty-Second Annual Meeting of the American Folklore Society, Report of the Committee on Policy," *JAF* 54 (1941): 76.

31. ECP, Gayton to ECP, n.d.

32. See Dwyer-Shick, "The American Folklore Society," "Appendix C, Annual Meetings of the American Folklore Society," pp. 359–62, for a listing of the professional societies with which the society held joint meetings.

33. ECP, Ann Gayton to ECP, 12 Jan. 19 [1941].

34. Alfred M. Tozzer, "Report of the Secretary," *AA* 23 (1921): 102.

35. ECP, Goddard to ECP, 21 Oct. 1920.

36. ECP, ECP to Tozzer, n.d.

37. Alfred V. Kidder, "Report of the Treasurer," and John R. Swanton, "Report of the Editor," *AA* 26 (1924): 123, 124. Parsons continued with her support. In 1925, she paid for her own work, *The Scalp Ceremonial of Zuñi* (Memoirs 30, $193.27), and in 1926 for a volume that she had edited, *A Pueblo Indian Journal, 1920–1921* (Memoirs 32, $723.24). In 1929, she again subsidized the publication of her own work, *The Social Organization of the Tewa of New Mexico* (Memoirs 36). In 1933, she paid for Leslie White's *The Pueblo of San Felipe* (Memoirs 38, $557.42), and for her own *Hopi and Zuñi Ceremonialism* (Memoirs 39, $425.88). In 1937, she paid for Leslie White's *The Pueblo of Santo Domingo, New Mexico* (Memoirs 43, $902.15); in 1939, she paid for half

the costs of Morris Opler's *Dirty Boy: Jicarilla Tale of Raid and War* (Memoirs 52, $172.78); in 1940, for E. Adamson Hoebel's *The Political Organization and Law-Ways of the Comanche Indians* (Memoirs 54, $250); and in 1941, for her *Notes on the Caddo* (Memoirs 57, $392.30). [See *AA:* A. V. Kidder, "Report of the Treasurer," and Robert H. Lowie, "Report of the Editor," 27 (1925): 176, 179; E. W. Gifford, "Report of the Treasurer," and Robert H. Lowie, "Report of the Editor," 29 (1927): 305, 306; Cornelius Osgood, "Report of Treasurer," 38 (1936): 304; 41 (1939): 298; ECP, list of checks to the Treasurer of the American Anthropological Association.]

38. ECP, ECP to Spier, 9 Apr. 1934.
39. ECP, Spier to ECP, 20 Apr. 1934.
40. ECP, Frank M. Setzler to ECP, 31 Dec. 1940.
41. ECP, anonymous to ECP, 21 Jan. 1941.
42. ECP, ECP to Fred Eggan, 31 Dec. 1940.
43. ECP, "An Anthropological Excursion."

15

A Legacy to Folklore and Anthropology

Just prior to her second trip to Peguche, in September, 1941, Elsie wrote to Robert Redfield: "I am off to Ecuador this week to amplify and check on my Andean Indian study including some very interesting written material I have been receiving during the past year from school-taught Indians in another valley. I have rarely seen such frank and credible reporting, but naturally I want to get a first hand picture also." Redfield had been handling the arrangements for the publication of *Peguche* by the University of Chicago Press. For this reason, Parsons appended to her letter the following note: "In case of accident, I am leaving directions to send you my original ms. on the Andean Indians of Ecuador which I am taking with me, also a duplicate which is in New York. Also a collection of pictures, some rough miscellaneous notes (of little or no value), and some things I collected in order to figure—the masks, incised food gourd, and necklace. The book is about four-fifths written, Preface and Chapter 1, the least written. However, I think the ms. is printable and my family would probably contribute to the publication."[1] Redfield responded, wishing her "an interesting time in Ecuador" and indicating his eagerness to hear more about the materials she had received from the school-taught Indians. He added, "We have used such Indians in Guatemala to some extent and the results have been excellent."[2]

As Parsons prepared to leave for her fieldtrip, she also organized details for the Fortieth Annual Meeting of the American Anthropological Association, to be held from December 27 to 30, 1941, in Andover, Massachusetts. The meeting, which would be in conjunction with the American Folklore Society and the Society for American Archaeology, would mark her retirement as president of the American Anthropological Association. As noted in the program, she was scheduled to deliver the presidential address on "Anthropology and Prediction," following the annual dinner (for which the appropriate attire was indicated as "Business suit") on December 29.[3] On September 18, 1941, she wrote to Fred Eggan, secretary of the American Anthropological Association, "I am off in a few days on a field trip to Ecuador, due back in New York on November 18, which I trust will not be too late for any questions that may come up in connection with the program."[4] On her return, Eggan welcomed her, "Glad to hear that you are back—you are just in time to help out on the program. . . . Hope you had a nice fieldtrip. I heard from one of our students that you had a fine place to work in Ecuador, and I am anxious to hear more about it."[5]

Prior to the 1941 meeting, Elsie attended to two seemingly unrelated matters. She wrote a letter of correction to *Who's Who* concerning an entry in the 1928 edition:

Dear Sirs:

My attention has been drawn to the entry of my name in Who's Who Vol. XV as Mrs. Herbert Parsons and to my demise in 1928.

As I am generally known as Elsie Clews Parsons and as I have been quite active in my profession, anthropology, since 1928 being this current year president of the American Anthropological Association, I suggest you send me a blank to fill out which, if you see fit, you can use in your next publication.[6]

She also prepared a list for the Committee on Resolutions of the American Anthropological Association, the last two entries of which read:

5. Record the deep sense of loss suffered by the Association through the deaths of Charles Amsden, Manuel J. Andrade, Helen Blish, W. T. Bush, Herbert C. Howe, Jackson S. Lincoln, Rufus A. McIlhenny, John E. Starkweather, Benjamin L. Whorf.

6. Any others?[7]

The irony, and eeriness, in these two matters lay in the fact that the 1928 *Who's Who* entry for Parsons would be correct for 1941 and that there would be an added name to the list of deceased members of the American Anthropological Association—her own.

When Elsie first returned from Ecuador, she resumed her normal schedule of activities. Franz Boas wrote her, "Gladys told me of your return from South America and that you feel satisfied with the results of your trip. I do hope I'll see you soon. At present I am a little under the weather and have to avoid all unnecessary steps, so that I take lunch in the office. Would it be convenient to you either to see me after lunch in Columbia or let me call on you in the afternoon about four o'clock (on Thursday)." He thanked her for the check that she had sent him for secretarial help and expressed a desire to show her his Cochiti manuscript, which he said was "ready in long hand except the vocabulary." He closed with the wish "to see you soon and to hear about your trip."[8]

Just over two weeks after Boas had written her, Elsie was in the hospital. When he heard she was not feeling well, A. Irving Hallowell wrote, "I'm very sorry indeed to hear of your illness. By all means go slow so that we can look forward to seeing you in Andover."[9] From her hospital bed, Elsie made plans to attend the American Anthropological Association Meeting. She wrote to Eggan, "On December 10 I came down with an attack of appendicitis and was operated on the next day. It has been an easy case and my surgeon thinks I can probably make the Andover trip. If I do make it I still want to take things rather easy, and I will be obliged if in any communication you make to Byers you ask him to assign me a room near the dining hall, that would save some steps." She added that she would "hate to miss the meetings, not because of any official routine, but because I really enjoy seeing people at our annual meetings."[10]

Two days later, on December 19, 1941, Elsie Clews Parsons was dead. Her son, McIlvaine Parsons, wrote the obituary that appeared the following day in the *New York Herald Tribune:*

> Dr. Elsie Clews Parsons Is Dead; Anthropologist and Sociologist, U.S. Association Head was Indian Authority, Tireless Traveler, Prolific Writer. Dr. Elsie Clews Parsons, president of the American Anthropological Association and widow of Herbert Parsons, attorney and Republican political leader, died yesterday morning at New York Hospital of uremia and other complications following an appendectomy six days earlier. She was sixty-six years old.
>
> Dr. Parsons, the only woman ever chosen to head a major American scientific association, was to have presided at the annual convention of the American Anthropological Association, which she had headed for a year, in Andover, Mass., on Dec. 27. She returned a month ago from a field trip among the Peguchi, a tribe of Andean Indians, in the province of Imbabura in northwest Ecuador.[11]

The day of Elsie's death Gladys Reichard wrote to Alfred Louis Kroeber, "You will doubtless have heard the shocking news of Elsie's death before you get this, but I thot you might want to know a little more than you read in the newspaper." Reichard continued: "She came back from Ecuador not so long ago, hardly a month, in excellent spirits but glad to get back because she had minded the discomforts more than usual. We decided on analyzing the situation that there were more discomforts than usual. Her good spirits & apparent good health were obvious even last Wed. night (Dec. 10) when she attended a Council meeting of the Am[erican] Ethnol[ological] Soc[iety]. On Thurs. she was taken to the New York Hospital for observation & was operated on that very day for appendicitis. From then on until last night she seemed to be doing extraordinarily well." At that point, Reichard said, "uremia was detected & she simply" slipped away. Gladys added, "She had her presidential speech ready—I have it now—& I think it ought to be read, don't you?"[12]

So it was that Gladys Reichard delivered Elsie Clews Parsons's presidential address on "Anthropology and Prediction" to the American Anthropological Association. Reichard wrote to Elsie's son, Herbert, telling him that the talk had been "very well received." She also noted the juxtaposition of Parsons's cautionary remarks on the involvement of anthropologists in the war effort with a gathering held to encourage just such participation—a gathering that sponsored the resolution "that the American Anthropological Association places itself and its resources and the specialized skills and knowledge of its members at the disposal of the country in the successful prosecution of the war."[13] Reichard recounted: "Two nights before we had had what I call a 'revival meeting.' You know 'rally round the flag, etc.' and I was thinking Elsie certainly would have put the quietus on some of the slop that was uttered. Then it happened that her speech—heard by almost the same crowd—took up some of the problems point by point but sanely whereas the other was just incitation." She added, "I am going to offer it to the Editor of the American Anthropologist for publication."[14]

A year prior to her death, Elsie had written to her daughter, Lissa, "Our thoughts being on death, I enclose a memorandum on my own."[15] Attached to the letter was the following:

Directions after death
    If convenient, cremation (ashes left at crematory); otherwise, if not convenient, burial, but not in a cemetery and without grave stone.
    No funeral, no religious services whatsoever.
    Relatives requested not to wear mourning.
    Dated 31 Jan. 1926
    O.K. 1940.

Her wishes were not followed for one request—there was a private funeral service—but they were for the others. Her body was cremated, and the ashes were scattered.[16]

The American Folklore Society and the American Anthropological Association both marked the passing of Elsie Clews Parsons. In the *Journal of American Folklore*, there were two resolutions. The first was a customary listing of members who had died during the year: "Be it resolved that The American Folklore Society record its deep sense of loss in the deaths of Dr. Elsie Clews Parsons, of Dr. George Lyman Kittredge, and of Reverend J. J. Williams, and desires to express its condolences to their surviving relatives." Following this was a separate resolution in recognition of her contributions to the discipline: "Be it resolved that The American Folklore Society expresses its profound appreciation for the encouragement and support given by Dr. Elsie Clews Parsons to the study of Folklore and to the work of our Society."[17] The American Anthropological Association set Parsons apart from the listing of deceased members—the resolution that she herself had prepared, and then had asked, "Is there anyone else?"

> *Be it resolved*, that the American Anthropological Association expresses its deep sorrow for the untimely death of our colleague and President, Dr. Elsie Clews Parsons. An able and tireless writer and field worker, she has made outstanding contributions, especially in the fields of folklore and Southwestern and Latin American ethnology. As a generous supporter of field work and publications, as a wise counsellor, and as a loyal friend, she exerted important constructive influence on American Anthropology for many years.[18]

Elsie's death was like a marker of change in anthropology, an end, as it were, of an era. Her friends and colleagues felt this. Cora DuBois wrote to Robert Lowie, "The loss of Elsie has meant far more to me than I was prepared for. Your comment about understanding discriminatingly through her a part of your personality is some of my sense of loss. Part of it too is a feeling of impoverishment as the ranks of nineteenth century personalities thin. There is in them a sense of integrity and of direction more absent than present in my age grade." DuBois added, "However much one might disagree with Elsie on any issue, there was a quality not to be denied."[19]

This aspect of the changing times was conveyed in a letter to Elsie written by Mary Simkhovitch, director of Greenwich House in New York City, on May 31, 1940: "What a rather uncanny feeling it gives one to be at the end of an epoch, but I suppose we are always at the end of an epoch although we didn't always know it as clearly as we do

now."[20] The end of an era in the founding and organization of settlement houses was the point of reference in the letter. The end of an
era in the discipline of anthropology was also at hand. The scepter of
power had passed from the aging Franz Boas to his students who
struggled to grasp it. And with the shift in control came new concerns
and a new frame of inquiry. The vantage point had changed.

In ways, Parsons straddled the divide: she had continued with insistence to collect minute details in her ethnographic works, to con-
struct, bit by bit, her mosaic; but she had combined this with a new
focus on acculturation. This dual perspective was present in notes
that Parsons had written shortly before her death. On a slip of paper,
she had penciled, "Anthropology is a descriptive science, selecting
and classifying facts about mankind from various viewpoints."[21] Her
anthropological approach was firmly rooted in the enduring concerns
of description and classification. However, she had also moved into a
new area, the study of culture change. In notes for the manuscript,
"The World Changes," Parsons wrote that acculturation involved
"knowledge of *both* cultures *and the point of view* that *what is happening
under his eyes is just as significant as what happened in earlier periods.*" She
added, "Too often fieldworkers have not been comparative-minded
enough about their own culture to be adequate observers of how that
culture was effecting another culture."[22]

A woman of clear mind and strong opinion, Parsons would not fix
her vision on what for younger students was the backbone of society,
the generalized study of social structure. She refused to adopt the label "Social Anthropology," which she regarded simply as another
name for sociology; and she most emphatically conveyed her view to
those who used it.[23] She was impatient with the influence of A. R.
Radcliffe-Brown on American anthropologists. In September, 1933,
she wrote Lowie, "Why the hell do people pay so much attention to
Radcliffe-Brown? All this 'functional' talk is nothing more than any
good ethnologist has always appreciated. Insistence on neglected
lines of observation is all right for the teacher, but shouldn't be
magnified into a position of new truth." She concluded, "We do love
catch words!"[24]

Elsie was skeptical of any approach that stressed theory over description and comparison. In her correspondence with other anthropologists, she argued this point. To Clyde Kluckhohn, she wrote,
"Don't you think these psychological conclusions should be presented
merely as hypotheses until they are tested in specific cultures?"[25] And
to Robert Zingg's proposal to study the Huichol from the perspective
of the "current theories of primitive social organization, religion, art,

and psychology," Parsons responded, "I hope you plan a thorough description of the Huichol before testing theories. . . . Most of us think that culture must be described before it can be used as a basis for testing theory, whether historical or psychological."[26]

However, the "most of us" of Parsons's assertion were the old guard, and their numbers were diminishing. The younger students, impatient with descriptions of culture, were eager to analyze society from a theoretical perspective. In such a vein, Fred Eggan wrote Parsons of his work on the pueblos, which he described as "an attempt at a sociological rather than a historical or psychological analysis." In another letter, he explained the intent of his doctoral dissertation: "to abstract the kinship *structure* from Hopi behavior, and compare it with other pueblo groups in an attempt to define the 'types' of social structure in the S.W. and elsewhere." As he said, his project was in "its infancy [and] the 'types' were not set up," but still he was able to suggest that "the 'western pueblos' seemed to be a unit in that they had similar kinship . . . structures." This, he said, held true "regardless of where the content came from or what languages they spoke."[27] Parsons remained unconvinced that such an approach was warranted. Penciled in the margin alongside Eggan's statement about his intent to work out the changes between the east and west pueblos along similar lines was Elsie's note, "But you are assuming there was once a homogeneous culture—in face of 4 different stock languages & no end of other cultural differences."[28]

While there was a sharp move away from the Boasian tradition—a tradition so clearly represented in Parsons's writings—still there was a recognition of her solid contributions to anthropology. In his assessment, Leslie Spier remarked on Parsons's crucial work in the Southwest. At the time when she had begun her investigations, Spier said, the existing literature had been random and disorganized. There were "voluminous reports on particular ceremonies of the Hopi, a badly organized account of Zuñi, and a scattering of observations on the Rio Grande Pueblos." At the end of her twenty-five years of research, Spier said, "We had from her . . . a monumental series of reports and syntheses for the entire field."[29]

According to Melville Herskovits, Elsie had brought the same force to the study of Negro folklore. Her contributions were "so extensive as to comprise, in themselves, the bulk of the available materials in this field." No future work could be done, Herskovits emphasized, without using her work as a foundation. Prior to Parsons's research, collectors had operated on an "accepted notion of Negro lore . . . that it consisted of animal tales and that it was 'the epitome of primitive naivete.' " Parsons had simply turned the field around. As Herskovits wrote: "The principle of collecting tales without selection based on preconceived categories, which she introduced into the study of Negro lore, is today universally accepted; that the story should be set down as narrated . . . is another commonplace of present procedure. Careful notation of time and place of collecting and, where feasible, the name of the storyteller and such facts about him as indicate his competence are today accepted by students as normal practice."[30]

In reflections on her colleague, Gladys Reichard drew together the strands of Elsie's life. She wrote, "With the sudden death on December 19, 1941, of Dr. Elsie Clews Parsons anthropology was deprived not only of a scientist, an indefatigable worker and a benefactor, but also of a friend and a great person." Reichard stressed the preeminent role that Parsons had played in anthropology: "The anthropologist usually depends upon an institution for the realization of his greatest potentialities; Elsie Clews Parsons was herself an institution, not in the material sense of the word for she did not erect buildings or accumulate material property. She was an anthropological institution because of her varied interests, her cooperation with many universities and museums, her incredible tolerance, her discrimination and her judgment, in short, because of her general philosophy of life."[31] Reichard stressed the "great influence" that Parsons had had on so many young ethnologists. Parsons supported "an incalculable amount of research work" and followed "through to publications in which even a sentence of appreciation sometimes became embarrassing to her." Reichard assessed "the great monument of Elsie Parsons' career [as] her 'teaching.' " She continued: "This consisted in long talks with young people about their work; such conferences included well-taken criticism and advice. It was followed by intensive correspondence, a means of furnishing constant stimulation and new direction. Never did Dr. Parsons have the idea that money alone would do a job." Further, Reichard stressed, Parsons never attempted to "exert pressure on a worker or his theories, as might have been expected because of the subsidy."[32]

In a letter to Alfred Tozzer, Boas had posed a question, "I wonder how many people really know how much anthropology owes to her."[33] He himself had provided an answer to this query years earlier, in his dedication of *Keresan Texts* to Elsie Clews Parsons. The inscription read:

Dear Elsie,

    I dedicate this book to you in sincere friendship and in remembrance of weeks of joint labors. Accept it as a slight expression of gratitude for your energetic and unselfish labors that have brought about a revival of interest in southwestern ethnology. Our indebtedness goes further. To your initiative is due the systematic exploration of the field of negro folk-lore and of many questions pertaining to processes of social life that illuminate our social behavior. Those who have had the good fortune to be associated with you owe much to the stimulus that your thoughtful investigations have given to them.

Yours faithfully,
FRANZ BOAS[34]

In his remarks on her death, Boas stressed Parsons's "unselfish devotion to science," which, he said, "has few equals." Always ready with help for young scientists, "the only return she demanded for her help was industry and serious work." Boas continued: "Without her help many of the important contributions of late years would not have seen the light. Her interest in folk-lore as a source of the understanding of culture and cultural processes led her to the most liberal support of the American Folk-Lore Society, whose broad field of publication and research was made possible almost entirely by her generous support." As if in answer to Tozzer's remark to him that "Elsie's death will come especially hard to you," Boas acknowledged, "We lament her loss, but the memory of her devotion to her ideals will live on among us and lead us to emulate her example."[35]

NOTES

1. Robert Redfield Papers, University of Chicago, ECP to Redfield, 16 Sept. 1941.
2. ECP, Redfield to ECP, 19 Sept. 1941.
3. NAA, Program, Fortieth Annual Meeting of the American Anthropological Association, Phillips Academy, Andover, Massachusetts, December 27–30, 1941.
4. ECP, ECP to Eggan, 18 Sept. 1941.
5. ECP, Eggan to ECP, 22 Nov. 1941.
6. ECP, ECP to Who's Who, Marquis Company, Chicago, Illinois, 1941.
7. ECP, "Memorandum for 1941 Committee on Resolutions."
8. ECP, Boas to ECP, 25 Nov. 1941.
9. ECP, Hallowell to ECP, 15 Dec. 1941.
10. NAA, ECP to Fred Eggan, 17 Dec. 1941.
11. McIlvaine Parsons, "Dr. Elsie Clews Parsons Is Dead," *New York Herald Tribune*, 20 Dec. 1941, p. 14, col. 5–6.
12. UCA, Reichard to Kroeber, 19 Dec. 1941. The cause of death listed on Parsons's estate tax return was "Embolism, complication ff. appendectomy" (ECP, estate tax return, executor's copy). Peter Hare reports that Parsons's

son, Herbert, who was a doctor, recalled the cause of death as pulmonary thrombosis. See Hare, *A Woman's Quest for Science* (Buffalo, N.Y.: Prometheus Books, 1985), p. 167.

13. "Proceedings of the American Anthropological Association for the Year Ending December, 1941," *AA* 44 (1942): 288.

14. ECP, Reichard to Herbert Parsons, Jr., 12 Jan. 1942.

15. ECP, ECP to Lissa, 11 Feb. 1940.

16. ECP, John Parsons to Richard Dorson, 8 Feb. 1960.

17. "Fifty-Third Annual Meeting of the American Folklore Society," *JAF* 55 (1942): 95.

18. "Proceedings of the American Anthropological Association for the Year Ending December, 1941," *AA* 44 (1942): 288.

19. Lowie Papers, Cora DuBois to Lowie, 4 Jan. 1942.

20. Mary Simkhovitch to ECP, 31 May 1940, ECP.

21. ECP, Peguche Notes, ECP.

22. ECP, "The World Changes," her emphasis.

23. ECP, Duncan Strong to ECP, 25 July 1939; H. Scudder Mekeel to ECP, 18 Jan. 1938; 22 Mar. 1938; ECP to Mekeel, 24 Mar. 1938; Mekeel to ECP, 29 Mar. 1938.

24. Lowie Papers, ECP to Lowie, 14 Sept. 1933.

25. ECP, ECP to Kluckhohn, 13 May 1941.

26. ECP, Robert Zingg to ECP, n.d.; ECP to Zingg, n.d.

27. ECP, Eggan to ECP, 20 July 1936; 22 June 1930.

28. ECP, Eggan to ECP, 29 Jan. 1937; ECP's penciled notes.

29. Leslie Spier, "Elsie Clews Parsons," *AA* 45 (1943): 247.

30. Herskovits, "Some Next Steps in the Study of Negro Folklore," *JAF* 56 (1943): 1.

31. Gladys Reichard, "Elsie Clews Parsons," *JAF* 56 (1943): 45.

32. Ibid., p. 48.

33. Boas Papers, Boas to Tozzer, 22 Dec. 1941.

34. Franz Boas, *Keresan Texts* (New York: G. E. Stechert & Company, 1928), p. v.

35. Franz Boas, "Elsie Clews Parsons, Late President of the American Anthropological Association," *Scientific Monthly* 54 (May 1941): 482; Boas Papers, Tozzer to Boas, 25 Dec. 1941.

Selected Bibliography

Manuscript Sources

American Folklore Society Papers, University of Pennsylvania Folklore and Folklife Archives, Philadelphia, PA

American Museum of Natural History, New York, NY

Franz Boas Papers, American Philosophical Society, Philadelphia, PA

Randolph Bourne Papers, Rare Book and Manuscript Library, Columbia University, New York, NY

Columbia University Oral History Collection, New York, NY

Department of Anthropology, Archives, University of California, Berkeley

Alfred Louis Kroeber Papers, Bancroft Library, University of California, Berkeley

Robert H. Lowie Papers, Bancroft Library, Univeristy of California, Berkeley

Mabel Dodge Luhan Papers, Beinecke Rare Book and Manuscript Library, Yale University, New Haven, CT

National Anthropological Archives, Smithsonian Institution, Washington, DC

Elsie Clews Parsons Papers, American Philosophical Society, Philadelphia, PA

Herbert Parsons Papers, Rare Book and Manuscript Library, Columbia University, New York, NY

Robert Redfield Papers, University of Chicago Library, IL

Rye Historical Society, Rye, NY

Anne Gayton Spier Papers, Bancroft Library, University of California, Berkeley

Leslie White Papers, Michigan Historical Collections, Bentley Historical Library, University of Michigan, Ann Arbor

Printed Material: Books, Journal Articles, and Dissertations

Amory, Cleveland. *The Last Resorts: A Portrait of American Society at Play.* New York: Harper and Brothers, 1952.

Anonymous. Review of *Fear and Conventionality. The Outlook*, 10 Feb. 1915, p. 348.

——— . Review of *The Old-Fashioned Woman. The Nation*, 7 Aug. 1913, p. 127.

——— . Review of *The Old-Fashioned Woman. The Outlook*, 30 Aug. 1913, p. 1011.

Babcock, Barbara A., ed. *Pueblo Mothers and Children: Essays by Elsie Clews Parsons 1915–1924*. Santa Fe, New Mexico: Ancient City Press.

Babcock, Barbara A. "Taking Liberties, Writing from the Margins, and Doing it with a Difference." *JAF* 100 (1987): 391–411.

——— , and Nancy J. Parezo. *Daughters of the Desert: Women Anthropologists and the Native American Southwest, 1880–1980*. Albuquerque: University of New Mexico Press, 1988.

Beals, Ralph L. "Anthropologist and Educator." Interview by Diane L. Dillon. Oral History Program, University of California, Berkeley, 1977.

Benedict, Ruth. "Franz Boas." *Science* 97, no. 2507 (1943): 60–62.

Boas, Franz. "Elsie Clews Parsons, Late President of the American Anthropological Association." *Scientific Monthly* 54 (May 1942): 480–82.

——— . *Keresan Texts*. New York: G. E. Stechert and Co., 1925–28. 2 parts.

——— . "The American Ethnological Society." *Science* 97, no. 2505 (1943): 7–8.

——— . "Recent Anthropology." *Science* 98, no. 2545 (1943): 311–14.

——— . "Recent Anthropology, II." *Science* 98, no. 2546 (1943): 334–37.

Bourne, Randolph. "The Handicapped." *Atlantic Monthly* 108 (Sept. 1911): 320–29.

Boyer, Paul S. "Elsie Clews Parsons." In *Notable American Women 1607–1950, a Biographical Dictionary*, Edward T. James et al., eds. Cambridge: Belknap Press of Harvard University, 1971, pp. 20–23.

Brew, J. O. "Hopi Prehistory and History to 1850." In *Handbook of North American Indians, Southwest*, Alfonso Ortiz, ed. Washington: Smithsonian Institution, 1979, pp. 514–23.

Brody, J. J. "Pueblo Fine Arts." In *Handbook of North American Indians, Southwest*, Alfonso Ortiz, ed. Washington: Smithsonian Institution, 1979, pp. 603–8.

Caffrey, Margaret M. *Ruth Benedict: Stranger in This Land*. Austin: University of Texas Press, 1989.

Capelle, Elizabeth L. "Elsie Clews Parsons: A New Woman." Master's thesis in History, Columbia University, 1977.

Chambers, Keith S. "The Indefatigable Elsie Clews Parsons—Folklorist." *Western Folklore* 32 (1973): 180–98.

Clayton, Bruce. *Forgotten Prophet: The Life of Randolph Bourne*. Baton Rouge: Louisiana State University Press, 1984.

Clews, Henry. *Fifty Years in Wall Street*. New York: Irving Publishing Company, 1915. Rpt. New York: Arno Press, 1973.

——— . *Twenty-Eight Years in Wall Street*. New York: Irving Publishing Company, 1887.

——— . *Financial, Economic, and Miscellaneous Speeches and Essays*. New York: Irving Publishing Company, 1910.

Collier, John. "The Crisis in the Affairs of the Ancient Pueblo Indians That Has Brought the Country's Federated Women to Their Aid." *The World*, 21 Jan. 1923, sec. cc, p. 1, col. 1–3.

———. *From Every Zenith*. Denver: Sage Books, 1963.

———. "Politicians Pillage the Pueblos." *The Searchlight*, 31 Jan. 1923, pp. 15–19.

———. "Robbing the Pueblo Indians," *The World*, 27 Nov. 1922, p. 12, col. 1.

Culleton, Fanny Parsons. Interview conducted by Rosemary Lévy Zumwalt, Boone, North Carolina, 6 July 1988.

Davenport, Frederick M. Review of *The Family: An Ethnographical and Historical Outline with Descriptive Notes*, by Elsie Clews Parsons. *Political Science Quarterly* 22 (1907): 744–47.

Day, Clarence. "Portrait of a Lady." *New Republic*, 23 July 1919, pp. 387–89.

Digby, Kenelm. "The Literary Lobby." *The Literary Review*, 9 Dec. 1922, p. 310.

Dorson, Richard. "Elsie Clews Parsons: Feminist and Folklorist." *AFFWord* 1–3 (1971): 1–4.

Dumarest, Father Noël. *Notes on Cochiti, New Mexico*, Elsie Clews Parsons, trans. and ed. Memoirs of the American Anthropological Association. Lancaster, Pa.: American Anthropological Association, 1919. Vol. 6, no. 3.

Dwyer-Shick, Susan. "The American Folklore Society and Folklore Research in American, 1888–1940." Ph.D. dissertation in Folklore and Folklife, University of Pennsylvania, 1979.

Elliott, Maud Howe. *This Was My Newport*. Cambridge, Mass.: The Mythology Company, 1944.

Espinosa, Aurelio M. *The Folklore of Spain in the American Southwest*. Norman: University of Oklahoma Press, 1985.

Fauset, Arthur Huff. *Folklore from Nova Scotia*. Memoirs of the American Folklore Society. New York: G. E. Stechert and Co., 1931. Vol. 24.

Friedlander, Judith. "Elsie Clews Parsons (1874–1941)." In *Women Anthropologists, Selected Biographies*, Ute Gacs et al., eds. Urbana: University of Illinois Press, 1989, pp. 282–90.

Gacs, Ute, Aisha Khan, Jerrie McIntyre, and Ruth Weinberg. *Women Anthropologists: Selected Biographies*. Urbana: University of Illinois Press, 1989.

Gillen, John L. "Franklin Henry Giddings." In *American Masters of Social Science*, Howard Odum, ed. New York: Henry Holt and Company, 1927, pp. 189–228.

Goldfrank, Ester Schiff. *The Artist of "Isleta Paintings" in Pueblo Society*. Washington, D.C.: Smithsonian Institution, 1967.

———. *Notes on an Undirected Life: As One Anthropologist Tells It*. Flushing, New York: Queens College Press, Queens College Publications in Anthropology, 1978. No. 3.

———. *The Social and Ceremonial Organization of Cochiti*. Memoirs of the American Anthropological Association. Menasha, Wis.: American Anthropological Association, 1927. No. 33.

Griscom, Lloyd C. *Diplomatically Speaking*. New York: The Literary Guild of America, 1940.

Hahn, Emily. *Mabel: A Biography of Mabel Dodge Luhan.* Boston: Houghton Mifflin Company, 1977.

Hare, Peter H. *A Woman's Quest for Science: Portrait of Anthropologist Elsie Clews Parsons.* Buffalo, N.Y.: Prometheus Books, 1985.

Hemenway, Robert E. *Zora Neale Hurston: A Literary Biography.* Urbana: University of Illinois Press, 1980.

Henderson, Alice Corbin. "The Death of the Pueblos." *New Republic,* 29 Nov. 1922, pp. 11–13.

Herman, Kali. "Parsons, Elsie Clews." *Women in Particular: An Index to American Women.* Phoenix, Ariz.: Oryx Press, 1984.

Herrick, Robert. *Wanderings.* New York: Harcourt, Brace and Company, 1925.

Herskovits, Melville J. "Some Next Steps in the Study of Negro Folklore." *JAF* 56 (1943): 1–7.

Hoebel, E. Adamson. *The Political Organization and Law-Ways of the Comanche Indians.* Memoirs of the American Anthropological Association. Menasha, Wis.: American Anthropological Association, 1940. No. 34.

Horowitz, Amy. "Franz Boas and Zora Neale Hurston: Resetting the Margins." American Folklore Society Meeting, Philadelphia, Pennsylvania, 1989.

Hoxie, R. Gordon, et al. *A History of the Faculty of Political Science, Columbia University.* New York: Columbia University Press, 1955.

Jackson, Bruce, Michael Taft, and Harvey S. Axlerod. *The Centennial Index: One Hundred Years of the Journal of American Folklore.* *JAF* 101 (1988).

Johnson, Alvin. *Pioneer's Progress.* New York: The Viking Press, 1952.

Journal of American Folklore. Elsie Clews Parsons Memorial Number, 56, No. 219 (1943).

Keating, Barbara. "Elsie Clews Parsons: Her Work and Influence in Sociology." *Journal of the History of Sociology* 1 (1978): 1–9.

Kelly, Lawrence C. *The Assault on Assimilation: John Collier and the Origins of Indian Policy Reform.* Albuquerque: University of New Mexico Press, 1983.

Kennedy, David. *Birth Control in America: The Career of Margaret Sanger.* New Haven: Yale University Press, 1970.

Kennedy, Elsie Parsons. "The Reminiscences of Mr. and Mrs. John D. Kennedy." Interview by Allan Nevins and Louis M. Starr. Oral History Research Office, Columbia University, 1966.

King, Moses. *Notable New Yorkers, 1896–1899.* New York: Bartlett and Company, The Orr Press, 1899.

Kroeber, Alfred Louis. "Elsie Clews Parsons." *AA* 45 (1943): 252–55.

Kroeber, Theodora. *Alfred Kroeber: A Personal Configuration.* Berkeley: University of California Press, 1970.

La Farge, Oliver. Review of *Mitla, Town of the Souls.* *Saturday Review of Literature,* 16 Jan. 1937, p. 16.

Lamphere, Louise. "Feminist Anthropology: The Legacy of Elsie Clews Parsons." *American Ethnologist* 16 (1989): 518–33.

Lasch, Christopher. *The New Radicalism in America, 1889–1963: The Intellectual as a Social Type.* New York: Alfred A. Knopf, 1965.

Leslie, Charles M. *Now We Are Civilized: A Study of the World View of the Zapotec Indians of Mitla, Oaxaca.* Detroit: Wayne State University Press, 1960.

Lippmann, Walter. *Drift and Mastery: An Attempt to Diagnose the Current Unrest.* New York: Kinnerly Press, 1914.

Lipset, Seymour M. "The Department of Sociology." In *A History of the Faculty of Political Science, Columbia University,* R. Gordon Hoxie, ed. New York: Columbia University Press, 1955, pp. 284–303.

Lowie, Robert H., and Leta Stetter Hollingworth. "Science and Feminism." *Scientific Monthly* 3 (Sept. 1916): 277–84.

May, Henry. *The End of American Innocence: A Study of the First Years of Our Own Time, 1912–1917.* New York: Alfred A. Knopf, 1959.

McCutcheon, John T. *Drawn from Memory.* New York: Bobbs-Merrill Company, 1950.

Mead, Margaret, and Ruth L. Bunzel, ed. *The Golden Age of American Anthropology.* New York: George Braziller, 1960.

Minger, Ralph Eldin. *William Howard Taft and United States Foreign Policy: The Apprenticeship Years, 1900–1908.* Urbana: University of Illinois Press, 1975.

Modell, Judith Schacter. *Ruth Benedict: Patterns of a Life.* Philadelphia: University of Pennsylvania Press, 1983.

Moore, Sally Falk. "The Department of Anthropology." In *A History of the Faculty of Political Science, Columbia University,* R. Gordon Hoxie, ed. New York: Columbia University Press, 1955, pp. 147–60.

Moreau, John Adam. *Randolph Bourne: Legend and Reality.* Washington, D.C.: Public Affairs Press, 1966.

Morrill, Claire. *A Taos Mosaic: Portrait of a New Mexican Village.* Albuquerque: University of New Mexico Press, 1973.

Moulton, F. R., ed. "The Sixth Philadelphia Meeting of the American Association for the Advancement of Science and Associated Societies." *Science* 93 (1941): 133–35.

Mumford, Louis. "The Image of Randolph Bourne." *New Republic,* 24 Sept. 1930, pp. 151–52.

Murphy, Robert F. *Robert H. Lowie.* New York: Columbia University Press, 1972.

Naumburg, Elsa Herzfeld. Review of *The Old Fashioned Woman. Survey,* 28 June 1913, pp. 437–38.

Nevius, Blake. *Robert Herrick: The Development of a Novelist.* Berkeley: University of California Press, 1962.

Noble, David W. *The Paradox of Progressive Thought.* Minneapolis: University of Minnesota Press, 1958.

Northcott, Clarence H. "The Sociological Theories of Franklin Henry Giddings: Consciousness of Kind, Pluralistic Behavior, and Statistical Method." In *An Introduction to the History of Sociology,* Harry Elmer Barnes, ed. Chicago: University of Chicago Press, 1948, pp. 744–65.

Null, Elizabeth F., W. K. McNeil, and Lynn Pifer. "The *Journal's* Editors." In *The Centennial Index: One Hundred Years of the Journal of American Folklore. JAF* 101 (1988): 20–49.

O'Connor, Richard. *The Golden Summers: An Antic History of Newport.* New York: Putnam, 1974.

Odum, Howard W, ed. *American Masters of Social Science: An Approach to the Study of the Social Sciences through a Neglected Field of Biography.* New York: Henry Holt and Company, 1927.

O'Neill, William. *The Last Romantic: A Life of Max Eastman.* New York: Oxford University Press, 1978.

Opler, Morris. *Dirty Boy: Jicarilla Tale of Raid and War.* Memoirs of the American Anthropological Association. Menasha, Wis.: American Anthropological Association, 1938. No. 52.

Ortiz, Alfonso, ed. *New Perspectives on the Pueblos.* Albuquerque: University of New Mexico Press, 1972.

——— . Review of Esther Goldfrank's *The Artist of "Isleta Paintings" in Pueblo Society. AA* 70 (1968): 838–39.

Paddock, John. *Ancient Oaxaca.* Stanford: Stanford University Press, 1966.

Pandey, Triloki Nath. "Anthropologists at Zuni." *Proceedings of the American Philosophical Society* 116, no. 4 (1972): 321–37.

Parsons, Elsie Clews. "The Aim of Productive Efficiency in Education." *Educational Review* 30 (Dec. 1905): 500–6.

——— , ed. *American Indian Life.* New York: Viking Press, 1922.

——— . "American 'Society,' I." *New Republic,* 16 Dec. 1916, pp. 184–86.

——— . "American 'Society,' II." *New Republic,* 23 Dec. 1916, pp. 214–16.

——— . "American Snobbishness in the Philippines." *The Independent* 61 (8 Feb. 1906): 332–33.

——— . "Americans in Haiti." *New York Times,* 18 Oct. 1920, sec. 1, p. 4, col. 5.

——— . "Americans They Have Met." *New York Times,* 30 May 1916, sec. 1, p. 8, col. 6.

——— . "Bermuda Folklore." *JAF* 38 (1925): 239–66, 267–93.

——— . "Ceremonial Defloration." *Psychoanalytic Review* 5 (1918): 339–40.

——— . "The Ceremonial of Growing Up." *School and Society* 2, no. 38 (Sept. 1915): 408–11.

——— . "Circumventing Darwinism." *Journal of Philosophy, Psychology and Scientific Methods* 12 (Oct. 1915): 610–12.

——— . "A Communication in Regard to the 'Discovery of Time.' " *Journal of Philosophy, Psychology and Scientific Methods* 12 (Dec. 1915): 713–15.

——— . "Congressional Junket in Japan, the Taft Party of 1905 Meets the Mikado." *New York Historical Society Quarterly* 41 (1957): 385–406.

——— . "Curanderos in Oaxaca, Mexico." *Scientific Monthly* 32 (Jan. 1931): 60–68.

——— . "The Dragon's Teeth." *Harper's Weekly,* 8 May 1915, p. 449.

——— . "Facing Race Suicide." *The Masses* 6, no. 9 (June 1915): 15.

——— . "The Family." In *America Now: An Inquiry into Civilization in the United States by Thirty-Six Americans.* Harold E. Stearns, ed. New York: Charles Scribner's Sons, 1938, pp. 404–8.

———. *The Family: An Ethnographical and Historical Outline with Descriptive Notes.* New York: G. P. Putnam's Sons, 1906.

———. "The Favorite Number of the Zuñi." *Scientific Monthly* 3 (Dec. 1916): 596–600.

———. *Fear and Conventionality.* New York: G. P. Putnam's Sons, 1914.

———. "Feminism and Conventionality." *Women in Public Life, Annals of the American Academy of Political and Social Science* 56 (1914): 47–53.

———. "Feminism and Sex Ethics." *International Journal of Ethics* 26 (1916): 462–65.

———. "Feminism and the Family." *International Journal of Ethics* 28 (1917): 52–58.

———. "Field Work in Teaching Sociology." *Educational Review* 20 (Sept. 1900): 159–69.

———. "Fiesta at Sant'Ana, New Mexico." *Scientific Monthly* 16 (1923): 178–83.

———. "Filipino Village Reminiscence." *Scientific Monthly* 51 (Nov. 1940): 435–59.

——— and A. M. Bacon. "Folk-Lore from Elizabeth City County, Virginia." *JAF* 35 (1922): 250–327.

———. *Folk-Lore from the Cape Verde Islands.* Memoirs of the American Folklore Society. New York: G. E. Stechert and Co., 1923. Vol. 15, parts 1–2.

———. "Folk-Lore of the Cherokee of Robeson County, North Carolina." *JAF* 32 (1919): 384–93.

———. *Folk-Lore of the Antilles, French and English.* Memoirs of the American Folklore Society. New York: G. E. Stechert and Co., 1933, 1936, 1943. Memoirs 26, parts 1–3.

———. *Folk-Lore of the Sea Islands, South Carolina.* Memoirs of the American Folklore Society. New York: G. E. Stechert and Co., 1923. Vol. 16.

———. *Folk-Tales of Andros, Bahamas.* Memoirs of the American Folklore Society. New York: G. E. Stechert and Co., 1918. Vol. 8.

———. "Friendship, a Social Category." *American Journal of Sociology* 21 (1915): 230–33.

———. "Getting Married on First Mesa, Arizona." *Scientific Monthly* 13 (Sept. 1921): 259–65.

———. "Gregariousness and the Impulse to Classify." *Journal of Philosophy, Psychology and Scientific Methods* 12 (Oct. 1915): 551–53.

———. "Half-Breed." *Scientific Monthly* 18 (Feb. 1924): 144–48.

———. "Hayti: Misunderstood." *The Independent* 72 (8 Aug. 1912): 322–24.

———. "Higher Education of Women and the Family." *American Journal of Sociology* 14 (1909): 758–63.

———. *Hopi and Zuñi Ceremonialism.* Memoirs of the American Anthropological Association. Menasha, Wis.: American Anthropological Association, 1933. No. 39.

———. "A Hopi Ceremonial." *Century Magazine* 101, n.s. 79 (Nov. 1920): 177–80.

———. "Injustice to Haitians." *New York Times,* 7 Jan. 1917, sec. 7, p. 2, col. 5.

———. "Ironies of Death." *New Republic,* 11 Mar. 1916, pp. 159–61.

————. *Isleta, New Mexico.* 47th Annual Report of the Bureau of American Ethnology. Washington, D.C.: U.S. Government Printing Office, 1932.

————. *Isleta Paintings.* Esther S. Goldfrank, ed. Washington, D. C.: Smithsonian Institution, 1962.

————. "Joel Chandler Harris and Negro Folklore," *The Dial* 66 (1919): 491–93.

————. *Kiowa Tales.* Memoirs of the American Folk-Lore Society. New York: G. E. Stechert and Co., 1929. Vol. 22.

————. *Laguna Genealogies.* Anthropological Papers of the American Museum of Natural History. New York: American Museum of Natural History, 1923. Vol. 19, part 5.

————. "The Lesser Evil." *Harper's Weekly,* 26 Feb. 1916, p. 215.

————. Letter to the editor. *New Republic* 21 Oct. 1940, p. 554.

————. "Lord Bateman." *JAF* 41 (1928): 585–88.

————. "Meetings." *The Masses* 6, no. 7 (Apr. 1915): 11.

————. *Mitla, Town of the Souls and Other Zapoteco-Speaking Pueblos of Oaxaca, Mexico.* Chicago: University of Chicago Press, 1936.

————. "Must We Have Her?" *New Republic,* 10 June, 1916, pp. 145–46.

————. "Mysticism in War." *Scientific Monthly* 3 (Sept. 1916): 285–88.

————. "New Morals for Old, Changes in Sex Relations." *The Nation* 118 (1924): 551–53.

————. "Notes on Acoma and Laguna." *AA* 20 (1918): 162–86.

————. *Notes on Ceremonialism at Laguna.* Anthropological Papers of the American Museum of Natural History. New York: American Museum of Natural History, 1920. Vol. 19, part 4.

————, trans. and ed. *Notes on Cochiti, New Mexico.* Father Noël Dumarest. Memoirs of the American Anthropological Association. Lancaster, Pa.: American Anthropological Association, 1919. Vol. 6, no. 3.

————. *Notes on the Caddo.* Memoirs of the American Anthropological Association. Menasha, Wis.: American Anthropological Association, 1941. No. 57.

————. "Notes on Isleta, Santa Ana, and Acoma." *AA* 22 (1920): 56–69.

————. *Notes on Zuñi.* Memoirs of the American Anthropological Association. Lancaster, Pa.: American Anthropological Association, 1917. Vol. 4, nos. 3–4.

————. "A Novel's Ethnology." *New Republic,* 23 Oct. 1915, pp. 314–15.

————. "Nursery and Savagery." *Pedagogical Seminary* 22 (1915): 296–99.

————. "Nursery Bugaboos." *Pedagogical Seminary* 22 (June 1915): 147–51.

————. *The Old-Fashioned Woman: Primitive Fancies about the Sex.* 1913; rpt. New York: Arno Press, 1972.

————. "On the Loose." *New Republic,* 27 Feb. 1915, pp. 100–101.

————. "Patterns for Peace or War." *Scientific Monthly* 5 (Sept. 1917): 229–38.

————. *Peguche, Canton of Otavalo, Province of Imbabura, Ecuador: A Study of Andean Indians.* Chicago: University of Chicago Press, 1945.

————. "Penalizing Marriage and Child-Bearing." *The Independent* 60 (18 Jan. 1906): 146–47.

———. "The Pueblo Indian Clan in Folk-Lore." *JAF* 34 (1921): 209–16.

———. *A Pueblo Indian Journal, 1920–1921.* Memoirs of the American Anthropological Association. Menasha, Wis.: American Anthropological Association, 1925. No. 32.

———. *Pueblo Indian Religion.* Chicago: University of Chicago Press, 1939, 2 vols.

———. *Pueblo Indian Religion.* 1939; rpt. Chicago: Midway Reprints, University of Chicago Press. 1974.

———. *The Pueblo of Jemez.* Papers of the Southwestern Expedition. Andover, Mass.: Yale University Press, 1925. No. 3.

———. "Reasoning from Analogy at Zuñi." *Scientific Monthly* 4 (Apr. 1917): 365–68.

———. *Religious Chastity: An Ethnological Study.* New York: Macaulay Company, 1913. Pseud. of John Main. Reprint, New York: AMS Press, 1975.

———. Review of *A History of the Family as a Social and Educational Institution,* by Willystine Goodsell. *School and Society* 4, no. 103 (1916): 934–36.

———. Review of J. A. Todd, *The Primitive Family as an Educational Agency. Science* 39 (May 1914): 654–56.

———. "A Romantic in Bengal and in New York." *Scientific Monthly* 21 (Dec. 1925): 600–612.

———. "Rough House." *Forum* 55 (Apr. 1916): 454–56.

———. *The Scalp Ceremonial of Zuñi.* Memoirs of the American Anthropological Association. Menasha, Wis.: American Anthropological Association. 1924. No. 31.

———. "The School Child, the School Nurse and the Local School Board." *Charities,* 28 Sept. 1905, pp. 1–8.

———. "Seniority in the Nursery." *School and Society* 3, no. 53 (Jan. 1916): 14–17.

———. "Sex." In *Civilization in the United States: An Inquiry by Thirty Americans.* Harold E. Stearns, ed. New York: Harcourt, Brace, 1922, pp. 309–18.

———. "Sex Morality and the Taboo of Direct Reference." *The Independent* 61 (16 Aug. 1906): 391–92.

———. "The Sin of Being Found Out." *New Review* 3, no. 19 (15 Dec. 1915): 361–62.

———. *Social Freedom: A Study of the Conflicts between Social Classifications and Personality.* New York: G. P. Putnam's Sons, 1915.

———. *The Social Organization of the Tewa of New Mexico.* Memoirs of the American Anthropological Association. Menasha, Wis.: American Anthropological Association. 1929. No. 36.

———. *Social Rule: A Study of the Will to Power.* New York: G. P. Putnam's Sons, The Knickerbocker Press, 1916.

———. "Some Mexican Idols in Folklore." *Scientific Monthly* 44 (May 1937): 470–73.

———. "Spirituals and Other Folk-Lore from the Bahamas." *JAF* 41 (1928): 453–524.

―――. "Spirituals from the 'American' Colony of Samana Bay, Santo Domingo." *JAF* 41 (1928): 525–28.

―――. "Spring Days in Zuni, New Mexico." *Scientific Monthly* 36 (Jan. 1933): 49–54.

―――. "The Strawberry Patch." *The Masses* 6, no. 12 (Sept. 1915): 8.

―――. "The Study of Variants." *JAF* 33 (1920): 87–90.

―――. "The Supernatural Policing of Women." *The Independent* 72 (8 Feb 1912): 307–10.

―――. *Taos Pueblo.* Memoirs of the American Folklore Society. Menasha, Wis.: George Banta Publishing Co., 1936. Vol. 34.

―――. *Taos Tales.* Memoirs of the American Folklore Society. New York: J. J. Augustin, 1940. Vol. 34.

―――. "The Teleological Delusion." *Journal of Philosophy, Psychology and Scientific Method* 14 (Aug. 1917): 463–68.

―――. *Tewa Tales.* Memoirs of the American Folklore Society. New York: G. E. Stechert and Co., 1926. Vol. 19.

―――. "To Abolish War." *New York Times,* 10 Jan. 1915, sec. 3, p. 2, col. 6.

―――. *The Scalp Ceremonial of Zuñi.* Memoirs of the American Anthropological Association. Menasha, Wis.: American Anthropological Association, 1924. No. 31.

―――. *The Social Organization of the Tewa of New Mexico.* Memoirs of the American Anthropological Association. Menasha, Wis.: American Anthropological Association, 1929. No. 36.

―――. "The Toy Soldier." *Educational Review* 50 (June 1915): 91–94.

―――. "Unconscious Feminism." *New York Times,* 28 Apr. 1915, sec. 1, p. 12, col. 5.

―――. "Waiyautitsa of Zuñi, New Mexico." *Scientific Monthly* 9 (Nov. 1919): 443–57.

―――. "Waiyautitsa of Zuñi, New Mexico." In *American Indian Life.* New York: Viking Press, 1922, pp. 157–73.

―――. "Why Holidays." *New Republic,* 2 June 1917, pp. 140–41.

―――. *Winter and Summer Dance Series in Zuñi in 1918.* University of California Publications in American Archaeology and Ethnology. Berkeley, Ca.: University of California Press. 1922. Vol. 17, No. 3.

―――. "Wives and Birth Control." *New Republic,* 18 Mar. 1916, pp. 187–88.

―――. "Women and War." *New York Times,* 23 July 1915, sec. 1, p. 8, col. 5.

―――. "The Woman Who Did." *Harper's Weekly,* 11 Sept. 1915, p. 255.

―――. "The Wonder." *New Republic,* 10 Nov. 1917, pp. 53–54, 56.

―――. "Zuni Inoculative Magic." *Science* 44 (1916): 469–70.

Parsons, McIlvaine. "Dr. Elsie Clews Parsons Is Dead." *New York Herald Tribune,* 20 Dec. 1941, p. 14, col. 5–6.

Parsons, William, Jr. "The Progressive Politics of Herbert Parsons." Master's thesis, Department of American Studies, Yale University, 1965.

Pringle, Henry F. *The Life and Times of William Howard Taft.* New York: Farrar and Rinehart, 1939.

Radin, Paul. Review of *Peguche, Hispanic American Historical Review*, 26 (1946): 245–46.

Reichard, Gladys E. "Bibliography of Elsie Clews Parsons." *JAF* 56 (1943): 48–56.

———. "Elsie Clews Parsons." *JAF* 56 (19–43): 45–48.

———. "Indian or Spanish?" *Survey Graphics*, Jan. 1934, p. 44.

———. Review of *Mitla, Town of the Souls. Barnard College Alumnae*, Feb. 1937, p. 15.

———. Review of *Mitla, Town of the Souls. Survey Graphics*, Jan. 1937, pp. 44–45.

———. "The Elsie Clews Parsons Collection." *Proceedings of the American Philosophical Society* 94, no. 3 (1950): 308–9.

Rohner, Ronald P. *The Ethnography of Franz Boas*. Chicago: University of Chicago Press, 1969.

Rosenberg, Rosalind. *Beyond Separate Spheres: Intellectual Roots of Modern Feminism*. New Haven: Yale University Press, 1982.

———. "The Primitive Side of Civilized Culture." In *Beyond Separate Spheres, Intellectual Roots of Modern Feminism*. New Haven: Yale University Press, 1982, pp. 147–77.

Rossiter, Margaret W. *Women Scientists in America: Struggles and Strategies to 1940*. Baltimore: Johns Hopkins University Press, 1982.

Rudnick, Lois Palken. *Mabel Dodge Luhan, New Woman, New Worlds*. Albuquerque: University of New Mexico Press, 1984.

———. "The Unexpurgated Self: A Critical Biography of Mabel Dodge Luhan." Ph.D. Dissertation in American Civilization, Brown University, 1977.

Sandeen, Eric J. *The Letters of Randolph Bourne: A Comprehensive Edition*. New York: Whitston Publishing Company, 1981.

Sanger, Margaret Higgens. *Margaret Sanger: An Autobiography*. New York: W. W. Norton and Company, 1938.

Shepherd, William R. "John William Burgess." In *American Masters of Social Science*. Howard W. Odum, ed. New York: Macmillan Co., 1927, pp. 21–57.

Sobel, Robert. *Panic on Wall Street*. New York: The MacMillan Company, 1968.

Spencer, Herbert. *The Principles of Biology*. New York: D. Appleton and Company, 1874. 2 vols.

Spier, Leslie. "Addenda to Bibliography of Elsie Clews Parsons." *JAF* 56, (1945): 136.

———. "Elsie Clews Parsons." *AA* 45 (1943): 244–51.

Stearns, Harold E. *America Now: An Inquiry into Civilization in the United States by Thirty-Six Americans*. New York: Charles Scribner's Sons, 1938.

———. *Civilization in the United States: An Inquiry by Thirty Americans*. New York: Harcourt, Brace, 1922.

———. *Liberalism in America: Its Origin, Its Temporary Collapse, Its Future*. New York: Boni and Liveright Inc., 1919.

Stephen, Alexander M. *Hopi Journal of Alexander M. Stephen.* Elsie Clews Parsons, ed. New York: Columbia University Press, 1936, 2 vols. Rpt. New York: AMS Press, 1969.

Taft, William Howard. *William Howard Taft Papers.* Washington, D.C.: Library of Congress, 1972.

Tax, Sol. Review of *Mitla, American Sociological Review* 2 (1937): 135–36.

Toksvig, Signe. "Elsie Clews Parsons." *New Republic,* 26 Nov. 1919, pp. 17–20.

Underhill, Ruth. "Note on Easter Devils at Kawori'k on the Papago Reservation." *AA* 36 (1934): 515.

Wertheim, Arthur Frank. *The New York Little Renaissance: Iconoclasm, Modernism, and Nationalism in American Culture, 1908–1917.* New York: New York University Press, 1976.

Wesser, Robert F. "Theodore Roosevelt: Reform and Reorganization of the Republican Party in New York, 1901–1906." *New York History* 46 (July 1965): 230–52.

White, Leslie A. *The Pueblo of San Felipe.* Memoirs of the American Anthropological Association. Menasha, Wis.: American Anthropological Association, 1932. No. 38.

——— . *The Pueblo of Santa Ana, New Mexico.* Memoirs of the American Anthropological Association. Menasha, Wis.: American Anthropological Association, 1942. Vol. 44, no. 4, part 2.

——— . *The Pueblo of Santo Domingo, New Mexico.* Memoirs of the American Anthropological Association. Menasha, Wis.: American Anthropological Association, 1935. No. 43.

——— . "Parsons, Elsie Worthington Clews." *Dictionary of American Biography,* Supp. 3 (1941–45).

——— . Review of *Hopi Journal of Alexander M. Stephen. AA* 40 (1938): 306–07.

Woodbury, Natalie. Discussant remarks at Feminist Perspectives on Elsie Clews Parsons and Her Works, American Anthropological Association Meeting, Phoenix, Arizona, November, 1988.

Zumwalt, Rosemary Lévy. *American Folklore Scholarship: A Dialogue of Dissent.* Bloomington: Indiana University Press, 1988.

Index

Abbott, Leonard, 128
Abell, Mrs., 106
Aberle, Sophie, 254–55
Acculturation, 220, 307, 310, 332
Acoma research, 242–43, 270
Adamson, Thelma, 317
Adolescence, 104
Age classes, 105
Agustina (*curandera*), 285
Alcoholic beverages, 302
Alen, James Val, 29
Amateur folklore collecting, 319
American Anthropological Association:
    American Folkore Society and, 319,
    320; annual meetings, 170, 314, 315,
    322, 327–28; Bursum bill and, 262;
    ECP and, 313, 320–22, 327–28;
    Modern Language Association and,
    315, 318
American Anthropologist (journal), 321
American Association for the Advance-
    ment of Science, 170, 262, 265, 314
American Colony of Samana Bay, 204–5
American Council of Learned Societies,
    317
American Ethnological Society, 260,
    261, 313
American Folklore Society: annual meet-
    ings, 164, 170, 314, 319–20; ECP
    and, 313, 314–15, 316, 317–20, 323–
    24n16; symposium (1935), 216
American Indian Defense Society, 261
American League to Limit Arma-
    ments, 131
American Museum of Natural History,
    150, 171, 260, 321
American Sociological Association, 51

Andrade, Manuel J., 324n16
Andrango, Francisco, 306
Andros Island folklore, 201, 202
Animal folklore characters, 198
Anthropological Society (Washington,
    D.C.), 77
Anthropologists, 159; associations of,
    313–26; Bursum bill and, 266; coor-
    dination of, 268; Taos mistrust of,
    240–41, 256; trained by Boas, 162–
    63; in Washington, D.C., 77; in Zuni
    Pueblo, 155
"Anthums" (spirituals), 204–5
Apache Indians, 150–51, 216
"An Appeal by Pablo Johnson of La-
    guna," 261
"An Appeal by the Pueblo Indians of
    New Mexico to the People of the
    United States," 260, 261
"The Appeal of the Acomas," 261
Armbrister, Jack, 201–2
*The Artist of "Isleta Paintings" in Pueblo
    Society* (Goldfrank), 276n65
Artistic pursuits, 118
Assimilation, cultural, 221–22, 223
Atwood, Stella M., 264
Augustin, Heinrich W., 317
Austin, Mary, 262

Baca, Pedro, 148
Bacon, A. M., 187
Bahamian folklore, 200
Bailey's Beach, 28, 29
Bakhmeteff, Boris A., 64
Balch, Ernesto, 280
Bannard, Otto, 74
Barnabas, Father, 243